D0400915

Canary Islands

Sally O'Brien, Sarah Andrews

Contents

La Palma p196

Tenerife p135

Lanzarote p113

La Gomera p176

El Hierro p218

Gran Canaria p56

Fuerteventura p89

Destination: Canary Islands

In a 'win the lottery' fantasy, you may dream of being so wealthy that you could affor[d] the good life on a different island each day. Guess what? This is actually possible in the [Canary] Islands – and you don't have to be a millionaire! The Islas Canarias, a Spanish archipela[go] more than 100km from the coast of Saharan Africa, are a varied and fascinating destina[tion] travellers intent on hedonism, the great outdoors, relaxation and recreation combined[.]

On the smaller, less-developed western islands, each scarcely trodden by English-spe[aking] visitors, you can walk through woods of Canary pine and follow centuries-old trails that link village upon village. On Tenerife, the stark, volcanic grandeur of the Parque Nacional del Teide beckons. Offshore are hidden rocks, caves and sunken wrecks ideal for diving or snorkelling. Along the islands' coastlines, the dominant trade winds provide power for windsurfing, kite-surfing and sailing, while surfers ride the perfect tubes off Lanzarote and Fuerteventura.

The island of Gran Canaria is an ever-changing pastiche: subtropical and fertile to the north, reminiscent of the desert to the south. Tenerife is more diverse still. La Gomera, La Palma and El Hierro are mountainous, green and dotted with brief strands of black sand, presenting a startling contrast to the desertscapes and sparkling white beaches of Lanzarote and Fuerteventura.

Amid the melting pot of Andalucian, Berber, Portuguese, Italian, French and even British migration, the Guanches, the indigenous islanders displaced during the Spanish conquest in the 15th century, also left their mark. No doubt the islands will leave their mark on you too.

Founded in the 17th century, picturesque Agulo, La Gomera, overlooks the Atlantic (p187)

DAMIEN SIMONIS

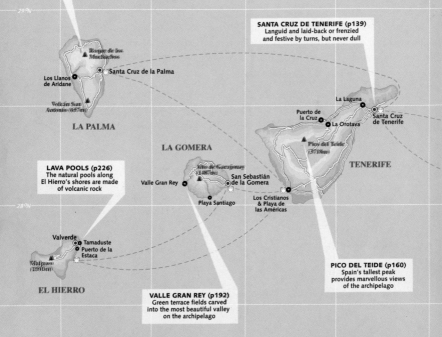

ROQUE DE LOS MUCHACHOS (p198)
Arguably the best stargazing spot in the world, it's a heavenly feast for the eyes

SANTA CRUZ DE TENERIFE (p139)
Languid and laid-back or frenzied and festive by turns, but never dull

LAVA POOLS (p226)
The natural pools along El Hierro's shores are made of volcanic rock

VALLE GRAN REY (p192)
Green terrace fields carved into the most beautiful valley on the archipelago

PICO DEL TEIDE (p160)
Spain's tallest peak provides marvellous views of the archipelago

LA PALMA

Roque de los Muchachos ▲

Los Llanos de Aridane ⊙

⊙ Santa Cruz de la Palma

Volcán San Antonio (657m) ▲

LA GOMERA

Alto de Garajonay (1487m) ▲

Valle Gran Rey ⊙

San Sebastián de la Gomera ⊙

Playa Santiago ⊙

TENERIFE

La Laguna ⊙

Puerto de la Cruz ⊙ ⊙ La Orotava

Pico del Teide (3718m) ▲

Santa Cruz de Tenerife ⊙

Los Cristianos & Playa de las Américas

EL HIERRO

Valverde ⊙

Tamaduste ⊙

Puerto de la Estaca ⊙

Malpaso (1501m) ▲

ATLANTIC OCEAN

ATLANTIC OCEAN

JAMEOS DEL AGUA (p126)
A groovy entertainment centre,
educational facility and natural
wonder all rolled into one

*To Cádiz
(mainland Spain)*

Isla de Alegranza

MONTAÑAS DEL FUEGO (p129)
An eerie, arid, volcanic landscape of
breathtaking proportions

Agujas Grandes (266m) ▲
Isla Graciosa
Monte Corona ▲
(609m)
Jameos
del Agua

Timanfaya (510m) ▲
Arrecife
LANZAROTE
*To Cádiz
(mainland
Spain)*
Playa Blanca

Corralejo
Isla de Lobos

PUERTO DE MÓGAN (p86)
With a waterfront decorated in exotic flora,
this small yachting harbour is nicknamed the
'Venice of the Canaries'

La Oliva

Betancuria
Puerto del
Rosario
Gran Montaña ▲
(708m)

FUERTEVENTURA

Puerto de
las Nieves
Las Palmas de
Gran Canaria
▲ Pico de las Nieves
(1949m)
San Bartolomé
de Tirajana
Puerto de
Mógan
GRAN CANARIA
Maspalomas & Playa
del Inglés

Morro Jable

**PLAYA DE SOTAVENTO
DE JANDÍA (p108)**
Mile upon mile of achingly beautiful
Atlantic beaches

MASPALOMAS (p80)
Four hundred hectares of rolling sand
dunes that are the perfect setting
for a Lawrence of Arabia play

ELEVATION	
	2000m
	1500m
	1000m
	500m
	200m
	0

0 ⊢──────┤ 60 km
0 ⊢──────┤ 40 miles

The Canary Islands' natural beauty is its greatest feature, with World Heritage–listed sites and diverse reserves competing for your attention. The archipelago's volcanic origins have produced the startling peak of the **Parque Nacional del Teide** (p160), the sizzling stones of the **Parque Nacional de Timanfaya** (p129) and the massive rock cauldron of the **Parque Nacional de la Caldera de Taburiente** (p212), where you can stargaze at the **Roque de los Muchachos** (p198). One of the planet's most ancient laurel forests lies in the heart of **Parque Nacional de Garajonay** (p188), while the protected sand dunes of **Maspalomas** (p80) are sure to inspire.

INGRID RODDIS

Summit of Pico del Teide (3718m), Parque Nacional del Teide, Tenerife (p160)

View of Parque Nacional de la Caldera de Taburiente from around Mirador Lomo de las Chozas, La Palma (p212)

DAMIEN SIMONIS

WAYNE WALTON

Montañas del Fuego (Mountains of Fire), Parque Nacional de Timanfaya, Lanzarote (p129)

Dramatic coastlines are a Canarian speciality, whether you're manoeuvring hairpin turns on the breathtaking drive between **Agaete** (p78) and **Aldea de San Nicolás** (p79), marvelling at the golden sands and the vibrant turquoise waters of **Playa de Sotavento de Jandía** (p108), swimming in the natural rock pools of **Tamaduste** (p226), lazing on the black-sand beach of **Puerto Naos** (p212) or surfing world-class waves at **La Caleta de Famara** (p128). If you need reminding of nature's forces, absorb the wild charms of mountainous **Punta de Teno** (p162) or carve up the isolated waves that roll onto **Isla Graciosa** (p127).

DAMIEN SIMONIS

The rocky coastline of Tamaduste, El Hierro (p226)

A small beach on Isla Graciosa, Lanzarote (p127)

GREG GAWLOWSKI

About to hit the surf on Fuerteventura (p90)

CHRISTIAN ASLUND

Cities, Towns & Villages

The Canary Islands possess some charming towns and villages. **La Orotava** (p155) and **La Laguna** (p145) are photogenic urban jewels, with rows of historic architecture. Fishing villages like **Garachico** (p158) are perfect for lazy seafood feasts, while in rustic hamlets such as **Pájara** (p98), traffic jams consist of your car and a herd of goats. **Puerto de Mogán** (p86) is a small-scale Venice bedecked in bougainvillea, and whitewashed **Yaiza** (p130) is the place to go for food and wine away from the crowds. The cities **Santa Cruz de Tenerife** (p139) and **Las Palmas de Gran Canaria** (p61) pick up the pace with eye-catching architecture, international and local cuisine, fun museums and internationally renowned partying.

TONY WHEELER

Casa/Museo de Colón, Las Palmas de Gran Canaria (p65)

Brightly coloured buildings, Santa Cruz de Tenerife (p139)

WAYNE WALT

The fishing harbour of Puerto de Mogán, Gran Canaria (p86)

GREG GAWLOWS

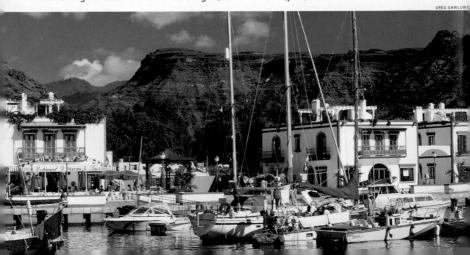

Getting Started

WHEN TO GO

When it comes to sunshine, the Canary Islands are caught in a kind of weather warp, with an eternal spring-summer climate. They're a year-round destination; you can pretty much take your pick of when to go.

See the Climate Charts (p237) for more information.

The winter months – December to March – *are* a tad cooler but still paradise compared to mainland Europe, the UK and most of North America. This makes winter the islands' busiest period – with crowds and higher prices – as young and old, gay and straight, family and friends decide to chase away the winter blues with a tan and a cocktail.

The summer period – July to September – is a rival high season, mainly because that's when mainland Spaniards elect to go on their annual holiday (for your average Madrileño, the Canaries can seem refreshingly cool in the height of a scorching mainland summer). English and German travellers also head to the Canaries in high numbers in August.

The Carnaval season in February/March is an intensely popular period, when anyone and everyone decides to partake in the fun – finding a place to stay can be difficult, and prices rise accordingly.

For maximum value on airfares and accommodation, the best periods are from November to mid-December and, better still, April to June (with the notable exception of the Easter rush). Spring especially is a great time to be around.

COSTS & MONEY

Daily living expenses on the Canary Islands are lower than those in most countries of western Europe. That said, they generally work out a little higher than those of peninsular Spain since just about everything has to be brought over from the mainland or from across the Atlantic.

Accommodation, which is plentiful, can be a bargain compared to other popular European holiday destinations. Food too is inexpensive for either self-caterers or avid restaurant-goers. Car hire is cheap, taxi transport good value over short distances and public transport (bus) very economical. Flying between the islands can be expensive but time-saving. Theme and amusement parks are all pricey, especially for large family groups.

A breakdown of average costs per person per day at the most standard level might be: €20 for a bed in a double room; €5 for breakfast (juice, coffee and a toasted ham-and-cheese sandwich); €8 for a *menú del día* (set menu) lunch; €20 for dinner. If money is no object you can easily spend €100 or more per person on accommodation.

HOW MUCH?

Sun lounge with big umbrella €3

Cocktail with little umbrella €6

Movie ticket €4.50

Local bus ticket €0.90

Apartment for two €45

Local newspaper €1.50

Aloe vera gel €7

Day of kitesurfing €100

LONELY PLANET INDEX

Litre of petrol (unleaded) €0.60

Bottle of water from €0.50

Bottle of beer €2

Serve of *papas arrugadas* (wrinkly potatoes) €3

Souvenir T-shirt €10

DON'T LEAVE HOME WITHOUT...

- Getting waxed
- Your local and international driving licence
- Booking a car or a hotel – if you're counting on good ones
- Sunscreen and a hat – remember, you're closer to Africa than Europe
- Adapter plug for electrical appliances
- A beach towel – many hotels will make you pay for the privilege of using theirs
- A good book – hard to find on the islands

TOP FIVES
FESTIVALS & EVENTS

Canarios *love* to celebrate, and almost any excuse will do. There's almost always a fiesta or local *feria* (fair), or even a wild carnival to enjoy somewhere on the islands. Patron saints and their special days enliven even the smallest one-goat *pueblo* (village), and the gender-bender antics of the citizens of Santa Cruz and Las Palmas during Carnaval are rivalled only by the gaudy celebrations of Rio de Janeiro. The following list is our Top Five, but for a more comprehensive listing of festivals and events see the Directory (p240).

- Carnaval (all islands), 10 to 14 days before Ash Wednesday
- El Entierro de la Sardina (The Burial of the Sardine; all islands), final day of Carnaval
- Fiesta de la Virgen del Pino (Feast of the Virgin of the Pine; Gran Canaria, p77), 6 to 8 September
- Festival de Música de Canarias (Canary Music Festival; all islands), January and February
- Romería de San Roque (Pilgrimage of Saint Roch; Tenerife, p159), August

MUST-SEE COASTAL STRETCHES

Seven islands and a whole lot of coastline to explore – whether it be a solitary walk along a pristine beach at sunset or an exhilarating drive punctuated by hairpin bends, you can find rolling dunes, empty coves, seaside hot spots and fishing villages if you feel like it. Following is a list of our favourites, but other scenic and pleasant coastal stretches are listed throughout the island chapters.

- Agate to Aldea de San Nicolas (p79)
- Playa de Sotavento (p108)
- Punta del Papagayo (p134)
- Sabinosa to La Dehesa (p231)
- Barlovento to Santo Domingo (p216)

MUST-SEE TOWNS

The Canary Islands are made up of some delightful towns, both large and small. If you're staying in a purpose-built resort it can be difficult to visualise real life existing away from the all-expenses-paid, all-you-can-eat, airport-transfer tourist strips, but authentic architecture, culture, restaurants and experiences are waiting to be savoured in the following places. Other towns and villages are featured throughout the destination chapters.

- La Orotava (p155)
- La Laguna (p145)
- Garachico (p158)
- Puerto de Mogán (p86)
- Santa Cruz de la Palma (p201)

WALKS

The Canary Islands really are a walker's paradise, with a wide variety of terrains that suit all tastes (and fitness levels). The near-constant good weather makes walking feasible year-round, and the sheer number of trails here ensures that you'll never get bored. More walking options and advice are in the Canary Islands Outdoors chapter (see p41) and scattered throughout the book.

- Roques de García (p160)
- Up to the Alto de Garajonay (p188)
- Mirador de Jinama to La Frontera (p227)
- Ruta de los Volcanes (p129)
- Cruz de Tejeda to Roque Nublo (p75)

TRAVEL LITERATURE

Lanzarote (Michel Houellebecq) This book contains Houellebecq's usual mix of trenchant cultural observation, spot-on critique and barren, yet graphic, sexcapades – this time in Lanzarote, where a Frenchman takes a package tour and gets to know some of his fellow travellers. By turns savage and clinical, hilarious and disturbing.

The Canary Islands (Florence du Cane) Written in 1911 by English du Cane, this book is rather charming, mostly because of the paintings by Ella du Cane. Sadly, this title can be very hard to find.

Todos los Mojos de Canarias (Flora Lilia Barrera Álamo & Dolores Hernández Barrera) Get hooked on *mojo* (spicy salsa sauce) before you even taste it, with this book devoted to the ubiquitous and delicious sauce of the Canary Islands. See the Food & Drink chapter for more on *mojo* (p48).

Handbook of Canary Folk Medicine (José Jaén) Even if you're not keen on alternative therapies, this interesting little book provides a glimpse into some aspects of traditional Canarian life that are in danger of disappearing. It's fascinating for anyone with a good general knowledge of flora.

Arquitecturas Contemporáneas Las Palmas de Gran Canaria 1960–2000 (José Luis Gago) This beautiful black-and-white coffee-table book contains stunning photographs of some of the most intriguing and arresting modern architecture in Las Palmas.

INTERNET RESOURCES

EcoTurismo Canarias (www.ecoturismocanarias.com) An interesting site covering wildlife, rural accommodation and related services.

El Hierro (www.el-hierro.org) A well-laid out site provided by the island's *cabildo* (government).

Fuerteventura (www.fuerteventura.com) You'll find a reasonable amount of news and reviews, festival dates, and an accommodation availability search.

Gran Canaria (www.turismograncanaria.com) An effective (and official) site, with good practical information (in Spanish).

La Gomera (www.gomera-island.com) The island's infrastructure, culture and ecology in one easy website.

La Palma (www.la-palma-tur.org) La Isla Bonita's very own website, with information on culture, history and cuisine.

Lanzarote (www.lanzarote.com) A very good and knowledgeable website, with strong transport, culture and events listings.

Tenerife (www.tenerife.net) A good general site with plenty of tourist-related information.

Vive Canarias (www.vivecanarias.com) An informative site with plenty of information on the local arts scene, a good festival directory and plenty of entertainment listings.

Itineraries

ISLAND HOPPING

THE EASTERN ISLES – GRAN CANARIA, FUERTEVENTURA & LANZAROTE
Two weeks / 275km

Gran Canaria is the logical starting point for an eastern-isles tour. From **Las Palmas de Gran Canaria** (p61), you can explore the pretty villages of **Arucas** (p77), **Teror** (p76) and **Vega de San Mateo** (p76). Travelling through the interior, chill out in **Tejeda** (p75) and then catch sight of the centre's rock formations. Head south to the delightful yachting town of **Puerto de Mogán** (p86). Moving east along the beautiful coastline you'll soon come across the booming, hedonistic holiday region of **Maspalomas** (p80) and **Playa del Inglés** (p80).

Over on Fuerteventura, **Morro Jable** (p109) is a breezy, easy-going resort that serves as a gateway to over 20km of glorious beach known as the **Playa de Sotavento de Jandía** (p108). Pleasant escapes include **Pájara** (p98) and **Ajuy** (p98). Up north, you can chill out or get active by turns in **El Cotillo** (p106) and **Corralejo** (p102).

On Lanzarote, the beaches of **Playa Blanca** (p133), **Papagayo** (p134) and **Puerto del Carmen** (p131) compete with inland attractions such as the **Parque Nacional de Timanfaya** (p129) and César Manrique's man-made delights at **Tahiche** (p125), **Jameos del Agua** (p126), **Cueva de los Verdes** (p126) and **Mirador del Río** (p128).

See the individual listings for these attractions throughout the book or refer to the Transport chapter (p247) for getting there and around.

The Canaries' easternmost islands are immensely popular holiday destinations for a good reason – sun, sand, surf and sociability combine to meet the needs of most travellers. You can do these islands as fast or as slow as you like. We recommend at least a week to do this trip, with two weeks the ideal time frame.

A WALKER'S PARADISE – FROM TENERIFE TO LA GOMERA & EL HIERRO
One week / 75km

Though you have a good chance of landing first in Tenerife, there's no reason you have to stay there. The smaller, less crowded isles of the west are just a half-hour plane ride (or a longer boat ride) away.

From **Los Cristianos** (p167) in southern Tenerife, catch one of the many ferries that leave daily for **La Gomera** (p176). Just 45 minutes later, you'll disembark in the capital, **San Sebastián de la Gomera** (p180), the city known as the last place Columbus walked before 'finding' America.

The **Parque Nacional de Garajonay** (p188), a green haven in the centre of this mountainous island, is going to be your first destination. Take a walk through the park's famous laurel trees to the **Alto de Garajonay** (p188), where on a clear day you'll have views of Tenerife and El Teide. Next, head down to the lush **Valle Gran Rey** (p192), where you can hike through palms or loll on the beach before catching the ferry to **Playa Santiago** (p190) and the airport.

The direct ferry to El Hierro takes two hours and drops you off near the capital, **Valverde** (p223). Skip it and head straight towards **La Restinga** (p228), where you can take a lovely walk through **El Pinar** (p228), a protected pine forest, before heading to **El Sabinar** (p233), further west, where twisted juniper trees create a haunted-looking landscape.

Though there are only some 75km between the eastern shores of Tenerife and the western tip of El Hierro, thousands of kilometres of trails crisscross these islands, and hiking all of them would take you the better part of the next decade. If you're looking for a somewhat shorter time commitment, a week or so will be just about right to try out two or three of the best walks on each island.

A HOP, SKIP & JUMP – TENERIFE TO GRAN CANARIA

One week / 305km

The archipelago's two biggest islands, Tenerife and Gran Canaria, are also the most suited to family travellers, with diverse landscapes and seascapes, plentiful shopping, international cuisine and tourist infrastructure galore.

From **Santa Cruz de Tenerife** (p139), you can scale the architectural heights of **La Laguna** (p145), get busy at **Puerto de la Cruz** (p150), soak up the atmosphere at **La Orotava** (p155), then scale the literal heights of the **Parque Nacional del Teide** (p159). Every possible entertainment option may well draw you to the international playground feel of **Costa Adeje, Playa de las Américas** and **Los Cristianos** (p167), or you may well feel like making a pilgrimage to **Candelaria** (p165).

From Gran Canaria's capital of **Las Palmas** (p61), you can bar crawl and beachcomb to your heart's content, although in landlocked escapes such as **San Bartolomé de Tirajana** (p75), **Fataga** (p75) and **Los Berrazales** (p79) getting away from it all may appeal. You may wish to take on the spectacular coastal drive between **Aldea de San Nicolás** (p79) and **Agaete** (p78), where a slap-up seafood lunch is assured. If it's family-friendly options you're after, look no further than the **Maspalomas** (p80) area.

See the individual listings for these attractions throughout the book or refer to the Transport chapter (p247) for details of getting there and around.

The archipelago's two biggest islands (and biggest rivals) offer the greatest geographical diversity and the widest range of options for visitors. Get in the car and cruise the beaches, towns, ports and dunes over seven days.

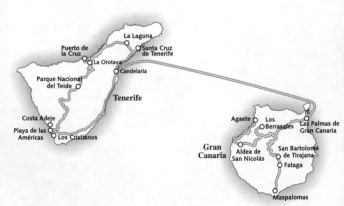

TAILORED TRIPS

LOVIN' LAVA

As the Canaries are volcanic in origin, it makes sense to go a little volcano crazy while here. The very islands are the tips of volcanoes that arose from the Atlantic Ocean millions of years ago, and some – Tenerife, El Hierro, Lanzarote and La Palma – are still active.

El Hierro is still home to a staggering 500 volcanic cones. The area known as **La Restinga** (p228) is a must – the volcanic *malpaís* (badlands; deeply eroded barren areas) showcase contorted lava shapes. With an eruption as recently as 1971, La Palma is probably the closest you'll get to wondering 'what if…?' while you're exploring volcanoes on the Canary Islands; visit **Los Canarios de Fuencaliente** (p208), where you do some great walks.

On La Gomera, you'll notice an absence of craters and cones, but you will find *roques* –odd-looking rock formations that were gradually exposed as volcanic fissures eroded the surrounding landscape – such as **Roque Cano** (p188). The big daddy of 'em all in this part of the world is **El Telde** (p160) on Tenerife, where you can revel in the awe-inspiring views and majestic power of Spain's highest peak.

Gran Canaria's colourful **Los Azulejos** (p88), on the road between Puerto de Mogán and Aldea de San Nicolas, demonstrate the unusual beauty to be found in the fiery leftovers. The **Malpaís de la Corona** (p125) on Lanzarote are a strikingly barren landscape redolent of destruction, where vegetation struggles to survive, while the **Parque Nacional de Timanfaya** (p129), also on Lanzarote, with its 'Mountains of Fire', as well as the spectacular **Ruta de los Volcanos** (p129), is a highlight of any visit here.

CANARIAN CUISINE

Amid the mountains of 'international' cuisine and fast-food joints, some fabulous dining experiences can be found in the Canary Islands. On the western-most isles, the *paradores* (state-owned up-market hotels) combine location, architecture and first-rate dining to create a wonderful experience that's well worth the travel. On El Hierro, the **Parador Nacional** (p226) is kitted out with big picture windows overlooking the ocean and offers traditional Canarian food. The **Parador Nacional** (p205) on La Palma boasts Manuel Martín Gutiérrez slaving over a hot stove, while **Parador Nacional Conde de la Gomera** (p185) is without a doubt the most refined establishment of San Sebastián de la Gomera. Staff dress in local costume and the few but consistently good dishes are creative versions of Canary favourites. Tenerife's **Parador Nacional** (p162) dishes up the sort of excellent cuisine that has travel writers gushing – and all in the most elegant surrounds, with jaw-dropping views.

Surprisingly, other great dining options can be found in the restaurants-cum-tourist-attractions designed by César Manrique around Lanzarote and in the **Mirador de la Peña** (p227) on El Hierro. You'll find incredible design features, quality local ingredients, reasonable prices, and, more often than not, wonderful views or sights to go with your meal.

THE WINE TRAIL

We have to be honest: you're not going to come across any Grand Crus in the Canaries. But you will find leafy volcanic vineyards to mosey around, some of them making rather tasty wines that in the 16th and 17th centuries even Shakespeare praised (see the boxed text on p209).

Head to Lanzarote, where the unusual planting style around **La Geria** (p130) is a unique adaptation to the soil and climate. After having a peek, try some local *vino del volcán* (wine of the volcano) at the wine bars.

Tenerife is known for its wines too, and the island has five *denominación de origenes*, or appellations certifying a high standard and regional origin. Start with a visit to the **Casa del Vino La Baranda** (p149) in El Sauzal to get a little background, then drive around the nearby Tacoronte vineyards or head south to El Médano, where you can visit the **Tasca Frontos winery** (p166).

Head south to Fuencaliente where the volcanic soil gives birth to sweet brews in wineries such as **Bodegas Teneguia** and **Vinos Carballo** (p209). The *malvasía* (Malmsey wine) of La Palma is worth a taste too (p209).

The Authors

SALLY O'BRIEN   Coordinating Author

Being Australian, Sally was already a fan of stunning landscapes, miles of beaches, cold beer, laid-back cities, friendly people, fresh seafood and plenty of sunshine. The opportunity to enjoy it all 'à la Canarias', and with tax-free shopping, proved hard to resist. Her only regrets involve airline baggage restrictions, not having good enough legs to become a drag act at Carnaval and wanting to spend more time surfing. Previous work for Lonely Planet that left her wilting in the heat and sleep-deprived includes Lonely Planet's *Madrid Condensed*.

Sally's Favourite Trip

After weeks spent amid the heaving crowds and blindingly white resorts of Gran Canaria and Fuerteventura, my low-key arrival on Lanzarote – to be met by a guy who handed me the keys to a rattling old Citroën and gave me a rudimentary map – was a welcome relief. My arrival in La Caleta de Famara (pp128–9) had me smiling with joy – after all, a handful of great seafood restaurants, some simple accommodation options and a superb stretch of beach was probably the basic recipe for the Canary Islands' success all those years ago, before inappropriate development, international menus and rented sun loungers took over. It may seem like a remote place to get to – but for a getaway *par excellence*, it's hard to beat.

La Caleta de Famara ○

Lanzarote

SARAH ANDREWS   Coauthor

North Carolina native Sarah Andrews has been writing about Spain since 1998, though she had never seen so much lava and so many weird rocks until she hit the Canary Islands. When not traipsing around the mountainous terrain of the western isles, she writes from her home base in Barcelona, publishing articles and guidebooks about Spain and working as the Associated Press correspondent in Catalunya. This book is her first for Lonely Planet.

CONTRIBUTING AUTHOR

Dr Caroline Evans wrote the Health chapter. Caroline studied medicine at University of London, and completed General Practice training in Cambridge. She is the medical adviser to Nomad Travel clinic, a private travel health clinic in London, and also a GP specialising in travel medicine. She has been an expedition doctor for Raleigh International and Coral Cay expeditions.

Snapshot

Some of the more interesting graffiti you'll find sprinkled about in the Canary Islands revolves around the topic of independence from 'the mainland', with the inadvertently amusing 'Spanish Go Home!' seeming to be the preferred slogan. With the Canary Islands full to bursting with Germans, the English and assorted Scandinavians, you'd think the islands' inhabitants would be sick of tourists; but no, for some it's the Spanish who are unwelcome. The region's flag is a yellow, blue and white tricolour – to which the few militant *independentistas* (people who are pro-independence) add seven stars to represent the islands, as a reminder that the Canary Islands are a separate land mass from the Iberian peninsula. Don't worry about getting caught in some kind of coup, though – Canarian nationalism has generally been a fringe phenomenon.

FAST FACTS

Population: 1,694,477

People aged over
100: 175

Coastline: about 1500km

Unemployment: 57,600

No matter what the occasional anti-goth (or *godo* in Spanish; goth is what the Canarios call the Spaniards) sentiment, Franco's decision in the 1960s to open up sunny Spain to foreign sun-lovers has provided the archipelago with its most pressing agendas. Millions upon millions of visitors have poured in here for the last 40 years, escaping the rainy skies of Munich, Manchester or Moscow. And it's that dry, sunny climate that causes the biggest pickle. You may well find yourself muttering 'Water, water everywhere' as you gaze upon acres of aquatic theme parks, miles of glorious beaches and seriously lavish thalassotherapy spas, but remember that particular poetic stanza ends with the line 'And not a drop to drink'. With no rivers and hardly any rainfall, the lack of water in the islands is a big deal. Desalinisation has been the only solution thus far (see p39 for more).

At the time of research, the most incendiary issue was the thorny, heated and heartbreaking subject of illegal boat people. Despite appearances, the Canaries are Spanish, and therefore European, and to many of northern and western Africa's inhabitants, they represent a chance to attain freedom, prosperity and hope.

For so long the Canary Islands lost many of its inhabitants to foreign shores (see p28). And, as the wheel turns full circle, the eastern islands in particular are now a staging post for a new generation of economic migrants – folk who risk their lives crossing illegally from the African mainland in fragile rowing boats. The motives are just the same: fleeing poverty in the hope of creating a new life on a new continent. Throughout the summer months, dozens of flimsy boats brave the waters between Morocco and Fuerteventura – and dozens of passengers never make it to dry land. The discovery of the drowned bodies of immigrants is a distressingly regular occurrence on Canary shores.

Despite hot-air platitudes and rhetoric about 'what to do' with this problem, and with the people who make it to shore, it appears that this issue is not going to resolve itself any time in the near future.

History

MISTS OF MYTH

The existence of the islands was known, or postulated, in ancient times. Plato (428–348 BC), in his dialogues *Timaeus* and *Critias*, spoke of Atlantis, a continent sunk deep into the ocean floor in a great cataclysm that left only the peaks of its highest mountains above the water. Whether Plato believed in the lost continent's existence or had more allegorical intentions remains a matter of conjecture. In the centuries since Plato's death, those convinced of the existence of Atlantis have maintained that Macronesia (the Canary Islands, the Azores, Cape Verde and Madeira) constitutes the visible remains of the lost continent.

Legend also has it that one of the 12 labours of Hercules (Heracles to the Greeks) was to go to the end of the world and bring back golden apples guarded by the Hesperides (daughters of evening), offspring of Hesperis and Atlas, the latter a Titan in Greek and Roman mythology who gave his name to the Atlantic Ocean and the Atlas mountain ranges in Morocco. Hercules supposedly had to go beyond the Pillars of Hercules (the modern Strait of Gibraltar), to reach the paradisiacal home of these maidens. Hercules carried out his task and returned from what many later thought could only have been the Canary Islands – about the only place to fit the ancients' description (see the boxed text on p59).

Classical writer Homer identified the islands as Elysium, a place where the righteous spent their afterlife. For all their storytelling, there is no concrete evidence that either the Phoenicians or Greeks ever landed on the Canaries. It is entirely possible, however, that early reconnaissance of the North African Atlantic coast by the Phoenicians and their successors, the Carthaginians, took in at least a peek at the easternmost islands of the archipelago. Some historians believe a Phoenician expedition landed on the islands in the 12th century BC, and that the Carthaginian Hanno turned up there in 470 BC.

The expanding Roman Empire defeated Carthage in the Third Punic War in 146 BC; but the Romans appear not to have been overly keen to investigate the fabled islands, which they knew as the Insulae Fortunatae (Fortunate Isles). A century-and-a-half later, shortly after the birth of Christ, the Romans received vaguely reliable reports on them, penned by Pliny the Elder (AD 23–79) and based upon accounts of an expedition carried out around 40 BC by Juba II, a client king in Roman North Africa. In AD 150, Ptolemy fairly accurately located the islands' position with a little dead reckoning, tracing an imaginary meridian line marking the end of the known world through El Hierro.

DID YOU KNOW?

The islands are estimated to be 30 million years old, relatively young in geological terms.

THE GUANCHES

That the Canary Islands were inhabited before the birth of Christ is undisputed. But by whom? Carbon dating of the sparse archaeological finds has pushed back the known date of the earliest settlement to around 200 BC, although earlier occupation is quite conceivable. For a long time, learned observers maintained that the islands were first inhabited by Cro-Magnon man, the Neolithic predecessor of modern *Homo sapiens*. Such conclusions have emerged from the comparison of ancient skulls of indigenous inhabitants with Cro-Magnon remains discovered in the Mediterranean.

Historians tend to wrinkle their noses up at the idea now, although the evidence either way is so flimsy that it cannot be completely ruled out. It

GUANCHE SOCIETY

For all their differences, the tribes of the Canary Islands had much in common. Their stone-age economy was reliant on limited farming, herding, hunting and gathering. The main sources of meat were goats and fish. Barley was grown and, once ground and toasted, formed *gofio*, the basic staple, which in one form or another is still eaten today.

Women made pottery, often decorated with vegetable dyes. Implements and weapons were fashioned roughly of wood, stone and bone. Goat-skin leather was the basis of most garments, while jewellery and ornaments were largely restricted to earthenware bead-and-shell necklaces.

The majority of islanders lived in caves, mostly artificial. On the eastern islands some built simple low houses, with rough stone walls and wood-beam roofs covered with stones and caked with wet earth.

Oddly enough, the Guanches seem to have known nothing of sailing, at best using simple dugouts for coastal fishing or to move occasionally between the islands. Among the Guanches' primitive weapons were the *banot* (lance), rocks and the *tenique* (a stone wrapped up in animal hide and used as a mace).

The Guanches worshipped a god, known as Alcorac in Gran Canaria, Achaman in Tenerife, and Abora in La Palma. It appears the god was identified strongly with Magec (the sun). Tenerife islanders commonly held that Hades (hell) was in the Teide volcano, and was directed by the god of evil, Guayota.

throws the doors of speculation wide open, since Cro-Magnon man came onto the scene as long as 40,000 years ago.

A disconcerting clue is provided by European descriptions of locals in the wake of conquest in the 15th century. They found, mainly on Tenerife, tall and powerfully built people, blue-eyed and with fair hair down to their waists. These lanky blond islanders were known as Guanches (from *guan*, 'man', and *che* or *achinch*, meaning 'white mountain' in reference to the snow-capped Teide volcano).

The Guanches – Survivors and their Descendants, by José Luis Concepción, is a fine tome that looks at the fate of the islands' first inhabitants. The author also wrote a volume on customs, called *Costumbres, Tradiciones Canarias* (published in English and German).

The Tenerife Guanches fascinated the Europeans (and ultimately put up the most tenacious resistance to them), but their origin is an open question. If they were not descendants of Cro-Magnon man, where did they come from? Some suggest they were Celtic immigrants from mainland Iberia, possibly even related to the Basques. More fancifully, it is tempting to see a drop of Nordic blood in the Guanches – did Norse raiding parties land here in the 8th or 9th centuries?

Whatever the explanation, the term Guanche came to be used for all the Canary Islands' indigenous people, although not all of them fit the description. On the eastern islands in particular, the original inhabitants were almost certainly Berber migrants from nearby Saharan Africa. Place names and the handful of words of the Canary Islands' languages (or dialects) that have come down to us bear a striking resemblance to Berber tribal languages. It has also been noted that the occasional case of blue eyes and blond-ish hair occurs among the Berbers too. This would lend still more credence to the feeling that the islands' original inhabitants were all Berber migrants, and so dispel more imaginative speculation of the kind mentioned above.

When, and in what number, these people occupied the islands remains a mystery, but it appears certain that they came from several tribes. One of them may have been the Canarii tribe, which could explain the islands' present name. Certainly, by the time European swashbucklers started nosing around the islands in the Middle Ages, they were peopled by a variety of tribes often more hostile to one another than to visiting strangers.

Although not as expert as the Egyptians, the Guanches mummified their dead chiefs and nobles before laying them out in burial caves, usually in barely accessible locations. The embalmers were treated as untouchables and excluded from community life.

The head of a tribe or region was the *mencey*, although on Gran Canaria the chief's title was more commonly *guanarteme*. His rule was almost absolute, although justice was administered through a council of nobles *(achimencey)*, sometimes known as a *taoro* or *tagoror*. The *taoro* would usually gather under the ancient branches of a dragon tree *(Dracaena draco)*. Between them, the chief and aristocrats owned all property, flocks and fields, leaving the *achicaxna* (plebs) to get along as best they could.

Although living in an essentially patriarchal society, women did have some power. On Gran Canaria in particular, succession rights were passed through the mother rather than the father. But when times got tough, they got tougher still for women. Infanticide was practised throughout the islands in periods of famine – and it was girls who were sacrificed, never boys.

The island clans were not averse to squabbling, and by the time the European conquest of the islands got under way in the 15th century, Tenerife was divided into no less than nine tiny fiefdoms. Gran Canaria had also been a patchwork of minor principalities, but by the 15th century these had merged to form two kingdoms, one based around the town of Gáldar, another around Telde. Fuerteventura was another island divided in two, and tiny La Palma boasted an astonishing 12 cantons (small, territorial divisions). The other islands were each ruled by one *mencey*.

FIRST ENCOUNTERS

Virtually no written record remains of visits to the Fortunate Isles until the 14th century. The first vaguely tenable account of a European landing comes in the late 13th or early 14th century when the Genoese captain Lanzarotto (or Lancelotto) Malocello bumped into the island that would later bear his name: Lanzarote. From then on, slavers, dreamers searching for the Río de Oro (the 'River of Gold' route for the legendary African gold trade that many thought spilled into the Atlantic at about the same latitude as the islands), and missionaries bent on spreading the Word all made excursions to the islands.

Of these missions, the most important and influential was the Italian-led and Portuguese-backed expedition of 1341. Three caravels (two- or three-masted sailing ships) charted a course around all seven islands and took note of even the tiniest islets: the Canary Islands were finally, and more or less accurately, on the map.

THE CONQUEST BEGINS

On 1 May 1402, Jean de Béthencourt, lord of Granville in Normandy (France) and something of an adventurer, set out from La Rochelle with a small and ill-equipped party bound for the Canary Islands. The avowed aim, as the priests brought along for the ride would testify, was to convert the heathen islanders. Uppermost in de Béthencourt's mind was more likely the hope of glory and a fast buck. With his partner, Gadifer de la Salle, he may have hoped to use the Canaries as a launch pad for exploration of the African coast in search of the Río de Oro. That project never got off the ground, and the buccaneers decided to take over the islands instead. So commenced a lengthy and inglorious chapter of invasion, treachery and bungling. Many Guanches would lose their lives or be sold into slavery in the coming century, the remainder destined to be swallowed up by the invading society.

De Béthencourt's motley crew landed first in Lanzarote, at that stage governed by Mencey Guardafía. There was no resistance and de Béthencourt went on to establish a fort on Fuerteventura.

DID YOU KNOW?

La Gomera was the last place Christopher Columbus touched dry land before setting sail to the New World (see the boxed text on p184).

That was as far as he got. Having run out of supplies and with too few men for the enterprise, he headed for Spain where he aimed to obtain the backing of the Castilian crown. What had started as a private French enterprise now became a Spanish imperialist adventure.

De Béthencourt returned in 1404 with ships, men and money. Fuerteventura, El Hierro and La Gomera quickly fell under his control. Appointed lord of the four islands by the Spanish king, Enrique III, de Béthencourt encouraged the settlement of farmers from his Norman homeland and began to pull in the profits. In 1406 he returned for good to Normandy, leaving his nephew Maciot in charge of his Atlantic possessions.

History of the Canary Islands, by José M Castellano Gil and Francisco J Macíos Martín, is a fairly straightforward summary of the islands' past. This book is published in various languages by the Centro de la Cultura Popular Canaria.

SQUABBLES & STAGNATION

What followed was scarcely one of the world's grandest colonial undertakings. Characterised by continued squabbling and occasional mutiny among the colonists, the European presence did nothing for the increasingly oppressed islanders in the years following de Béthencourt's departure.

The islanders were heavily taxed and many were sold off into slavery; Maciot also recruited them for abortive raids on the remaining three independent islands. He then capped it all off by selling to Portugal his rights – inherited from his uncle – to the four islands. This move prompted a tiff with Spain, which was eventually awarded rights to the islands by Pope Eugene V. Low-key rivalry continued for years, with Portugal only recognising Spanish control of the Canaries in 1479 under the Treaty of Alcáçovas. In return, Spain agreed that Portugal could have the Azores, Cape Verde and Madeira.

Maciot died in self-imposed exile in Madeira in 1452. A string of minor Spanish nobles proceeded to run the show, all eager to sell their rights to the islands almost as soon as they had acquired them.

Numerous commanders undertook the business of attacking the other islands with extraordinarily little success. Guillén Peraza died in an attempt to assault La Palma in 1443. In 1464 Peraza's brother-in-law Diego de Herrera, appointed lord of La Gomera, attempted a landing on Gran Canaria and another near present-day Santa Cruz de Tenerife. By 1466 he had managed to sign a trade treaty with the Canarios, and won permission to build a defensive turret in Gando Bay.

The Canary Islands Through History, by Salvador López Herrera, attempts to trace the story of the Guanches and the Spanish conquest of the archipelago. This is a quirky volume of at times dubious academic worth.

THE FALL OF GRAN CANARIA

In 1478 a new commander arrived with fresh forces (including, for the first time, a small cavalry unit), and orders from the Catholic Monarchs of Spain, Fernando and Isabel, to finish the Canaries campaign once and for all. Juan Rejón landed and dug in at the site of modern Las Palmas de Gran Canaria. He was immediately attacked by a force of 2000 under Doramas, *guanarteme* (island chief) of the island's Telde kingdom. Rejón carried the day but fell victim to internal intrigue by making an enemy of the spiritual head of the conquered territories, Canon Juan Bermúdez, accusing him of incompetence.

The investigator sent from Spain, Pedro de Algaba, sided with Bermúdez and had Rejón transported to the mainland in chains. But, once there, Rejón convinced the Spanish authorities that he'd been unjustly treated and was given carte blanche to return to the Canaries to re-establish his control. One of his first acts was to have Algaba, his erstwhile accuser, arrested and executed. However, this act of vengeance proved his final undoing, as Queen Isabel believed the punishment unwarranted and had Rejón replaced by Pedro de Vera.

De Vera continued the campaign and had the good fortune to capture the island's other *guanarteme*, Tenesor Semidan (known as Don Fernando Guanarteme after his baptism), in an attack on Gáldar by sea. Tenesor Semidan was sent to Spain, converted to Christianity and returned in 1483 to convince his countrymen to give up the fight. This they did and de Vera subsequently suggested that some might like to sign up for an assault on Tenerife. Duly embarked, de Vera committed the umpteenth act of treachery that had marked the long years of conquest: he packed them off to be sold as slaves in Spain. But the Canarios learnt of this and forced the ships transporting them to put in at Lanzarote.

After the frightful suppression of a revolt in La Gomera in 1488 (p180), de Vera was relieved of his post as Captain-General of the conquest.

THE FINAL CAMPAIGNS

De Vera's successor was Galician Alonso Fernández de Lugo, who in 1491 received a royal commission to conquer La Palma and Tenerife. He began in La Palma in November and by May of the following year had the island under control. This he achieved partly by negotiation, though the last *mencey* of La Palma, Tanausú, and his men maintained resistance in the virtually impregnable crater of the Caldera de Taburiente. Only by enticing him out for talks on 3 May and then ambushing him could de Lugo defeat his last adversary on the island. For La Palma, the war was over.

Tenerife provided the toughest resistance to the Spaniards. In May 1494 de Lugo landed in Tenerife, together with 1000 infantry soldiers and a cavalry of 150, among them Guanches from Gran Canaria and La Gomera.

In the ensuing months the Spaniards fortified their positions and attempted talks with several of the nine *menceys*, managing to win over those of Güímar and Anaga. Bencomo, *mencey* of Tahoro and sworn enemy of the invaders, was sure of the support of at least three other *menceys*, while the remaining three wavered.

In spring of the following year, de Lugo sent a column westwards. This proved a disaster. Bencomo was waiting in ambush in the Barranco de Acentejo ravine. The Spanish force was decimated at a place now called La Matanza de Acentejo (Slaughter of Acentejo). De Lugo then thought better of the whole operation and left Tenerife.

By the end of the year, he was back to engage in the second major battle of the campaign – at La Laguna on 14 November 1494. Here he had greater success, but the Guanches were far from defeated, and de Lugo fell back to Santa Cruz. At the beginning of the new year a plague known as the *modorra* began to ravage the island. It hardly seemed to affect the Spaniards but soon took a serious toll on the Guanches.

On 25 December 1494, 5000 Guanches under Bencomo were routed in the second battle of the Acentejo. The spot, only a few kilometres south of La Matanza, is still called La Victoria (Victory) today. By the following July, when de Lugo marched into the Valle de la Orotava to confront Bencomo's successor Bentor, the diseased and demoralised Guanches were in no state to resist. Bentor surrendered and the conquest was complete. Pockets of resistance took two years to mop up, and Bentor eventually committed suicide.

Four years after the fall of Granada and the reunification of Christian Spain, the Catholic Monarchs could now celebrate one of the country's first imperial exploits – the subjugation in only 94 years of a small Atlantic archipelago defended by Neolithic tribes. Even so, the Spaniards had some difficulty in fully controlling the Guanches. Many refused to

Jews in the Canary Islands: Being a Calendar of Jewish Cases Extracted from the Records of the Canariote Inquisition in the Collection of the Marquess of Bute was translated by Lucien Wolf. If the title hasn't filled you in, nothing will.

DID YOU KNOW?

The modorra of 1495 was probably a lethal mix of influenza, pneumonia and encephalitis.

settle in the towns established by the colonists, preferring to live their traditional lives out of reach of the authorities.

Nevertheless, the Guanches were destined to disappear. Although open hostilities had ceased, the conquistadors continued shipping them as slaves to Spain. Remaining Guanches were converted en masse to Christianity, taking on Christian names and the surnames of their new Spanish godfathers.

Some of the slaves would be freed and permitted to return to the islands. Although the bulk of them were dispossessed of their land, they soon began to assimilate with the colonisers. Within a century, their language had all but disappeared: except for a handful of words, all that comes down to us today are the islands' many Guanche place names.

The Canary Islands After the Conquest, by Felipe Fernández-Armesto, a leading authority on the islands' history, is a fairly specialised work concentrating on 16th-century life in the Canaries.

ECONOMIC & FOREIGN CHALLENGES

From the early 16th century, Gran Canaria and Tenerife in particular attracted a steady stream of settlers from Spain, Portugal, France, Italy and even Britain. Each island had its own local authority, or *cabildo insular*, although increasingly they were overshadowed by the Royal Court of Appeal, established in Las Palmas in 1526. Sugar cane had been introduced from the Portuguese island of Madeira, and soon sugar became the Canaries' main export.

The 'discovery' of the New World by Christopher Columbus in 1492, who called in to the archipelago several times en route to the Americas, proved a mixed blessing. It brought much passing transatlantic trade but also led to sugar production being diverted to the Americas, where the cane could be grown and processed more cheaply. The local economy was rescued only by the growing export demand for wine, produced mainly in Tenerife; *vino seco* (dry wine), which Shakespeare called Canary Sack, was much appreciated in Britain.

Poorer islands, especially Lanzarote and Fuerteventura, remained backwaters, their impoverished inhabitants making a living from smuggling and piracy off the Moroccan coast – the latter activity part of a tit-for-tat game played out with the Moroccans for centuries.

Spain's control of the islands did not go completely unchallenged. The most spectacular success went to Admiral Robert Blake, one of Oliver Cromwell's three 'generals at sea'. In 1657, a year after war had broken out between England and Spain, Blake annihilated a Spanish treasure fleet (at the cost of only one ship) at Santa Cruz de Tenerife.

British harassment culminated in 1797 with Admiral Horatio Nelson's attack on Santa Cruz. Sent there to intercept yet another treasure shipment, he not only failed to storm the town but lost his right arm in the fighting.

ISLAND RIVALRIES

Within the Canary Islands, a bitter feud developed between Gran Canaria and Tenerife over supremacy of the archipelago. The fortunes of the two rested largely with their economic fate.

When the Canaries were declared a province of Spain in 1821, Santa Cruz de Tenerife was made the capital. Bickering between the two main islands remained heated and Las Palmas frequently demanded that the province be split in two. The idea was briefly but unsuccessfully put into practice in the 1840s.

In 1927 Madrid finally decided to split the Canaries into two provinces: Tenerife, La Gomera, La Palma and El Hierro in the west; Fuerteventura, Gran Canaria and Lanzarote in the east.

FRANCO'S SPAIN

In the 1930s, as the left and the right in mainland Spain became increasingly militant, fears of a coup grew. In March 1936 the government decided to 'transfer' General Franco, a veteran of Spain's wars in Morocco and beloved of the tough Spanish Foreign Legion, to the Canary Islands.

Suspicions that he was involved in a plot to overthrow the government were well-founded; when the pro-coup garrisons of Melilla (Spanish North Africa) rose prematurely on 17 July, Franco was ready. Having seized control of the islands virtually without a struggle (the pro-Republican commander of the Las Palmas garrison died in mysterious circumstances on 14 July), Franco flew to Morocco on 19 July. Although there was virtually no fighting on the islands, the Nationalists wasted no time in rounding up anyone vaguely suspected of harbouring Republican sympathies.

The postwar economic misery of mainland Spain was shared by the islands, and again many Canarios opted to emigrate. In the 1950s the situation was so desperate that 16,000 migrated clandestinely, mainly to Venezuela, even though by then that country had closed its doors to further immigration. One-third of those who attempted to flee perished in the ocean crossings.

DID YOU KNOW?

General Franco stayed in the Hostal Madrid in Las Palmas de Gran Canaria the night before launching his coup.

TOURISM & 'NATIONALISM'

When Franco decided to open up the doors of Spain to northern European tourists the Canaries benefited as much as the mainland. Millions of holiday-makers now pour into the islands year-round.

Always a fringe phenomenon, Canaries nationalism started to resurface in opposition to Franco. MPAIC (Movimiento para la Autodeterminación e Independencia del Archipiélago Canario), founded in 1963 by Antonio Cubillo to promote secession from Spain, embarked on a terrorist campaign in the late 1970s; Cubillo was expelled, though later he was allowed to return.

In 1978 a new constitution was passed in Madrid with devolution as one of its central pillars. Thus the Canary Islands became a *comunidad autónoma* (autonomous region) in August 1982, yet they remained divided into two provinces.

The main force in Canary Islands politics since its first regional election victory in 1995 has been the Coalición Canaria (CC). Although not bent on independence from Spain (which would be unlikely), the CC nevertheless puts the interests of the islands before national considerations. Don't be surprised to see graffiti along the lines of 'Spanish Go Home'.

The Culture

REGIONAL IDENTITY

Most of the Canary Island locals have the classic Mediterranean looks of the Spaniards (with perhaps a little Berber mixed in) – dark hair, flashing eyes and olive complexion. But talk to some for a while and you might find that they don't think of themselves as all that Spanish.

The *godos* (goths), as the Canarios refer to Spaniards from the peninsula, are not automatically thought of as being part of the family. While mainlanders like to joke about the Canarios being African, there are some in the islands who actually prefer to think of themselves that way (at least insofar as this distinguishes them from the rest of Spain). After all, they are geographically much closer to the African continent than to the Spanish mainland.

Well before the Canary Islands were declared a single province of Spain in 1821, competition for primacy between the two main islands, Tenerife and Gran Canaria, was already intense. The selection of Santa Cruz de Tenerife as the provincial capital infuriated politicians and other worthies in Las Palmas de Gran Canaria, and marked the beginning of a long fight to have the province split in two. Tried and shelved in the 1840s, the idea only became reality in 1927. Lanzarote, Fuerteventura and Gran Canaria formed one province, with Las Palmas as the capital, while Tenerife, La Palma, La Gomera and El Hierro were grouped under the leadership of Santa Cruz de Tenerife.

Soon after the 1982 electoral victory of the socialists at national level, the Canary Islands were declared a *comunidad autónoma,* one of 17 autonomous regions across Spain. And plenty of Canarios would like to see their islands become completely autonomous – keep an eye peeled for splashes of graffiti declaring 'Spaniards Go Home'.

The region's flag is a yellow, blue and white tricolour, to which the few militant *independentistas* add seven stars to represent the islands. The provincial division remains intact, as does the bitter rivalry between the two provinces – so much so that the regional government has offices in both provincial capitals, which alternate as lead city of the region every four years!

LIFESTYLE

The greatest lifestyle change that has come to the Canary Islands has been the tourism industry. In a matter of decades a primarily agricultural society became a service industry. Traditional lifestyles on small *fincas* (farms) or in fishing villages have been supplanted by employment in the tourism sector. This may go some way to explaining a certain reticence in the local population – after all, work is work – so don't take offence when it seems there's a distance between you and the locals a lot of the time.

NAMING NAMES

Although the term 'Canario' has come to designate all of the islanders, it once referred more strictly to the people of Gran Canaria alone (now more often as not referred to as Grancanarios or Canariones). The people of Tenerife are Tinerfeños; those of Lanzarote are not Lanzaroteños but Conejeros; Fuerteventura, Majoreros (from the Guanche name for much of the island, Maxorata); La Gomera, Gomeros; La Palma, Palmeros; and El Hierro, Herreños.

Making casual friends on the islands is not difficult. You don't need to be overly outgoing to strike up a chat with locals (particularly if you speak passable Spanish), but don't expect it to go much further than that. Hearty farewells and promises of further meetings, while not to be dismissed, are to be taken with a sizable grain of salt.

People socialise in cafés, bars, restaurants and public places. Dinner parties and intimate gatherings in people's homes are the exception rather than the rule. Canarios are a pretty relaxed lot but, like mainland Spaniards and most Latin peoples, they like to dress well, at least when on show.

POPULATION

The total resident population of the Canary Islands is growing at a slow rate. Mind you, for every Canario, five foreigners visit the islands each year! The bulk of the country's population is concentrated on the two main islands – Gran Canaria (730,620) and Tenerife (806,000). Of the remaining islands, the population ranges from 97,000 in Lanzarote to just 10,002 in El Hierro.

Only a fraction of all the people who visit the Canaries decide to stay for good. Of the Europeans who do stay, the Germans and Brits are by far out in front. Many of the 35,000-odd from the Americas are descendants of Canarios who migrated there generations ago. Venezuelans, their country the most favoured destination for migrants from these often less-than-fortunate isles, are by far the most numerous.

SPORT

The Canary Islands are a sport-friendly destination, as they have a balmy, sunny climate, plenty of coastline and a laid-back, outdoor lifestyle that rewards activity. As part of Spain, there are no prizes for guessing the top sport here: football (soccer). There are two teams in the national competition – for details, see p144 and p73.

Lucha Canaria

The Guanches of Tenerife were a particularly robust and war-like crowd who loved a trial of strength. Any island party was an excuse for indulging in tests of manhood. Apart from jumping over steep ravines and diving into the ocean from dizzying heights, one favourite pastime was wrestling. Rooted in this ancient diversion lies the essence of the modern *lucha canaria* (Canarian wrestling).

One member of each team faces off his adversary in the ring and, after a formal greeting and other signs of goodwill, they set about trying to dump each other into the dust. No part of the body except the soles of the feet may touch the ground, and whoever fails first in this department loses. Each pair fight it out in a best of three competition (each clash is known as a *brega*), and the team with the most winning wrestlers wins the whole show.

Size and weight are not the determining factors (although these boys tend to be as beefy as rugby front-row forwards), but rather the skill with which the combatants grapple and manoeuvre their opponents into a position from which they can be toppled. Kicking, punching, pinching and so on are not permitted. Historically, the *lucha* was staged for fiestas and also as a means of resolving disputes.

There is a major league competition known as the Copa Presidente del Gobierno Canarias. Clashes at this level are often televised.

If you want to find out if any matches are due to be held locally, ask at the nearest tourist office.

Stick Fighting

The *juego del palo* (literally 'stick game') started off in preconquest days as anything but a game. Two combatants would arm themselves with heavy staves and stones, and attempt to break as many bones in their opponents' bodies as possible. After the arrival of the Spaniards, the 'game' became increasingly marginalised to rural areas and became more a trial of skill than a violent blood sport.

The sport, if it can be called such, is still practised throughout the islands, and there is even a federation devoted to it. The staff is now made of sturdy wood and is about 2m long. The stick goes by various names, *banot* in Tenerife and *lata* in Fuerteventura. You are most likely to see a demonstration of the *juego del palo* at local fiestas.

A related sport involving poles is the *lucha al garrote*, where opponents wield even longer staves.

EMIGRATION

The Canarios have long looked across the Atlantic to farther shores, and a high proportion of Cubans and continental Americans can claim a Canarian gene or two.

Following in the wake of Christopher Columbus, Canarios were among the earliest colonisers. In the early days, the most popular destinations were Cuba, La Hispañola (today's Dominican Republic and Haiti) and Puerto Rico in the Caribbean. On the mainland, pioneers settled around Buenos Aires in Argentina, Montevideo in Uruguay, and Caracas in Venezuela. Further north, Canarios were well represented in Florida, Louisiana, Yucatán and Nueva España (Texas) – it was a group of Canaries emigrants who, on 9 March 1731, founded San Fernando (today's San Antonio, Texas).

There were two later surges in emigration, both spurred as much by poverty on the islands and the need to escape as by hope of a new life and new deal over the waters. In the Canaries, the 1880s are called the decade of *la crisis de la cochinilla* (the cochineal crisis), when synthetic dyes swamped the international market and killed off the local cochineal cottage industries. Later, the hard times that Spain endured following the Spanish civil war and WWII were even harder on the archipelago, and lasted right through until the 1960s.

In the Franco era, many Canarios left without a passport or papers and arrived illegally in the new land (the Americas). Here, they were interned in camps and then set to work, cutting cane in the sugar plantations in order to earn their keep – arduous labour from which they escaped to better-paid work at the first opportunity.

Venezuela is often called the 'eighth island' of the Canaries. So strong are business, family and cultural links that each day many Canarian newspapers carry a whole page of news from Caracas, and Televisión Autonómica, the islands' TV channel, has a similar daily news programme.

Nowadays the Canary Islands, for so long a region of net emigration, admit more people than they export – workers for the hotel, restaurant and construction industries, and migrants from northern Europe seeking a place in the near-perpetual sun.

RELIGION

One of the primary concerns of the conquistadors from Spain was to convert what they perceived to be the heathen of these far-flung islands to the one true faith. As the conquest proceeded, the indigenous inhabitants were swiftly converted to Christianity, usually as part of the terms of surrender.

Catholicism has left a deep-rooted impression on the Canaries. Although the depth of the average Canario's religiosity may be a subject of speculation, the Church still plays an important role in peoples' lives. Most Canarios are baptised and confirmed, have church weddings and funerals, and attend church for important feast days – although fewer than half regularly turn up for Sunday Mass. Many of the colourful and often wild fiestas that take place throughout the year have some religious context or origin.

You may come across references to cults on one or two of the islands. The Order of the Solar Temple, or something like it, has been known to have a base in Tenerife. No need to worry about being brainwashed, though – they're more interested in UFOs.

ARTS
Architecture
The Guanches lived more often than not in caves; nothing of the rudimentary houses they built remains today.

Spaniards, Portuguese, French, Flemish, Italian and English masters all injected something of their own architectural wealth into the Canaries. By the time the conquest of the islands was completed at the end of the 15th century, the Gothic and *mudéjar* (type of Islamic architecture) styles already belonged more to the past than the present. The interior of the Catedral de Santa Ana in Las Palmas (p66) is nevertheless a fine example of what some art historians have denominated Atlantic Gothic. The bell tower of the Basílica de la Virgen del Pino (p77) in Teror, Gran Canaria, retains its Portuguese Gothic identity.

Only a few scraps of *mudéjar* influence made it to the islands. Probably the best examples are the fine wooden ceilings (known as *artesonado*) in the Iglesia de Nuestra Señora la Concepción (p147) in La Laguna, Tenerife. Not far behind are those of the Iglesia de Santa Catalina (p149) in Tacoronte, on the same island.

You can get the merest whiff of *plateresque* (meaning silversmith-like, so called because it was reminiscent of intricate metalwork) energy at the Catedral de Las Palmas in Gran Canaria and the Iglesia de Nuestra Señora la Concepción in La Laguna, Tenerife – the latter a veritable reference work of styles from Gothic, through *mudéjar* to *plateresque*. The Casa/Museo de Colón (p65) in Las Palmas also has *plateresque* features. Baroque, the trademark of the 17th century, left several traces across the archipelago and is best preserved in the parish church of Betancuria (p97), Fuerteventura.

Neoclassical, neogothic and other styles demonstrating a perhaps less creative, more derivative era are represented from the late 18th century onwards in imposing public buildings in the bigger cities. The Iglesia de San Juan in Arucas (p77) is an impressive piece of neogothic architecture – a shame it's not the genuine article.

Modernism makes an appearance along the Calle Mayor de Triana and in the private houses of the Triana district of Las Palmas de Gran Canaria.

Rural houses were, and still are, simple affairs. Their outstanding element is usually an internal courtyard or patio, where a great deal of family life is played out. Another singular element about these houses, usually brilliantly whitewashed, is their wooden upstairs balconies. At their most elaborate, such balconies are intricately carved works of art.

Private houses and mansions in the towns might incorporate various styles with, say, a *plateresque* entrance, wooden balconies of various types and a striking variety of broad windows. These windows are, in some cases, true works of art: multipaned and with varied combinations of wooden shutters, frames and panels.

MILITARY ARCHITECTURE

From the earliest days of the conquest well into the 18th century, the single most common construction efforts – apart from churches – were castles and forts. This lasted well into the 18th century. The bulk of these forts were (and are) rough-and-ready affairs, and few have particular artistic merit. Among those to look out for though are the Torre del Conde (p183), San Sebastián de la Gomera, Castillo de la Luz (p67), Las Palmas de Gran Canaria and the Castillo de San Juan (p142), Santa Cruz de Tenerife.

The patio, again, remains a paramount element – usually the most striking and beautiful part of Canario houses. The mix, in many cases, bears signs of Portuguese and Andalucían influence.

Literature

Until the arrival of the conquering Spaniards in the 15th century, the Guanches appear not to have known writing. Very much a frontier world even after the conquest, the Canaries were not an immediate source of world-renowned writers.

Little, if anything, that the islands have produced in the way of literature has made it into English translation.

This is not to say the islanders have been inactive. The Guanches themselves did not write down their verses but some of their oral ballads were transcribed by an Italian historian, Leonardo Torriani. And with the conquistadors came storytellers to chronicle their exploits.

Various historians and poets followed. The first of note beyond the islands was the Tinerfeño writer José de Viera y Clavijo (1731–1813), an accomplished poet but known above all for his painstaking history of the islands, *Noticias de la Historia General de Canarias*. His contemporary, Tomás de Iriarte (1750–91), born in Puerto de la Cruz, was for years something of a dandy in Madrid court circles. He wrote several plays, but his *Fábulas Literarias*, poetry and tales charged with a mordant wit, constituted his lasting work.

Ricardo Murphy (1814–40) led the way for Romantic poetry on the islands, but succumbed at an early age, as did so many ardent poets of the time, to tuberculosis (which he contracted in London).

Nicolás Estévanez (1838–1914) spent much of his life outside the Canaries, first as a soldier and politician in Madrid and then in exile for 40 years in France. His poems, in particular 'Canarias', marked him as the motor behind the so-called Escuela Regionalista, a school of poets devoted to themes less universal and more identifiable with the archipelago.

Another of the islands' great historians emerged about the same time. Agustín Millares Torres (1826–96) is remembered for his monumental *Historia General de las Islas Canarias*.

Benito Pérez Galdós (1843–1920) grew up in Las Palmas de Gran Canaria, moving to Madrid in 1862. A prolific chronicler of his times, he produced 46 novels and numerous other books and plays.

Ángel Guimerá (1849–1924), born in Santa Cruz de Tenerife, moved to the mainland to become one of Barcelona's great lyric poets and a leading figure in Catalan theatre.

Dr Tomás Morales (1885–1921) became, in his short life, one of the islands' leading exponents of Modernist poetry. A contemporary of his, also of some note, was Alonso Quesada (1886–1925).

The poet Josefina de la Torre (1907–2002) first achieved fame in the late 1920s. As the 20th century wore on, the poets of the Vanguardia took the

Among Benito Pérez Galdós' masterpieces is the four-part *Fortunata y Jacinta*, which recounts the lives of two unhappily married women of different social classes during the period of the Alfonsine revolution of 1875.

centre stage. Among the Canaries' exponents were Pedro Perdomo Acedo (1897–1977) and Felix Delgado (1904–36).

Carmen Laforet Díaz's (1921–) *Nada*, written in the wake of the Civil War, is the partly autobiographical account of a young girl's move from her home in the Canary Islands to study in post–Civil War Barcelona, where she is obliged to live in squalor with her grandmother. She has followed this up with other novels of lesser impact and, in 1961, *Gran Canaria*, a guide to her home island.

One of the most creative talents to emerge among the postmodern poets of the 1980s was Yolanda Soler Onís (1964–). *Sobre el Ámbar*, written from 1982 to 1986, is a collection of pieces whose images are sourced largely from an exploration of the islands' poetic traditions.

Other contemporary novelists to look out for are Roberto Cabrera and E Díaz Marrero.

Music

The symbol of the Canarios' musical heritage is the *timple*, a ukulele-style instrument of obscure origin. Although many thought it was a variation of the Italian mandolin or the Spanish and Portuguese *guitarillo*, it now appears that Berber slaves, shipped in for farm work by the early Norman invaders under Jean de Béthencourt, might have introduced it to the islands.

It's a small, wooden, five-stringed instrument with a rounded back (it is said the original Berber version was made of a turtle shell) and a sharp tone. There is also a four-string version known as the *contra* or *requinto*, prevalent in Lanzarote.

The *timple* has travelled widely, as emigrants from the islands took it with them to Latin America, where it was incorporated into their instrumental repertory.

Whenever you see local traditional fiestas, the *timple* will be there accompanying such dances as the *isa* and *folía* or, if you're lucky, the *tajaraste* – about the only dance said to have been passed down from the ancient Guanches.

Los Sabandeños is one of the most widely known folkloric groups in the Canary Islands, and their CDs of light, melodic music are widely available.

Over the centuries there has been no shortage of immigration from Andalucía in the south of Spain, and with it came another musical tradition. Popular Andalucían dances such as the *malagueña* have become part of the local island folk tradition.

Rosana Arbelo, born in Lanzarote in 1962, is a fine *cantautor* (singer-songwriter) whose lyrics tend to the melancholy, accompanied by an appealing mix of Cuban, Spanish and African rhythms. However, the islands' most established *cantautor*, and one appreciated across all Spain, is Tenerife's Pedro Guerra.

Visual Arts

The Guanches left behind a number of cave paintings and petroglyphs (rock carvings), notably in the *cuevas* (caves) of Gáldar (p78) on Gran Canaria, Belmaco (p208) and Parque Cultural La Zarza (p216) on La Palma and Los Letreros (p228) on El Hierro. The paintings appear to date from at least the 13th and 14th centuries. Some depict human and animal figures, while others (such as in Cueva Pintada de Gáldar, p78) are essentially geometric figures and decorative designs. Circles and ovals seem to have been the preferred symbols, and feature among funerary inscriptions on Lanzarote and La Palma.

Isaac de Vega was one of the 20th century's outstanding novelists in the Canaries. His *Fetasa* (1957) is a disturbing study of alienation and solitude and is without doubt the book that kick-started other typically 'Canarian' works of the period.

SHOE BIZ

The Canary Islands aren't exactly brimming with top-flight fashion designers (indeed, it would seem that the Canaries' greatest fashion statement is more of a question: 'Does my bum look big in this?'). That said, arguably the greatest shoe designer in the world, Manolo Blahnik, was born in Santa Cruz de Tenerife in 1943. Blahnik still drops by to see his mother in between bursts of creativity that encourage the wealthy and beautiful women of New York, London and Paris to part with big money for spike heels. He discovered his passion for female footwear as a child growing up on a banana plantation – how, we're not sure, but that's how the story goes.

In the 17th century, Gaspar de Quevedo from Tenerife was the first major painter to emerge from the Canary Islands. Quevedo was succeeded in the 18th century by Cristóbal Hernández de Quintana (1659–1725), whose paintings still decorate the Catedral de la Laguna (p147) in Tenerife. More important was Juan de Miranda (1723–1805), among whose outstanding works is *La Adoración de los Pastores* (The Adoration of the Shepherds) in the Iglesia de Nuestra Señora la Concepción (p142) in Santa Cruz de Tenerife. His best known acolyte was Luis de la Cruz y Ríos (1776–1853), born in La Orotava and above all a portraitist.

In the 19th century, Valentín Sanz Carta (1849–98) was among the first Canarios to produce landscapes. Others of his ilk included Lorenzo Pastor and Lillier y Thruillé, whose work can be seen in the Museo de Bellas Artes (p141) in Santa Cruz de Tenerife.

The Canaries' main exponent of Impressionism was Manuel González Méndez (1843–1909), whose *La Verdad Venciendo el Error* hangs in the *ayuntamiento* (town hall; Map pp140–1) of Santa Cruz de Tenerife.

Néstor Martín Fernández de la Torre (1887–1938), whose speciality was murals, is best represented by his *Poema del Mar y Poema de la Tierra* (Poem of the Sea and Poem of the Earth). This and other works can be seen in the Museo Nestor (p67), a gallery dedicated mainly to his artwork, in Las Palmas de Gran Canaria.

The Cuban-Canario José Aguiar García (1895–1976), born of Gomero parents, grew up in Cuba. A prolific painter, he too reached the apogee of his craft in his murals. His works are spread across the islands; the *Friso Isleño* hangs in the casino in Santa Cruz de Tenerife.

All the great currents of European art filtered through to the Canary Islands. Of the so-called Coloristas, names worth mentioning include Francesco Miranda Bonnin (1911–63) and Jesús Arencibia, who created the big mural in the Iglesia de San Antonio Abad (p66) in Las Palmas de Gran Canaria.

The first surrealist exhibition in Spain was held on 11 May 1935 in Santa Cruz de Tenerife. The greatest local exponent of surrealism, Tinerfeño surrealist Óscar Domínguez (1906–57), ended up in Paris in 1927 and was much influenced by Picasso. Others of the period include Cubist Antonio Padrón (1920–68), Felo Monzón (1910–89) and Jorge Oramas (1911–35).

Leading the field of abstract artists is Manuel Millares (1921–72), native of Las Palmas de Gran Canaria. Lanzarote's César Manrique (1919–92) also enjoyed a considerable degree of international recognition.

Canarios currently working hard at the canvas include Cristino de Vera (born 1931, lives in Madrid), who displays elements of a primitive expressionism in his paintings, and María Castro (born 1930), and José Luis Fajardo (1941–), who uses just about any materials that come to hand in his often bizarre works.

Environment

THE LAND

The seven islands and six islets that make up the Canary Island archipelago are little more than the tallest tips of a vast volcanic mountain range that lies below the ocean. Just babies in geological terms, the islands were thrown up 30 million years ago when great slabs of the Earth's crust (called tectonic plates) collided, crumpling the land into mammoth mountains both on land, as in the case of Morocco's Atlas mountain range, and on the ocean floor, as in the case of the Cape Verde islands, the Azores and the Canaries. These Atlantic islands are collectively referred to as Macronesia. After the initial creation, series of volcanic eruptions put the final touches on the islands' forms.

There is still plenty of activity across the floor of the Atlantic Ocean and many peaks lie out of sight below the surface. Occasionally new volcanic islands are puffed up into the light of day, but they are generally little more than feeble mounds of loose ash and are quickly washed away.

These days in the Canary Islands you can best get a feel for the rumblings below the surface on Lanzarote, where the Montañas del Fuego (p129) still bubble with vigour – although the last eruptions took place way back in 1824. Of the remaining islands, not an eruptive burp has been heard from Fuerteventura, Gran Canaria, La Gomera or El Hierro for centuries; Tenerife's most recent display was a fairly innocuous affair in 1909, and it was La Palma that hosted the most recent spectacle – a fiery outburst by Volcán Teneguía in 1971 (p208).

The seven main islands have a total area of 7447 sq km. Their size may not be great, but packed into them is just about every imaginable kind of landscape, from the long sandy beaches of Fuerteventura and dunes of Gran Canaria to the majestic Atlantic cliffs of Tenerife and mist-enveloped woods of La Gomera. The easternmost islands have an almost Saharan desertscape, while corners of La Palma and La Gomera are downright lush. The highest mountain in all of Spain is the Pico del Teide (Teide peak; 3718m; p160), which dominates the entire island of Tenerife.

None of the islands has rivers, and lack of water remains a serious problem. Instead of rivers, webs of barrancos (ravines) cut their way from the mountainous interior of most of the islands to the coast. Water flows along some, but others remain dry nearly year-round.

Lanzarote and Fuerteventura, the two most easterly islands, would be quite at home if attached to the nearby coast of continental Africa (which is just 115km away). Their hilly landscapes are otherworldly, though neither island is blessed with impressive mountains. Long stretches of beach, like the Playa de Sotavento de Jandía (p108) are Fuerteventura's greatest tourist drawing card.

Lanzarote, last rocked by a volcanic eruption in 1824, takes its present appearance from a series of massive blasts in 1730. The lava flow was devastating in many ways, but it created fertile ground where before there was nothing. Today Lanzarote produces a wide range of crops grown mostly on volcanic hillsides. Another by-product of that eruption are the Montañas del Fuego (Mountains of Fire) in the Parque Nacional de Timanfaya, where volcanic rocks still give off enough heat to sizzle a steak (literally – see it being done at the Restaurante del Diablo, p129). North of the island are clustered five of the archipelago's six little islets (the other is Isla de Lobos, p106, just off the northern tip of Fuerteventura).

DID YOU KNOW?

La Palma is the steepest island in the world, relative to its height and overall area.

www.canarias.org has extensive information on the archipelago's flora, fauna and volcanic origins.

Gran Canaria is roughly a circular-based volcanic pyramid. Its northern half is surprisingly green and fertile, while south of the peak of Pozo de las Nieves (1949m; p76) the territory is more arid, reminiscent of Gran Canaria's eastern neighbours. For the variety of its geography, flora and climate, the island is often dubbed a 'continent in miniature'.

Gran Canaria's big brother, at least in terms of size, is Tenerife – every bit as much a 'mini-continent' and last redoubt of the Guanches (indigenous Canarios). Almost two-thirds of the island is taken up by the rugged slopes of the volcanic mountain peak and crater Teide, which is not only Spain's highest peak, but also the third-largest volcano in the world, after Hawaii's Mauna Loa and Mauna Kea. A further string of mountains, the Anaga range, spreads along the northeastern panhandle. The only real lowlands are around La Laguna and alongside parts of the coast. The staggering cliffs of the north coast are occasionally lashed by Atlantic rain squalls, which are arrested by the mountains in such a way that the southwestern and southeastern coasts present a more serene weather picture.

The remaining western islands have much in common with one another. Better supplied with spring and/or rain water, they are green and ringed by rocky, ocean-battered coastlines. La Palma's dominant feature is the yawning funnel known as the Caldera de Taburiente (pp212–15), whose highest peak is the Roque de los Muchachos (2426m). The centre of La Gomera's high *meseta* (plateau) is covered by a Unesco-listed laurel forest, the Parque Nacional de Garajonay (p179). El Hierro, smallest of the Canary Islands and a Unesco-listed biosphere reserve (see the boxed text on p222), is mountainous – the highest peak is Malpaso at 1501m – with a coastline that seems designed to be a fortress.

El Teide & Other Volcanoes

El Teide (p160) is what's known as a shield volcano – huge and rising in a broad, gently angled cone to a summit that holds a steep-walled, flat-based crater. Although seemingly quieter than Italy's Vesuvius, Etna and Stromboli, all of which still have it in them to cause quite a fright, Teide is by no means finished.

Wisps of hot air can sometimes be seen around the peak of Teide. Where the lava is fairly fluid, steam pressure can build up to the point

---

VOLCANIC ORIGINS

You don't have to be long in the Canary Islands to notice the astonishing variety of volcanic rock. Towering cones, tiny lightweight pebbles, rough untameable badlands (deeply eroded barren area), smooth and shiny rock, red rock, black rock…they're all scattered about, blasted out of the Earth's surface by the countless eruptions that have rocked the archipelago over its history.

The way a volcano erupts is largely determined by its gas content. If the material seething beneath the surface has a high gas content, the effect is like shaking a bottle of fizzy drink; once the cap's off, the contents spurt out with force. In the case of volcanoes, what are called pyroclasts – cinders, ash and lightweight fragments of pumice – are hurled high into the air and scatter over a wide area.

On the other hand, if the mix is more viscous, the magma wells up, overflows a vent, then slows as it slithers down the mountain as lava flow, cooling all the while until its progress is stopped. You'll see several such congealed rivers, composed of spiky and irregular clinker (volcanic slag), in the Parque Nacional de Timanfaya on Lanzarote and around the slopes of Teide. Look also for obsidian (fragments or layers of smooth, shiny material, like black glass) and scoria (high in iron and magnesium and reddish brown in colour since it's – quite literally – rusting).

of ejecting lava and ash or both in an eruption through the narrow vent. The vent can simply be blown off if there is sufficient pressure.

Stratovolcanoes, similar to the shield volcanoes, are found on the islands too, and sometimes they literally blow their top. Massive explosions can cause the whole summit to cave in, blasting away an enormous crater. The result is known as a caldera, within which it is not unusual for new cones to emerge, creating volcanoes within volcanoes. There are several impressive calderas on Gran Canaria, most notably Caldera de Bandama (p76). Oddly enough, massive Caldera de Taburiente (p212) on La Palma does not belong to this group of geological phenomena, although it was long thought to.

When volcanoes do erupt, they belch out all sorts of things: ash, cinders, lapilli (small, round bombs of lava) and great streams of molten rock. Volcanic eruptions, however, don't just come through one central crater. Often subsidiary craters form around the main cone as lava and other materials force fissures into the mountain and escape that way.

The Volcanoes of the Canary Islands, by Vivente Araña and Juan Carracedo, is a series of three volumes about – what else? – Canary Island volcanoes. Lovely photos and informative text.

WILDLIFE
Animals
Perhaps 'wildlife' is a little misleading. Sure, there are wild lives out there in the natural areas of even the most populated islands, but they tend to be small and shy, and largely undetected by the untrained eye. Bugs abound, and lizards and birds are the biggest things you'll see – in some cases they are quite big indeed, like the giant lizard of El Hierro (p221). There are some 200 species of birds on the islands, though many are imports from Africa and Europe. Among the indigenous birds are the canary (those in the wild are a muck-brown colour, not the sunny yellow colour of their domesticated cousins) and a few large pigeons.

To see something more thrilling (no offence to birds), you'll have to head out to the ocean, where it's likely that you can observe whales and dolphins in the wild. The stretch between Tenerife and La Gomera is a traditional feeding ground for as many as 26 species of whales, and others pass through during migration. The most common are pilot whales, sperm whales and bottlenose dolphins.

Whale-watching is big business around here, and 800,000 people a year head out on boats to get a look. A law regulates observation of sea mammals, prohibiting boats from getting closer than 60m to an animal and limiting the number of boats following schools at any one time. The law also tries to curb practices such as using sonar and other devices to attract whales' attention. Four small patrol boats attempt to keep a watchful eye on these activities.

Try to join an outfit that respects the regulations. You could also contact the organisation Whales & Tales in Tenerife (see p40).

Aside from the majestic marine mammals, there are many other life forms busy under the ocean. The waters around the Canary Islands host 350 species of fish, and about 600 species of algae. You can see them up close by signing up for a scuba diving or snorkelling excursion. See the activities sections of individual island chapters for more information.

DID YOU KNOW?

The giant lizard of El Hierro grows as long as 45cm.

ENDANGERED SPECIES
The giant lizard of El Hierro (p221) was once common on the island, though its numbers began seriously dwindling in the 1900s. By the 1940s nary a trace was to be found, and the species was given up for lost. Miraculously, a tiny population of these 45cm-long lizards managed to survive on a precipice, and a pair was discovered and captured by a local

---

NOT-SO-FRIENDLY FIDO

If you come across a solid-looking dog with a big head and a stern gaze, you are probably getting to know the Canary dog, known in Spanish as the *presa canario*. This beast is right up there with the pit bull as a tenacious guard dog, loyal and chummy with its owners but rarely well disposed to outsiders.

The breed is also known as the *verdino* (from a slightly greenish tint in its colouring), and opinion is divided regarding its origins. Probably introduced to the islands in the wake of the Spanish conquest in the 15th century, and subsequently mixed with other breeds, the Canary dog has been used for centuries to guard farms and cattle. When it comes to stopping human intruders in their tracks, no other dog is so full of fight. It is prized by owners for its fearlessness and loyalty.

One can only speculate about the dogs mentioned in Pliny's description of ancient King Juba's expedition to the islands in 40 BC. These dogs were said to be exceptionally robust and there are those who are convinced that the *verdino's* ancestors were indeed present on the islands 2000 years ago. But as usual, the accounts are conflicting.

Some academics maintain that the conquistadors were none too taken with these animals, considering them wild and dangerous, and eventually set about having the majority of them destroyed.

Other accounts suggest that the Spaniards found no such animals on their arrival and, hence, later introduced their own. Whatever the truth, the Canary dog is now prized as a local island breed.

---

herdsman. Now there is a recovery programme working to breed the lizards in captivity and slowly introduce them into the wild.

Plants

The islands' rich volcanic soil, varied rainfall and dramatic changes in altitude support a surprising diversity of plant life, both indigenous and imported. The Canary Islands are home to about 2000 species, about half of them unique to the islands. The only brake on what might otherwise be a still more florid display in this largely subtropical environment is the shortage of water. Even so, botanists will have a field day here, and there are numerous botanical gardens scattered about where you can observe a whole range of local flora.

Up to an elevation of about 400m, the land is home to plants that thrive in hot and arid conditions. Where farmland has been irrigated, you'll find bananas, oranges, coffee, sugar cane, dates and tobacco. In the towns, bougainvillea, hibiscus, acacia, geraniums, marigolds and carnations all contribute to the bright array. Of the more exotic specimens, the strelitzia, with its blue, white and orange blossoms, stands out. These exotics have all been introduced to the islands. The dry, uncultivated scrublands near the coast, known as *tabaibales*, host various indigenous plants such as *cardón* (*Euphorbia*).

At elevations of around 700m, the Canaries' climate is more typical of the Mediterranean, encouraging crops such as cereals, potatoes and grapes. Where the crops give way, stands of eucalyptus and cork take over. Mimosa, broom, honeysuckle and laburnums are also common.

Higher still, the air is cooler, and common plants and trees include holly, myrtle and the laurel. The best place to explore forest land is in La Gomera's Parque Nacional de Garajonay (p179), host to one of the world's last remaining Tertiary-era forests and declared a Unesco World Heritage site. Known as *laurisilva*, it is made up of laurels, holly, linden and giant heather, clad in lichen and moss and often swathed in swirling mist.

DID YOU KNOW?

More than half of Spain's endemic plant species are found in the Canary Islands.

Up to 2000m high, the most common tree you're likely to encounter is the Canary pine *(Pinus canariensis)*, which manages to set down roots on impossibly steep slopes that would defeat most other species. It is a particularly hardy tree whose fire-resistant timber makes fine construction material.

Up in the great volcanic basin of the Parque Nacional del Teide (p159) on Tenerife are some outstanding flowers. Apart from the feisty high-altitude Teide violet, one of the floral symbols of the Canaries is the flamboyant *tajinaste rojo*, or Teide viper's bugloss *(Echium wildpretii)*, which can grow over 3m high. Every other spring it sprouts an extraordinary conical spike of striking red blooms like a great red poker. After its brief, spectacular moment of glory, all that remains is a thin, desiccated spear-shaped skeleton, like a well-picked-over fish. Leave well alone; each fishbone has thousands of tiny strands, itchy as horsehair.

Although much of the vegetation is common across the islands, there are some marked differences. Fuerteventura, Lanzarote and the south of Gran Canaria distinguish themselves from the rest of the islands with their semidesert flora, where saltbush, Canary palm and other small shrubs dominate. Concentrated in a couple of spots – the cliffs of La Caleta de Famara in Lanzarote, and Jandía in Fuerteventura – you will find more abundant flora. This includes the rare *cardón de Jandía* (a cactus-like plant), several species of daisy and all sorts of odd cliff plants unique to these islands.

National Parks and Flora of the Canary Islands, published by Otermin Ediciones, is an easy-to-read overview of the Canaries' four national parks and the plants found in them.

NATIONAL PARKS

With more than 40% of its territory falling under one of eight categories of parkland, the Canary Islands are one of the most extensively protected territories in all of Europe.

At the top of the park pyramid are the four *parques nacionales* (national parks), administered at state level from Madrid. The regional government handles the other seven varieties of protected spaces, which range from rural parks to the more symbolic 'site of scientific interest'.

Only since the late 1980s have real steps been taken to protect the islands' natural diversity. A series of laws establishing and then enforcing protected spaces pushed the effort from merely a good intention to a solid structure of parks and protected spaces.

THE TREE WITH A LONG, SHADY PAST

Among the more curious trees you will see in the Canary Islands is the *drago* (dragon tree; *Dracaena draco*), which can reach 18m in height and live for centuries.

Having survived the last ice age, it looks different – even a touch prehistoric. In shape it resembles a giant posy of flowers, its trunk and branches the stems, which break into bunches of long, narrow silvery-green leaves higher up. As the plant (technically it is not a tree, though it's always referred to as one) grows, it becomes more and more top heavy. To stabilise itself, the *drago* ingeniously grows roots on the outside of its trunk, eventually creating a second, wider trunk.

What makes the *drago* stranger still is its red sap or resin – known, of course, as 'dragon's blood' – which was traditionally used in medicine.

The plant played an important role in Canary Island life, for it was beneath the ancient branches of a *drago* that the Guanche Council of Nobles would gather to administer justice.

The *drago* is one of a family of up to 80 species *(Dracaena)* that survived the ice age in tropical and subtropical zones of the Old World, and is one of the last representatives of Tertiary-era flora.

CANARY NATIONAL PARKS & UNESCO RESERVES

Park Name	Features	Activities	For Kids	Page
Parque Nacional del Teide, Tenerife	Spain's highest mountain, the volcanic peak of Teide, volcanic landscapes	Riding the cable car to the peak, hiking around Los Roques de García	The little ones will love the cable car	159
Parque Nacional de Garajonay, La Gomera	A prehistoric laurel forest, horizontal rain, pines	Hiking to the top of the Alto de Garajonay, cycling down from the summit	The La Laguna Grande has a playground and recreational area	188
Parque Nacional de Timanfaya & Montañas del Fuego, Lanzarote	Volcanic activity, warm volcanic rocks due to molten lava beneath the surface	Eating at the Restaurante del Diablo, touching and walking on hot volcanic lava	A camel ride at the Museo de las Rocas	129
Parque Nacional de la Caldera de Taburiente, La Palma	Towering rock walls, slopes of pines	Hiking into the cauldron-like Caldera in the park's centre	The walks around La Cumbrecita are ideal for short legs	212
Los Tilos Biosphere Reserve, La Palma	Lush laurel forest, a watery gorge	Hiking along the gorge, stopping in the informative visitors centre	The lookout point near the visitors centre is a short walk away	216
Lanzarote, Biosphere Reserve (Unesco has declared the entire island a biosphere reserve)	Unique plants, marine reserve, volcanic landscape	Walking among some of the archipelago's most dramatic volcanic landscapes, relaxing on volcanic beaches	Older kids will gawk at César Manrique's weird architecture	114
El Hierro, Biosphere Reserve (Unesco has declared the entire island a biosphere reserve)	Aboriginal etchings, pine forests, twisted juniper trees	Driving through El Pinar, walking among the junipers in El Sabinar	Stop in the Hoya del Morcillo recreation area	222

The islands' four national parks, for instance, are largely protected from human interference by rules banning visitors from free camping or straying from defined walking paths. You can contribute by obeying the rules on where you are permitted to hike and keeping all your trash with you – what you take in you should also take out.

There are also several World Heritage Sites, declared and protected by Unesco.

ENVIRONMENTAL ISSUES

As in mainland Spain, the 1960s saw the first waves of mass sea-and-sun tourism crash over the tranquil shores of the Canary Islands. The government of the day rubbed its hands in anticipation of filling up the state coffers with easy tourist dollars, and local entrepreneurs enthusiastically leapt aboard the gravy train. Few, however, gave a thought to what impact the tourists and the mushrooming coastal resorts might have on the environment.

The near-unregulated building and expansion of resorts well into the 1980s has created some monumental eyesores, particularly on the southern side of Tenerife and Gran Canaria. Great scabs of holiday villas, hotels and condominiums have spread across much of the two islands' southern coasts. And the problem is not restricted to the resorts – hasty cement extensions of towns and villages mean that parts of the interior of the islands are being increasingly spoiled by property developers and speculators.

The massive influx of visitors to the islands over recent decades has brought or exacerbated other problems. Littering of beaches, dunes and other areas of natural beauty, both by outsiders and locals, remains a burning issue. Occasionally ecological societies organise massive clean-ups of rubbish along beaches and the like – worthy gestures but equally damning evidence of the extent to which the problem persists.

For the islands' administrators, it's a conundrum. Tourism has come to represent an essential pillar of the Canaries' economy, which quite simply it cannot do without. They argue that profits from the tourist trade are ploughed back into the community. However, this is still fairly haphazard and there have long been calls for more regional planning – and, every year more insistently, for a total moratorium on yet more tourism development. Some of the damage done over the years, especially to the coastline, is irreversible.

www.gobcan.es/medioambiente/eng is the Canary government's informative environment page, where you'll find news and information on everything from whales to forest fires.

Water

One of the islands' greatest and most persistent problems is water, or rather the lack of. Limited rainfall and the few natural springs have always restricted agriculture in the islands and water is a commodity still in short supply.

Desalination appears the only solution for the Canaries, which already accounts for 2% of the world's desalinated water production. Pretty much all potable H_2O on Lanzarote and Fuerteventura is desalinated sea water.

In summer, the corollary of the perennial water problem is the forest fire. With almost clockwork regularity, hundreds of hectares of forest are ravaged every summer on all the islands except the already bare Lanzarote and Fuerteventura.

Organisations

The islands are swarming with environmental action groups, some more active than others. Most are members of the **Federación Ecologista Canaria Ben-Magec** (Ben-Magec Ecological Foundation of the Canaries; ☎ 928 31 01 04; Calle de las Botas 5, Las Palmas). Some of the individual groups you'll find on the islands are

---

RESPONSIBLE TOURISM – WATER CONSERVATION

Though the use of desalinated sea water is on the rise, we all should do our part to conserve H_2O, starting with some common-sense strategies, such as limiting shower time, turning off the tap when not using water and requesting that hotel towels not be laundered every day – instead, hang them up to dry and re-use.

listed below. The word 'Apdo' followed by number indicates a postbox number only.

El Hierro Asociación Para la Defensa de la Naturaleza e Identidad del Hierro (☎ 922 55 82 19; Calle de la Ola 7, La Restinga)

Fuerteventura Asociación Canaria de Amigos de la Naturaleza (☎ 928 85 20 71; Calle Juan Tadeo, Puerto del Rosario)

Gran Canaria Asociación Canaria de Amigos de la Naturaleza (☎ 928 27 36 44; Calle Presidente Alvear 50, Las Palmas)

La Gomera Asociación Ecologista y Cultural Guarapo (☎ 922 80 07 10; Apdo 74, 38800 San Sebastián de la Gomera)

La Palma Asamblea Irichen (☎ 922 44 06 62; Apdo 170, 38700 Santa Cruz de la Palma)

Lanzarote Asociación Cultural y Ecologista El Guincho (☎ 928 81 54 32; fax 928 81 54 30; Apdo 365, 35580 Arrecife)

Tenerife Asociación Tinerfeña de Amigos de la Naturaleza (☎ 922 27 93 92; www.atan.org; Calle Santo Domingo 10, 38080 Santa Cruz de Tenerife); Whales & Tales (☎ 922 82 05 59; Apdo 7, 38080 La Laguna)

Canary Islands Outdoors

Being outdoors is what the Canary Islands are all about. With temperatures ranging from about 18°C in winter to 24°C in summer, and an average rainfall hovering around 250mm, you're almost guaranteed the perfect weather for whatever activity suits your fancy. And the astonishing variety of landscapes here – from La Gomera's humid and verdant Parque Nacional de Garajonay to the vast lunarscapes of Lanzarote – means that the same pursuit will be different on each island.

Most trekkers and adventure seekers head towards the smaller islands, especially La Gomera, La Palma and, for water sports, Lanzarote, but it's possible to get away from the crowds and test your adventuresome spirit on any of the seven islands. All boast excellent hiking and biking trails, and the abundance of water sports is obvious. Countless outfitters offer guidance for just about any activity that comes to mind (details are provided in the individual island chapters), but if you decide to set out on your own it's essential to be well-informed about possible dangers, route length and difficulty, and the appropriate gear and clothing.

WALKING & HIKING

Hundreds of trails, many of them historic paths used before the days of cars and highways, crisscross the islands. A good place to start is the national parks – the Parque Nacional del Teide (p159), in Tenerife, the Parque Nacional de Garajonay (p188) in La Gomera and the Parque Nacional de la Caldera de Taburiente (p212) in La Palma all have excellent hiking.

It's also possible, though much more complicated, to walk in Lanzarote's volcanic Parque Nacional de Timanfaya (p129), but you won't be able to wander far. Each of these parks offers a variety of walks and hikes, ranging from easy strolls ending at lookout points to multiday treks across mountains and gorges.

To get a feel for the destruction and power of volcanoes, head to El Teide (p159). Here you can walk across the barren *cañadas* (flatlands) that surround the base of the volcanic peak, or you can hike up to the mouth of El Teide itself, where on clear days you'll gasp at the views of the valley below, the ocean and the islands in the distance. For

---

SAFETY GUIDELINES FOR WALKING & HIKING

Before embarking on a walking trip, consider the following points to ensure a safe and enjoyable experience in the Canary Islands:

- Be sure you are healthy and feel comfortable walking for a sustained period.
- Obtain reliable information about physical and environmental conditions along your intended route (eg from park authorities).
- Be aware of local laws, regulations and etiquette about wildlife and the environment.
- Walk only in regions, and on trails, within your realm of experience.
- Seasonal changes – yes, even in the mild Canary Islands – can vary, so be sure you're not headed to a slippery slope after spring rains or to a snow-capped peak in wintertime.
- Before you set out, ask about the environmental characteristics that can affect your walk and how local, experienced walkers deal with these considerations.

RESPONSIBLE WALKING

To help preserve the ecology and beauty of the Canary Islands, consider the following tips when walking:

- Carry out *all* your rubbish. Don't overlook easily forgotten items, such as silver paper, orange peel, cigarette butts and plastic wrappers. Empty packaging should be stored in a dedicated rubbish bag. Make an effort to carry out rubbish left by others.

- Never bury your rubbish: digging disturbs soil and ground cover and encourages erosion. Buried rubbish will likely be dug up by animals, who may be injured or poisoned by it. It may also take years to decompose.

- Minimise waste by taking minimal packaging and no more food than you will need. Take reusable containers or stuff sacks.

- Sanitary napkins, tampons, condoms and toilet paper should be carried out despite the inconvenience. They burn and decompose poorly.

- Contamination of water sources by human faeces can lead to the transmission of all sorts of nasties. Where there is a toilet, please use it. Where there is none, bury your waste. Dig a small hole 15cm (6in) deep and at least 100m (320ft) from any watercourse. Cover the waste with soil and a rock. In snow, dig down to the soil.

- Ensure that these guidelines are applied to a portable toilet tent if one is being used by a large trekking party. Encourage all party members, including porters, to use the site.

something in between, take the 1½-hour walk around the Roques de García, just south of the peak, where the landscape is varied and not too challenging.

If you like some shade every now and again, try Garajonay (p188), home to one of the last vestiges of the ancient *laurisilva* (laurel) forest that once covered southern Europe. Thanks to a near-permanent mist in the air (called horizontal rain), this green forest is dripping with life and moss. It's beautiful, but the dampness makes walking around here downright cold, so be sure to bring a jacket. From the park's highest point, the Alto de Garajonay, you can see Tenerife and El Teide – if the clouds don't interrupt the view.

The Caldera de Taburiente (p213) offers a landscape somewhere between the verdant Garajonay and the stark Teide. You can hike along the rock walls of the park's interior or meander among the pine forests on the outer slopes of the park. Accessing the caldera's interior is a bit more complicated than accessing other parks, simply because no road runs through it. Be prepared to commit no less than four hours if you want to do anything more than drive up to a *mirador* (lookout point) and walk around.

National parks aren't the only spots with good hiking trails. Among our other favourites are the Ruta de los Volcanos (p210) in La Palma, the descent from the Mirador de Jinama to La Frontera (p227) in El Hierro, the dunes of Maspalomas (p80) and the hike to El Cedro (p187) in La Gomera. The Unesco-protected Los Tilos biosphere reserve (p216) in La Palma is worth a stop too. For a truly spectacular walk, sign up for the 'Tremesana' guided hike in the Parque Nacional de Timanfaya (p129); you'll have to plan in advance, but the effort will be well spent.

You can walk in the Canary Islands any time of year, but some trails become dangerous or impossible in rainy weather, and others (like the trek up to the peak of El Teide) are harder to do in winter, when parts of the trail are covered in snow. Be aware that while along the coast and in the lowlands it's normally warm and sunny, as you head into higher altitudes, the wind, fog and air temperature can change the situation drastically, so always carry warm and waterproof clothing. Don't forget to take water along with you, as there are few fountains or vendors out along the trails.

SCUBA DIVING & SNORKELLING

The variety of marine life and the warm, relatively calm waters of the Canary Islands make this a great place for scuba diving or snorkelling. You won't experience the wild colours of Caribbean coral, but the volcanic coast is made of beautiful rock formations and caves. As far as life underwater goes, you can espy some 350 species of fish and 600 different kinds of algae.

Scuba schools and outfitters are scattered across the islands, so you won't have trouble finding someone willing to take you out. A standard dive, with equipment rental included, costs around €30, but a 'try dive' (a first-timer diving with a teacher) can be double that. Certification classes start at €200 and generally last between three days and a week, though they can be much more expensive depending on the certification level. Many scuba outfitters also offer snorkelling excursions for nondivers, and prices tend to be about half the cost of a regular dive.

The southern coast of El Hierro is considered one of the top spots for scuba diving. There is a wealth of marine life there, thanks in part to the lack of development on the island. Also, the waters in the Mar de las Calmas (Sea of Calm) are among the warmest and calmest of all the archipelago, which increases visibility and makes the whole experience more enjoyable.

Lanzarote offers enviable diving conditions as well, with visibility up to 20m and especially warm waters. One word of warning – all divers

Any of the *Discovery Walking Guides*, which cover all islands except Fuerteventura, will prove to be a helpful hiking companion.

Diving in Canaries by Sergio Hanquet is a big hardback book with luscious photographs of the underwater life you'll find around the Canaries

---

RESPONSIBLE DIVING

The popularity of diving is placing immense pressure on many sites in the Canary Islands. Please consider the following tips when diving and help preserve the ecology and beauty of the marine world:

■ Avoid touching living marine organisms with your body or dragging equipment across reefs. Polyps can be damaged by even the gentlest contact.

■ Be conscious of your fins. Even without contact, the surge from heavy fin strokes can damage delicate organisms.

■ Practise and maintain proper buoyancy control. Make sure you are correctly weighted and that your weight belt is positioned so that you stay horizontal. If you have not dived for a while, have a practice dive in a pool before taking to the reef. Be aware that buoyancy can change over the period of an extended trip: initially you may breathe harder and need more weight; a few days later you may breathe more easily and need less weight.

■ Take great care in underwater caves. Spend as little time within them as possible as your air bubbles may be caught within the roof and leave previously submerged organisms high and dry. Taking turns to inspect the interior of a small cave will lessen the chances of causing damage.

■ Ensure that you take home all your rubbish and any litter you may find as well. Plastics in particular are a serious threat to marine life.

■ Resist the temptation to feed fish. You may disturb their normal eating habits, encourage aggressive behaviour or feed them food that is detrimental to their health.

GETTING YOUR SEA LEGS: BOATING IN THE CANARIES

Ah, so much ocean, so little time! There's no reason to stay land-locked when it's so easy to hire a sailboat, take a day cruise or try sea kayaking. The waters around the island vary greatly, and some places may be too rough for a novice navigator, but there are areas where you'll have no problem. The Mar de las Calmas (Sea of Calm) off El Hierro's southern coast has still waters that draw sea kayakers, while the southern coast of Tenerife is popular with sailors and yachters.

Tacorón, El Hierro (p228) The jagged volcanic coast here makes a surprisingly peaceful backdrop for the small recreational area along the shore, where you can swim in a natural lava rock pool or grill out under the rustic picnic hut. Out on the tranquil waters of the Mar de las Calmas is an ideal place for even beginner kayakers. A paddle along the shore will lead you past towering cliffs, ragged rocks and quiet pools. Nearest town: La Restinga. For information contact **@ctivos** (☎ 922 55 71 71; activos@ya.com).

Puerto Colón, Tenerife (p169) You won't have to sail far from shore before the hotel jungle of Tenerife's largest resort melts into the gentle slopes of the island. Rent a boat or sign up for an excursion with companies in Puerto Colón (listed below) and navigate the waters between Tenerife and La Gomera with the shadow of El Teide behind you. Nearest town: Playa de las Américas & Costa Adeje. For information contact **Water Sport Club** (☎ 922 71 54 04; www.tenerife.com/wsc) or **Excursion Shop** (☎ 922 71 41 72; www.tenerife-direct.com).

Valle Gran Rey, La Gomera (p192) Setting off from the resort's port you'll float past kilometre after kilometre of impenetrable rock cliff before arriving at one of the island's most unique sites, Los Órganos (The Organs), a rock formation seen only from the water that does indeed looks just like an enormous pipe organ carved into the rock. To see it, take one of the cruises that leaves Valle Gran Rey daily. For information contact **Tina** (☎ 922 80 58 85) or **Siron** (☎ 922 80 54 80).

Puerto de Mogán, Gran Canaria (p87) This relatively secluded, discreet resort boasts a first-class marina and plenty of pretty yachts – many available for charter or a simple cruise on the sapphire-coloured waters of southern Gran Canaria. For information contact **Bar Marina** (☎ 928 56 50 95; www.barmarina-mogan.com; Plaza Mayor).

Puerto Calero, Lanzarote (p133) Skippered by the well-regarded Tino García, the boat *Mizu I* will transport you to the nearby depths as you search for mako sharks and other big fish on a fishing trip you'll never forget. The company will pick you up from your hotel and transport you to the port, and all equipment is included in the price. For information contact **Mizu I** (☎ 636 47 40 00; fax 928 51 43 78).

---

here must be registered, though the permit price is usually included with your equipment rental. Some of the best areas for diving are around Isla Graciosa and along Puerto Calero (p127), where you will find marlin, barracuda and a host of other fish. There are spots of orange coral and interesting underwater caves nearby too.

In Tenerife, most diving outfitters are congregated around the southern resorts, though the area around Los Gigantes (p163) has the reputation of having the best diving conditions of the lot. It's possible to do wreck dives (where you explore sunken boats and the like), cave dives and old-fashioned boat dives. Marine life in these waters ranges from eels to angel sharks and stingrays.

In Gran Canaria, Puerto de Mogán (p86) is the main dive centre on the island, and there are plenty of boats heading out to dive in and around the caves and wrecks that lie not far offshore. A popular diving destination is Pasito Blanco, about a 30-minute boat ride from Puerto Rico and considered the best reef dive on the island. The place is teeming with marine life and you can see stingrays on the sand and moray eels slithering about.

SURFING, WINDSURFING & KITESURFING

Surfing, windsurfing and, a new edition, kitesurfing, are popular water sports on most of the islands. Schools offering classes and equipment rental are scattered around the windier Canary coasts, and there are a variety of spots to choose from, ranging from the beginner-friendly sandy beaches of Fuerteventura to the wilder waves of eastern Tenerife. Group surf classes can be as cheap as €5 per hour, though private lessons will be more, and surf board rental is usually about €15 per day. Windsurfing and kitesurfing are pricier; equipment rental costs around €40 per day, and a three-hour private lesson will be somewhere in the vicinity of €125.

La Caleta de Famara (p128) and Isla Graciosa (p127) on Lanzarote offer world-class surf breaks. There's great windsurfing around the Bahía de Pozo Izquierdo (p83) on Gran Canarias, and the Las Palmas area (p68) offers decent waves for surfers too. On Fuerteventura, head to the area around El Cotillo (p107), Corralejo (p102) and the Isla de Lobos (p106), where waves really start pumping around late September and continue throughout the winter. The southern coast of Fuerteventura, in particular Playa de Sotavento (p108) and Playa de Barlovento (p111), are also great windsurfing spots.

On Tenerife, Roque de las Bodegas (p149) attracts local surfers, wind-surfers and boogie boarders. Playa de las Américas (p169) and Las Galletas (p174) are popular windsurfing spots and nearby El Médano (p166) is considered one of the best places in the world for windsurfing. International competitions are held here every year, and enthusiasts from all over the long, sandy beaches to test the waters. Be-ginners beware – it's harder than it looks, and before renting equipment, invest in one of the classes offered by numerous local companies. Courses last between two days and a week, and prices vary widely according to how much you're aiming to learn.

True thrill-seekers can try the latest surfing trend, kitesurfing, which involves being connected to a huge parachute-like kite, standing on a short board and letting the wind take you where it will. Watching the people with know-how leap and flip is amazing, but you have to be a real daredevil to try it. Areas with several windsurfing outfitters are likely to be home to a kitesurfing school or two.

GOLF

In the past decade, southern Tenerife has become the golf hotspot of the Canary Islands. Golfers who love the balmy temperatures that let them play year-round have spawned the creation of a half-dozen courses in and around the Playa de las Américas alone (p170). The courses are aimed at holiday golfers and are not known for being particularly challenging.

You'll also find a few courses around Las Palmas in Gran Canaria, and a course or two dotted around Lanzarote and Fuerteventura.

The lack of water on the islands (see p33) makes golf a rather envir-onmentally unfriendly and difficult sport to sustain. Golf course owners say that the water for those lush greens comes from run-off and local water purification plants, but environmental groups say the golf courses take water from agriculture. The truth is in there somewhere, and local politicians, golf supporters, environmentalists and farmers are still argu-ing about where.

In winter, green fees hover around €75, but in midsummer they could be half that. Renting a golf cart will cost you up to €40, and club rental can cost up to €20.

www.surfcanarias.com

www.traildatabase.org

www.linksgolf.co.uk

www.tenerifegolf.es

CYCLING

If you've got strong legs, then cycling may be the perfect way to see the Canary Islands. Bike rental is available across the islands, and numerous companies offer guided excursions of a day or even longer. If you think you're in very good shape, try the climb up to El Teide (p160) or the Alto

ACTIVITIES FOR THE LITTLE ONES

While cycling and long-distance trekking may be too much of a strain on your shorter-legged companions, the great outdoors offers plenty for kids too. Shorter hikes are an option, and many guides offer easy walks especially aimed at families or the elderly who, like children, may have problems with distances and altitude changes. Ask around at the excursion companies listed in the individual island chapters.

Boat trips are an obvious option, and either the whale-watching trips mentioned in the Environment chapter (p40) or the sailing excursions mentioned in the boxed text on p44 suit kids – just be sure to pack some seasickness drugs for the ride.

Finally, there are a host of organised activities aimed at kids, ranging from camel rides to parasailing (yes, parasailing – kids weighing at least 20kg can try it). See listings in individual island chapters for details.

de Garajonay (p188). But if constantly heading uphill on a bicycle isn't your idea of a good time, sign up with one of the companies that carts you (and your bike) up to the top then turns you loose to race downhill, with nary a peddle push between you and the end of the route.

Less-extreme routes can be found on the eastern islands. Outside Maspalomas on Gran Canaria (p83) there are a few excellent bike trails, and Fuerteventura has decent cycling areas too.

The price of renting a bike depends largely on what kind of bike you get – suspension and other extras will cost more. In general, a day's rental starts at about €15, and a guided hike will be around €35.

Food & Drink

The cuisine of the Canary Islands reflects a wide range of influences, from Spanish regional to global fast food. It would indeed be a shame to stick with the safety of what you know in terms of food – a little investigation into the local dishes pays culinary dividends. The Canaries are not a seaside outpost of northern Europe but a fascinating archipelago whose culinary delights are too often overlooked. If you have an even slightly adventurous approach to your travel, then your taste buds can have just as much of a holiday.

A good range of typical Spanish food is widely available in the islands, partly to satisfy the *godos* (Spaniards) who live here, and partly to widen the choice on offer for locals and visitors alike. Latin American influences are also evident, and the Muslim heritage in sweets and the use of certain spices such as cumin and saffron is a reminder of the centuries of Arab control of southern Spain (right up until the time of the conquest of the islands).

The basis of the truly local cuisine is, however, rather narrow, traditionally restricted to what the islands produce for themselves. If you take the time to circulate around the islands, though, you'll find many variants on standard dishes and quite a few local specialities. Experiment and enjoy!

STAPLES & SPECIALITIES

The staple product *par excellence* is *gofio*, a uniquely Canario product. A roasted mixture of wheat, maize or barley, *gofio* takes the place of bread in the average Canario's diet. There is no shortage of bread these days, but *gofio* remains common. It is something of an acquired taste and, mixed in varying proportions, is used as a breakfast food or combined with almonds and figs to make sweets. The Spanish author Antonio Muñoz Molina recalled in *Ardor Guerrero*, his recollections of conscript days in the Basque city of San Sebastián in northern Spain in the 1980s:

> Pepe Rifón had organised a kind of Leninist cell, a clandestine commune to which we all contributed... The only thing we never managed to share was *gofio*, that passion of our chums from the Canaries...(who) would tear open the packets of *gofio* and shove fistfuls of the stuff into their mouths... 'You mainlanders are the dopes not liking *gofio*,' they'd say. 'It's God's own food'.

Pleasures of the Canary Islands: Wine, Food, Beauty, Mystery, by Ann and Larry Walker, is one of the few introductions to Canarian cuisine in English.

Other basic foods long common across the islands are bananas and tomatoes, but nowadays the markets are filled with a wide range of fruit and vegetables. Beef, pork and lamb are widely available (usually imported), but the traditional *cabra* (goat) and *cabrito* (kid) remain the staple animal protein. Most local cheeses come from goat's milk too.

The Canary Islands owe a lot to Columbus; it was from South America that elementary items such as potatoes, tomatoes and corn were introduced. From there also came more exotic delights such as avocados and papayas, while sweet mangoes arrived from Asia. Look out for all three in the valleys and on supermarket shelves.

Away from the standard Spanish fare, and the tourist-oriented, international-style restaurants in the resorts, there is a genuine local cuisine. The most obvious Canarian contribution to the dinner table is the *mojo* (spicy salsa sauce made from red chilli peppers). This sauce has many variants and is used to dip pretty much anything in – from chicken legs to *gofio*.

Papas arrugadas (wrinkly potatoes) are perhaps the next best-known dish, although there is really not much to them. They're small new potatoes boiled and salted in their skins and only come to life when dipped in one of the *mojos*.

Of the many soups you'll find, one typically Canarian variant is *potaje de berros* (watercress soup). Another is *rancho canario*, a kind of broth with thick noodles and the odd chunk of meat and potato – it's very hearty.

Conejo en salmorejo is rabbit in a marinade made of water, vinegar, olive oil, salt, pepper, sweet black pudding and avocado. Although now considered a pillar of local cuisine, the dish's origins actually lie in distant Aragón, in Spain.

Sancocho canario is a salted-fish dish with *mojo*. On La Gomera you might get a chance to tuck into *buche gomero*, basically salted tuna stomach – it tastes a lot better than it sounds!

Almogrote, a starter from La Gomera, is a goat-cheese spread, flavoured with garlic, chilli pepper and salt.

Some of the classic mainland Spanish dishes widely available include paella (saffron rice cooked with chicken and rabbit or with seafood – at its best with good seafood), *tortilla* (omelette), gazpacho (a cold, tomato-based soup usually available in summer only), various *sopas* (soups) and *pinchos morunos* (kebabs).

Dining in the Canary Islands

First adjustment: locals eat at times of day when most of us wouldn't dream of it! Breakfast *(desayuno)* is about the only meal of the day which takes place about the same time for everyone – that is, when you get up!

The serious eating starts with lunch *(la comida* or, less commonly, *el almuerzo)*: the famous siesta time, the midafternoon, is actually reserved by many locals for this, the main meal of the day. While Canarios tend to eat at home with the family, there is plenty of action in the restaurants too, starting at about 2pm and continuing until 4pm.

This late start sets the tone for the evening procedures too. If you turn up for dinner at 6pm or 7pm, you'll be eating alone – if the restaurant is even open. Of course, in the most heavily touristed areas the restaurants will be open to cater for the strange habits of foreigners, but you'll be unlikely to see a single Canario dining in them.

Dinner *(cena)* is often a lighter meal for your average Canario, although this is not to say that they eschew restaurant outings. In any event, dinner begins, at the earliest, at about 9pm. The bulk of locals wouldn't seriously consider wandering into their favourite eating house until 10pm. As with lunch, the evening meal can easily last two or three hours – a leisurely and highly social affair.

Main meals will generally consist of some form of *carne* (meat), otherwise you will have the choice of many kinds of *pescado* (fish) or *mariscos* (seafood).

MENÚ DEL DÍA

The traveller's friend in the Canary Islands, as in mainland Spain, is the *menú del día*, a set meal available at most restaurants for lunch and occasionally in the evening too. Generally you get a starter or side dish, a main dish, a simple dessert and a drink, all for a modest price – which hovers around €6 at budget establishments and can rise to €13 at posher places.

Your main dish can be preceded by *entremeses*, or starters of various kinds. *Ensaladas* (salads) commonly figure as either starters or side dishes.

Snacks are an important part of the Spanish culinary heritage, particularly the bar snacks known as tapas (see p51). You can usually pick up a quick bite to eat to tide you over until the main meal times swing around.

Canarian Cheese

Goat cheese is produced across several of the islands, but the best-known cheese is probably the *queso de flor*. This is made of a mix of cow's and sheep's milk, which is infused with the aroma of flowers from a type of thistle (the *cardo alcausí*). It is produced exclusively in the Guía area of northern Gran Canaria. Another prizewinning cow and sheep cheese mix is the *pastor*, from around Arucas.

Of the goat cheeses, Fuerteventura's *majorero* – a slightly acidic, creamy cheese – is probably the most highly sought after.

The smoked cheese of El Hierro, *queso herreño*, is also much prized, and outside the island costs considerably more than at home.

Desserts

On an ordinary day in a no-nonsense eatery, you may find your dessert options (*postres*) limited to timeless Spanish favourites such as *flan* (crème caramel), *helado* (ice cream) or a piece of fruit.

But the Canarios do have a sweet tooth. And if you are disappointed after your meal, the best thing you can do is head for the local *pastelería* (cake shop) and indulge yourself.

Some of the better-known sticky sweets are *bienmesabes* (a kind of thick, sticky goo made of almonds and honey – deadly sweet!), *frangollos* (a mix of cornmeal, milk and honey), *tirijaras* (a type of confectionery), *bizcochos lustrados* (a type of sponge cake) and *turrón de melaza* (molasses nougat).

La Palma's honey-and-sugar *rapaduras* are a favourite tooth-rotter, and you shouldn't miss the *quesadillas* from El Hierro – they've been making this cheesy cinnamon pastry (sometimes also made with aniseed) since the Middle Ages. *Morcillas dulces* (sweet blood sausages), made with grapes, raisins and almonds, are a rather odd concoction; perhaps the closest comparison is the Christmas mince pie.

DRINKS
Coffee

The Canary Islanders like coffee strong and slightly bitter. A *café con leche* is about 50% coffee, 50% hot milk; ask for *sombra* if you want lots of milk. A *café solo* is an espresso (short black); *café cortado* (or just *cortado*) is an espresso with a splash of milk. If you like your coffee piping hot, ask for any of the above to be *caliente*.

There are some local variations on the theme. *Cortado de condensado* is an espresso with condensed milk; *cortado de leche y leche* is the same with a little standard milk thrown in. It sometimes comes in a larger cup and is then called a *barraquito*. You can also have your *barraquito con licor* or *con alcohol*, a shot of liquor usually accompanied by a shred of lemon and sometimes some cinnamon – this is the authentic *barraquito*, as any Canario will tell you.

Strangely, these options are all but unknown in the province of Las Palmas, while in the western islands they are coming out of your ears.

Todos los Mojos de Canarias, by Flora Lilia Barrera Álamo and Dolores Hernández Barrera, is one to look out for if you get hooked on *mojo* (salsa sauce). The various recipes that'll let you practise your skills when you get back home are to be treasured.

In the easternmost islands you will be asked if you want your milk *condensada* or *líquida*.

For iced coffee, ask for *café con hielo*: you'll get a glass of ice and a hot cup of coffee, to be poured over the ice – which, surprisingly, doesn't all melt straight away.

Wine

The local wine-making industry is relatively modest, but you can come across some good drops. Wine comes in *blanco* (white), *tinto* (red) or *rosado* (rosé). Prices vary considerably. In general, you get what you pay for and can pick up a really good tipple for about €5.

If it's kick not quality you're after, a bottle of basic wine need cost no more than €2 (especially if you buy it at a supermarket). In restaurants, if you are not too particular about brands, you can simply order the *vino de la casa* (house wine), the cheapest option, which varies from very drinkable to one up on vinegar, depending upon the restaurant.

One of the most common wines across the islands is the *malvasía* (Malmsey wine, also produced in Madeira, Portugal). It is generally sweet *(dulce)*, although you can find the odd dry *(seco)* version. It is particularly common on La Palma.

DID YOU KNOW?

The La Dorada brewing company makes a thoroughly local beer from *gofio* called Volcan beer.

Tenerife is the principal source of wine, and the red Tacoronte Acentejo was the first Canarian wine to earn the grade of DO (*denominación de origen*; an appellation certifying high standards and regional origin). This term is one of many employed to regulate and judge wine and grape quality. Other productive vineyards are in the Icod de los Vinos, Güímar and Tacoronte areas of Tenerife. In Lanzarote, the vine has come back into vogue since the early 1980s, and in late 1993 the island's *malvasías* were awarded a DO.

Wine is produced on the other islands too, but the quality is generally not as good. See the Wine Trail tailored trip on p16 for more details.

Beer

The most common way to order a beer *(cerveza)* is to ask for a *caña*, which is a small draught beer *(cerveza de barril* or *cerveza de presión)*. La Dorada, brewed in Santa Cruz de Tenerife, is a very smooth number. It's as good as – if not superior to – any beer imported from the mainland. Tropical, produced on Gran Canaria and a little lighter, is a worthy runner-up and the preferred tipple of the eastern isles. Volcan beer by the La Dorada company is also worth sampling.

Spirits

Apart from the mainland Spanish imports, which include the grape-based *aguardiente* (similar to schnapps or grappa), *coñac* (brandy) and a whole host of other *licores* (liqueurs), you could try some local firewater if you come across it.

NEVER MISS YOUR WATER...

The tap water *(agua del grifo)* won't do you any harm; it just tastes a little unpleasant and makes vile tea. Exceptions are what flows from the cold tap on El Hierro and La Palma, where the water's sweet as any you've had. Elsewhere, most people go for bottled water from island springs such as Fuente Alta, Teide and Pinalito on Tenerife, or Firgas, Toscal and Breñalta on Gran Canaria. Water is water and local brands put cheaper than H_2O imported at cost from the mainland. *Agua mineral* (bottled water) comes in several either *con gas* (fizzy) or *sin gas* (still).

Although the sugar plantations have all but gone, what remains is put to good use in the production of *ron* (rum). Ron Aldea of La Palma is considered the best. *Ron miel* (honey rum) is more liqueur than rum, but interesting enough to taste. Quite a few liqueurs are produced in the islands, including the banana-based *cobana*. Both this and *ron miel* are produced mainly on Gran Canaria. Another one is *mistela* from La Gomera, a mixture of wine, sugar, rum and sometimes honey – a potent taste!

WHERE TO EAT & DRINK

Hanging around in bars and cafés, or simply dropping by for a quick caffeine or alcohol injection, is an integral part of life in the Canaries. The distinction between cafés and bars is negligible; coffee and alcohol are almost always available in both. Bars take several different forms, including *cervecerías* (beer bars, a vague equivalent of the pub, although some bars take on the name 'pub' too, as seems to happen right across Western Europe). In *tabernas* (taverns) and bodegas (old-style wine bars) you can sometimes get a decent meal too.

Variations on the theme include the *mesón* (traditionally a place for simple home cooking, although this is often no longer the case), *comedor* (literally a dining room, usually attached to a bar or hotel), *venta* (road-side inn) and *marisquería* (seafood specialist).

Standing at the bar rather than sitting down can often save you 10% to 20% of the bill, especially where the tables are outside on a picturesque terrace or in a smart attached dining room.

In restaurants, it is common practice to display a *carta* (menu), usually with prices, out the front. Any taxes and service charges should also be advertised, but quite often they are not.

Restaurants generally open for lunch and dinner, from 1pm to 4pm and then 8pm to midnight, unless they have a bar attached, in which case they may be open right through the day. Most restaurants close one day per week and advertise this fact with a sign in the window. We've provided closing-day information or unusual opening hours in our reviews for individual restaurants in the destination chapters.

The Best of Canary Island Cooking, produced by the Centro de la Cultura Popular Canaria, is a great, handy little volume that is readily available at various shops around the islands, in a number of languages.

Quick Eats

Bar snacks, or tapas, are a well-established mainland importation. They range from a tiny saucer with an olive or two and a thin slice of cheese through to quite substantial and delicious mouthfuls of anything from potato chips to seafood. These are provided at most bars as an accompaniment to your beer or wine. The idea is to stimulate your thirst, and it generally works. Quite often now there is a small charge, and more and more you actually have to ask the barman for the tapas. Generally they are on display – the barman will usually choose unless you make a specific request.

A larger version of the tapas is the *ración*. You always pay for this and three or four *raciones* makes a pretty decent meal.

The other standard snack (or *merienda*) is the *bocadillo*, or long bread stick. Typically this will be a rather dry affair with a slice of *jamón* (ham) and/or *queso* (cheese), or a wedge of *tortilla española* (potato omelette).

VEGETARIANS & VEGANS

The Canary Islands may seem like paradise to some, but they can be more like purgatory for vegetarians, and worse still for vegans. This is meat-eating country, so you will find your choices (unless you cater for yourself) a little limited. Salads are OK, and you will come across various side dishes such as *champiñones* (mushrooms, usually lightly fried in olive oil and garlic). Other possibilities include *berenjenas* (aubergines), *menestra* (a hearty vegetable stew), *espárragos* (asparagus), *lentejas* (lentils) and other vegetables that are sometimes cooked as side dishes.

WHINING & DINING

Eating with children is no hassle in the Canary Islands. Places will often include a children's menu (especially in tourist resorts) at a very reasonable price (say, €3 for a burger with chips or portion of spaghetti). Children are treated with a mix of indulgence and respect – like special little adults, really. Many rural or isolated places will not have highchairs, although tourist resorts will be able to accommodate them and set them up for you at the table. All the usual baby food products are readily available at the supermarkets, and there are no particular Spanish foods that you should avoid – although your kids may want to be consulted first before you start trying to broaden their palates.

HABITS & CUSTOMS

Rushing meals (other than the perfunctory breakfast ritual) is a no-no in the Canary Islands. Giving yourself over to a long lunch and a civilised dinner, punctuated with conversation, is the norm, as eating is very much a social exercise designed to allow people to meet, reaffirm connections and enjoy themselves. You'll find manners no different from those at home, but if you're from a place where smoking at the table is frowned upon, you're in for a rude shock.

EAT YOUR WORDS

Want to know the difference between a *salchida* and a *salchichón*? Get behind the cuisine scene by getting to know the foodies' language. For pronunciation guides, see p257.

Useful Phrases

Table for..., please.
oo·na me·sa pa·ra..., por fa·vor
Una mesa para..., por favor.

Can I see the menu please?
pwe·do ver el me·noo, por fa·vor
¿Puedo ver el menú, por favor?

What is today's special?
kwal es el pla·to del dee·a
¿Cuál es el plato del día?

What's the soup of the day?
kwal es la so·pa del dee·a
¿Cuál es la sopa del día?

I'll try what she/he's having.
pro·ba·ray lo ke e·lya/el es·ta ko·myen·do
Probaré lo que ella/él está comiendo.

What's in this dish?
ke een·gre·dyen·tes tye·ne es·te pla·to
¿Qué ingredientes tiene este plato?

Can I have a (beer) please?
oo·na (ser·ve·sa) por fa·vor
¿Una (cerveza) por favor?

Is service included in the bill?
el ser·vee·syos es·ta een·kloo·ee·do en la kwen·ta
¿El servicio está incluido en la cuenta?

Thank you, that was delicious.
moo·chas gra·syas, es·ta·ba bwe·nee·see·mo
Muchas gracias, estaba buenísimo.

The bill, please.
la kwen·ta, por fa·vor
La cuenta, por favor.

TABLE TALK

Here are some basic words that can come in handy whatever kind of meal you're eating:

aceite de oliva	a·*sey*·te de o·*lee*·va	olive oil
almuerzo or comida	al·*mwer*·so or ko·*mee*·da	lunch
azúcar	a·*soo*·kar	sugar
bollo	*bo*·lyo	bread roll
caliente	ka·*lyen*·te	hot (temperature)
camarero/a	ka·ma·re·ro/a	waiter/waitress
cambio	*kam*·byo	change
carta	*kar*·ta	menu
cena	*se*·na	dinner
comida	ko·*mee*·da	food, meal
cuchara	koo·*cha*·ra	spoon
cuchillo	koo·*chee*·lyo	knife
cuenta	*kwen*·ta	bill (check)
desayuno	des·a·*yoo*·no	breakfast
frío/a	*free*·o/a	cold
hielo	*ye*·lo	ice
leche	*le*·che	milk
mantequilla	man·te·*kee*·lya	butter
menú del diá	me·*noo* del *dee*·a	set menu
mermelada	mer·me·*la*·da	jam
mesa	*me*·sa	table
pan	pan	bread
pimienta	pee·*myen*·ta	pepper
plato	*pla*·to	plate
postre	*pos*·tre	dessert
sal	sal	salt
salsa	*sal*·sa	sauce
taza	*ta*·tha	cup
tenedor	te·ne·*dor*	fork
vaso or copa	*va*·so or *ko*·pa	glass
vinagre	vee·*na*·gre	vinegar

I am a vegetarian.   *Soy vegetariana/o.*
soy veg·khe·ta·*rya*·na/o

Food Glossary

Deciphering a menu in the Canaries is always tricky. However much you already know, there will always be dishes and expressions with which you're not familiar. The following list should help you with the basics at least.

PESCADO & MARISCOS (FISH & SHELLFISH)

almejas	al·*me*·khas	clams
anchoas	an·*cho*·as	anchovies
atún	a·*toon*	tuna
bacalao	ba·ka·*lao*	salted cod
bonito	bo·*nee*·to	tuna
boquerones	bo·ke·*ro*·nes	raw anchovies pickled in vinegar
calamares	ka·la·*ma*·res	squid
cangrejo	kan·*gre*·kho	crab
gambas	*gam*·bas	shrimps
langostinos	lan·gos·*tee*·nos	large prawns

lenguado	len·*gwa*·do	sole
mejillones	me·khee·*lyo*·nes	mussels
ostra	*os*·tra	oyster
pez espada	pes es·*pa*·da	swordfish
pulpo	*pool*·po	octopus
vieira	vee·*ey*·ra	scallop

CARNE (MEAT)

cabra	*ka*·bra	goat
cerdo	*ser*·do	pork
chorizo	cho·*ree*·so	spicy red cooked sausage
conejo	ko·*ne*·kho	rabbit
cordero	kor·*de*·ro	lamb
hígado	*ee*·ga·do	liver
jamón	kha·*mon*	ham
lomo	*lo*·mo	pork loin
pato	*pa*·to	duck
pavo	*pa*·vo	turkey
riñón	ree·*nyon*	kidney
salchicha	sal·*chee*·cha	fresh pork sausage
salchichón	sal·chee·*chon*	peppery cured white sausage
sesos	*se*·sos	brains
vacuno	va·*koo*·no	beef

FRUTAS & NUECES (FRUIT & NUTS)

aceituna	a·sey·*too*·na	olive
aguacate	a·gwa·*ka*·te	avocado
almendras	al·*men*·dras	almonds
cacahuete	ka·ka·*we*·te	peanut
cereza	se·*re*·sa	cherry
fresa	*fre*·sa	strawberry
lima	*lee*·ma	lime
limón	lee·*mon*	lemon
mandarina	man·da·*ree*·na	tangerine
manzana	man·*sa*·na	apple
melocotón	me·lo·ko·*ton*	peach
naranja	na·*ran*·kha	orange
piña	*pee*·nya	pineapple
plátano	*pla*·ta·no	banana
sandía	san·*dee*·a	watermelon
uva	*oo*·va	grape

HORTALIZAS (VEGETABLES)

calabacín	ka·la·ba·*seen*	zucchini, courgette
cebolla	se·*bo*·lya	onion
champiñones	cham·pee·*nyo*·nes	mushrooms
espárragos	es·*pa*·ra·gos	asparagus
espinaca	es·pee·*na*·ka	spinach
guisante	gee·*san*·te	pea
haba	*a*·ba	broad bean
lechuga	le·*choo*·ga	lettuce
lentejas	len·*te*·khas	lentils
pimiento	pee·*myen*·to	pepper, capsicum
puerro	*pwe*·ro	leek
zanahoria	sa·na·*o*·rya	carrot

TARTAS & POSTRES (CAKES & DESSERTS)

flan	flan	crème caramel
galleta	ga·*lye*·ta	biscuit, cookie
helado	e·*la*·do	ice cream
pastel	pas·*tel*	pastry, cake
torta	*tor*·ta	round flat bun, cake
turrón	too·*ron*	almond nougat

TÉCNICAS (COOKING TECHNIQUES)

a la brasa	a la *bra*·sa	to barbecue
a la plancha	a la *plan*·cha	grilled
al horno	al *or*·no	baked
asar	a·*sa*	to roast
frito	*free*·to	fried
rebozado	re·bo·*sa*·do	battered
relleno	re·*lye*·no	stuffed

Drinks Glossary

CAFÉ (COFFEE)

café con leche	ka·fe kon *le*·che	50/50 coffee and hot milk
café cortado	ka·fe kor·*ta*·do	short black with a splash of milk
café solo	ka·fe *so*·lo	a short black
café con hielo	ka·fe kon *ye*·lo	iced coffee

REFRESCOS (SOFT DRINKS)

agua potable	a·*gwa* pot·*ab*·le	drinking water
agua mineral	a·*gwa* mee·ne·*ral*	bottled water
con gas	kon gas	fizzy
sin gas	sin gas	still
batido	ba·*tee*·do	flavoured milk drink/milk shake
zumo de		
naranja	*soo*·mo de na·*ran*·kha	orange juice

VINO (WINE)

blanco	*blan*·ko	white
de la casa	de la *ka*·sa	house
rosado	ro·*sa*·do	rosé
tinto	*teen*·to	red

CERVEZA (BEER)

botellín	bo·tel·*yin*	bottled
caña	ka·*nyah*	draught
jarra	*kha*·ra	in a pint glass

OTHER ALCOHOLIC DRINKS

aguardiente	a·*gwa*·*dyen*·te	grape-based spirit (similar to schnapps or grappa)
coñac	ko·*nyak*	brandy
licor	*lee*·kor	liqueur
ron	ron	rum
sangría	san·*gree*·a	a wine and fruit punch usually laced with red wine

Gran Canaria

CONTENTS

The Canariones, as the islanders tend to refer to themselves, like to think of Gran Canaria as a 'continent in miniature'. You'll come across this phrase with great regularity on your visit here, and the startling range of terrain – from the fertile north to the arid interior and desert south – largely justifies the claim.

The island is the third largest of the archipelago but accounts for almost half the population. In many respects this is perhaps the least attractive of the Canary Islands, although this is, like most things, a matter of personal taste and preference. If you're after a boobs-out, balls-to-the-wall, beach-side holiday with the one-week charter-flight crowd, then the Playa del Inglés (p80) scene will have you sunburnt, hung over and wondering how to get a money transfer organised in record time.

The capital, Las Palmas de Gran Canaria (p61), is a busy, happening city and worth a visit for its historic old quarter, bar-hopping scene and the golden sands of Playa de las Canteras. Surfers can pick up some waves here and off Maspalomas, and windsurfers are in heaven on the southeastern coast.

The interior is a world away from both the capital and the southern resorts, and worth exploring, if only to recapture a little peace and quiet. It is nevertheless a somewhat arid affair and frankly less captivating than the volcanic or verdant attractions of the other islands.

HIGHLIGHTS

- **Strolling**

  The historic Vegueta quarter of Las Palmas is full of charm (p65)

- **Saharan Sands**

  The expansive and stunning dunes of Maspalomas are a great place to wander (p83)

- **Driving**

  The scenic coastal route from Agaete to Aldea de San Nicolás is full of twists and turns (p79)

- **Mooching**

  Puerto de Mogán is a bougainvillea-bedecked gem for the yachterati (p86)

- **One Hump or Two?**

  A camel ride in a palm-fringed oasis (p75)

| TELEPHONE CODE: 928 | POPULATION: 730,620 | AREA: 1560 SQ KM |

GRAN CANARIA

HISTORY

Gran Canaria was known to its original inhabitants as Tamarán, which scholars have linked with the Arabic name for date palms (*tamar*). This sounds feasible but could not go back much beyond the 7th century, when the Muslim Arabs invaded Morocco. The Romans – who, as far as is known, never landed here – first called the island Canaria (see the boxed text on p59). How Canaria came to be Gran (Big) is also open to question: some say it was because the Spaniards thought the locals put up a big fight while resisting conquest, and others that the island was thought to be the biggest in the archipelago.

Conquest began in earnest with the landing of a Spanish force led by Juan Rejón in 1478. Despite carrying the day and beating off a furious counterattack by Doramas, the *guanarteme* (chief) of the island's Telde kingdom, Rejón was supplanted by Pedro de Vera, who pressed home the campaign in the following five years. The turning point was the conversion of the Guanche chief Tenesor Semidan to Christianity. In April 1483 he convinced his countrymen to submit.

The island was soon colonised by a ragtag assortment of adventurers and landless hopefuls from as far away as Galicia, Andalucia, Portugal, Italy, France, the Low Countries and even Britain and Ireland.

Initially, the island boomed on the back of sugar exports and transatlantic trade between Spain and the Americas. But, as

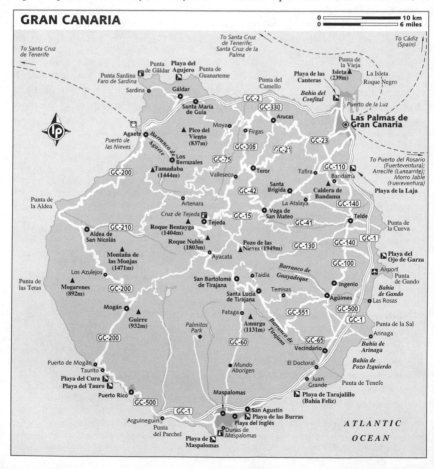

DOGS, BIRDS & PURPLE PROSE

To the ancient Greeks, the fabled islands beyond the Pillars of Hercules (today's Straits of Gibraltar) were known as the Hesperides or Atlantes, after the daughters of Atlas who Hercules supposedly visited. Long thought to be abundant in every possible kind of fruit, the islands were also often referred to as the Garden of Hesperides. Some writers have also identified Elysium, the field of perfect peace where the ancient Greeks believed the good and great spent the afterlife, with the Canaries.

The Romans, who apparently never set foot on the islands, knew them as the Insulae Fortunatae (Fortunate Isles). The Spaniards, when they set about conquering them in the 15th century, also began by calling them the Islas Afortunadas.

Juba II, the North African king who told Pliny the Elder about the islands, referred to them as the Insulae Purpuriae (Purple Isles) because of the purple dyes extracted from the orchil lichens on Fuerteventura and Lanzarote. Juba's report can't have been all fiction as he at least got the number of islands right – seven. The Romans gave them the following names: Canaria (Gran Canaria), Nivaria (Tenerife), Capraria (Lanzarote), Planaria (Fuerteventura), Junonia Mayor (La Palma), Junonia Minor (La Gomera) and Pluvialia (El Hierro).

The Guanches (indigenous Canarios) had their own names for the islands, some of them preserved to this day: Tamarán (Gran Canaria), Achinech (Tenerife), Tyterorgatra (Lanzarote), Maxorata (Fuerteventura), Benahoare (La Palma), Gomera (La Gomera) and Hero (El Hierro).

Why Canaria? One improbable tale talks of an adventuresome Latin couple, Cranus and Crana, who went off in search of a challenge, bumped into what is now Gran Canaria and liked it so much they stayed. They dubbed the island Cranaria, which was later simplified to Canaria.

Another theory suggests the name was inspired by the trilling canary birds, thought by some to be native to the islands. However, most ornithologists claim the bird took the name from the islands rather than the other way around.

Others reckon the name came from the Latin word for dog (canus) because members of Juba's expedition came across what they considered unusually large dogs. On the other hand, there was a minority school of thought which held that the natives of the island were dog-eaters!

And maybe none of these fanciful solutions to the riddle is near the mark. Yet another theory claims that the people of Canaria, who possibly arrived several hundred years before Christ, were in fact Berbers of the Canarii tribe living in Morocco. The tribal name was simply applied to the island and later accepted by Pliny. Canaria became 'great' (gran), according to some chronicles, after its people put up a tough fight against the Spanish conquistadors.

Equally unclear is at precisely what point the islands came to be known collectively as Las Islas Canarias, although this probably came with the completion of the Spanish conquest of the islands at the end of the 15th century.

the demand for Canary Islands sugar fell and the fortunes of wine grew, the island declined before its main rival and superior wine-grower, Tenerife. It was not until the late 19th century that Gran Canaria recovered its position. To this day the two islands remain rivals and, between them, are home to most of the islands' permanent populace.

INFORMATION
Books & Maps

One of the best among competing maps of the island is *Gran Canaria*, published by Distrimapas Telstar (€2.50). It comes with accurate city maps of Las Palmas, Maspalomas, Playa del Inglés and various other towns.

Michelin map No 220 *Gran Canaria* (€2.30) can be found in bookshops or general tourist shops throughout the island.

Discovery Walking Guides produces two titles for walkers: *Gran Canaria Mountains Walking Guide* and *Gran Canaria South & Mountains Walking Guide*, both written by DA Brawn.

Landscapes of Gran Canaria by Noel Rochford gives more ideas for walks, car tours and picnic sites.

Newspapers

The most widely read local newspapers on Gran Canaria and the two most eastern islands are *Canarias 7* and *La Provincian*.

GRAN CANARIA

TO MARKET, TO MARKET...

Gran Canaria's towns and villages are the scene of some interesting little markets that mix tourist trinkets and local products with an easy-going morning away from the bustle of the resort towns. Markets generally last from 9am to 2pm. Following is a list of some mercantile diversions:

Puerto de Mogán Friday
San Fernando Wednesday & Saturday
Arguineguin Tuesday & Thursday
Teror Sunday
Vega de San Mateo Saturday & Sunday

Of the English-language weeklies, *Island Connections* – for sale at newsagents but available free from most tourist offices – is the most widely distributed.

ACTIVITIES

Many visitors come to simply relax and escape the workaday world, but if you're looking for something more active, there is ample potential. The Bahía de Pozo Izquierdo, on the southeastern coast, has demanding, world-class windsurfing, while Maspalomas and Playa de las Canteras (Las Palmas) have more gentle waves. There are several diving and deep-sea fishing outfits in the southern resorts, while on land you can bike or trek independently or join a guided group. Details are provided under specific towns.

Thalassotherapy

To save you looking it up – it's a health treatment based on warmed-up sea water, designed to remove stress and other more physical aches. Whether or not it works (some of its claims for cellulite control seem a tad dubious), it's quite a sensual experience in its own right and often does wonders for skin ailments. There are centres scattered around the island, including at the Hotel Puerto de las Nieves (p79), and at the Hotel Gloria Palace near Playa del Inglés (p83).

ACCOMMODATION

Away from Las Palmas and the southern coastal resorts, accommodation is remarkably thin on the ground. As a rule you should not have too much trouble in the capital, but the resorts can be full to overflowing in high season.

For something a thousand metaphorical miles from the package tour resorts, consider renting a *casa rural* (house in the country). Contact **Gran Canaria Rural** (☎ 928 46 25 47; www.grancanariarural.com), **AECAN** (☎ 922 24 08 16; www.aecan.com), who have an all-islands remit, or **RETUR** (☎ 928 66 16 68; www.returcanarias.com).

GETTING THERE & AWAY
Air

Along with the two airports on Tenerife, Gran Canaria's **airport** (☎ 928 57 91 30), 16km south of Las Palmas, is the main hub in the islands. From here there are connections to all other islands as well as regular flights to mainland Spain, and a raft of international scheduled and charter flights.

Binter (☎ 902 39 13 92; www.bintercanarias.com) flies between Gran Canaria and Tenerife Norte (€45, 30 minutes, 18 daily), Tenerife Sur (€45, 35 minutes, twice daily), La Palma (€73, 50 minutes, four daily), El Hierro (€79, 50 minutes, seven weekly), La Gomera (€73, 45 minutes, twice daily), Fuerteventura (€53, 45 minutes, 23 daily) and Lanzarote (€60, 45 minutes, 20 daily).

Isla Airways (www.islasairways.com in Spanish) has flights to Fuerteventura (at least four daily), Tenerife (one daily) and La Palma (one daily).

Iberia (www.iberia.com) has six flights daily to Madrid while **Spanair** (www.spanair.com) has three and **Air Europa** (www.air-europa.com) has two. Iberia and Spanair fly daily to Barcelona.

There are weekly flights to Morocco and Senegal with **Royal Air Maroc** (www.royalairmaroc.com) and **Air Senegal International** (www.air-senegal-international.com), respectively.

At the airport you'll find a tourist information office on the ground floor (open whenever flights arrive), airline offices, car-rental outlets, a post office, a pharmacy that stays open until 10pm and money-changing facilities (including a Western Union representative). Disabled access is very good at the airport.

Boat

Ferries and jetfoils link Gran Canaria with Tenerife, Lanzarote and Fuerteventura, using Las Palmas and Agaete ports. See the

Getting There & Away sections under each port for more details and p249 for details of the ferry to/from Cádiz (mainland Spain).

GETTING AROUND
To/From the Airport
Taxis and buses service the airport and will get you to whichever part of the island you need to reach. See individual listings under separate locations for further details.

Bus
Blue, turquoise or green **Global** (☎ 902 38 11 10; www.globalsu.net in Spanish) buses provide the island with a first-class network of routes, although the number of runs per day to many rural areas is pretty thin. In Las Palmas, yellow municipal buses provide a similarly efficient service that deserves to be the envy of many a larger city.

If you're travelling around the island, it's probably worthwhile investing in a Tarjeta Insular, an island-wide discount card, for €12. Instead of buying individual tickets on the bus for each trip, you stick your card in the machine, tell the driver your destination and he endorses your card. When compared to the standard fare for a journey, it represents at least a 30% saving on each trip. Cards are on sale at bus stations and from many newsagents and *estancos* (tobacconists).

Car
Car rental is abundant and can work out very economically if you book in advance. All the usual international companies have representation at the airport, but you can also find local companies at resorts and towns.

Taxi
Taxis are plentiful, especially in Las Palmas and the tourist Mecca of Maspalomas. Fares are more than reasonable for local trips, but not so good if you're travelling longer distances from, say, the airport to the other side of the island.

DÍA DE SANTA LUCIA

On 13 December, make a point of checking out any church you can on Gran Canaria, when they are all illuminated in honour of the Día de Santa Lucia (St Lucy's Day).

LAS PALMAS DE GRAN CANARIA

pop 354,865

Las Palmas is the big smoke, the only place in the Canary Islands, apart from Santa Cruz de Tenerife, with that unmistakable big-city feel. While it oozes the kind of sunny languor you'd associate with the Mediterranean or North Africa, the snarled traffic, bustling shopping districts, chatty bars and thriving port all give off the energy of a city, Spain's seventh largest.

The historic centre, though small, is rich in interest and undergoing a rebirth as an entertainment precinct, and combined with the Playa de las Canteras could keep the average hedonist busy for days. The flavour is Spanish, with a heavy international overlay. You'll find a lively mix of Chinese, African, Indian and Spanish people, plus an eclectic mix of tourists, container-ship crews and the flotsam and jetsam that tends to drift around port cities.

If you've come to the Canaries to experience something of Spain, away from the all-day English breakfast and time-share scene, and like some city bustle plus a museum or two and a cultural life that doesn't revolve around karaoke, this place rewards your attention.

HISTORY
Although Jean de Béthencourt's partner in mischief, Gadifer de la Salle, sailed past here in 1403, it wasn't until 1478 that Europeans made a determined landing in the area. That year Juan Rejón and his troops set up camp just south of La Isleta, naming it Real de las Palmas. As the conquest of the island proceeded, the original military camp began to take on a more permanent look, and so the *barrio* (district) of San Antonio Abad, later known as Vegueta, began to expand.

By the time Christopher Columbus sailed by on his way to the Americas in 1492, the busy little hub of the old town had already been traced out. Everybody likes to claim a hero for their very own and the Gran Canarian version of history has it that Columbus briefly put in here for repairs before pushing on to La Gomera.

LAS PALMAS (NORTH)

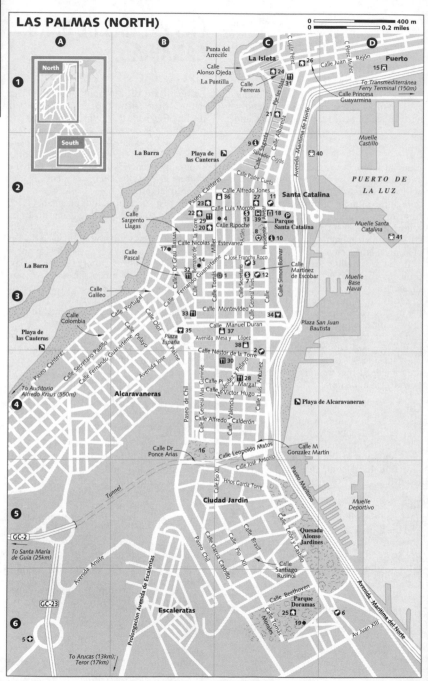

0 _____ 400 m
0 _____ 0.2 miles

North

South

Ⓐ   Ⓑ   Ⓒ   Ⓓ

Punta del
Arrecife

Calle
Alonso Ojeda

La Puntilla

La Isleta

Puerto

C Luis Pérez
C Pérez Muñoz
Calle Juan Negrín Rejón
15

To Transmediterránea
Ferry Terminal (150m)
Calle Princesa
Guayarmina

Calle
Ferreras

26
24
31

Playa de
las Canteras

La Barra

Muelle
Castillo

PUERTO DE
LA LUZ

Santa Catalina

Paseo Canteras

Calle Padre Cueto

Calle Alfredo Jones

Calle Sargento
Llagas

La Barra

Calle
Pascal

Calle
Galileo

Playa de
las Canteras

Calle
Colombia

Muelle Santa
Catalina

Muelle
Base Naval

Parque
Santa Catalina

Alcaravaneras

Plaza
España

Avenida Mesa y López

Calle Néstor de la Torre

Plaza San Juan
Bautista

Playa de Alcaravaneras

To Auditorio
Alfredo Kraus (550m)

Calle Leopoldo Matos

Calle Dr
Ponce Arias

Calle M
Gonzalez Martín

Ciudad Jardín

Tunnel

Muelle
Deportivo

GC-2

To Santa María
de Guía (25km)

GC-23

Escaleratas

To Arucas (13km);
Teror (17km)

Quesada
Alonso
Jardines

Parque
Doramas

5
6

Las Palmas grew quickly as a commercial centre, and in recognition of its importance the seat of the bishopric of the Canary Islands was transferred here from Lanzarote halfway through the 16th century.

The city, along with the rest of the archipelago, benefited greatly from the Spanish conquest of Latin America and the subsequent transatlantic trade. But you have to take the good with the bad, and the islands were a favourite target for pirates and buccaneers of all nations. In 1595 Sir Francis Drake raided Las Palmas with particular gusto. Four years later a still more determined band of Dutch adventurers reduced much of the town to ruins.

In 1821, Santa Cruz de Tenerife was declared capital of the single new Spanish province of Las Islas Canarias. This left the great and good of Las Palmas disgruntled but redress was some time in coming.

The fortunes of the port city fluctuated with those of the islands as a whole as boom followed bust in a chain of cash-crop cycles. However, Las Palmas began to go its own way towards the end of the 19th century, due in no small measure to the growing British presence in the city.

The trading families of the Millers and the Swanstons were already well established by the time Sir Alfred Lewis Jones set up the Grand Canary Coaling Company in Las Palmas. The city flourished as a crucial refuelling stop for transatlantic shipping. It was the British who introduced the first watermains, electricity company and telephone exchange to the city in the early 20th century. However, it all came apart before the outbreak of WWII, as coal-fired ships gradually made way for more modern vessels.

Still, the city's prosperity had become such that Madrid could no longer resist calls for the islands to be divided into two provinces. Las Palmas thus became capital of Gran Canaria, Fuerteventura and Lanzarote in 1927.

It was from Las Palmas that Franco launched the coup in July 1936 that sparked the Spanish Civil War.

Since the 1960s, when the tourism boom was first felt in the islands, Las Palmas has grown from a middling port city of 70,000 souls to a bustling metropolis of over 300,000 people. And while it shares evenly the status of regional capital with Santa Cruz de Tenerife, there is no doubt that Las Palmas packs the bigger punch in terms of bulk.

ORIENTATION

Las Palmas stretches from the old historical centre in the south, centred on the Vegueta and Triana districts, up a series of long boulevards towards bustling Santa Catalina and the port, Puerto de la Luz – a good 3km. From there it continues up to what was once a islet off the island, still called La Isleta.

Most of what will be of interest to sightseers is concentrated in Vegueta, and you'll find plenty of authentic bars and restaurants here too.

The heavier, more international action is around Santa Catalina, which has a slightly seedy vibe at times. The bulk of the hotels are around here, close to the 3km-long golden sands of Playa de las Canteras, the bars, shops and port.

Maps

You'll find a free map sponsored by the El Corte Inglés department store all over

GRAN CANARIA

LAS PALMAS (SOUTH)

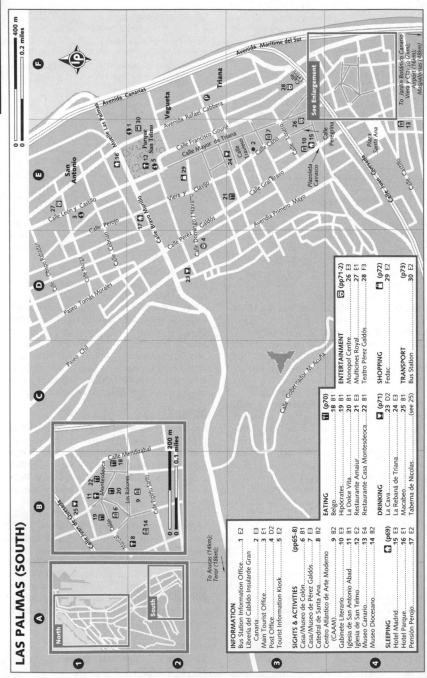

INFORMATION
Bus Station Information Office.................1 E2
Librería del Cabildo Insularde Gran
Canaria..2 E3
Main Tourist Office.................................3 E1
Post Office..4 D2
Tourist Information Kiosk.......................5 E2

SIGHTS & ACTIVITIES   (pp65-8)
Casa/Museo de Colón..............................6 B1
Casa/Museo de Pérez Galdós...................7 E3
Catedral de Santa Ana.............................8 B2
Centro Atlántico de Arte Moderno
(CAAM)...9 B2
Gabinete Literario.................................10 E3
Iglesia de San Antonio Abad.................11 B1
Iglesia de San Telmo.............................12 E2
Museo Canario......................................13 E4
Museo Diocesano..................................14 B2

SLEEPING   (p69)
Hotel Madrid...15 E3
Hotel Parque..16 E1
Pensión Perojo......................................17 E2

EATING   (p70)
Belgo..18 B1
Hipócrates...19 B1
La Dolce Vita..20 B1
Restaurante Amaiur...............................21 E3
Restaurante Casa Montesdeoca.............22 B1

DRINKING   (p71)
La Cava...23 D2
La Rebaná de Triana..............................24 E3
Macabeo..25 B1
Taberna de Nicolas...........................(see 25)

ENTERTAINMENT   (pp71-2)
Monopol Centre....................................26 E3
Multicines Royal....................................27 E1
Teatro Pérez Galdós..............................28 F3

SHOPPING   (p72)
Fedac..29 E2

TRANSPORT   (p73)
Bus Station..30 E2

the place. For bus travel, pick up the local public-transport map, called *Guaguas Municipales* (yellow cover). Both are available from tourist offices.

INFORMATION
Bookshops
Librería del Cabildo Insular de Gran Canaria (Map p64; Calle Travieso 15) This bookshop will help you learn all you ever wanted to know about the Canary Islands. Most titles are in Spanish but there are a few shelves of English titles.

Emergency
Police station (Map pp62-3; ☎ 928 44 64 00; Parque Santa Catalina) Just west of the nearby tourist office.

Internet Access
Cybernet (Map pp62-3; cnr Calles Martínez de Escobar & Tomás Miller; per hr €1.20; ☯ 10am-3pm & 5pm-1am Mon-Thu & Sun, 10am-3pm & 5pm-midnight Fri & Sat)

Laundry
Las Palmas has plenty of dry-cleaners and *lavanderías*, traditional laundries where you leave your washing and collect it later the same day.
Hersoji (Map pp62-3; Calle Ripoche 22) Conveniently central, located beside Hostal Residencia Majorica.

Medical Services
Hospital General de Las Palmas Dr Negrin (Map pp62-3; ☎ 928 45 00 01; Calle Barranco de la Ballena s/n)

Money
Viajes Insular (Map pp62-3; ☎ 928 22 79 50; Calle Luis Morote 9) Represents American Express.
Office Services (Map pp62-3; Calle los Martínez de Escobar 5) Represents Western Union and also has an office at the airport.

Post
Main post office (Map p64; ☎ 928 36 21 15; Avenida Primero de Mayo 62; ☯ 8.30am-8.30pm Mon-Fri, 9.30am-2pm Sat)

Tourist Offices
Bus station information office (Map p64; ☎ 928 36 83 35; ☯ 6.30am-8.30pm Mon-Fri, 7.30am-1pm Sat & Sun) Great for island-wide transport info and also provides a general service.
Main tourist office (Map p64; ☎ 928 21 96 00; Calle León y Castillo 17; ☯ 8am-2pm Mon-Fri) An island-wide remit but scant opening hours.

Tourist information kiosk (Map p64; Parque San Telmo; ☯ 3.30-8pm Mon-Fri, 10am-3pm Sat)
Tourist information kiosk (Map pp62-3; Playa de las Canteras; ☎ 10am-7.30pm Mon-Fri, 10am-1pm Sat)
Tourist office (Map pp62-3; ☎ 928 26 46 23; Parque Santa Catalina s/n; 9am-2pm Mon-Fri) Has an island-wide remit.
Tourist office (Map pp62-3; Pueblo Canario; ☯ 9am-2.30pm Mon-Fri)

DANGERS & ANNOYANCES
Las Palmas is not only the largest city in the islands but palpably the dodgiest. There's drug abuse and, as a major port, Las Palmas attracts its share of shady characters.

All this means is that you should take the standard city streetwise precautions. Carry as little money and as few valuables on you as possible. Leave nothing of value (preferably nothing at all) in cars, especially the hired variety.

At night, avoid dark, quiet streets and parks. Parque San Telmo (Map p64) and Parque Santa Catalina (Map pp62-3) are safe enough in daylight, although even then down-and-outs wander among the courting couples and playing children.

If hookers with attitude hanging around in doorways are your type of scene, head for Calle Molinos de Viento, a block west of Calle León y Castillo. Otherwise, it's perhaps best to avoid this louche zone.

SIGHTS
Vegueta & Triana   Map p64
The most architecturally and atmospherically appealing part of the city, this is also where the bulk of historic sights are found. Wandering around the streets is a pleasant way to spend the time, and eating options are excellent (see p70).

CASA/MUSEO DE COLÓN
This **museum** (☎ 928 31 23 73; Calle Colón 1; admission free; ☯ 9am-7pm Mon-Fri, 9am-3pm Sat & Sun) is a glorious example of Canarian architecture, built around two patios overlooked by fine wooden balconies. The exterior itself is something of a work of art, with some showy *plateresque* (silversmith-like) elements mixed in with the brown-stained balconies so typical of the islands.

Although it's called Columbus' House (it's possible he passed by here to present his credentials to the governor in 1492), most of what you see was the residence of Las Palmas' early governors.

The museum's four sections present Columbus' voyages, the Canary Islands as a staging post for transatlantic shipping, pre-Columbian America and the city of Las Palmas. Upstairs is an art gallery whose most interesting canvases are from the Hispanic-Flemish school.

CATEDRAL DE SANTA ANA & MUSEO DIOCESANO

The city's big, grey, main **cathedral** (☎ 928 33 14 30; Calle Obispo Codina 13; admission free; ✆ 10am-5pm Mon-Fri, 10am-2pm Sat) was begun in the early 15th century, soon after the Spanish conquest, but took what must be a record 350 years to complete. The neoclassical facade contrasts with the interior, which is a fine example of what some art historians have denominated Atlantic Gothic that betrays the earlier beginnings of construction. The Gothic retable above the high altar comes from Catalunya (mainland Spain) and the exquisite lamp hanging before the altar was made in Genova (Italy). It also holds a number of paintings by Juan de Miranda, the islands' most respected 18th-century artist.

The **Museo Diocesano** (☎ 928 31 49 89; Calle Espíritu Santo 20; admission €3; ✆ 10am-5pm Mon-Fri, 10am-2pm Sat) is set on two levels around the Patio de los Naranjos (Orange Tree Courtyard), once home to the Inquisition. It contains a fairly standard collection of religious art and memorabilia, including centuries-old manuscripts, a good number of wooden sculptures and other ornaments.

You can also access the cathedral's **tower** (admission €1.50; ✆ 9.15am-6pm Mon-Fri) if you fancy a stunning and wide-ranging view of the surrounds from the city to the coast – it's a private enterprise though.

IGLESIA DE SAN ANTONIO ABAD

Just behind the Casa/Museo de Colón (p65), heading towards the waterfront, this little **church** (Plaza San Antonio Abad 4) of modest Romanesque-Canarian design is where, according to tradition, Columbus prayed for divine help before sailing for the Americas.

MUSEO CANARIO

The island's main **museum** (☎ 928 33 68 00; www.elmuseocanario.com; Calle Dr Verneau 2; adult/under 12s/concession €3/free/1.20; ✆ 10am-8pm Mon-Fri, 10am-2pm Sat & Sun) chronicles Gran Canaria's preconquest history. It claims to be home to the biggest collection of Cro-Magnon skulls in the world – no mean boast! Some heads come attached to other body parts in the form of mummies. There is also a fair collection of pottery and other Guanche implements. The material comes from across the island, offering history buffs a good range of experience. The gift shop here is certainly attractive, and a good spot to pick up some excellent educational gifts for kids.

CENTRO ATLÁNTICO DE ARTE MODERNO

The city's main **museum of modern art** (CAAM; ☎ 902 31 18 24; www.caam.net; Calle los Balcones 11; admission free; ✆ 10am-9pm Tue-Sat, 10am-2pm Sun) hosts some wonderful temporary exhibitions, and its permanent collection focuses on 20th-century art from both Canarian and international artists. It is housed in a beautifully rejuvenated 18th-century building, which is flooded with natural light. You'll find works by such local artists as José Jorge Oramas, Plácido Fleitas, Eduardo Gregorio, Felo Monzón, Santiago Santana and César Manrique on display.

GABINETE LITERARIO

This sumptuous **historical building** (Plazoleta Cairasco), with its gracious interior patio, is a national monument. It's an old-world display of faded elegance, illuminated by chandeliers and lined with bookcases crammed with learned-looking volumes. The place was once a theatre and now functions as a kind of well-to-do club.

CALLE MAYOR DE TRIANA

Traditionally, this street, now a pedestrianised mall, was the main shopping street in Las Palmas. As you browse the shop windows, keep your head up and eyes peeled to enjoy the little architectural gems, among them some nice examples of modernism, that line this busy thoroughfare.

CASA/MUSEO DE PÉREZ GALDÓS

In 1843 the Canary Islands' greatest writer, Benito Pérez Galdós (see p30), was born in this **house** (☎ 928 36 69 76; Calle Cano 6; admission free; ✆ 9am-7pm Mon-Fri) in the heart of old Las Palmas. He spent the first 19 years of his life here before moving on to Madrid and literary greatness.

The house contains a reconstruction of the author's study, various personal effects and other objects related to his life. It's a really attractive sight in the old quarter – with a lovely central courtyard that whispers 'oasis' – and guided tours are available every hour (in Spanish).

PARQUE SAN TELMO

The **Iglesia de San Telmo**, on the southwestern side of the park, was one of the first religious buildings in the nascent town. Beside it is a tourist information kiosk (p65) and, in the northwestern corner, a beautiful modernist **kiosk** which these days functions as an open-air *terraza* (terrace) – a thoroughly pleasant, shady spot for a drink.

The square can be a bit dodgy after dark and dusk seems to be the preferred time for panhandlers to appear and importune the kiosk's customers. They're rarely aggressive though.

Ciudad Jardín   Map pp62–3

The **Parque Doramas** is the nucleus of this area of the city, laid out by the British towards the end of the 19th century, when British businessmen dominated the economic life of Las Palmas. That said, this leafy, upper class suburb is a decidedly eclectic mix of architectural styles, ranging from British colonial to Andalucian.

PUEBLO CANARIO

Designed by the artist Néstor Martín Fernández de la Torre and built by his brother Miguel, the Pueblo Canario borders the gardens of the Parque Doramas. With a restaurant, terraces, shops and kids' play area, it is designed as a pleasant bit of escapism in a clearly Canarian architectural style. The small central plaza, surrounded by buildings reflecting that traditional style, makes for an agreeable drinks stop.

MUSEO NÉSTOR

An **art gallery** (928 24 51 35; Pueblo Canario; adult/student €2/free; 10am-8pm Tue-Sat, 10.30am-2.30pm Sun) originally dedicated purely to the works of Néstor, who died in 1938, the Museo Néstor was later expanded to accommodate a broader collection of works – displayed in the Gallery of Contemporary Canarian

Art (rooms 11 to 13). It also houses period furniture and other memorabilia.

CASINO DE LAS PALMAS

If you remembered to bring along your black-tie evening wear and want to have a flutter in style, head for the **casino** (8pm-4am). It's within the city's prestigious Hotel Santa Catalina (p69), built in 1904 in the heart of the Parque Doramas.

Santa Catalina   Map pp62–3

Santa Catalina is a sometimes intriguing mix of city beach, multicultural melting pot, seedy port and business hub. At times you'll feel like you're in the developing world; at other times you'll think you're on mainland Spain.

PLAYA DE LAS CANTERAS

The 3km stretch of narrow, golden, sandy beach attracts the world and his wife, and with so many sunny days, you'll have to wait until hell freezes over to find solitude on this stretch of sand. It has made the Santa Catalina district the city's main tourist draw card. There's an attractive *paseo marítimo* (seaside promenade) – the Paseo Canteras – which allows walkers, cyclists, joggers and rollerbladers to cover the entire length, free from traffic. The whole area fairly hums with the activity of bars, restaurants, nightclubs and shops.

MUSEO ELDER DE LA CIENCIA Y LA TECNOLOGÍA

This 21st-century **museum of science and technology** (928 01 18 28; www.museoelder.org; Parque Santa Catalina s/n; adult/child €4.50/3; 11am-9pm Tue-Sun) is full of things that whirr, clank and hum. It occupies a revamped docks warehouse to the east of Parque de Santa Catalina and is a great space to spend a few hours. Kids will be rapt in some of the displays – a space pod, interactive chromakey screen and very graphic depiction of a baby's birth all provoked wide-eyed stares. It's wheelchair accessible.

CASTILLO DE LA LUZ

Built in the 16th century (as were most other such fortresses around the Canary Islands) to ward off pirate attacks, the **castle** has traditionally been used for occasional art exhibitions. It was closed at the time of writing, but its environs have been extensively landscaped with some charming rose bushes and shady trees, and woe betide anyone who dares sit on the grass!

Jardín Botánico Canario Viera y Clavijo

About 9km southwest of the city, just before the village of Tafira Alta, this vast **botanical garden** (☎ 928 35 36 04; admission free; ⏱ 9am-6pm) – Spain's largest, encompassing 27 hectares – hosts a broad range of Macronesian flora from all seven Canary Islands, including many species on the verge of extinction. Wear stout shoes as some of the stony paths are uneven.

Bus Nos 301, 302 and 303 all pass by the garden's upper entrance. By car, take the C-811 road from Las Palmas.

ACTIVITIES
Surfing

Playa de las Canteras is not the world's greatest surf break but you can catch some good waves, and plenty of locals are out there at the weekend. It is one of the better beaches on the island. Unfortunately, there's nowhere to hire gear so pack your own board.

Diving

Buceo Canarias (Map pp62-3; ☎ 928 26 27 86; Calle Bernardo de la Torre 56-58) organises courses at all levels and rents and sells diving gear.

Walking

Las Palmas has two great *paseos marítimos* that hug the coast. For the shorter one, see p67; the other extends from the northern limit of Playa de Alcaravaneras for nearly 5km, the downside being that it's sandwiched between the shore and a six-lane highway for too much of its length.

LANGUAGE COURSES

There are a dozen or so language schools in Las Palmas, some of which offer Spanish classes – check the *Paginas Amarillas* (Yellow Pages). The **Gran Canaria School of Languages** (Map pp62-3; ⏱ 928 26 79 71; www.grancanariaschool .com; Calle Dr Grau Bassas 27), offers intensive courses from €115 per week – and you can enrol for as short a period as one week. It has a good reputation too, and has been in business for more than 40 years. Lodging can also be arranged through the school.

LAS PALMAS FOR CHILDREN

Las Palmas represents no difficulties for parents travelling with their offspring – but with the resorts of the south offering nonstop kid-friendly entertainment, you'll generally find that attractions are limited to play sets in public plazas. Children stay out quite late at night, and even though child-friendly menus are not widely available, child-friendly policies exist at most restaurants.

PLAIN SAILING

In the 1880s, when Puerto de la Luz (Las Palmas) was developing as a port, merchant and passenger ships had to moor some way from the docks. A local variety of shuttle boat, or *bote*, equipped with oars and sails up to 13m high, was developed to service offshore vessels. From poop to prow these boats measured no more than 7m, and they were soon doing a brisk trade ferrying people and goods from ship to shore.

Like any business, these little *botes* knew both busy and slack times. During the latter their captains and crews organised regattas in the port area. An idea born to ease the boredom of empty days sitting on the docks slowly transformed itself into a regular competition, and the tradition has been maintained.

Eighteen of these curious craft remain today and they regularly gather for an afternoon's racing on Saturday (usually from 5pm) and Sunday (around noon) from April to October. Crewed by eight to 12 people, each boat represents a *barrio*, or district, of Las Palmas.

Apart from the odd appearance of the participating vessels, the race itself is a little peculiar in that competitors race only *en bolina* (against the wind), but in such a way as to get maximum power from it. The fact that the prevailing wind is pretty much the same in the competition months off the east coast of Gran Canaria makes it the ideal spot for such races. The *botes* start at Playa de la Laja, a few kilometres south of the southern suburbs of Las Palmas, and finish at Playa de Alcaravaneras.

FESTIVALS & EVENTS

Although overshadowed by its more famous version in Santa Cruz de Tenerife, **Carnaval** is nevertheless a big event in Las Palmas. Three to four weeks of madness and fancy dress mark the first rupture with winter in February (the dates move depending on when Lent falls) – not that winter out here is any great trial! The bulk of the action takes place around Parque de Santa Catalina.

In late June the **Fiesta de San Juan**, in honour of the patron saint of the city, coincides with Midsummer's Day. Cultural events are staged across the city while big fireworks displays and concerts take place on Playa de las Canteras.

Corpus Christi, another feast with movable dates that takes place around June, is marked in particular by the laying out of extraordinary floral 'carpets' in some of the central streets of the old city.

Among the oldest religious festivals in Las Palmas is the **Romería de Nuestra Señora de la Luz** (Pilgrimage of Our Lady of Light), held in October. Most of the action takes place around Playa de las Canteras and in La Isleta. The battle with Sir Francis Drake is commemorated at the same time.

Las Palmas hosts a range of international festivals including:

Festival de Música de Canarias (January and February)
Festival de Ópera (February to March)
Festival de Ballet y Danza (May)
Festival Internacional de Cine (October to November) An international film festival held every two years.

SLEEPING

The bulk of the accommodation of all classes is around Santa Catalina beach and the port.

Vegueta & Triana   Map p64
BUDGET

Hotel Madrid (☎ 928 36 06 64; fax 928 38 21 76; Plazoleta Cairasco 4; s/d €36/48) The pick of the budget crop, in a ramshackle sort of way, has to be friendly Madrid, right by the Gabinete Literario. Simple rooms with bathroom are lacking in luxuries but are full of history – after all, General Franco spent the night here before the start of the Civil War. Ask for a room overlooking the square or Franco's favourite – No 3. Service is as slow as a wet weekend, but the ground-floor bar's a good place to wait for it.

Pensión Perojo (☎ 928 37 13 87; Calle Perojo 1; s/d without bathroom €15/24) A scrupulously clean and acceptable budget option in this part of the world is the friendly Perojo, although it's situated on an intersection that cops the full brunt of the peak-hour traffic noise.

MID-RANGE

Hotel Parque (☎ 928 36 80 00; www.hparque.com; Muelle Las Palmas 2; s/d €65/100; P ⊠ ⊠) What breakfast views this place commands from its 6th-floor perch above the park! Rooms are supremely comfortable, with great big bathrooms and excellent management. Plus, it's a hop, skip and a jump from the historic Vegueta and Triana *barrios* and the bus station.

Ciudad Jardín   Map pp62–3
Hotel Santa Catalina (☎ 928 24 30 40; www.hotels antacatalina.com; Calle León y Castillo 227; s/d €117/183) At the heart of Parque Doramas, this five-star lovely is *the* address in Las Palmas. Everything here is of the highest standard, and no luxurious stone goes unturned. It exudes the class of another era, with its own casino and *hamam* (Turkish bath), and delightful views of either the sea or a subtropical garden.

Santa Catalina & the Port   Map pp62–3
BUDGET

Pensión Plaza (☎ 928 26 52 12; Calle Luis Morote 16; s/d €24/36) Many of the clientele here might have tumbled off the latest container ship, but it's OK and there's usually a room going, although solo women travellers may find it a bit ropey. Basic rooms are clean and serviceable, and the management's a bit gruff.

MID-RANGE

Hotel Concorde (☎ 928 26 27 50; www.hotelconcorde .org; Calle Tomás Miller 85; s/d €85/100; P ⊠ ⊠) A recipient of millennium renovations and efficient on the management front. You will find very good rooms here, with a decent swimming pool and a superb beach just nearby – plus air-con! – making this an extremely comfy option.

Hotel Tenesoya (☎ 928 46 96 08; fax 928 46 02 79; Calle Sagasta 98; s/d €49.90/56.20) Close to the beach and the action of the northern end of the city, this is a modern, well-run hotel with an international clientele and good standards. All rooms have TV and a safe.

Apartamentos Luz Playa (☎ 928 26 75 50; e.t.c.@ terra.es; Calle Sagasta 66; d/studio €45/60) Stacked atop a Chinese restaurant on the Playa de las Canteras, these apartments have some great ocean views and spick-and-span (although a little dour) rooms. Larger apartments are also available, but it's the studios that command the sea views.

Apartamentos Playa Dorada (☎ 928 26 51 00; fax 928 26 51 04; Calle Luis Morote 69; apt 1-2 people €55, 3-4 people €67-80) Near the beach and firmly entrenched in the 1970s, these apartments are an endearing mix of kitsch, earth tones and crafty tiles. Go for a balcony room and breathe in the sea air and sun-splashed hedonism. Like several places, it's around 25% cheaper in May and June.

Apartamentos Catalina Park (☎ 928 26 41 20; Calle Tomás Miller 67; studio €36.10-42.10) If you want to stay in this neck of the woods and fit three people into a good-sized studio with a handy kitchenette, then stay here. Service is friendly and the space is nicely kitted-out.

TOP END

Hotel Imperial Playa (☎ 928 46 88 54; www.nh-hoteles.com; Calle Ferreras 1; s/d €118/165; P 🔁 🖵 🖳) This great hotel has an unbeatable location and wonderful modern rooms with a nautical feel and balcony doors that can be opened to take full advantage of the sea air. Business travellers are well looked after, as are children.

EATING

Eating out in Las Palmas will be a highlight of your time in the city – with most tastes catered to and high standards. For the most atmospheric eating, head to the Vegueta and Triana *barrios*.

Vegueta & Triana   Map p64

Hipócrates (☎ 928 31 11 71; Calle Colón 4; mains €5.70-9; ☺ closed Mon) Just opposite the entrance to the Museo Colón, this is a charming vegetarian restaurant with a glittery DIY décor and some wonderful, organic, cruelty-free feeds. Small portions are available for kids, and just to include everyone, you can drink and smoke too!

Belgo (Calle Mendizabal 28; mains €7-25) Oh-so-hip, this could be straight out of Barcelona, with its keen eye for cutting-edge design flourishes (such as a red L-shaped bar and interesting designs on the walls). It's a slick

package, advertising *'tapas con arte'* and other more substantial meals.

Restaurante Casa Montesdeoca (☎ 928 33 34 66; Calle Montesdeoca 10; mains €12.50-24; ☺ closed Sun) Set in an exquisitely maintained, 16th-century, Canarian colonial-style house, this restaurant also boasts a cool and relaxing patio (internal courtyard). Any of the meat or seafood dishes can be sincerely recommended and it's a good spot to conduct a business lunch.

Restaurante Amaiur (☎ 928 37 07 17; Calle Pérez Galdós 2; mains €11.50-17; ☺ closed Mon) Another very good upmarket establishment (and popular, so you may well want to make reservations) which offers mainly Basque cuisine. Try any of the seafood dishes, and enjoy the vegetable sides, which should placate most vegetarians.

La Dolce Vita (☎ 928 31 04 63; Calle Agustín Millares 5; mains €5-12; ☺ closed Sun) With some lovely home-made pasta on the menu and plenty of Italian film posters on the walls, this sweet place is as close to Rome as you can get in Las Palmas. There's a pretty decent selection of vegetarian-friendly options too.

Santa Catalina & the Port   Map pp62–3

Anthuriun (☎ 928 24 49 08; Calle Pi y Margall 10; mains €14.20-16.50; ☺ closed Sat afternoon & Sun) This smart restaurant has a fine reputation throughout the island and combines reworked interpretations of Canarian cuisine and Catalan kitchen experimentation amid subdued, low-key décor. Exquisite good taste all round – so reservations are advised.

Mesón Condado (☎ 928 46 94 43; Calle Ferreras 22; mains €5-17) This better than decent, middle-of-the-road (décor-wise) eatery serves up a mix of Galician food (concentrating on shellfish) from northwestern Spain, Canarian fare and more mainstream Spanish dishes. A very satisfying *menú del día* (set menu) will set you back a piffling €5 or thereabouts.

Casa Pablo (☎ 928 26 81 58; Calle Tomás Miller 73; mains €9-41; ☺ closed Mon; P) A deservedly popular little spot, oozing atmosphere and charm, with plenty of Spanish celebrity pics adorning the walls to leave you in no doubt that this is *the* place to come in Las Palmas (Eurovision's Dana ate here!) for a great feed (with Spanish, Basque and French influences). Hell, just popping in for some tapas and a cold beer is a more enjoyable exercise than at many eating options in this part of the world. There's free parking available too.

Restaurante Tehran (☎ 928 22 28 17; Calle Bernardo de la Torre 1; mains €7-market price) For Middle Eastern food with a difference, head to this place, which specialises in Iranian cuisine. There's even caviar on the menu, which will set you back at least €30 a serve. Still, if you ever had fantasies about hanging out in the Shah's compound, this'll be the closest you get to it in Las Palmas. If your budget's more restrained, the *menú del día* costs about €9.

Restaurante Balalaika (☎ 928 27 44 83; Calle Fernando Guanarteme 27; mains €9-11; ☺ closed Sun night) If you're hankering for something international but a little more exotic than the standard menus, this cosy place, with low lights, lots of warm colours and a Russian menu, will get you glowing – and they have caviar (it'll cost ya)! Live piano is played from 9pm.

Self-Catering

If you're cooking for yourself, shun the big supermarkets and take your custom to the **covered market** (Map pp62–3) between Calles Barcelona and Néstor de la Torre. Open mornings only, daily except Sunday, it's relatively small for such a large city yet full of atmosphere.

DRINKING & ENTERTAINMENT
Bars & Pubs

There is no shortage of watering holes in Las Palmas. There are popular *terrazas* on **Plaza España** (Map pp62–3), good for a daytime drink or as places to kick off the evening's fun in the Santa Catalina area. The Vegueta area also gets busy, and is the most attractive and interesting port of call for night owls.

Macabeo (Map p64; ☎ 928 32 17 28; Calle La Pelota 18) This place is a wonderfully kitted-out (with marble-top tables and high ceilings), funky bar/*taberna* (tavern) in the historic quarter, which takes its design cues from the Barcelona school of bar décor. It's smooth, slick and stylish, and so is the crowd. The tapas is great too.

Taberna de Nicolas (Map p64; ☎ 928 33 34 35; Calle La Pelota 15; tapas & raciónes €2.85-11.20) A great, atmospheric old haunt with chandeliers, dark wood, great ham and plenty of locals sharing snacks and gossip.

La Rebaná de Triana (Map p64; ☎ 928 36 10 51; Calle Constantino 15) One of the closest things you'll get to a Madrid-style tapas bar, in the heart of the Triana area. Settle in for a *ración* (large tapas) of *jamón* (cured ham), get a beer poured and admire the tiles.

La Cava (Map p64; Avenida Primero de Mayo 57; ☺ 9pm-3am Tue-Sat) Easy to miss and with a rather conspiratorial air about it, this is the sort of place you might choose for an assignation with your secret lover. Make that low-key and low-rent secret lover.

One great entertainment space is the **Monopol Centre** (Map p64; La Plazuela), which has a cinema, *terrazas*, bars and small clubs. Our favourite? Lounge Bar, which doesn't get going until after midnight, but has funky DJ sounds (the name Lounge is telling) and a spacey, industrial vibe.

Late-Night Bars & Discos

The late-night bars and discos are mostly in the Santa Catalina beach–Puerto de la Luz area. Don't expect to pay less than €5 per glass, whatever's in it.

Pick Up (Map pp62-3; ☎ 928 37 32 43; Calle Montevideo 3; ☺ midnight-5am Tue-Sat) This cool club melds a luxe industrial décor with DJ-spun sounds at the house end of things. It gets popular, and attracts a funky crowd.

Live Music

You can enjoy free performances of Canarian folk music in the Pueblo Canario (p67) every Sunday morning from about 11.30am.

Classical Music & Opera

Auditorio Alfredo Kraus (☎ 928 49 17 70), a spectacular auditorium designed by the Catalan architect Óscar Tusquets, is what one French expert described as 'a boat of air, sea and light'. Constructed partly of volcanic rock and with a huge window affording the spectators (up to 1700) broad ocean views, it is the dominant feature of the southern end of Playa de las Canteras.

Concerts are also sometimes performed in the Teatro Pérez Galdós (see p72).

Cinemas

The chances of getting to see undubbed versions of foreign movies are slight. **Multicines Royal** (Map p64; Calle León y Castillo 85; admission €4.50) is central.

Theatre

Teatro Pérez Galdós (Map p64; ☎ 928 36 15 09; Calle Lentini 1) has some theatrical performances and more frequent music recitals.

Football

The Union Deportiva de Las Palmas (UD; www.udlaspalmas.net in Spanish) celebrated the new millennium and its 50th anniversary by being promoted to the first division. What gave added piquancy was that the team's ascent coincided with relegation to Division Two for Tenerife – arch rivals on the football pitch and in every other field. The good times didn't last though, and at the time of writing both teams were in Division Two. To see UD in action, join the throng heading for the 20,000-odd seat **Estadio Insular** (Map pp62-3; ☎ 928 24 09 10; Calle Pio XII).

SHOPPING

Fedac (Fundación para la Etnografía y el Desarollo de la Artesanía Canaria; Foundation for Ethnography and the Development of Canarian Handicrafts; Map p64; ☎ 928 36 96 61; Calle Domingo J Navarro 7; ☟ 9.30am-1.30pm & 4.30-8pm Mon-Fri) Before buying handicrafts and other souvenirs, make your way to this shop, a government-sponsored, nonprofit-making outfit, where prices and quality are a good standard by which to measure those of products sold elsewhere. You'll find all sorts of traditional handicrafts here, such as pottery, baskets and leatherwork.

Boxes & Cigars (Map pp62-3; ☎ 928 26 71 78; Calle Tomás Miller 80; ☟ 10am-2pm & 4-9pm Mon-Sat) If it's cigars you're after, this place has a dazzling range on offer, with the boxes just about as attractive as the contents.

The traditional shopper's street has for centuries been **Calle Mayor de Triana** (Map p64). The street is nowadays also as interesting for its jumble of modernist architecture that houses some of the stores. Other great shopping strips include Calle Cano, Calle Viera y Clavijo and the surrounding streets (all Map p64).

Las Palmas' self-promoted chic shoppers' hangout is **Avenida Mesa y López** (Map pp62-3). Here you'll find the gigantic department store **El Corte Inglés** (Map pp62-3; ☎ 928 26 30 00; Avenida Mesa y López 15 & 18; ☟ 10am-10pm Mon-Sat) as well as a host of other shops and boutiques. Nearby, Indians have moved into many of the shops around Parque Santa Catalina to sell cheap electronic goods (or sell electronic goods cheaply, depending on how you view these things). You can pick up some great deals on cameras, watches, computing equipment and mobile phones – but remember you generally get what you pay for.

GETTING THERE & AWAY
To/From the Airport

Bus No 60 runs between the airport and Las Palmas bus station every hour around the clock and twice hourly between 7am and 7pm. The journey takes about 25 minutes, traffic permitting, and costs €1.70 to Estación San Telmo or €2.15 to Intercambiador (Interchange) Santa Catalina. A taxi between the airport and central Las Palmas is likely to cost you about €20.

Boat

For details of the weekly ferry to/from Cádiz (mainland Spain), see p249.

The quickest way to Santa Cruz de Tenerife is by **Trasmediterránea** (☎ 902 45 46 45; www .trasmediterranea.com) jetfoil. The 80-minute trip departs at least twice daily and the standard *butaca* (armchair seating) fare is from €49.35 to €62.65. Trasmediterránea also runs one service daily on to Morro Jable in Fuerteventura (€49.35 to €62.65, 1½ hours).

For a bus/ferry combination to Santa Cruz de Tenerife with Fred Olsen, see p79. The Fred Olsen bus (Map pp62–3) leaves from Parque Santa Catalina.

If you enjoy the sea trip for its own sake, you might want to take Trasmediterránea's weekly standard ferry, which sets sail from Las Palmas for Santa Cruz de Tenerife on Thursday (from €22.40, 3½ hours) and continues on to Santa Cruz de la Palma (from €37, 20 hours).

Three Trasmediterránea ferries per week serve Puerto del Rosario on Fuerteventura (€28, eight hours) and two serve Arrecife on Lanzarote (from €28, 10 hours).

Naviera Armas (Map pp62-3; ☎ 928 26 77 00; www.navieraarmas.com in Spanish) has a daily ferry to Morro Jable (Fuerteventura, €29.50, 3¾ hours), twelve weekly to Santa Cruz de Tenerife (€15.40, 3¼ hours), two weekly ferries to Puerto del Rosario (€31.90, 6½ hours) and at least three weekly to Arrecife (Lanzarote, €31.90, 7¼ hours).

View of Puerto de Mogán, Gran
Canaria (p86)

TONY WHEELER

DAMIEN SIMONIS

Café in Parque San Telmo in the Vegueta
district of Las Palmas de Gran Canaria (p67)

Sand dunes of Maspalomas, Gran Canaria (p80)

GREG GAWLOWSKI

PAUL KENNEDY

Fishing boats in Corralejo, Fuerteventura
(p102)

The small fishing village of El Cotillo,
Fuerteventura, a base for various sea
activities (p106)

PAUL KENN

A windmill in Tiscamanita, central Fuerteventura (p98)

MARTIN LLA

Bus

The **bus station** (Map p64; ☎ 928 36 83 35, 902 38 11 10 for timetable enquiries; Parque San Telmo) is located at the northern end of the Vegueta district. You should be able to get a copy of Global's island-wide schedules from any tourist office.

Bus Nos 30 and 50 (nonstop) go to Maspalomas (€4.50), No 1 to Puerto de Mogán (€5.55), Nos 12 and 80 to Telde (€1.10) and Nos 101, 102, 103 and 105 to Santa María de Guía and Gáldar (€2.25). There are frequent services to all these destinations.

A night owl bus, No 5, links the capital and Maspalomas. It leaves on the hour from Las Palmas, from 8pm to 3am, and on the half-hour from Maspalomas, from 9.30pm to 4.30am. If you plan to travel much outside town, a Tarjeta Insular (see p61) may well save you money.

Car

There are many car rental firms at the airport, at the jetfoil terminal and scattered across the city's Santa Catalina district.

GETTING AROUND
Bus

Yellow buses serve the metropolitan area. Pick up a route map from the tourist office at the bus station or from one of the other information offices around town.

The Tarjeta Insular (see p61) also works on urban routes. Just stick it in the machine and it will deduct €0.60. A standard single ticket, bought on the bus, costs €0.85.

Yellow bus Nos 1, 12, 13 and 15 all run from Triana northwards as far as the port and the northern end of Playa de las Canteras, calling by the bus station and Parque Santa Catalina.

For €8 you can buy a ticket giving you unlimited hop-on-hop-off travel for one day on the Bus Turística (Tourist Bus). It departs from Parque Santa Catalina irregularly 12 times daily, making it almost impossible to plan a day around Las Palmas and rely on it for getting around. This said, if you just jump on and stay aboard for the round trip, it's an excellent way of getting an initial overview of the town.

Car

Driving and parking in Las Palmas are a pain. It's not really any worse than many mainland Spanish cities, but rush-hour traffic jams are frustrating, as is the sometimes misleading one-way street system. Most of the centre operates meter parking. Otherwise there are several private car parks, where you pay around €2 per hour.

Taxi

If you need a **taxi** (☎ 928 46 00 00, 928 46 56 66, 928 46 22 12), you can call, flag them down or pick them up at one of the plentiful taxi stands across the city.

AROUND LAS PALMAS

With your own transport, you can get a reasonable look at the entire island in two to three days. Buses connect most towns and villages, but you will use up more time this way. Cyclists not averse to some tough inclines will enjoy the lightly trafficked roads of the interior.

Starting from Las Palmas you can enjoy a one-day circuit, heading first south and then cutting inland to take in the mountainous Tejeda region before swinging northeastwards back towards the capital.

TELDE
pop 99,500

Telde is the island's second city. It was founded before the Spanish conquest, by monks from Mallorca seeking to set up a bishopric in the Fortunate Isles, and is known for its production of string instruments, above all the *timple* (a kind of ukulele) – the islands' musical emblem.

The 12km trip south from Las Palmas passes through an arid, semi-industrialised landscape. But it's worth taking the trouble to visit Telde's San Juan and San Francisco areas, the nucleus of the old town.

Here the houses positively gleam with whitewash as the town preens itself and tries quite hard to live down its industrial image.

The **tourist office** (☎ 928 13 90 55; Calle León y Castillo 2; ☯ 8am-3pm Mon-Fri) is just off Plaza de San Juan.

Among the well-aged noble houses of the San Juan area, the 15th-century **Basílica de San Juan** stands out. As you enter, your eye is drawn to the elaborate 16th-century altarpiece, all gilt and gold, with a Crucifixion at its heart. On the large silver cross the Christ figure, made of a corn-based plaster by Tarasco Indians in Mexico, dates from the earliest days of cultural contact between the two continents.

The **Museo León y Castillo** (Calle León y Castillo 43; admission free; 🕑 8am-2pm Mon-Fri) is devoted to the family of the same name and in particular a late-19th-century politician – you'll want to be a serious Spanish history buff to get much out of this.

More interesting for most is the short walk to the **Iglesia de San Francisco**. From the Plaza San Juan, take cobbled Calle Inés Chanida westwards as it runs alongside an old aqueduct with orange and banana groves below. In the church, note the three polychrome stone altars on the northernmost of the twin naves and the fine *artesonado* (coffered ceiling).

Bus Nos 12 and 80 run to/from Las Palmas every 20 minutes.

INGENIO & AGÜIMES

A short bus ride south of Telde brings you to the towns of Ingenio and Agüimes, separated from one another by the Barranco de Guayadeque (see following) and in themselves of little interest.

Of the two, Agüimes boasts a marginally more attractive town centre, the centrepiece of which is shady Plaza Rosario, bounded on one side by the **Iglesia de San Sebastián**, considered one of the best examples of Canarian neoclassicism.

Festivals & Events

What does make Agüimes special is the **Encuentro Teatral Tres Continentes** (www.festivaldelsur.com), an annual gathering of theatre companies from Europe, South America and Africa. During this festival, held 1–15 September, an otherwise fairly quiet place becomes a temporary hotbed of international creativity. For advance information, you could try ringing Agüimes' **Concejalía de Cultura** (Cultural Council; ☎ 928 78 41 00).

Getting There & Around

A number of buses connect the two towns with Telde and Las Palmas. From Agüimes, bus No 22 heads southeast to the coast and **Arinaga**, a popular local spot for swimming even though there is no real beach to speak of.

BARRANCO DE GUAYADEQUE

The real reason for being hereabouts lies between Ingenio and Agüimes. The Barranco de Guayadeque (Guayadeque Ravine) rises up into central Gran Canaria in a majestic sweep of crumpled ridges, its close-cropped vegetation softening the otherwise arid terrain with a little green. Most curiously, about halfway along the 9km road leading into the barranco (ravine) from Agüimes (there is another road from Ingenio) you'll find an odd relic of bygone ages – a troglodyte hamlet. Some of the handful of inhabitants here live in cleverly decked-out caves.

Another 4km and the road peters out in an impassable (for vehicles) track and a couple of restaurants. **Restaurante Tagoror** (☎ 928 17 20 13; mains €4-9) is both recommended and modestly priced, with Canarian staples featuring heavily on the menu.

TEMISAS

If you have a vehicle, you can take a back road from Agüimes to Santa Lucía de Tirajana. The C-815 highway, which all the buses and coaches take, also heads this way.

If you decide to opt for the narrow, little-frequented and only *just* two-lane back road, as it weaves its way around the mountains notice the terracing up each side valley and incised into many of the flanks.

All the terraces were worked until relatively recently. Then came mass tourism and with it plenty of less gruelling, better-paid work.

The setting for sleepy Temisas, with its backdrop of impenetrable cliffs, is impressive. And the village itself has preserved a good deal of its older stone houses.

SANTA LUCÍA DE TIRAJANA

Despite its pretty position in the upper reaches of a palm-studded valley, this place is something of a tourist-fuelled travesty. Someone has seen fit to build a very cheap-looking Disney castle and shoved inside, any which way, several hundred Guanche artefacts and a jumble of more modern tools and implements.

Admission costs €3, but you need a healthy sense of the downright ridiculous to savour this 'Castillo de la Fortaleza'. Various restaurants can be found surrounding the 'castle' and near the western exit of the village.

Bus No 34 connects Santa Lucía with San Bartolomé de Tirajana and El Doctoral (in the southeast) semiregularly.

SAN BARTOLOMÉ DE TIRAJANA

pop 3620 / elevation 850m

San Bartolomé has no notable sights, but the views out over the Tirajana valley are certainly pleasing and you could choose a worse spot to get stuck for the night.

Hostal Santana (☎ 928 12 71 32; Calle Tamaran 10; s/d €18/24), housed in an unattractive modern building on the main street, has simple rooms. Fight to be heard over the dull roar of the soaps on the TV in the downstairs bar and be rewarded with sweet service.

Viño Tinto (Calle Tamaran 20; ☺ 9am-5pm Sat-Thu) is a great spot to stock up on funky local straw hats (so retro!), scrummy local cheese and wine, or a bottle of rum or *licor de moras* (blackberry liquor).

Along the same street are several eatcries and bars. If you're planning a visit, make it on Sunday morning, when there's a lively farmers market known as Mercatunte.

FATAGA

A 7km detour south from San Bartolomé (or a pleasantly winding 30-minute drive north from Playa del Inglés on good roads) brings you to the charming hamlet of Fataga, sitting squat on a small knoll, humbled by the tall cliffs that overhang it to the west. Its narrow, car-free, cobbled lanes are a joy to roam. Several houses have already been tastefully renovated, without succumbing to toy-town sterility.

Bar Restaurante La Albericoque (☎ 928 79 86 56, Calle Nestor Álamo 4; mains €4-10) On the main road, this place has good local fare and a nice atmosphere. Next door is a small bar/café that is the closest thing to an arty, bohemian hangout in these parts.

El Molino del Agua (☎ 928 17 23 03; Carretera Fataga; s/d €35/45) About 1.5km north of the village, this is something of a package-tour circus during the day, with camel rides and a good-quality, feed-the-5000 restaurant. But, set amid a mature palm grove, it's a very pleasant, tranquil place – once the coaches have rolled off into the distance.

The rooms are good value. If the camels (€8 per ride) fail to turn you on, you can always hire a bike for the day for the same price.

Casa Rural Falcón (☎ 928 39 01 69; fax 928 39 01 70; Calle El Rio 4; house €100) This delightful rural house, just near the Plaza de Josefetta Alemana, can sleep up to six people and is well appointed. You'll need to book in advance though – it is not a 'turn up with your bags' kind of place. Disabled access is also possible.

Bus No 18 (from Maspalomas to San Bartolomé) calls by four times daily.

TEJEDA & AROUND

pop 890 / elevation 1050m

Tejeda is 33km north of San Bartolomé along a road that twists its way through splendidly rugged scenery of looming cliffs and deep gorges. It is a quiet, unprepossessing hill village whose main attraction is its marvellous setting. There are a few good places for a hearty lunch in town – all much of a muchness.

One gastronomic highlight of our visit here was the discovery of **Dulceria Nublo Tejeda** (☎ 928 66 60 30; Calle Hernández Guerra 15), a sublime pastry shop with delicious local treats – all freshly baked on the premises. If you're a fan of marzipan or *bienmesabe* (an almond and honey concoction), this place will love you right up.

If you want to stay in the area, try nabbing some digs at **Casa Rurale Servando** (☎ 928 38 21 31; www.usuarlos.lycos.es/casaruralservando in Spanish; Calle Heraclio Sanchez s/n).

Cruz de Tejeda

The greenish/greyish stone cross – from which this spot, north of Tejeda, takes its name – marks the centre of Gran Canaria and its old *caminos reales* (king's highways), along which it is still possible to cross the entire island.

From the lookouts here you can contemplate the island's greatest natural wonders: to the west the Roque Bentayga (see p76) and in clear weather the great cone of Teide on Tenerife; to the south Pozo de las Nieves (the island's highest point, p76) and the odd-looking **Roque Nublo** (1803m), which as often as not is truly is enveloped in a cloud; and dropping away to the northeast Vega de San Mateo (Plains of San Mateo; p76).

Walking this part of the world doesn't present any great challenges, but take plenty of water and wear sturdy shoes. Generally, you'll follow well-paved (and well-signed) roads that snake their way around rock formations that are often obscured by clouds (wear suncream though – you can still get burnt!). The walk from Cruz de Tejeda to Roque Nublo is especially recommended. You can get information and tips from Hotel El Refugio (see below).

You can also buy souvenirs and ride donkeys if you feel the urge.

The **Hotel El Refugio** (☎ 928 66 65 13; elrefu gio@canariasonline.com; Cruz de Tejeda s/n; s/d €52/64; P ♨) is a cheery, rural hostelry that makes a great base for a few days' walking. It has solid, comfortable rooms and a handy, good restaurant.

Bus No 305 from Las Palmas (via Santa Brígida and Vega de San Mateo) passes by five times daily on its way to Tejeda. From the south of the island you're better off by bike or car, although bus No 18 connects the two.

Roque Bentayga

About 10km southwest of Tejeda village rises up the Roque Bentayga (1404m). It's signposted – you need your own transport. Around the Roque itself, and further afield, there are various reminders of the Guanche presence here – from rock inscriptions to granaries and a sacred ritual site.

Pozo de las Nieves

Those with their own wheels can drive the 15km southeast of Tejeda to this, the highest peak on the island at 1949m. Follow the signs for Los Pechos and keep an eye on the military communications post which sits atop the rise. The views are breathtaking on a clear day. Directly west is the distinctive Roque Nublo.

VEGA DE SAN MATEO

Descending from the barren, chilly heights of Tejeda, you'll notice the scene around you quickly transforming itself as you approach San Mateo. The plain (*vega*) of San Mateo is a sea of green. As with most of the northern strip of the island (but especially the northeast), the area is busily cultivated and receives enough rain to keep local farmers well occupied.

You'll notice too that the area is much more densely populated – most of the island's population lives in the north. There's not an awful lot to San Mateo but it makes a pleasant stop.

If you happen to be around in September, try to make it for the *romería* (pilgrimage) and celebrations of the patron saint, St Matthew, on 21 September.

Statistically, you've a greater chance of catching the large weekend market. Held every Saturday and Sunday just south of the bus station, it pulls in regulars from all over the island.

Bus No 303 comes up from Las Palmas every 30 minutes.

SANTA BRÍGIDA & BANDAMA

About 9km further east on the road to Las Palmas, the next town of any note is Santa Brígida, whose centre repays a wander. The narrow streets are tree-lined and attractive, and from the parish church there are nice views inland over fields and palm groves to the central mountains.

Back on the road to Las Palmas, after 4km there's a turn-off for the **Caldera de Bandama**, one of the biggest extinct volcanic craters on the island, which offers superb views. Close by is **La Atalaya**, the largest pottery-producing village on the island, with plenty of opportunities to buy breakables and work out how to transport them back home.

Bus No 311 from Las Palmas to the village of Bandama passes through La Atalaya and takes you close to the crater – get off at the end of the line.

THE NORTH

As on most of the islands, the rain-blessed fertile north of Gran Canaria presents a radically different picture from its rugged, monochrome interior and south. Rolling hills, intensively tilled fields and terraces, and myriad villages and hamlets make up a busy and interesting picture as you wind along twisting roads, negotiating ravines and an ever-changing terrain. Only as you reach the west does the green give way to a more austere, although no less captivating, landscape – the west coast is the most dramatic on the island.

TEROR

pop 6100 / elevation 543m

In spite of its name, Teror, 22km southwest of Las Palmas, does anything but inspire fear. The central Plaza Nuestra Señora del Pino and Calle Real, leading from it and lined with fine old houses, have survived the modern age more or less intact and make a lovely spot to go for a wander.

Among the houses is **Casa de los Patronos de la Virgen** (admission €3; ✪ 11am-6.30pm Mon-Thu & Sat, 10.30am-2pm Sun), which generally serves as a museum. Smelling pleasantly musty, it's full of all sorts of intriguing odds and ends, mostly from the Las Palmas families who owned it and used it as their second home in the hills. The ancestors of Simón Bolívar's wife, the Venezuelan María Teresa Rodríguez del Toro, lived here at one point. At the time of research it was closed for restoration, but should be open by late 2004.

Dominating the square is the **Basílica de la Virgen del Pino** (admission free; ✪ 8am-noon & 2-6pm), a neoclassical 18th-century edifice. The interior, a lavishly gilt-laden affair, features the compelling 15th-century carving of the enthroned Virgen de la Nieve, illuminated in her place of honour at the heart of a particularly ornate altarpiece. If that doesn't distract you too much, make time to study the church's dome. It gets extra points for the sign at the front asking that visitors turn off their mobile phones, as 'you don't need a mobile to talk to God'!

Festivals & Events
The Virgen is the patron of the island and Teror is the religious capital. The **Fiesta de la Virgen del Pino** (Feast Day of the Virgin of the Pine), held in the first week of September, is not only a big event in Teror – it's the most important religious feast day on the island's calendar.

Sleeping & Eating
Casa Rural Doña Margarita (☎ 928 35 00 00; www.margaritacasarural.com; Calle Padre Cueto 4; house €70-95) This is a beautifully restored local house from the 18th century, with wooden beams, stone walls and solid furniture, just off the main plaza. It sleeps up to four people and has a tendency to get fully booked very quickly. Wonderful.

El Rincón de Magüi (Calle Diputación 6; mains €5-10) Just off the central square, and decorated with ceramic plates, this is a good-value local eatery that has an unheard-of no-smoking section! Avowedly local dishes such as *carne de cabre en salsa* (goat in sauce; €6.50) are a weekend staple.

Getting There & Away
Bus No 216 connects with Las Palmas and No 215 with Arucas. Both run hourly.

ARUCAS
pop 32,900
Nicknamed the 'pearl of Gran Canaria', Arucas makes a thoroughly pleasant day trip from Las Palmas. The extraordinary, grey, neo-Gothic **Iglesia de San Juan** (✪ 9.30am-12.30pm & 4.30-7.15pm), begun in 1917 and completed more than 60 years later, stands sullen watch over the bright white houses of Arucas in a striking display of disproportion. Inside, a fine 16th-century Italian Crucifixion, hanging above the altar, and the wooden Cristo Yacente (Reclining Christ), behind in the ambulatory, are the most noteworthy artworks.

From the church, walk down Calle Gourié then Calle León y Castillo and turn right into Plaza Constitución, whose most interesting building is its restrained modernist **ayuntamiento** (town hall). Opposite are the spruce **municipal gardens** and, within them, the lackadaisical **tourist office** (☎ 928 62 31 36; ✪ 8am-4pm Mon-Fri).

Calle Heredad flanks the gardens on the southern side of the plaza. It's dominated by the neoclassical **Heredad de Aguas de Arucas y Firgas** building, completed in 1908.

More to the taste of many visitors is the **Destilerías Arehucas** (Arehucas Rum Distillery; ✪ 10am-2pm Mon-Fri). Free guided visits, culminating in a little tipple, take place during opening hours.

A great spot for a snack or coffee is **Siroco** (Calle León y Castillo 7; ✪ 7am-11pm Mon-Thu, 7am-midnight Fri & Sat), in a high-ceilinged, well-restored 19th-century building. With a nice upstairs *comedor* (dining room), where it's easy to unwind, and a no-smoking section, it's the most stylish spot in town. Sandwiches cost about €2.50.

If you have wheels – it's a fairly hard grind, mind you, if you have only two – take the well-signed route to **La Montaña de Arucas**, 2.5km north of the town. From here there's a splendid panorama of Las Palmas to the northeast, the northern coast of the island, fruit orchards, banana groves – and hectare upon hectare of plastic greenhouses. The restaurant here – which controls access to the finest views westwards – is among the best in town.

About 1.5km west of town is the glamorous **Hacienda de Buen Suceso** (☎ 928 62 29 45; fax 928 62 29 42; Carretera de Arucas a Bañaderos; s/d €95/140), a fine Canarian rural hotel that will have you playing plantation owner in no time, and the equally splendid **Jardín de las Hespérides** (Jardín de la Marquésa; admission €5; ☼ 9am-noon & 2-6pm Mon-Fri) botanical garden. Owned by the Marquésa de Arucas, they may not be to every democrat's taste but both are very beautiful.

Bus Nos 205 and 206 provide a regular service to/from Las Palmas, while No 215 runs hourly to Teror.

MOYA
pop 900 / elevation 490m

The spectacular 13km drive between Arucas and Moya follows a corniche, incised into the flank of the mountain, which gives spectacular views of the northern coast. Moya hasn't a lot to hold you except for the **Casa/Museo Tomás Morales** (☎ 928 62 02 17; admission free; ☼ 8am-8pm Mon-Fri, 10am-2pm & 5-8pm Sat), which is opposite the 16th-century church on the main road through town. Once home to the Canarian poet, who died in 1922 when he was only 37, it also promotes temporary art exhibitions.

Bus Nos 116 and 117 between them run 15 times daily to/from Las Palmas.

SANTA MARÍA DE GUÍA
pop 8430

Just off the main C-810 highway 25km west of Las Palmas, Santa María de Guía (or just Guía) was for a while home to the French composer Camille Saint-Saëns (1835–1921), who occasionally tickled the ivories in the town's 17th-century neoclassical church.

In the 18th century, the town and surrounding area were devastated by a plague of locusts.

To rid themselves of this blight, town and country people got together to implore the Virgin Mary for help. This has remained a tradition and on the third Sunday of September the townsfolk celebrate La Rama de las Marías, in which they dance their way to the doors of the church to make offerings of fruits of the earth to Mary. The town is also known for its *queso de flor* (flower cheese).

Bus Nos 101, 102, 103 and 105 all pass through on their way from Las Palmas.

GÁLDAR
pop 22,600 / elevation 124m

One of the most important archaeological finds in the islands is the **Cueva Pintada** (Painted Cave), near the Agaete exit of this town. Its walls bear deteriorating designs in red, black and white that were left behind by the Guanches. The area around it, which has yielded some remains of a Guanche settlement, has been declared an archaeological park and a museum, **Museo Etnográfico de Barranco Hondo de Abajo** (☎ 928 55 51 20; ☼ noon-5.30pm Mon-Fri), has been constructed, although you'll need to call and request a guided visit.

A couple of kilometres out of town at Playa del Agujero is the **Necrópolis de Gáldar** (closed to the public). Mummies, objects used in Guanche funeral rites and domestic items have been discovered among these tombs. The area has, however, been fenced off and seems likely to stay that way.

Gáldar's **tourist office** (☎ 928 89 58 55; Plaza Heredamientos s/n; ☼ 8am-2.30pm Mon-Fri) is in the Edificio Heredad de Agua building.

Bus Nos 101, 102, 103 and 105 head east for Las Palmas (€2.25). Southbound, No 103 links Gáldar with Agaete and Puerto de las Nieves (€3.20).

AGAETE & PUERTO DE LAS NIEVES
pop 5640

The town of Agaete, just 10km south of Gáldar, is a relaxing small town with a handful of seafood restaurants and some low-key sights. Nearby Puerto de las Nieves – until the 19th century the island's principal port and nowadays the terminal for the ferry to Santa Cruz de Tenerife – isn't easy to demarcate at all: the two towns seem to bleed into each other. It's nothing to go overboard about and the beaches are small, black and pebbly, but buildings are low, the Atlantic thunders in and there are great eating options by the port. It was there before tourism, and now coexists with, but is not overdominated by, it.

Just in from the beach is the striking **Iglesia de Nuestra Señora de la Concepción**. Built in 1874, it is unique in the islands for its pronounced Mediterranean style. For a moment it feels like you've landed in Greece! Inside are two parts of a 16th-century Flemish triptych by Joos van Cleve. The middle panel is preserved in nearby **Ermita de las Nieves**, a small chapel.

Around Agaete the coast begins to take on a sterner countenance than further north. From the jetty you can see the **Dedo de Dios** (God's Finger), thrusting up from the sea beneath the cliffs to the east of the port. This basalt monolith has weathered the elements for 100,000 years.

Festivals & Events
If you manage to be in Agaete around 4 August you'll witness the **Fiesta de la Rama**, whose origins lie in an obscure Guanche rain dance. Nowadays locals, accompanied by marching bands, parade into town brandishing tree branches and then get down to the serious business of having a good time.

Sleeping & Eating
Hotel Puerto de las Nieves (☎ 928 88 62 56; Avenida Alcalde José de Armas s/n; s/d €60.70/90.20) This is a newish four-star joint with wonderful facilities, including a thalassotherapy centre. Think large beds, wooden floors, good service and cellulite treatments.

Apartamentos El Angosto (☎ 928 55 41 92; Paseo Obispo Pildaín 11; apt €42; P) Near the cemetery, in Puerto de las Nieves, there are decent, simple apartments here, suited to self-caterers.

Fronting the port and surrounding it, you have a choice of seafood restaurants.

Cofradía de Pescadores (☎ 928 88 62 50; Muelle Puerto de las Nieves; menú del día €5.75) Located smack-bang next to the port and low on fancy decorative touches – but finding fresher fish (this *is* the fishermen's eating house, after all) is nigh impossible.

La Granja (mains €4.80-12) Cheap and cheerful La Granja, right by the dock entrance, does a *menú del día* for a bargain €5.50 and offers fantastic, simply prepared fish dishes to a ravenous, rowdy crowd at lunch times. It's friendly too, with outdoor seating.

Restaurante el Cápita (☎ 928 55 41 42; Calle Nuestra Señora de las Nieves 37; mains €5-12.50) This is a slightly smarter proposition, but it also has a *menú del día* for €4.65 (you'll do better picking à la carte). Fresh fish dishes abound and can't be faulted, although service can be a tad slow when it gets crowded.

Restaurante Dedo de Dios (☎ 928 89 85 81; Carretera Puerto de las Nieves s/n; mains €6.20-18.50) This family-friendly restaurant gets absolutely packed at lunch time on weekends, and with good reason. It's a breezy, bright and relaxing place to gather everyone together

DETOUR

An 8km flower-lined diversion up the tight Barranco de Agaete (follow the signs for El Valle) leads you to **Los Berrazales** (325m), whose mineral waters have curative qualities. At the end of the road is the two-star **Hotel Princesa Guayarmina** (☎ 928 89 80 09; www.hotelguayarmina.com; Los Berrazales s/n; s/d €37/57, ste €60/87; 🍴), a healthy place which grows its own vegetables and lays on all kinds of water treatment. The atmosphere is from another world – it's the sort of place where you imagine creative types convalescing from TB – thanks to the architecture and the fresh air. The Princesa also makes a good base for a few days' walking in the surrounding hills. Pop into the bar for a drink if you're not planning on staying – it's a nice little break. Bus No 102, which runs between Gáldar and Puerto de las Nieves, pushes on to Los Berrazales seven times daily.

for a long lunch, and is close to the miniscule strip of sand and sea that claims to be the 'beach'. Disabled access is good too.

Getting There & Away
Bus Nos 102 and 103 link the town and port with Las Palmas at least hourly. Bus No 101 heads south for Aldea de San Nicolás three times daily.

Fred Olsen (☎ 928 55 40 05; www.fredolsen.es) operates six fast ferries per day to Santa Cruz de Tenerife from Agaete/Puerto de las Nieves. The standard one-way fare is €29.70/14.90 per adult/child, plus €39 per car. There is a free bus connection to Las Palmas (Parque Santa Catalina). Going the other way, the bus leaves Las Palmas 1½ hours before the ferry is due to depart.

ALDEA DE SAN NICOLÁS
Usually known as San Nicolás de Tolentino, this town is the kind of place where you might well arrive in the evening and then stop and recharge your batteries before heading on round the island – although you won't find anything to see or do that's of any real interest.

The lure here is the travelling, not the arriving. The road between Agaete and San Nicolás takes you on a magnificent cliff-side journey. If you head southwest in the late afternoon, the setting sun delights the eyes with a soft-light display, marking out each successive ridge in an ever-darker shadowy mantle. There are numerous lookouts along the way to take in the rugged views.

The approach from Mogán and the south (see p86), though lacking the seascapes, is almost as awesome.

The rather scruffy town has little to excite the senses. In fact, it's the sort of place you only stay in because the arse has fallen out of your car. However, **Hotel Los Cascajos** (☎ 928 89 11 65; Calle Cascajos 9; s/d/tr €34/38/42) offers decent, spotlessly clean digs, and includes breakfast. The owner also has **Pensión Segundo** (☎ 928 89 09 09), nearby on the main square, and the bar/restaurant beneath it.

Bus No 38 runs regularly between Puerto de Mogán and Gáldar.

ARTENARA

A back road climbs eastwards up the valley from Aldea de San Nicolás to the hilltop village of Artenara, from where you are only a short distance from Tejeda. The sparsely populated countryside of bare ridges and rugged hills is dotted with troglodyte caves, some still inhabited.

Bus No 220 runs three times daily from Las Palmas via Teror. No buses connect the village with Aldea de San Nicolás.

PLAYA DEL INGLÉS & MASPALOMAS

pop around 40,000

This is the international party end of the island, with hundreds of thousands of international guests treating it like home. A good chunk of the coast has basically been converted into a giant holiday resort, with drinks, lots of drinks. You come here for sun (especially if escaping the European winter) and nocturnal fun. Of course, there is nothing to stop you exploring the rest of the island – and we'd recommend hiring a bike or car and breaking free for a day or two to do just that.

But don't come to Maspalomas and Playa del Inglés (Maspalomas wasn't an Englishman at all, but a French fellow who was one of the first foreigners to live in the area early

in the 20th century) for the history and impressive monuments – there aren't any, unless enormous swimming pools count as impressive monuments. And don't come expecting to savour Spain. Playa del Inglés in particular is a foreign-tourist destination, where mainland Spanish visitors are very much in a minority.

The heart of the resort is Playa del Inglés, and the heart of the heart is generally the Yumbo Centrum, a big four-level shopping jungle. You could spend your entire holiday in here. By day it's like an Arab bazaar, bursting with all sorts of goods from rags to radios, while innumerable restaurants compete for your attention with international food. Here you will also find banks, doctors, telephone and fax offices, a laundrette and supermarkets. The main tourist office is just outside the centre, on the same block.

As day gives way to night the scene transforms itself so that by the wee small hours the leather handbags and wallets in the stores have been replaced by leather gear in steamy gay bars. The vaguely wholesome, bustling family atmosphere evaporates as the discos, straight and gay, swing until dawn, barrels and bottles are drained by the dozen in pubs and bars, and the drag shows, saunas and sex shops all do a roaring trade.

Beyond Yumbo is the rest, which in many respects is not unlike Yumbo. This is, of course, an artificial settlement and you feel it immediately – the neatly traced boulevards and roundabouts betraying all the spontaneity in town design of a Five-Year Plan. It's all hotels, apartments, restaurants and bars, and then some.

The only natural items of genuine interest are the deeply impressive dunes of Maspalomas, which fold back from the beach. Covering 400 hectares, their inland heart has been declared a nature reserve with restricted access.

STREETSCAPES

In Maspalomas the street names are revealing – Avenida del Touroperador Saga Tours, Avenida del Touroperador Alpitours, Neckermann, Tui, Thomson and so on and so on. No plain old streets (*calles*) either – all avenues, no matter how small.

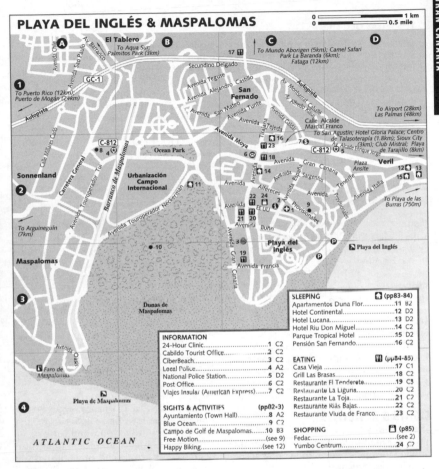

PLAYA DEL INGLÉS & MASPALOMAS

INFORMATION	
24-Hour Clinic..............................1	C2
Cabildo Tourist Office...................2	C2
CiberBeach..................................3	A2
Local Police.................................4	A2
National Police Station.................5	D2
Post Office...................................6	C2
Viajes Insular (American Express)....7	C2

SIGHTS & ACTIVITIES	(pp82-3)
Ayuntamiento (Town Hall)..............8	A2
Blue Ocean..................................9	C2
Campo de Golf de Maspalomas......10	B3
Free Motion............................(see 9)	
Happy Biking..........................(see 12)	

SLEEPING	(pp83-84)
Apartamentos Duna Flor................11	B2
Hotel Continental........................12	D2
Hotel Lucana..............................13	D2
Hotel Riu Don Miguel....................14	D2
Parque Tropical Hotel...................15	D2
Pensión San Fernando..................16	C2

EATING	(pp84-85)
Casa Vieja.................................17	C1
Grill Las Brasas...........................18	C2
Restaurante El Tenderete.............19	C3
Restaurante La Liguria..................20	C2
Restaurante La Toja.....................21	C2
Restaurante Rías Bajas.................22	C2
Restaurante Viuda de Franco.........23	C2

SHOPPING	(p85)
Fedac...................................(see 2)	
Yumbo Centrum.........................24	C2

ORIENTATION

The Playa del Inglés is right next to the centre of the triangle-shaped urban area, and to the southwest are the beaches and dunes of Maspalomas. Maspalomas itself is the quieter (you might say more exclusive) western perimeter of the resort. East of Playa del Inglés the resort continues, but thins out in the areas known as Veril and San Agustín.

There are bus stops all over the resorts, a couple of them right by Yumbo.

INFORMATION
Emergency

The **local police** (☎ 928 14 15 72; Plaza de la Constitución 2) are near the *ayuntamiento* beside the Barranco de Maspalomas. The national police station is beside the C-812 highway.

Internet Access

CiberBeach (Apartamentos Taidia, Avenida Tirajana 11; per 15 min €1.25; ☺ 8am-2pm & 5-10pm)

Laundry

Laundrette (Lot 411, 4th fl, Yumbo Centrum; ☺ 8am-8pm Mon-Fri, 8am-1pm Sat) Coin-operated, self-service and reliable.

Medical Services

The resort is swarming with clinics, their business no doubt enhanced by the aftermath of shattering hangovers and third-degree sunburn. A **24-hour clinic** (☎ 928 76 12 92; cnr

---

IT'S A GAY OLD LIFE

Gran Canaria is gay Europe's winter escape playground. Or, rather, the Playa del Inglés on the southern side of the island is. A seemingly endless string of bars, discos and clubs are crammed into the Yumbo Centrum (p85), right smack in the heart of the Playa del Inglés. It is predominantly a gay men's scene, although of course this doesn't stop small numbers of lesbians and straights from wading in.

Little happens before midnight. From then until about 3am the bars on the fourth level of the Yumbo Centrum bear the brunt of the fun, after which the nightclubs on the second level take over.

At dawn people stagger out for some rest. Some make for the beach at Maspalomas across the dunes, which are themselves a busy gay cruising area.

Avenida España & Avenida EE UU) is opposite the tourist office – English is spoken.

Money
Viajes Insular (☎ 928 76 05 00; Avenida Moya 14; ☺ 9am-8pm Mon-Fri, 9am-2pm Sat) Represents American Express.

Post
Post office (Avenida Tirajana)

Tourist Offices
Cabildo tourist office (☎ 928 77 15 50; cnr Avenida España & Avenida EE UU; ☺ 9am-2pm & 3-8pm Jul-Sep, 9am-9pm Mon-Fri & 9am-1pm Sat Oct-Jun) Just outside the Yumbo Centrum, this has plenty of brochures but no great interest in bestowing answers on questions that stray outside said brochures.

SIGHTS & ACTIVITIES
Theme Parks
There's a multitude of theme parks in the south of the island. You'll soon know about them because brochures and advertising are everywhere. They are a great way of keeping the young, and young-at-heart, entertained for a full day.

Palmitos Park (☎ 928 14 02 76; adult/child €17/12; ☺ 9.30am-6pm) A few kilometres north of the resort area, this is a subtropical oasis crammed with exotic flora and 1500 species of birds, along with a butterfly house, an aquarium and 15 performing parrots. Buses run here regularly from various stops in Playa del Inglés.

Mundo Aborigen (☎ 928 17 22 95; Carretera Playa del Inglés-Fataga; adult/child €12/free; ☺ 9am-6pm) Located 6km along the road north to Fataga, 100 or so model Guanches stand in various ancient poses designed to give you an idea of what life was like here before the con-

quistadors turned up to build theme parks about how the Guanches once lived. Take bus No 18.

Aqua Sur (☎ 928 14 05 25; Carretera Palmitos Park; adult/child €20/14; ☺ 10am-5pm daily, 10am-6pm 1 Jul-30 Sep) This enormous water park can boast its own surf beach with seven types of waves and miles of rides and slides. You can take bus Nos 45 and 70 to get here from Playa del Inglés and Puerto Rico, respectively.

Sioux City (☎ 928 76 25 73; Cañon del Aguila; ☺ 10am-5pm) Fancy a shoot-out or a trip to Miss Kitty's whorehouse? This is where good guys and bad guys shoot 'em up, round 'em up and generally get (mildly) wild for your entertainment. What it has to do with the Canary Islands, we'll never know. Take bus No 29 to get here.

Camel Safari Park La Baranda (☎ 928 79 86 80; Carretera Playa del Inglés-Fataga; ☺ 9am-6pm) After the Wild West, water rides and Guanches – a trip to the Orient? According to the brochure you can come and enjoy the oasis of palms and 'relax listening to the singing of the birds and the murmur of the camels'. Murmur?!

Swimming
For many, the only energy left after partying at night will be just enough to get down to the beach and collapse for the day. Beaches from east to west are Playa de las Burras, Playa del Inglés and Playa de Maspalomas. They all link up to form the one beach.

The best part about Maspalomas is the dunes. A camel trip, which is well worth the effort, costs €30/15 per adult/child.

There is a nudist area about where the dunes begin if you are approaching from Playa del Inglés. Although mixed, it's a popular gay cruising area.

Diving

Blue Ocean (☎ 928 77 05 46; Hotel Sandy Beach, Avenida Alfreces Provisionales s/n; dives from €60; ⓨ 9am-7pm) A reputable, friendly place that can organise dive courses, excursions and hire.

Surfing & Windsurfing

Although surfing is possible here (the best waves tend to break off the western end of Maspalomas by the lighthouse, or *faro*), this is not mind-blowing surfing territory. Windsurfers hang around in the same spot, but are better off heading east beyond the resorts to Bahía Feliz, Juan Grande and, best of all, Pozo Izquierdo, which is for experienced windsurfers. **Club Mistral** (☎ 928 15 71 58; www.club-mistral.com; Carretera Sur, Playa de Tarajillo), in Bahía Feliz, rents equipment and offers courses, including beginners instruc tion in kitesurfing.

Thalassotherapy

Centro de Talasoterapía (☎ 928 76 56 89; talasot erpia@hotelgloriapalace.com; Hotel Gloria Palace, Calle Las Margaritas s/n) Europe's largest, this cen tre occupies a huge complex attached to Hotel Gloria Palace, and is nothing short of breathtaking. Fabulous sea-water treat ments leave your skin as smooth as a baby's bum and your mind as light as a feather. A day's dunking and use of the various ap pliances costs from €50, but can climb far higher if you're convinced that cellulite can be cured by being horizontal.

Golf

Greens freaks can satisfy their needs at **Campo de Golf de Maspalomas** (☎ 928 76 25 81; www.maspalomasgolf.net; Avenida Touroperador Neck ermann), where 18 holes (from €50 to €75, depending on the time of year) are never enough and the ocean views are superb.

Cycling

Happy Biking (☎ 928 76 68 32; www.happy-biking.com; Hotel Continental, Avenida Italia 2; bike hire per day from €7) Now there's a nice name! Happy Biking rents out a range of cycles. Take your pass port along. It also organises cycle tours, mostly quite gentle, which start at €27, in cluding bike hire, transport to and from the ride, and a picnic.

Free Motion (☎ 928 77 74 79; www.free-motion.net; Hotel Sandy Beach, Avenida Alfereces Provisionales s/n; bike hire per day from €11.90) This outdoor-

loving operation has a range of tours (small groups) starting from €39 per day and can also hire out equipment. Hire prices rise to €25.90 per day for a bike with all the bells and whistles.

The *cabildo* (government) tourist office (see p82) has a brochure in Spanish describ ing four recommended day routes radiating from Maspalomas.

Walking

There's really no excuse for not pulling on those trainers and heading inland into the spectacularly rocky and wild interior of the island, where you'll wonder if you've wan dered into Nevada or Colorado at times!

Free Motion (see Cycling, previous) has a choice of three hiking trips in the country side. La Manzanilla, Roque Nublo and the Green North. Check which one is best suited to your needs. They all cost €39.90.

Rutas Canarias (☎ 928 67 04 66; full-day walk €27) Full-day walks set out by bus from the *cabildo* tourist office beside the Yumbo Centrum at 10am on Monday, Wednesday and Friday. Just turn up or ring for infor mation.

For all the above, transport to/from the walk is included within the fee. To enjoy an exhilarating 5km and more for free and without the need of a guide, simply follow the promenade, which, sometimes at shore level, sometimes above it, extends eastwards from Playa del Inglés.

SLEEPING

There are more than 500 hotels, apartment blocks and bungalows in Playa del Inglés and Maspalomas; in peak periods many are full to bursting. It's much safer and certainly cheaper to book a package outside Spain; the rate some hotels and apartments quote to independent visitors can be as much as 100% more than what a tour operator offers. Travel agents in Britain, Ireland, Germany and the Netherlands brim with deals and special last-minute offers.

If you're going it alone, it's almost im possible to assess where you should head. You get, in reasonable measure, what you pay for. In moderate to high season you are unlikely to find an apartment (cheaper than a hotel) for less than €40 for two people.

All we can do is give some indicative places and prices. With no taxi fare in the urban area above €7 – and taxis rolling through the night – consider taking a place away from the beach, even away from Playa del Inglés itself.

If you haven't reserved in advance, pick up an accommodation list and town map from one of the tourist offices and let your fingers do the walking. Many apartments don't have anyone in permanent attendance so it's often useless to simply turn up with hope in your heart.

Budget

A true budget scene doesn't exist in these parts.

Pensión San Fernando (☎ 928 76 39 06; Calle La Palma 16; d €18) There's precisely one *pensión* in town and if you can get in, it's excellent one-star value.

A basic room here, just south of San Fernando's Centro Comercial, will not have you thinking that you're in the lap of luxury, but it's tidy, friendly and far removed from the enforced 'costa del lager lout' vibe of some places.

Mid-Range

The bulk of apartments and hotels will fall into this category, but remember, they're usually booked by tour operators.

Parque Tropical Hotel (☎ 928 77 40 12; Avenida Italia 1; s/d/tr €75/125/175; ⊠) This hotel looks quite charming, which is no mean feat in these parts. The design is best described as 'Canarian', meaning that it has some attractive wood finishes against the blinding white walls. For a four-star hotel, prices are extremely reasonable.

Hotel Lucana (☎ 928 77 40 40; www.hotellucana.com in Spanish; Plaza del Sol 4; s/d €85/109; P ⊠ ⊠) Pleasant four-star Hotel Lucana, one block back from the shore, has quality rooms and a pretty spiffy selection of swimming pools. Baby-sitting is available on request and low-season reduction will generally save about 30% of the prices quoted above.

Apartamentos Duna Flor (☎ 928 76 76 75; fax 928 76 94 19; Avenida Touroperador Neckermann s/n; d €65) Getting mixed reviews, but looking perfectly acceptable when we paid a visit, this huge complex with central swimming pool is like a minivillage.

Its 400-plus pleasantly appointed bungalows and apartments cater for families, and the location is handy.

Top End

There's no such thing as a budget hotel hereabouts, so why not throw in the penny-pinching towel and go all out with a no-holds-barred accommodation wonderland? The premier top-end establishments are out by the dunes in Maspalomas.

Hotel Continental (☎ 928 76 00 33; fax 928 77 23 47; Avenida Italia 2; s/d/tr €168/268/376; ⊠) A great deal in this category is the three-star Continental, which offers half board (one meal per day is included in the price) into the bargain, has plenty of space for everyone and enough water features to seem indecent on such a rain-starved island. Children are very welcome and catered for. The above-quoted tariffs drop by over 50% in the lower seasons, which are most of the time.

Hotel Riu Don Miguel (☎ 928 76 15 08; hotel .donmiguel@riu.com; Avenida Tirajana 30; s/d/tr €186/259/369) Offering a smidgen over 280 rooms on five levels, this extremely well-managed holiday compound caters to everyone searching for a solid, very comfortable choice in the thick of things. Rooms are in great condition, and sporting facilities first-rate. Don't be fooled by the rack rates though – they are for absolute peak season, and you can get well over 50% off at other times.

EATING

The place is predictably swarming with eateries. The bulk of them serve up a pretty bland array of 'international' dishes designed to keep any stomach filled without upsetting any palates.

Restaurante Rías Bajas (☎ 928 76 40 33; cnr Avenida de Tirajana & Avenida EE UU; mains €11.60-24; ⏰ 1-4pm & 7.30pm-12.30am) This is primarily a solid fish and seafood place and has a strong island-wide reputation for great Cantabrian seafood delights. The décor continues the nautical theme, and it's often a good idea to show up earlyish, as this place can get busy on weekends.

Restaurante El Tenderete (☎ 928 76 14 60; Avenida Tirajana s/n; mains from €2.35 per 100g; ⏰ closed Sun) For quality Canarian seafood, you can't beat this joint. Its walls feature plenty of framed certificates and awards it has picked up. Recommended, especially for the fresh fish – pick your piece (dentex, sardines, sea bass, hake etc) from the fridge.

Restaurante Viuda de Franco (☎ 928 76 98 28; Calle Marcial Franco 11; mains €8-22; ⏰ 6am-midnight)

On the roundabout where the C-812 highway intersects with Avenida Tirajana in the area known as San Fernando, this stalwart of Canarian eating has been serving up tapas and solid meals since WWII. Nowadays – and despite the fact that the menu's available in seven different languages – the food still makes no concessions to non-Canary palates and is excellent value. Grab a table in the vine-covered patio and relax.

Casa Vieja (☎ 928 76 90 10; Calle El Lomo 139, Carretera de Fataga; mains €6.50-18; ☻ 1pm-midnight) Just north of the GC-1 motorway, along the road to Fataga. OK, so it's a little out of the way, but the effort to get here is well repaid. The 'old house' is indeed a charmingly bucolic affair. Plants – real, not the ubiquitous plastic – festoon the low roof, canaries trill and a particularly hearty meal (such portions!) won't hurt the wallet at all. Any grilled meat dish will get the thumbs up.

Restaurante La Toja (☎ 928 76 11 96; Edificio Barbados II, Avenida Tirajana 17; mains €14-21; ☻ closed Sun lunch) A quality establishment blending the best of cuisines from France and Galicia. Try the Galician-style boiled hake and revel in the smart, subdued-looking surrounds and smooth service.

Grill Las Brasas (☎ 928 76 29 05; Avenida Tirajana 28; mains €13-22; ☻ 6pm-midnight) Various grills and other meat dishes are the main reason for coming to this rustic-looking, cosy place. But there are some decent vegetarian options too – try the asparagus dishes and forget that whole thing about it not being easy being green.

Restaurante La Liguria (Avenida Tirajana 24; pizza €5.50-9) Of the myriad Italian joints, this is not a bad choice for those nights when it can only be pizza (a universal affliction it would seem). Most pasta and pizza dishes are authentic enough, but you're never going to believe you're in Naples while in the Canary Islands.

DRINKING & ENTERTAINMENT
Naming particular bars and discos is as pointless as listing hotels. You could stagger around Yumbo Centrum – as many do – for weeks and not have sampled all the nightlife options. Quite a few are gay venues, but there are plenty of straight places too.

If you ever break out beyond Yumbo Centrum, all the big *centros comerciales*

(shopping centres) have at least some bars and discos in them. And beyond them, there are still more bars and discos on offer.

SHOPPING
About the only interruption to the hectares of apartments, hotels, restaurants and bars comes in the form of the aforementioned shopping centres. In them you can buy everything from children's wear to electronics. A good tip is to keep on looking, despite the enormous temptation to buy everything as soon as you see it – you may well save even more money if you shop around.

Yumbo Centrum (www.cc-yumbo.com; Avenida EE UU; ☻ 24hr) There are more than 200 businesses in this four-level commercial centre. You can buy shoes, leather goods, perfume and anything else you fancy tax-free, although the quality should be checked. There are also supermarkets on the premises.

Fedac (☎ 928 77 24 45; Centro Insular del Turismo, cnr Avenida España & Avenida EE UU; ☻ 10am-2pm & 4-7.30pm Mon-Fri) If you're after local handicrafts, visit the small Fedac shop co-located with the *cabildo* tourist office. Fedac is a government-sponsored non-profit-making store, whose prices and quality are a good standard by which to measure those of products sold elsewhere. You'll also get a guarantee with your purchase.

GETTING THERE & AWAY
To/From the Airport
Bus No 66 runs to/from Gando airport (€2.95) hourly until about 9.15pm. For a taxi, budget for about €28 for Playa del Inglés and €31 for Maspalomas.

Bus
Buses link regularly with points along the coast, westwards as far as Puerto de Mogán and eastwards to Las Palmas. For Las Palmas (€4.50, about 50 minutes), take No 5 (night bus), 30 or 50 (nonstop). Pick up *horarios* (timetables) at the tourist office – one for south of the island and one for north.

GETTING AROUND
Bus
Global (☎ 902 38 11 10; www.globalsu.net in Spanish) runs buses to many of the theme parks listed earlier. The fare for a standard run

within town is €0.90. If you plan to travel out of town, a Tarjeta Insular (see p61) is a good investment.

Car

If you really must take your car down to the beach, there's a large paying car park beside Playa del Inglés. Street parking costs a reasonable €0.30 for 30 minutes to €2.40 for four hours (between 10am and 9pm).

Taxi

You can call a **taxi** (☎ 928 76 67 67), and taxi stands abound and are reliable. From Playa del Inglés, no destination within the urban area costs more than €7.

AROUND PLAYA DEL INGLÉS & MASPALOMAS

PUERTO RICO & ARGUINEGUÍN

If Maspalomas has redeeming features in the shape of its great dunes and nightlife, a little less good can be said of the chain of its resort cousins further west along the coast. The coastline here has been consumed by serried white cement resorts and tourism galore. It's a family-friendly part of the world, but independent travellers or the permanently cynical will want to look elsewhere for their holiday.

Parts of the port area of Arguineguín still remain true to its roots as a small, active fishing settlement, but it's a nondescript town with no genuine beach to speak of.

Good seafood can be had at modest prices in the down-to-earth restaurant of the Cofradía de Pescadores, the fishing co-operative within the port. It even does *gofio* (a roasted mixture of wheat, maize or barley), which you rarely find in big city restaurants or the resorts.

The original fishing town of Puerto Rico must be in there somewhere, but it's been submerged below compacted ranks of apartment blocks scaling the harsh, barren cliffs and hills of what must once have been a spectacular coastline, perfect for a 'spaghetti western' by the sea.

Not even the beach is particularly noteworthy (nor are those further west still, such as Playa del Cura, Playa del Tauro and the resort of Taurito). They do cater to family

holiday-makers though, with sun lounges, umbrellas, snacks and beach-side activities all provided (for a fee). Plus the waters are flat and smooth as glass, and safe for swimming.

There is no point in singling out specific apartments, hotels and the like. As in Maspalomas, you're much better off booking ahead from outside the islands.

Buses connect both places with Maspalomas and Playa del Inglés (€1.90) regularly and with Puerto de Mogán and Las Palmas (€5.45) less frequently.

Lineas Salmon (☎ 649 91 93 83) and Blue Bird have about eight services each day to/from Puerto de Mogán, and the former runs every hour between 9.30am and 4.30pm eastwards to Arguineguín. Prices for all are €5 one way or €8 return.

PUERTO DE MOGÁN

After Taurito, a couple of kilometres of rugged and pretty much unspoiled coastline recall what this whole southern stretch of the island must have been like 40 years ago before mass tourism came to the Canaries.

Finally you round a bend; below you is a smallish crescent of sandy beach and next to it a busy little yacht harbour and fishing port. Puerto de Mogán, although now largely given over to the tourist trade, is light years from its garish counterparts to the east and is worthy of its nickname, the 'Venice of the Canaries'.

The waterfront is a purpose-built holiday zone, but very tastefully done with low two- and three-storey apartments, covered in pretty bougainvillea and other exotic flora, the whole exuding an air of quiet charm despite the artificiality of the place. Here there really is a fishing port and small town clustered behind the tourist facade.

It's a fairly admirable balance – but how long can the balancing act last? When we visited, there were signs of increased development, as the town inches further back inland. It looks like four- and five-storey tourism complexes are about to make their presence felt.

The charm is agreeably disturbed on Friday morning (until 2pm) by the weekly market in the main plaza, where you'll also find a little bandstand – the scene of a few low-key live-music gigs, especially on Saturdays in August.

Activities

Puerto de Mogán is the main centre for diving on Gran Canaria, with caves and wrecks just offshore.

Atlantik Diving (☎ 689 35 20 49; atdiving@club demar.com; Hotel Club de Mar) offers courses at all levels, from a Discover Scuba experience (three hours, €90) to Dive Master (minimum 20 days, €570). For a single dive with full equipment provided, you're looking at €40.

Submarine Adventure (☎ 928 56 51 08; adult/child €26.50/13.25) has a yellow submarine that submerges eight times daily – and its owners run a free bus as far as Playa del Inglés to pick up punters. There's enough oxygen in there for 72 hours, in case you're nervous.

Sleeping

The apartments along the waterfront are generally let by local people. Start by asking around the shops below them – even if they don't let themselves, they can point you in the right direction.

La Venencia de Canarias (☎ 928 56 56 00; www .laveneciadecanarias.net; Local 328, Urb Puerto de Mogán; 1-/2-bedroom apt €60/95) Right in the thick of the resort's 'Venetian' quarter, this well-managed and charming business has great apartments that sleep between three and five people. Low-season reductions are excellent too.

Hotel Club de Mar (☎ 928 56 50 66; www.club demar.com; Playa de Mogán s/n; d €48, apt €59-84, villa €150; ☒ ☑) Right by the harbour, this hotel complex has large, airy rooms (doubles), apartments (between three and five people) and villas (up to six people) with all the trimmings. Our favourite bit is the staircase that goes straight down to the sea. You may well feel out of place if you're not German or Dutch though.

Apartamentos Marina (☎ 928 56 50 95; www.bar marina-mogan.com; Avenida General Franco s/n; 1-/2-bedroom apt €30/50; P) On the road into town, this place, owned by the proprietor of Bar Marina (which you'll find in Puerto de Mogán's central plaza), offers sunny, nicely furnished apartments that sleep between three and five people, and include solariums!

Pensión Eva (☎ 928 56 52 35; Calle Lomo Quiebre 35; d €15) About 750m inland as you head north and on the corner of Avenida General Franco, this simple place has ordinary but adequate rooms at bargain prices, and Eva is certainly deserving of your business.

Eating

The yacht harbour is lined with cafés and restaurants with pleasant *terrazas* offering fresh fish.

Cocina Creativa (Plaza Mayor s/n; tapas mains €15-25; ☺ noon-3pm Tue-Fri, 7.30-11.30pm Mon-Sat) Proudly advertising the fact that there are NO burgers and chips on the menu, this is a delightful place to eat. Run by two German women and avoiding any hint of tourist cheese, here you can feast on imaginatively prepared tapas dishes (that will easily satisfy the hungers of between two and six people). Easily our favourite dining option in this neck of the woods.

Restaurante Cofradía (☎ 928 56 53 21; mains €9.90-22) You'll not find it fresher than at the no-frills fishing cooperative eatery in the southwestern corner of the quay. It's a cheery, casual spot and popular to boot. Start with some nibbles and then proceed to a plate of plump, juicy grilled sardines.

Getting There & Away

There is no shortage of buses heading east to Puerto Rico and Playa del Inglés (€3). There are also regular departures for Las Palmas (€6.30).

Between them, **Lineas Salmon** (☎ 649 91 93 83) and Blue Bird run 15 ferry boats daily to/from Puerto Rico, costing €5/8 one way/return. To Arguineguín, it's €10/16 one way/return.

NORTH OF PUERTO DE MOGÁN

Just as Puerto de Mogán is a relief from the south coast's relentless armies of apartments, bungalows and 'true British pubs', so the GC-200 road north from the port is another leap away from the crowds.

As it ascends gradually up a wide valley towards **Mogán**, you pass orchards of subtropical trees such as papaya, mango and avocado. Mogán is a pleasant place with a handful of restaurants and bars, but nothing in particular to see or do. From here you can retrace your steps or travel the north or central routes listed earlier in this chapter (by car; see p76 and p73). If you choose to stay in Mogán, you can't beat **El Sirocco B&B** (☎ 928 56 93 01; Calle San Antonio 8; d €50), a beautifully decorated and painted B&B, which gets good word of mouth and is an ideal base for those keen on walking through the area.

To press on, you have two choices. The GC-200 winds off to the northwest through some spectacularly austere landscapes to Aldea de San Nicolás (26km; p79). It passes through **Los Azulejos**, a colourful rock formation that is supposed to look like an example of blue-tile work, but more closely resembles the colour of fungus in our opinion. Still, it's an eye-catching diversion on the winding drive.

Alternatively, a minor turn 2.5km north of Mogán heads northeast up to Ayacata. About 5km of this road, which climbs torturously up the barren and lonely barranco, is dirt track. From Ayacata you can head to Tejeda and the highest peaks on the island.

Fuerteventura

Lapped (and sometimes lashed) by the Atlantic, the dunes, shrub-studded plains, and arid, knife-edge mountain ridges of Fuerteventura present a parched, atmospheric picture. Its villages and towns, with their bundles of whitewashed, flat-roofed houses would be right at home cast across the semidesert wastes of northern Africa.

Fuerteventura is the second-largest island in the archipelago but one of the least populous and it seems relatively flat. The empty interior, where for centuries tough herdsmen have scratched out a living with their equally hardy flocks of goats, holds a certain fascination, although for most visitors the miles of white sandy beaches are the true delight.

Perhaps it's just a question of time, but for the moment the official line seems to be to keep development under control, and Fuerteventura avoids some of its eastern neighbours' monstrosities. The two main resorts are at opposite ends of the island. At the northern tip (and the point of entry if you're coming in by boat from Lanzarote) is Corralejo – beloved of the British sunseekers. Deep down south is Morro Jable, where a knowledge of German is almost as useful as Spanish. It's an altogether more sophisticated place, and ideal if you have a passion for surfing or sand. Locals are known as Majoreros or Maxoreros, from the Guanche (indigenous Canario) name for the northern kingdom of the island – Maxorata.

HIGHLIGHTS

- **Beachcombing**

  The endless strands of the Playa de Sotavento de Jandía (p108) will have you supine in no time

- **Walking**

  The parched, spectacular interior offers a range of stunning strolls (p92)

- **Surfing**

  On a board, with a kite or via the wind – the perfect conditions attract all types. Try it out at Isla de Lobos (p106), El Cotillo (p107) and Bubbles (p107)

- **Escaping**

  Isla de Lobos (p106) feels like the end of the earth – in a good way

- **Tilting at Windmills**

  Fuerteventura's interior landscape (p96) is littered with them

■ TELEPHONE CODE: 928	■ POPULATION: 60,275	■ AREA: 1660 SQ KM

HISTORY

The island was known (at least in theory) to the Romans as Planaria, but the Guanches called it (or most of it at any rate) Maxorata. What the Europeans came to dub Fuerteventura (Strong Winds) was in fact divided into two tribal kingdoms: Jandía, which took up the southern peninsula as far north as La Pared, and Maxorata, which occupied the rest of the island.

Fuerteventura was the second island to fall to the initial wave of conquerors under Jean de Béthencourt in January 1405. He had already established a fort there in 1402, but had been obliged to seek aid for his ambitions from the Castilian crown in Spain before proceeding. Although the islanders resisted the Spaniards, they could not hold out for long.

De Béthencourt set up a permanent base in the mountainous zone of what came to be known as Betancuria. He had a chapel built and the village that grew up around it, Santa María de Betancuria, became the island's capital. The choice of location was determined not by aesthetics but by hard reasoning. The area provided one of the island's few water supplies and the terrain gave a measure of natural defence against attacks from Guanches and, later, pirate raids.

New settlements spread slowly across the island but not until the 17th century did the Europeans occupy El Cotillo, once the seat of the Guanche Maxorata kingdom. At this

time the Arias and Saavedra families took control of the *señorío* (the island government deputising for the Spanish crown). By the following century, however, officers of the island militia had established themselves as a rival power base in La Oliva. Los Coroneles (the Colonels) gradually took virtual control of the island's affairs, enriching themselves at the expense of both the *señores* and the hard-pressed peasantry.

The militia was disbanded in 1834 and in 1912 the island, along with others in the archipelago, was granted a degree of self-administration with the installation of the *cabildo* (local authority).

INFORMATION
Books & Maps
Landscapes of Fuerteventura, by Noel Rochford and published by Sunflower Books, gives some useful suggestions for drives and walks around the island that are of varying duration.

See Maps on p242 for details on the maps available.

ACTIVITIES
The sea offers most of the action. From Caleta de Fuste, Morro Jable and Corralejo, you can both dive and windsurf (Morro Jable regularly hosts a leg of the Windsurf World Cup). The waters off Corralejo are good for deep-sea fishing and the curling waves nearby draw in surfers. Kitesurfing is gaining in popularity too, thanks to regular gusts of wind on the island's coast.

Walking
Fuerteventura's peaceful but stark landscape offers some great walking opportunities, with oases, volcanic craters, abandoned haciendas and rugged coastlines available to the intrepid. **Norte y Solana** (☎ 928 87 03 60; norteysolana@jazzfree.com; Calle Princesa Tibiabín 43, Gran Tarajal; walks €45-85) can organise a variety of walks on any day of the week. Lunch is included and transport to the start of each walk is arranged by the company. Monday's Panorama tour, taking in Pájara, Vega del Río de Palmas, Betancuria and Pozo Negro, is recommended.

ACCOMMODATION
Finding a place to stay in the coastal resorts can be problematic. In the case of many apartments you can't even book ahead as they deal exclusively with tour operators and their clientele.

If things look grim, head for Puerto del Rosario where you should encounter few problems getting a room. With a roof over your head you can work out your next strategy (hiring a vehicle of some sort will simplify life greatly).

There is only one camp site on the island, although plenty of people seem content to pitch a tent or plonk a caravan indescriminantly along the coastline near the beaches, and no-one seems too fussed about stopping it.

GETTING THERE & AWAY
Air
The **airport** (☎ 928 86 05 00) is 6km south of Puerto del Rosario.

Binter (☎ 902 39 13 92; www.bintercanarias.com) has 23 flights daily to Gran Canaria (€53, 45 minutes) and at least five daily to Tenerife Norte (€74, 45 minutes).

Otherwise, charter flights, generally operating only two or three days per week, connect the island with mainland Spanish cities and several European centres (including London, Manchester, Amsterdam, Munich and Frankfurt).

There is a reasonably helpful **tourist information office** (☎ 928 85 12 50; ☷ 9am-7pm Mon-Sat, 11am-4pm Sun) in the arrivals area at the airport.

Boat
Five ferries weekly link Puerto del Rosario and Las Palmas de Gran Canaria, while faster jetfoils speed between Morro Jable and Las Palmas.

There *are* boats between Puerto del Rosario and Arrecife on Lanzarote (see p122), but you're better off taking one of the regular ferries that make the 35- to 45-minute crossing between the more scenic Corralejo in the north and Playa Blanca in Lanzarote's south (see p105).

GETTING AROUND
Given the scant public transport cover on most routes, having your own wheels will greatly enhance your capacity to get around the island. Car hire will work out substantially cheaper than catching taxis hither and thither.

To/From the Airport

You can get taxis (€7) or buses to Puerto del Rosario and, from there, buses to other parts of the island.

Taxis from the airport to Corralejo cost around €33, to El Cotillo around €35, to Costa Calma around €52 and to the Jandía beaches around €70.

Bus

Tiadhe (☎ 928 85 21 66) provides a limited service, with 13 lines operating around the island. The most frequent links Puerto del Rosario with Corralejo (No 6) in the north and with Caleta de Fuste via the airport (No 3) to the south. Bus No 5 from Morro Jable to Costa Calma is also fairly regular.

On other routes, check times carefully before setting out. A number have only one service daily, primarily to transport school children and workers into Puerto del Rosario and bring them back at the end of the day. They tend to leave the village about 6.30am and return from Puerto del Rosario shortly after 4pm – little help if you're planning a day in the country.

If you intend to use the buses fairly frequently, or even for one return trip between Morro Jable and Corralejo, changing at Puerto del Rosario, it is worth investing in a Tarjeta Dinero, a discount card that costs €12. Instead of buying individual tickets on the bus for each trip, you tell the driver your destination and he endorses your card – it represents about a 30% saving on each trip.

Buses do not accept €20 or €50 notes, so it's a good idea to stock up on change or small notes if that's your preferred mode of transport.

Taxi

You can belt around in taxis, but it soon becomes an expensive habit. It's better to hire a car from one of the many rental offices.

PUERTO DEL ROSARIO

pop 22,650

Puerto del Rosario, the island capital – and the only place of consequence that exists for reasons other than tourism – is home to almost half the island's population. It's a relatively modern little port town that only really took off in the 19th century. If you fly to the island or use the buses, you may well find yourself passing through. It's a scruffy, dull sort of place, spreading like a thick clump of white clotted cream over the dusty earth. Mediocre, higgledy-piggledy concrete housing developments seep slowly into the surrounding dry country.

When Spain pulled out of the Sahara in 1975, it sent about 5000 Legión Extranjera (Foreign Legion) troops to Fuerteventura to keep a watch on North Africa. The huge barracks in Puerto del Rosario – a cross between a prison and a Beau Geste fort – are still in use, although remaining troops now number under 1000.

HISTORY

Puerto del Rosario, for long little more than an insignificant cluster of houses, became the island's capital in 1860, due to its growing importance as a harbour.

Until 1956 it was known as Puerto de las Cabras, named after the goats for which it had long been a watering hole (before becoming the main departure point for their export in the form of chops). In an early rebranding exercise, it was renamed Puerto del Rosario (Port of the Rosary) – altogether more dignified, you must agree, and be fitting a capital! All the same, it remains unexciting.

ORIENTATION

The centre of town backs away from the port, and anything you might need is within fairly easy strolling distance. The capital's main street is Calle León y Castillo, which runs in a downward direction to the port. Running across this is Avenida Primero de Mayo, somewhat of a commercial hub (don't get your hopes up though).

Maps

If you can find a copy of *Guia de Comercios y Servicios de Puerto del Rosario* (Guide to Businesses and Services of Puerto del Rosario; free) you may find it handy. Try the tourist office.

INFORMATION

Emergency

Police station (☎ 928 85 06 35; Calle Fernández Castañeyra 2)

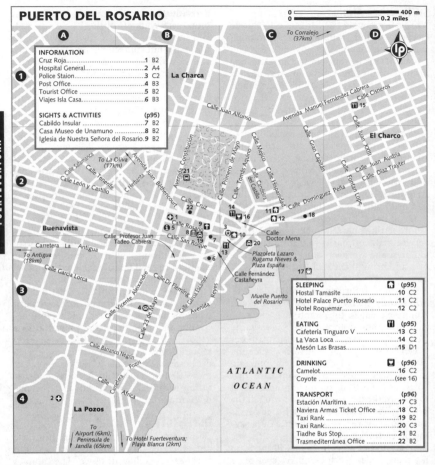

PUERTO DEL ROSARIO

INFORMATION		
Cruz Roja	1	B2
Hospital General	2	A4
Police Staion	3	C2
Post Office	4	B3
Tourist Office	5	B2
Viajes Isla Casa	6	B3

SIGHTS & ACTIVITIES		(p95)
Cabildo Insular	7	B2
Casa Museo de Unamuno	8	B2
Iglesia de Nuestra Señora del Rosario	9	B2

SLEEPING		(p95)
Hostal Tamasite	10	C2
Hotel Palace Puerto Rosario	11	C2
Hotel Roquemar	12	C2

EATING		(p95)
Cafetería Tinguaro V	13	C3
La Vaca Loca	14	C2
Mesón Las Brasas	15	D1

DRINKING		(p96)
Camelot	16	C2
Coyote	(see	16)

TRANSPORT		(p96)
Estación Marítima	17	C3
Naviera Armas Ticket Office	18	C2
Taxi Rank	19	B2
Taxi Rank	20	C3
Tiadhe Bus Stop	21	B2
Trasmediterránea Office	22	B2

ATLANTIC OCEAN

Medical Services

Hospital General (☎ 928 53 17 99; Carretera General al Aeroporto s/n) On the highway towards the airport.
Cruz Roja (Red Cross; ☎ 928 85 13 76; Avenida Constitución 19) Near the tourist office.

Money

Banks with mutlitlanguage ATMs line Avenida Primero de Mayo.

Post

Post office (☎ 928 85 04 12; Calle 23 de Mayo 76; 🕐 8.30am-8.30pm Mon-Fri, 9.30am-1pm Sat)

Telephone

There are plenty of public telephones throughout town and near the port area.

Tourist Offices

The **main tourist office** (☎ 928 53 08 44; Avenida Constitución 5; 🕐 8am-2pm Mon-Fri) is a fairly desultory, dingy place. It opens strictly civil servants' hours and has an attitude to match – that is, go figure it all out for yourself by flipping through some of their out-of-date brochures and try not to disturb their conversation.

If you fly in, you're much better off consulting the airport's **tourist information office** (☎ 928 85 12 50; 🕐 9am-7pm Mon-Sat, 11am-4pm Sun)

Travel Agents

Viajes Isla Casa (☎ 902 10 04 25; Calle Juan Tadeo Cabrera 3; 🕐 9.30am-2pm & 5-8pm Mon-Sat) Good for charter flights and tours to the other islands.

SIGHTS

About the only place to visit is **Casa Museo de Unamuno** (☎ 928 85 14 00; Calle Rosario 11; admission free; ☒ 9am-2pm Mon-Fri, 9am-1pm Mon-Fri Aug). The philosopher Miguel de Unamuno, exiled for his opposition to the dictatorship of Primo de Rivera, briefly stayed in this house, then the Hotel Fuerteventura, in 1924. He later escaped to France before returning to his position at Salamanca University when the Republicans came to power in 1931.

Part of the house has been turned into a period piece, with furnishings and other odds and ends from Unamuno's day, including his desk. You'll get a warm smile at the entrance, but if you're after information in anything other than Spanish, you're short on luck.

During his exile, Unamuno used to seek solace on the **Playa Blanca**, about a 45-minute walk south of the town centre.

FESTIVALS & EVENTS

The town puts on its party clothes on the first Sunday of October to celebrate the **Fiesta de la Virgen del Rosario**, the capital's patron.

SLEEPING

There are few good reasons for staying but if you have a hard time getting a room elsewhere on the island, you're more likely to find something here.

Budget

Hotel Roquemar (☎ 928 85 03 59; roquemar@tiscali.es; Avenida Marítima s/n; s/d €30/37) New to the port and well worth a stay is this immaculate and intimate 12-room, two-star hotel. Charming rooms have telephone, TV, minibar, bathroom and some pleasing sea views, and laundry facilities are available.

The management don't speak much English, but the sweet service makes up for everything.

Hostal Tamasite (☎ 928 85 02 80; fax 928 85 03 00; Calle León y Castillo 9; s/d €27/36) The Tamasite is a well-situated, very fragrant two-star *pensión* (guesthouse) with rather plain but clean rooms with bath, phone and TV.

This guesthouse is one of the better budget choices in town (it smells mighty clean), but not if you are a light sleeper, as the noise from nearby bars can be intrusive on weekends.

Mid-Range

Hotel Fuerteventura (☎ 928 85 11 50; Calle Playa Blanca 45; s/d €55/75; P ☒ ☒) Previously a *parador* (state-run chain) hotel, but now a privatised accommodation concern, this very nice hotel overlooks Playa Blanca, 3km south of the town centre. Unfortunately, it's also right under the flight path for the nearby airport, which can lead to some noisy intrusions on your quiet time. Still, rooms are beautifully appointed and airy, with old-fashioned charm and wooden floors.

Hotel Palace Puerto Rosario (☎ 928 85 94 64; fax 928 85 22 60; Avenida Ruperto González Negrín 9; s/d €55/83; ☒) A solid choice, this hotel comprises 88 rooms that are far more attractive than its harsh modern exterior would suggest. Beds are big, bathrooms are plush and amenities are in good nick. It's probably the closest thing you'll get to a centrally located business hotel in Puerto del Rosario.

EATING

Eating out in Puerto del Rosario is easy enough. There are some reasonable local restaurants throughout town and prices are certainly modest. That said, it's not a must-do on a gastronomic tour.

Restaurante Hotel Fuerteventura (☎ 928 85 11 50; Calle Playa Blanca 45; mains €8-20) Though no longer a *parador*, the restaurant of this excellent hotel maintains that chain's high culinary standards. Try their local speciality, *cabrito en adobo Majorero* (marinated kid). They also do a good value *menú del día* (set menu) and have a great local and Spanish wine list.

La Vaca Loca (Calle Cruz s/n; mains €7-18) If big serves of hearty meat dishes tempt you, then ignore the 'mad cow' implications of this restaurant's name and tuck in, bib at the ready. The setting is suitably western and portions will have you wondering if you're up to the challenge.

Mesón Las Brasas (☎ 928 53 09 98; Calle Juan XXIII 68; mains €6.50-11) This is a handy enough place, serving a fair range of fish and meat dishes in casual, unpretentious style, with a loyal local following. The *menú del día* is a bargain at €6.

Cafetería Tinguaro V (Plaza España 7) For *churros* (doughnuts) and chocolate, stop by this place – everyone else seems to! Don't expect anything flash though.

FUERTEVENTURA

DRINKING & ENTERTAINMENT

Puerto del Rosario has a modest nightlife scene, which is local, rather than touristy.

Camelot (Calle Ayose 6; ☾ 11pm-3am Mon-Sat) This bar has a medieval theme mixed in with a bit of disco and some strip-show sleaze, making for a curious combo.

You can catch live music performances in this place too, although the quality can be patchy.

Coyote (☎ 670 85 08 30; Calle León y Castilla 14; ☾ 9pm-3am Mon-Wed, 9pm-5am Thu-Sat) Right next door to Camelot, despite the disparity in addresses, this is an odd little spot, that has a good list of cocktails, some live music and a boisterous weekend crowd after midnight.

GETTING THERE & AWAY
To/From the Airport

Take bus No 3 (see Bus, below). It stops at the airport about 10 minutes before reaching Caleta de Fuste. The trip between town and the airport takes 10 to 15 minutes and costs €0.90. A taxi will rack up about €7.

Boat

Trasmediterránea (www.trasmediterranea.com) ferries leave from the *estación marítima* (ferry terminal) at 1pm on Tuesday, Thursday and Saturday for Las Palmas de Gran Canaria (€28.10, eight hours). The company also has an **office** (☎ 928 85 08 77; Calle León y Castillo 58) in town.

Naviera Armas (☎ 928 85 00 32; www.naviera armas.com) runs to Las Palmas at noon on Wednesday and Friday (€31.90, 6½ hours). Its office is in the grey- and white-striped building just east of the port entrance.

You can also buy tickets at any travel agency.

Bus

Tiadhe (☎ 928 85 21 66) buses leave from the main bus stop just past the corner of Avenida León y Castillo and Avenida Constitución. The following services operate from Puerto del Rosario:

No 1 Morro Jable via Tuineje (€7, 2 hours, at least nine daily)
No 2 Vega del Río de Palmas via Betancuria (€2.65, 50 minutes, twice daily Monday to Saturday)
No 3 Caleta de Fuste via the airport (€1, 20 minutes, at least 14 daily)
No 6 Corralejo (€2.40, 40 minutes, at least 14 daily)

No 7 El Cotillo via La Oliva (€3.50, 45 minutes, three daily)
No 10 Morro Jable via the airport (€7, 1½ hours, three daily Monday to Saturday)

GETTING AROUND
Bus

One municipal bus does the rounds of the town every hour, but you are unlikely to need it. If you do, you can catch it at the *guagua* (station).

Taxi

If you need a **taxi** (☎ 928 85 00 59, 928 85 02 16) you can call or grab one from the two taxi ranks in town – one near Casa Museo de Unamuno and the other near the entrance to the port area.

THE CENTRE

The central chunk of Fuerteventura offers some of the most varied countryside a desert island can manage. The mountains of the Parque Natural de Betancuria are sliced in their southern reaches by a palm-studded ravine starting at Vega del Río de Palmas (p97). The west and east coasts are mostly rocky cliffs interspersed with small, jolly black-sand beaches and unpretentious fishing hamlets. In contrast, the central, copper-coloured plains around Antigua (p97) are dotted with old windmills in various states of repair and dating back a couple of centuries. If you're driving, it's the sort of landscape that will inspire thoughts of making your own music video.

BETANCURIA

Jean de Béthencourt thought this the ideal spot to set up house in 1405, so he had living quarters and a chapel built. To this nascent settlement he gave his own name, which with time was corrupted to Betancuria (or the Villa de Santa María de Betancuria in the unexpurgated version). During the course of the century, Franciscan friars moved in and expanded the town, which remained the island's capital until 1834. The island's proximity to the northern African coast made it easy prey for Moroccan and European pirates who, on numerous occasions, managed to defy Betancuria's natural mountain defences and sack it. Tucked prettily into the protective folds of the basalt hills, the town is now home to fewer than 700 people.

Arrive on a Sunday morning and you'd be forgiven for thinking the place had been deserted long ago.

Sights

If you approach from the north, your gaze will be drawn down to the left, where ruins of the island's first **monastery**, built by the Franciscans, stand proud.

The centre of the settlement is watched over by the 17th-century **Iglesia de Santa María** (☎ 928 87 80 03; Calle Alcalde Carmelo Silvera s/n; 11am-5pm Mon-Sat). Pirates had destroyed its Gothic predecessor in 1593, but this 1620 construction contains some architectural features of note, including its stone floor, wooden ceiling and elaborate Baroque altar.

A short walk away is the **Museo de Arte Sacro** (☎ 928 87 80 03; Calle Alcalde Carmelo Silvera s/n; 10am-5pm Mon-Sat). This contains a mixed bag of religious art, including paintings, gold and silverware. Admission to both the church and this museum is covered by one €2 ticket; the custodian moves back and forth to open the church and museum alternately every half hour from 11am to 4pm, daily except Sunday.

Of modest interest also is the **Casa Museo de Betancuria** (☎ 928 87 82 41; Calle Roberto Roldán s/n; admission €1; 10am-5pm Tue-Sat, 11am-2pm Sun), which houses a simple collection of Guanche artefacts plus antique objects from the time of the early colonisers. The **Betancuria Craft Centre** is attached to the museum and worth visiting if you're after local souvenirs of good quality.

Festivals & Events

On 14 July, townspeople celebrate the **Día de San Buenaventura**, honouring the patron saint of the town, a fiesta dating from 1456.

Eating

Restaurante Casa de Santa María (☎ 928 87 82 82; Plaza Santa María de Betancuria 1; mains €9-17.50) Part of the tourist complex opposite the main portal of the church and open lunchtimes only, this lovely looking restaurant wins hands-down on atmosphere. It has seating both indoors and out and all manner of goaty offerings – from cheese to roast. A hearty *menú del día* costs €9.

Getting There & Away

Bus No 2 passes through here twice daily (except Sunday) on its way between Puerto del Rosario (€2.65) and Vega del Río de Palmas, a short distance south.

AROUND BETANCURIA

A couple of kilometres north of Betancuria, there's a handy lookout (on both sides of the road) that explains the various mountain peaks that loom on the horizon. Further on, the **Mirador Morro Velosa** offers mesmerising views across the island's weird, disconsolate moonscape. Here you'll find toilets, souvenir shops and a **restaurant** (mains €5.40-15.40; 9am-7pm) with dazzling views, good dishes made from local ingredients, but – on this occasion – atrocious coffee. If the barrier to the lookout is closed, the view is almost as spectacular at the col over which the FV-30 highway climbs before it twists its way north through the barely perceptible settlements of Valle de Santa Inés and Los Llanos de la Concepción.

In the pretty village **Casillas del Ángel** the petite Iglesia de Santa Ana contains an 18th-century wooden carving of St Anne.

For a hearty meal of goat meat, try the appropriately named **El Cabrito** (☎ 928 53 81 80; Caserío Tesjuates 38; mains €7-14.50) at the western end of the town. It has an outdoor eating area and good disabled access.

Heading south of Betancuria for Pájara, you soon hit the small oasis-like settlement of **Vega del Río de Palmas**. As you proceed, the reason for the name becomes clear – the road follows the course of a near-dry watercourse, still sufficiently wet enough below the surface to keep a stand of palms alive.

ANTIGUA

This is one of the bigger inland villages but there is not much to do except make a quick visit to the 18th-century church, which is one of the island's oldest. **Nuestra Señora de Antigua** has a pretty pink- and green-painted altar, and you stand a better chance of finding it open when you visit than many of the other churches on the island.

Scarcely 1km north of the sun-bleached, deserted-seeming village is the **Molino de Antigua** (☎ 928 87 80 41; admission €1.80; 9.30am-5.30pm

FUERTEVENTURA

Tue-Fri & Sun), a fully restored windmill that will inspire thoughts of Don Quixote's tilting at windmills.

Bus No 1 passes through here en route between Puerto del Rosario and Morro Jable.

Festivals & Events
The local feast day is **Nuestra Señora del Pino**, which takes place on 8 September.

AROUND ANTIGUA
You'll want your own transport to access these small towns.

La Ampuyenta
If it's open, the 17th-century **Ermita de San Pedro de Alcántara** merits a quick stop. The *ermita* (chapel) is surrounded by a stout, protective wall built by the French from the Normandy area. Within, the walls of the nave are decorated with large, engagingly naive paintings, contrasting with the more sophisticated works embellishing the wooden altarpieces.

Tiscamanita
Visit this tiny hamlet, 9km south of Antigua, to see a working restored mill (and find out what a hard grind it all was). The **Windmill Interpretation Centre** (☎ 928 85 14 00; admission €1.80; ☼ 9.30am-5.30pm Tue-Fri & Sun) highlights a praiseworthy restoration project and offers more information about windmills than you may ever want to know – in Spanish. You can buy *gofio* (a roasted mixture of wheat, maize or barley) here too, for €1.20, and gobble it down under the courtyard pomegranite tree. Ask for the English version of the explanatory leaflet if it's in stock.

PÁJARA
What makes the 17th-century **Iglesia de Nuestra Señora de Regla** unique in the islands is the pair of retables behind the altar, simpler and more subdued than the Baroque excesses of mainland Spain (stick a coin in the machine on the right after you enter the church to light them up). They are an example of influences flowing back from Latin America – in this case, Mexico. Lift your gaze to the fine wooden ceiling. Outside, the decoration above the main portal is said to be of Aztec inspiration, with its animal motifs.

DETOUR

If you have your own wheels, a 9km side trip from Pájara takes you northwest to **Ajuy** and contiguous **Puerto de la Peña**. A blink-and-you'll-miss-it fishing settlement, its black-sand beach makes a change from its illustrious golden neighbours to the south in the Jandía peninsula. The locals and fishing boats take pride of place here, and the strand is fronted by a couple of simple seafood eateries serving up the day's catch.

There's a low-key coastal walking track heading right as you face the water, leading for a few minutes along the windy rocks, with some lovely views.

Across the road from the church is **Restaurante La Fonda** (☎ 928 16 16 25; Calle Nuestra Señora de Regla 25; mains €6.50-12.50), which has a wonderful ambience, and features stone walls and wooden ceilings, as well as ropes of garlic, legs of ham and strings of chilli all hanging from the ceiling. The food here is good, honest and hearty, and the service is friendly. Restaurante La Fonda is also a good spot to pop in for a drink whilst on your tour of the surrounding countryside.

Pop into **La Casa del Artesano** (Calle Real 2; ☼ 9am-1pm Mon-Sat) for handmade lace items, local ceramics, wickerwork and woodwork. Local artisans make the goods and quality is high.

Two to three buses daily (No 13) run between Pájara and Gran Tarajal, then on to La Lajita.

The trip to Gran Tarajal takes about 30 minutes. The bus calls in at the beach villages between Gran Tarajal and La Lajita. There are no services to the north.

AROUND PÁJARA
The drive directly north towards Betancuria is one of the most spectacular on the island and the journey south towards the Jandía peninsula via La Pared is almost as attractive. Fuerteventura ranks as relatively flat when compared to Lanzarote and the other islands to the west, but you would never think so as you wend your way through this lonely and spectacularly harsh terrain.

CALETA DE FUSTE

Of the main resorts on the island, this is the most convenient for the airport but the least attractive for the independent traveller. If you're travelling with a family though, and want the convenience of a wide range of restaurants and easily accessible hotels and apartments, this is a good choice – although you'll want a car so you can access the most stunning scenery the island offers.

The well-stocked **tourist office** (☎ 928 16 32 86; Centro Comercial Castillo; 9am-3pm Mon-Fri) wins the prize for the most attractive tourist office on the island.

The squat, little, round tower (hyperbolically known as El Castillo) has been turned into an appendage of the Barceló Club El Castillo bungalow complex. The beach, while perfectly pleasant, is a poor relation compared with what's on offer at Corralejo and Jandía, although its flatness and calmness are ideal for those with small children.

A local market is held here every Saturday between 9am and 1pm, just near the tourist office.

Activities

DIVING

Conscientious **Deep Blue** (☎ 928 16 37 12, 606 27 54 68; www.deep-blue-diving.com) is conveniently situated beside the port. A single dive costs €27 and a pack of 10 costs €200. They do beginners courses for Professional Association of Diving Instructors (PADI) certification and a wide range of specialist courses, including ones for children (€36).

WINDSURFING

Between the port and beach, **Fanatic Fun Center** (☎ 928 53 59 99; Barcelo Club El Castillo; 10am-5pm) offers beginners courses costing €92/143 for six/12 hours, including equipment hire. Gear hire alone costs €30/42/150 per half-day/day/week.

SAILING & SUBBING

From the port, **Catamaran Excursions** (☎ 928 16 35 14; Puerto Castillo) sails daily at 12.30pm, returning at 4.30pm. The price of €42/21 per adult/child includes lunch on board, the use of snorkelling equipment and also a visit to their small oceanarium. With any luck (well, you'll need quite a lot of luck actually), you might catch sight of dolphins and whales.

Nautilus, a small yellow submarine, sets out on the hour daily for a 45-minute dive. Tickets cost €15 (children under 12 are free).

THALASSOTHERAPY

Thalasso-buffs can get their seawater fix at **Thalaventura** (☎ 928 16 09 61; thalaventura@eur othermes.com; Calle Sávila 10; 9am-8pm), where a massage starts at €28 and continues all the way to the splendour of a six-day pampering orgy for €482. Thalassotherapy is also available at the Barceló Club El Castillo (below).

Sleeping & Eating

As in other resorts, most places fill with package guests and some deal only with tour operators.

Hotel El Mahay (☎ 928 16 33 53; mhr@idecnet.com; s/d €40/65) Located 150m southwest of the tourist office, this has very limited capacity once the tour operator has taken its slice. Rooms are good value and include breakfast. Its mid-priced restaurant offers a good range of Spanish and international cuisine and gets the thumbs-up from many travellers spending time here.

Aparthotel Castillo de Elba (☎ 928 16 36 00; www.hoteleselba.com; Urbanazion Costa Antigua; studios €48, apt €55; P) Golf lovers should note that they're a mere 2km from this hotel chain's splendid greens, and the three-star apartments and studios here are attractive enough in themselves, with all the mod-cons and tasteful décor.

Low-season reductions and specials are available, depending on the time of year.

Barceló Club El Castillo (☎ 928 16 31 00; elca stillo@barcelo.com; Avenida Castillo s/n; bungalows from €72) Top of the range is this franchise, which is extremely popular with families, as it's right beside the beach and port. It's a veritable mini-village that deserves it's own postcode in many ways, with entertainment programmes, activities, plush accommodation, smooth service and a thalassotherapy centre.

Puerto Castillo Restaurante (Avenida Castillo s/n; mains €9-12; closed Sun) Just by the *castillo*, this place has good local fish dishes and plenty of meat cuts prepared in a variety of international ways. A children's menu (€3 to €5) is available and wheelchair access is good.

FUERTEVENTURA

THE SOUTHEAST

GINIGINAMAR & TARAJALEJO

These two quiet fishing hamlets go about their business largely undisturbed by tourists – though Tarajalejo, with a couple of hotels and apartment blocks at its southern limit, is under siege. Their brief, grey beaches make a dull show compared with their brilliant white cousins further south – but at least they're far less crowded.

If you'd like to learn to sail a catamaran, **Tarajalejo's Cat Company** (☎ 928 16 13 76; www.learn-catamaran-sailing.com; Avenida Palmers 6) offers taster, basic and advanced courses from a very reasonable €60.

Just west of the FV-2 highway outside Tarajalejo, El Brasero has a tiny **aquarium** (☎ 928 87 20 70; adult/child €4.50/2.25; 10am-7pm) with some brightly coloured fish that may well capture the kids' interest. It also offers **horse riding** (per hour/three hours €15/35). **Camping** (☎ 928 16 10 01; fax 928 16 10 28; camp site/person/tent €7.20/2.70/2.70) is available; sites are reasonable but far from luxurious, as they bear the full brunt of the noonday sun. Still, there's an excellent swimming pool on the premises

and good bathroom facilities. The pricing system is complicated to say the least. To get here, from the north, continue past the entrance to the nearest roundabout, and then head back to the entrance.

Bus No 1 between Puerto del Rosario and Morro Jable stops at Tarajalejo, but not in Giniginamar.

LA LAJITA

This little fishing village presents yet another black-sand and pebble beach. It's just starting to get built up, so may be a lot more bustling by the time you read this. At its southern exit is one of those theme-park arrangements that have so utterly overrun Fuerteventura's big-sister island, Gran Canaria.

At **Oasis Park** (☎ 928 16 11 35; Carretera General de Jandía s/n; adult/child €12/6; 9am-6pm) you can wander around the little zoo, populated by monkeys, exotic birds and other caged unfortunates, and/or join a 30-minute **camel trek** (adult/child €7.50/3.75). If plant life is more your thing, visit its botanical garden, which has over 2300 types of cacti.

Bus No 1 stops at the highway exit to town, from where it's a short walk south to the complex.

THE BIG CHEESE

Goats milk is curdled by stirring in rennet, an enzyme that was traditionally taken from the stomach of a kid. The liquid whey is squeezed from the resultant soggy blob. Then, the still damp (and usually circular) cheese is left to mature between two wooden disks; look for the characteristic multiple 'V' shaped imprint on the top and bottom.

Three islands in particular produce this white, usually flaky, musty-scented delicacy and each has its own distinctive flavour.

So renowned is Majorero, the cheese from Fuerteventura, that, just like a fine wine, it bears a *denominación de origen* label, certifying that it's indeed from the island and the genuine article. It's the first Canary Island cheese to receive this accolade – and the first goats cheese in the whole of Spain to bear the label.

At the heart of the process is the Majorero goat, a high-yielding hybrid of indigenous goats and those that were originally imported from the Spanish mainland, which can give as much as 750L of milk in one year. Whole cheeses weigh between one and six kilos but shop assistants will happily cut you a slice as thick or as thin as you like. You can buy it young and soft with a powdery white rind, which becomes yellow with ageing. Cheeses that are to be stored for some time are often given a coating of oil, corn meal or paprika to preserve them.

The cheeses of La Palma, whether young and fresh or more mature, are usually smoked. Nowadays they're mostly produced in large dairies but the smoking reflects an earlier practice where families would leave a cheese hanging above the fireplace to cure.

Milk from all over the island of El Hierro is brought to the cooperative outside the village of Isora and transformed into a cheese which is particularly prized.

None are easy to obtain outside the Canaries, so if you're a cheese lover, stock up before you leave – and perhaps add an extra slab for friends back home.

THE NORTH

ROAD TO LA OLIVA

The FV-10 highway shoots westwards away from Puerto del Rosario into the barren interior of the island. Before crossing the ridgeback that forms the island's spine, it passes through the sleepy hamlets of **Tetir** and **La Matilla**. The demure chapel in the latter is a good example of the simple, bucolic buildings of the Canaries – functional, relatively unadorned and aesthetically pleasing.

About 7km south of La Matilla along the FV-207 and 1km beyond the village of Tefía is the **Ecomuseo la Alcogida** (☎ 928 85 14 00; adult/child €4.20/0.60; ☺ 9.30am-5.30pm Tue-Fri & Sun) – a restored agricultural hamlet complete with furnished houses, outbuildings and domestic animals. There's an optional audio commentary in English (€3). It's a fascinating look into the tough rural life of the not-too-distant past, and is definitely worth stopping the car for. Local artisans work side-by-side in some of the settlement's buildings making lace and wicker baskets, so it's a handy spot to appraise Canarian craftsmanship and make a purchase.

Follow the road out of Tefía and swing right (west) on the FV-211 for **Los Molinos**. On the way you can't miss the old mill, sitting squat in the grounds of what is now a handicrafts school. Los Molinos itself is little more than a few simple houses overlooking a small black-pebble beach. If you do stop here, make a point of having a seafood lunch at **Restaurante La Terraza** (mains €5.50-24; ☺ 11am-7pm, 11am-10pm in summer) while gazing over Atlantic breakers.

Tindaya is a sprawling centre where much of the island's goat cheese (Queso Majorero) is produced. See the boxed text on p100 for more information on this renowned cheese.

Just to its north lies the site where the Basque sculptor, Eduardo Chillida, caused considerable controversy with his officially-supported plan to bore a huge hole into Montaña de Tindaya in 2000. The 50-cubic-metre space was designed to make its visitors 'feel small in their physical dimension, and brotherhood with all other people'. However, the plan did not go ahead, due to vociferous local protests about the fact that the mountain is believed to have been a sacred site of the Guanche people, who left about 200 *podomorphs* (footprint carvings designed to ward off evil spirits).

Geologists also warned that such an excavation would result in the mountain's certain collapse, and would cause grave environmental damage to the surrounding area. In 2002, the death of Chillida himself marked the final curtain for the ambitious plan, with Tindaya able to sleep soundly once more.

The No 7 bus from Puerto del Rosario to El Cotillo passes through all but Tefía and Casa de los Molinos three times daily. Bus No 2 between Puerto del Rosario and Vega del Río de Palmas passes by Tefía twice daily. There are no buses to Los Molinos.

LA OLIVA
pop 2300

One-time capital of the island, in fact if not in name, La Oliva still bears a trace or two of grander days. The weighty bell tower of the 18th-century **Iglesia de Nuestra Señora de la Candelaria** is the town's focal point of sorts, as its black volcanic bulk contrasts sharply with the bleached-white walls of the church itself (which was built in 1711). To the south, the 18th-century **Casa de los Coroneles**, more foreign-legion fortress than simple *casa* (house) – its name means House of the Colonels – stands in decrepit isolation, overrun with goats. Its promised restoration is still unfulfilled after many years. Still, it's an interesting enough sight as it stands.

From the early 1700s, the officers who once presided here virtually controlled the affairs of the island. Amassing power and wealth, they so exploited the peasant class that in 1834 Madrid, faced with repeated bloody mutinies on the island, disbanded the militia. Problem was, the now ex-colonels still held onto their appropriated wealth.

About 250m north of the church is the **Casa de la Cilla** (☺ 9.30am-5.30pm Tue-Fri & Sun), a small museum devoted to grain – both its production and the harsh life of the farming cycle in general.

Bus No 7 between Puerto del Rosario and El Cotillo passes through three times daily.

CORRALEJO

pop 5860

Tourism (generally for the English) is what makes this place tick. And while the area's hotels and apartments do a roaring trade, tourism seems to have been kept to manageable levels – the town has its tacky side but the bulk of the holiday apartments remain low rise and the town centre still retains the faintest resonance of what was once a simple fishing village.

What makes Corralejo is the blinding white sand dunes to the south of town, sweeping back in gentle sugar-loaf rolls from the crystal blue ocean. Protected as a nature park, no one can build on or near them.

The beaches that these dunes front are an excellent attraction in themselves, with plenty of room for everyone.

Orientation

Corralejo's east is bordered by its small passenger harbour, with the bulk of its businesses and eateries clustered around this area.

The streets of the town are organised on a grid, making it a simple navigational prospect.

Information

EMERGENCY

Police Station (☎ 928 86 61 07; Paseo Atlántico s/n)

INTERNET ACCESS

Internet Saloon (cnr Calle Juan Sebastián Elcano & Calle Fahía; per hr €4; 🕙 10am-2pm & 6-10pm Mon-Sat) Wired and ready to sort out your email situation.

MEDICAL SERVICES

Centro de Salud (☎ 928 86 61 43; Avenida Juan Carlos I) Next to the main bus station.

Clínica Médica Brisamar (☎ 928 53 64 02; Avenida General Franco; 🕙 24hr) One among several private clinics set up primarily for tourists.

POST

Post office (☎ 928 53 50 55; Calle Isaac Peral 55; 🕙 8.30am-2.30pm Mon-Fri, 9.30am-1pm Sat)

TOURIST OFFICES

Tourist office (☎ 928 86 62 35; Plaza Grande de Corralejo; 🕙 8am-2pm Mon-Fri) Can easily be found – it sits under a large windmill in the town's main plaza. Don't expect much information, though.

Sights & Activities

PARQUE NATURAL DE CORRALEJO

The beach dunes of this protected nature park stretch along the east coast for about 10km from Corralejo. It can get breezy here (it's no accident that kitesurfing is proving to be a popular activity along this stretch), and your predecessors have already applied their ingenuity to the problem – the little fortresses of loose stones, most commonly erected atop shrub-covered sandy knolls, are designed to protect sun-worshippers from the wind. The area is free to enter, and the business of providing sun loungers and umbrellas in front of the luxury hotels is a popular one (but that's no reason to believe that rubbish collectors will be cleaning up after you).

DIVING

Dive Center Corralejo (☎ 928 53 59 06; www.divecentercorralejo.com; Calle Nuestra Señora del Pino 22; dives from €45), just back from the waterfront, organises trips for both beginner and experienced divers. It also rents out equipment and offer courses, and can accommodate disabled divers with an advanced booking. It's a highly regarded and multilingual operation.

WINDSURFING

Conditions along much of the coast and in the strait between Corralejo and Lanzarote – the Estrecho de la Bocaina – are ideal for windsurfing. The **Ventura Windsurf Center** (☎ 928 86 62 95; www.ventura-surf.com; Calle Fragata s/n) is one of several in the area that cater for beginners – or you can just hire the gear. Prices for hire start at €19 an hour, with a €50 deposit required, and you can also hire surfboards and boogie boards. The centre is on the beach at the end of the street.

Out at Grandes Playas, **Flag Beach Windsurf Center** (☎ 928 86 63 89; www.flagbeach.com; Calle General Linares 31) has beginners windsurfing courses for €120 for three days and windsurf hire from €20 per hour. The staff are also excellent kitesurfing instructors, and there is a fantastic introductory two-day course available (€200).

SURFING

Corralejo is a justifiably popular base for surfers, with phrases like 'the Hawaii of

CORRALEJO

0 — 300 m
0 — 0.2 miles

FUERTEVENTURA

INFORMATION
Centro de Salud...........................1 B4
Clínica Médica Brisamar.............2 C6
Internet Saloon...........................3 B4
Police Station..............................4 C4
Post Office..................................5 B4
Tourist Office..............................6 B4

SIGHTS & ACTIVITIES (pp102-4)
Celia Cruz Ticket Kiosk to Isla de
  Lobos......................................7 C4
Dive Centre Corralejo.................8 C3
El Majorero Boat Ticket Kiosk......9 C3
Matador Surf School...................10 B5
Ventura Windsurf Center............11 C5
Vulcano Biking...........................12 B4

SLEEPING (p104)
Apartamentos Corralejo Beach...13 C4
Apartamentos Hoplaco...............14 C5
Hesperia Bristol Playa................15 B3
Hotel Corralejo..........................16 C4

EATING (p105)
Avenida.....................................17 B3
Café de Viena............................18 C5
Poco Loco..................................19 C5
Restaurante Avelino....................20 C3
Restaurante El Tío Bernabé.........21 C4
El Rincón de Perico.....................22 C4

DRINKING (p105)
Antiguo Café del Puerto.............23 C4
Cafe Latino................................24 C3
Centro Comercial Atlántico........25 C4
The Venue..............................(see 25)
Waikiki.......................................26 C5
Zumbar..................................(see 25)

SHOPPING (p105)
Market......................................27 C6
No Work Team...........................28 C5

TRANSPORT (pp105-6)
Bus Station................................29 B4
Estación Marítima.......................30 D3
Fred Olsen Ferries......................31 C3
Mal Fun Club (Motorbike Hire)....32 B4
Naviera Armas Ferries................33 D3
Taxi Rank..................................34 C4

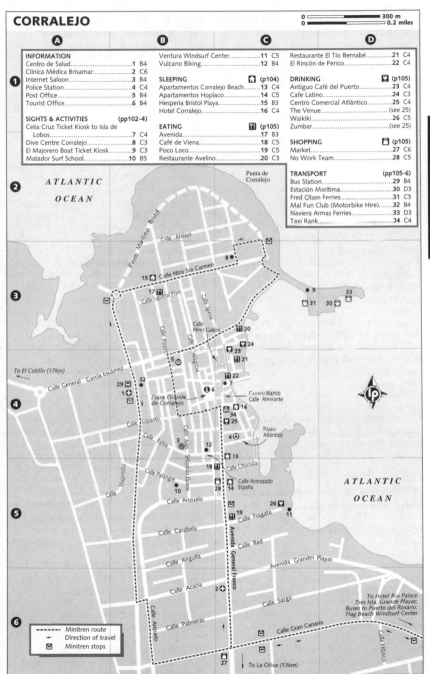

Europe' popping up in every second sentence. One excellent business worth giving custom to is the thoroughly professional **Matador Surf School** (☎ 928 86 73 07; www.matador surfschool.com; Calle Palangre 4; ☷ 10am-noon & 6-8pm Mon-Sat), which has great courses from €120 for three days. All courses include equipment and insurance, plus transport to the waves. Check them out for accommodation arrangements too.

Flag Beach Windsurf Center (☎ 928 86 63 89; www.flagbeach.com; Calle General Linares 31) also rents out boards (from €12 per day) and boogie boards (from €10 per day), plus they have a great surfing beginner's course for €25.

BOAT TRIPS

Three-hour mini-cruises aboard **El Majorero** (adult/child €11/5.50) allow a couple of hours on the Isla de Lobos (see the boxed text on p106). They leave at 10am and noon. Alternatively, simply use the boat to get across to the islet for €8/6 per adult/child return. The last boat back leaves at 4pm. Get tickets from the kiosk at the port.

The **Celia Cruz Catamaran** (☎ 639 14 00 14) does a similar return trip to Isla de Lobos (€8, daily at 9.45am) and also offers one-hour mini-cruises (€10, daily at 5.15pm except Sunday).

FISHING

At the port, you can sign up for deep-sea fishing trips for €45/40 per fisher/spectator. Trips take place between 8.30am and 2.30pm Monday to Saturday, and all of the operators will cook your catch for lunch.

CYCLING

Vulcano Biking (☎ 928 53 57 06; Calle Acorazado España 10; ☷ 10am-1pm & 6-8pm Mon-Sat) rents bikes from €6/15/30 per day/three days/week and roller blades for €3/6/12 per hour/day/three days.

Sleeping

It can be a real hassle finding somewhere to stay. Without wheels it can be worse as a lot of the apartments are strung out along the beach south of town. Still more of a pain, many deal only with tour operators. So, if you don't come with a package, be prepared to move on to, say, Puerto del Rosario until you can organise something in one of the resorts.

BUDGET

Hotel Corralejo (☎ 928 53 52 46; Calle Colón 12; s/d/t €20/25/30) This is a one-star seaside bargain right in the heart of town, with spacious rooms with bathrooms. Most rooms overlook the little town beach, but don't go expecting Lifestyles of the Rich and Famous décor. That said, it's often full.

MID-RANGE

Apartamentos Hoplaco (☎ /fax 928 86 60 40; Avenida General Franco 7; studios €36, apt €42-48) Within its shady compound, well-located Hoplaco could do with a lick of paint, but its apartments and studios are definitely worth considering. Studios sleep one to two people, while apartments can hold up to three. Reception opens between 10am and 2pm Monday to Friday, so let them know when you'll be arriving.

Apartamentos Corralejo Beach (☎ 928 88 63 15; www.corralejobeach.com; Avenida General Franco 3; studios €54, apt €60-75; ☲) Studios and apartments (sleeping two to four people) are handy for accessing the town centre but far enough away not to be disturbed by the whoops of the partying.

There's a nice swimming pool on the premises and a host of activities on offer, with gym, sauna, squash and mini golf available. Discounts of 20% are available for stays of a week or longer.

TOP END

Hesperia Bristol Playa (☎ 928 86 70 20; www.hes peria-bristolplaya.com; Urbanizacion Lago de Bristol 1; apt €119; ☲) Flash as a rat with a gold tooth, this is a shiny, smart 'aparthotel' complex that's brimming with style. Great rooms, fabulous swimming pools and excellent views of the Isla de Lobos, plus a central Corralejo location. Children are well catered for, with lots of entertainment options should you feel like doing little more than lounging poolside.

Hotel Riu Palace Tres Islas (☎ 928 53 57 00; www.riu.es; Avenida de las Grandes Playas; r €75-95) Part of the massive Riu chain, this marble-trimmed palace is a luxury seaside fortress on the edge of the dunes. Every effort goes into making guests decide that they'd prefer to live here than at home. Prices include half board (one meal per day is included in the price), which is well above the usual standard of hotel food.

WAYNE WALTON

Bodega (traditional wine bar), La Geria, Lanzarote (p130)

PAUL KENNEDY

The surf beach of La Caleta de Famara, Lanzarote (p128)

Cactus in César Manrique's garden, Lanzarote (p125)

DAMIEN SIMONIS

GREG GAWLOWSKI

The emerald green waters of the Charco de los Clicos, El Golfo, Lanzarote (p131)

Breakwater at sunset, Puerto
de la Cruz, Tenerife (p150)

Museo de Artesanía Iberoamericana, La Orotava,
Tenerife (p156)

The startling and solitary mountains of Punta de Teno, Tenerife (p162)

Eating
The pedestrianised area around the town's small port offers plenty of seafood eating options, with outdoor seating adding to the fun.

Restaurante El Tío Bernabé (☎ 928 53 58 95; Calle Iglesia 17; mains €7.65-22.85) This restaurant carries a wide range of Canarian cuisine and a superb array of fish. It's perfectly positioned to catch the sea breezes too, making this an excellent choice. Credit cards are accepted and live music is sometimes on offer.

Avenida (cnr Calle Pizarro & General Prim; mains €6.50-14; ☾ closed Sun & Mon) Crammed to the rafters with locals – yes, locals – and not a tourist in sight, this place serves enormous steaks and has an unpretentious, up-to-your-elbows-in-food vibe.

Restaurante Avelino (☎ 928 53 51 95; Calle General García Escámez s/n) Away from the tourist mainstream and still very Spanish (the Guardia Civil drink and eat here) is this great local fave. Ask for a recommendation and you'll generally be advised to go for the *mejillones en salsa* (mussels and sauce) – and with good reason.

Poco Loco (☎ 928 86 66 62; Avenida General Franco 16) This macho-looking den of meat consumption is great for grills – a healthy T-bone costs about €13. Wash it all down with beer and red wine and forget about seafood – you can get that elsewhere.

El Rincón de Perico (Calle Iglesia s/n; mains €7-14.50; ☾ closed Wed) If you want to try *gofio*, followed by a plate of *cabrito* (an island speciality for reasons which have probably become apparent by now) head to this solid local haunt, where Calle Iglesia runs into Plaza Chica.

Café de Viena (Calle Juan de Austria 27) For breakfast or a civilised cup of coffee, this place hits the spot.

Drinking & Entertainment
Finding a drink in Corralejo doesn't pose a problem. Bars take up much of the Centro Comercial Atlántico, on Avenida General Franco, as well as the custard-yellow shopping centre further down the road, on the corner of Calle Anguila.

Zumbar (Centro Comercial Atlántico, Avenida General Franco) The décor is bog-standard, but this place has the biggest party vibe. Happy hour starts at 9pm, and DJs play funk, soul, R&B, drum & bass and the usual screeching hits of summer.

The Venue (Centro Comercial Atlántico, Avenida General Franco) In the same complex as Zumbar and featuring a singing Alsatian, 'as seen on TV', as part of the night's entertainment.

Antiguo Café del Puerto (Calle Ballena 10; tapas €1.50-4.20) A classy place with rag-washed walls and some tasty tapas on offer amidst the smiles. It's a great choice for a drink and a snack without being deafened by euro-cheese music.

Cafe Latino (Calle Ballena; cocktails €4.80; ☾ closed Wed afternoon) For a relaxed cocktail just out of earshot of the main hurly burly, sample from the range at this shore-side place, which has great canned jazz and, at weekends, a DJ.

Waikiki (Calle de la Fragata 11) This is an excellent place to party, where a mix of surfers, party animals, families and friends gather in a hibiscus-fringed setting to scoff pizza (€5 to €6) and sip cocktails, day or night.

Shopping
No Work Team (☎ 928 53 51 11; Avenida General Franco 46; ☾ 10am-2pm & 5-8pm Mon-Sat) One local surfwear label to look out for (and it seems that every second man in Corralejo is wearing one of their T-shirts) is No Work Team. In its shop you'll find good-quality, comfy duds for men, women and children, with an unmistakeable surfwear feel.

There's also a rather tame local **market** (cnr Calle Gran Canaria & Avenida General Franco; ☾ 9am-1pm Mon & Fri) that is heavier on African arts and crafts than it is on Canarian specialities. Still, it's a pleasant diversion if the beaches aren't calling.

Getting There & Away
BOAT
Fred Olsen (☎ 902 53 50 90; www.fredolsen.es) ferries leave five times daily for Playa Blanca in Lanzarote. The trip takes 35 to 45 minutes and a one-way ticket costs €14.20 (car from €18.90).

You can buy tickets at the port. Otherwise, hop onto one of the five to six daily boats of **Naviera Armas** (☎ 928 54 21 13; www.naviera armas.com; adult/child/car €11.40/5.70/16.50).

At the Lanzarote end, Fred Olsen puts on a free connecting bus as far as Puerto del Carmen for its 9am and 5pm services. The 9am run continues to Lanzarote's airport. This free bus operates in the other direction too (see p133).

FUERTEVENTURA

DETOUR

The bare, 4.4-sq-km **Isla de Lobos** takes its name from the *lobos marinos* (seawolves) that lived there. They were, in fact, *focas monje* (monk seals), which have since disappeared thanks to the hungry crew of French explorer de la Salle, who ate them to stave off starvation in the early 15th century.

You can go on an excursion to the islet from Corralejo.

Once you've disembarked there's little to do but go for a short walk, order lunch at the quayside *chiringuito* (kiosk) – reserve when you arrive if you intend to lunch there – and head for the pleasant little beach.

It's a popular bird-watching destination, and there are hammerhead sharks in the waters around the island. Surfers often carve up the mean breaks when the waves are pumping.

The cheapest and fastest way to get there is on the Isla de Lobos ferry. Departing Corralejo at 10am, it leaves the island at 4pm. A return ticket costs €8/6 per adult/child.

A mini-cruise is another option; see p104.

BUS

The bus station is located on Avenida Juan Carlos I. Bus No 6 runs regularly from Corralejo's bus station to Puerto del Rosario (€2.40, 40 minutes).

You can also pick up the bus at the last Minitren stop southeast of town and at the Hotel Riu Palace Tres Islas.

Bus No 8 heads west to El Cotillo via La Oliva (€2.20, 40 minutes, six daily).

CAR & MOTORCYCLE

There's a string of car rental companies, most of them acting as agents for the same supplier, near the Centro Comercial Atlántico on Avenida General Franco.

If you want only two motorised wheels, one option is the authentically dirty **Mal Fun Club** (☎ 928 53 51 52; Avenida Juan Carlos I 35; ☯ 9am-1pm & 5-8pm Mon-Sat, 9am-1pm Sun), opposite the bus station. You can rent scooters and motorcycles from €32 and €58, respectively, with full cover insurance.

Getting Around
MINITREN

You know those irritating little trains that often transport sheepishly grinning tourists around resorts and theme parks? Well, you will find one in Corralejo and it actually comes in quite handy. It runs every 30 minutes, from 9am to 11.50pm, from Avenida General Franco and takes in the port, the bus station and the majority of the apartments at the northern end of the dunes in its circuit of the town. A ride costs €1 and the circuit takes around 25 minutes.

TAXI

Call ☎ 928 86 61 08 for a taxi. One from the town centre to the main beaches will cost about €5.

EL COTILLO

Once the seat of power of the tribal chiefs of Maxorata, the northern kingdom of Guanche Fuerteventura, El Cotillo has been largely ignored since the conquest. The exceptions to the rule were cut-throat pirates who occasionally sought to land here and the slowly growing invasion of less violent sun-seekers who prize the area's unaffected peacefulness. The developers have so far largely left this small fishing village on Fuerteventura's northwestern coast alone, but for how long? Get here quick, in case things change for the worse.

It's a lovely place to wander around or to choose as a base for a few days.

Apart from the delights of the sea (the better beaches stretch out south of town), the only object of note in El Cotillo is the tubby little **Fortaleza del Tostón**. Built in 1797, the fort now seems oddly out of place, sitting isolated above the modest cliffs south of the port. The beaches between El Cotillo and Corralejo are generally small and pebbly.

It's a quiet spot; if you're after some frenzied nightlife, you should head over to Corralejo (p105).

Activities
DIVING

The friendly and supremely helpful staff at **Dive Inn** (☎ 928 86 82 63; Calle Felix de Vera Guerra s/n) will take you to all the best spots for scuba diving (courses and equipment hire available) and can also help out with tips about the surrounding area. Snorkelling gear is available for those who prefer to float on the water's surface, and there's a nifty snorkelling course available too (for €60).

KITESURFING
If learning to kitesurf with a champ appeals, you must head to **Krunk** (☎ 696 28 77 97; Calle del Castillo 9; ☻ 10am-1pm & 6-8pm), where a three-day beginner's course costs €300 and a private hour-long lesson costs €65.

SURFING
Experienced surfers should make for a spot known as Bubbles, which is certainly not as innocuous as it sounds. Waves break over reef and rocks; you can pick out the casualties on the streets of El Cotillo and Corralejo during the surfing season. To get to Bubbles, you'll need your own transport. If you need to hire gear or buy equipment, visit **Onit Surf Shop** (☎ 928 53 86 76; www.onitsurf.com; Calle 3 de Abril de 1979 16; ☻ 10.30am-1.30pm & 5-8pm Mon-Sat), a friendly little shop with surfboards available for €10/50 per day/week and boogie boards for €8/40. If you'd rather ride a bike, they can provide these too.

Sleeping
El Cotillo is a rather nondescript, comparatively undeveloped haven with several groups of apartments. That said, what you'll get is great value for money and the feeling that you're not just one of the many thousand on the other stretches of tourist coast.

La Gaviota (☎ /fax 928 53 85 67; d €32) This laid-back, neo-hippy place which flies the Jolly Roger is really something special, with a lot of love and hard work poured into the décor and the ambience. It's small, but perfectly formed, so you should definitely book in advance.

Hotel Maria Hierro (☎ 928 53 85 98; hotelmariquitahierro@wanadoo.es; Calle Maria Hierro s/n; s/d €34.65/47.25; P ⊠ ⊠) This is a newish hotel right near the town's bus stop. It's a good choice too, with tidy rooms, relatively snazzy communal areas and a rooftop pool. Prices for the facilities represent very good value for money (breakfast is included).

Apartamentos Juan Benítez (☎ 928 53 85 03; victorianobenit@hotmail.com; Calle La Caleta 4; apt €45-75) Closer to the fort and the southern beaches are Juan's apartments, which are easy to find in this small place. The apartments themselves are very clean and sleep between one and four persons, plus they have satellite TV.

Eating
Marealta (Calle 3 de Abril de 1979 25; mains €9-13.20; ☻ 6pm-midnight Thu-Tue) This strikingly attractive restaurant features stone walls, lots of bougainvillea, a pretty courtyard and a good menu of tasty staples.

Restaurante La Vaca Azul (☎ 928 53 86 85; mains €6-23; ☻ closed Tue) A most pleasant spot to eat and drink and presided over by a surreal model cow (floodlit in lurid blue at night), right on the small pebble beach in the middle of town. Sample a good paella or the mixed fish grill (minimum two people) and sit back on the sun-drenched terrace.

El Veril (☎ 928 53 87 80; Muelle Pescadores; mains €10.50-15; ☻ closed Sun evening) Offering good service and easy-on-the-eye décor, this charming rural-meets-the-seaside eating house has some great local dishes. We loved La Castreña – peppers stuffed with anchovies.

Drinking & Entertainment
Heaven (Calle 23 de Abril de 1973 50; ☻ 9.30am-2am Wed-Mon) Pop in here for drinks, snacks and a picnic hamper. It's a nice little place, with beer on tap, some decent music playing in the background and probably the longest opening hours in town.

There's also some good little places around the tiny port to get a cold beer.

Getting There & Away
Bus No 7 for Puerto del Rosario (€3, 45 minutes) leaves at 6.45am, noon and 5pm daily. No 8 leaves for Corralejo (€2.20, 40 minutes, six daily). The dirt road that follows the coast to Corralejo is normally passable for ordinary cars.

AROUND EL COTILLO
Zoo Safari (☎ 928 86 80 06; ☻ 10am-5pm Mon-Sat) Located 1.5km northwest of the village of Lajares and 12km from Corralejo, this place offers half-hour camel rides for €6/3 per adult/child and a 1½-hour trip into the

caldera of the long-extinct Calderón Hondo volcano for €15/7.80. The latter trip departs from Zoo Safari at noon and 2pm Monday to Saturday.

The nearby town of **Villaverde** has the amusing (and, we're guessing, ironic) reputation as the Beverly Hills of Fuerteventura. It's a nice little area too, with tastefully renovated houses and the like, but there's no need to feel intimidated. Here you'll find **La Rosita** (☎ 928 17 53 25; Carretera La Oliva-Corralejo; ☽ 10am-6pm Mon-Sat), where you can take a camel ride through a local rural landscape. It also has a cactus garden, a farm animal display and some displays of rural life.

If you fancy staying in the area, it's impossible to beat the stunning **Hotel Rural Mahoh** (☎ 928 86 80 50; www.mahoh.com; Sitio de Juan Bello; per person s €61-77 d €36-45 tr €25-31; P ☒) where you'll feel very much the pampered gaucho. Rooms (they sleep up to three) are brimming with romantic character and are extremely comfortable. The attached **restaurant** (per person €20-30; ☽ closed Tue) is reason enough to stay, although it's also possible to just drop in for a filling Canarian meal. Bus No 8 stops right outside the premises.

PENÍNSULA DE JANDÍA

Most of the peninsula is protected by its status as the Parque Natural de Jandía, a designated nature park. The southwest is a canvas of craggy hills and bald plains leading to cliffs west of Morro Jable. Much of the rest is made up of dunes, scrub and beaches.

Somewhere along this peninsula, they say, German submarine crews used to hole up occasionally during WWII. You think these beaches are paradise now – just imagine them with not a single tourist, not one little apartment block, only you and your mates from the U-boat!

According to other stories, Nazi officials passed through here after the war to pick up false papers before heading on to South America. One version of the story even has hordes of Nazi gold buried hereabouts – so bring your bucket and spade!

COSTA CALMA
Costa Calma, about 25km northeast of Morro Jable, is a 'Tidy Town' version of

Caleta de Fuste. The beach is truly desirable and the developments are generally more tasteful. It's a superior resort but it lacks soul; its whole existence is due to tourism.

Activities
WINDSURFING
If catching the breeze with a sail and a board appeal, **Fanatic Fun Centre** (☎ 928 53 59 99; www.fanatic-surf.com; ☽ 9.30am-6pm summer, 10am-5pm winter) on the beach has hire rates from €12 per hour and private lessons from €36 per hour. English and German are spoken.

Sleeping & Eating
As with many places on the peninsula, the following places to sleep cater primarily to German package tourists. If you want to stay in one of the larger resort-style complexes, that all seem to be owned by the one operator, contact www.sunrisebeachhotels.com.

Bungalows Bahía Calma (☎ 928 54 71 58; fax 928 54 70 31; bungalows €50, apt €38) At the southern end of the resort, this business offers natty little apartments and bungalows amid well-tended gardens that are close to the pleasant beach.

It gets booked quickly with prepaid tour groups, but they'll certainly squeeze you in if there's a room. Management are clued-up and helpful.

Apartamentos Maryvent (☎ /fax 928 87 55 28; 2-3 person apt €42-78) A block north, cascading down the cliff and within a spit of the beach, this slightly more upmarket place has self-contained apartments with nice touches and very good security.

Chances are, if you're staying in this part of the world, you're on a package that includes meals. If you want to try something else, go to the Centro Comercial Costa Calma. In this centre you'll find **Mamma Mia** (pizza €3.65-5.95, mains €8-18), a deservedly popular little pizzeria with a casual, friendly atmosphere.

For a cocktail, head to **Bar Synergy** (Centro Comercial Costa Calma), which is about as hip as Costa Calma gets, with funky chairs and good music.

PLAYA DE SOTAVENTO DE JANDÍA
The name is a catch-all for the series of truly stunning beaches that stretch along the south coast of the peninsula. For swimming, sunbathing and windsurfing, this strand is

the most beautiful in the Canaries (the dunes of Corralejo in the north of the island run a close second). It's a coastal paradise – miles and miles of fine white sand that creeps its way almost imperceptibly into the turquoise expanse of the Atlantic.

For 10 hyperactive days each July, its drowsy calm is shattered by daytime action and frantic nightlife as the beach hosts a leg of the **Windsurf World Cup** (www.fuerteventura -worldcup.org). Kitesurfing is also a part of this wind-powered display of prowess.

Various driveable trails lead down off the FV-2 highway to vantage points off the beach – its generous expanses mean you should have little trouble finding a tranquil plot for yourself.

If you want to do a bit of cyberspace research before arriving, check out www .playasdejandia.com.

MORRO JABLE
pop 6070
Competing with Corralejo for the title of Fuerteventura's premier tourist resort is Morro Jable, the island's southernmost

town, which is extremely popular with German holiday makers in search of sunshine. It claims to be more low-key and sophisticated than its northern rival, but there's plenty of glitzy shops and crowded apartments that are almost identical to any other resort on the island or in the archipelago.

Orientation
Approaching Morro Jable from the north, you'll arrive via Avenida Saladar. The town centre, up the hill, is a maze of narrow, steep streets with few parking opportunities.

Information
EMERGENCY
Police station (☎ 928 54 10 22; Calle Laurel)

INTERNET ACCESS
Cosmo Office (☎ 928 54 50 67; Cosmo Centro Comercial, Avenida Saladar; per hr €4; ☽ 9am-1pm & 5-10pm Mon-Fri, 5-10pm Sun) Offers speedy connection.

LAUNDRY
You don't have to be a guest to use the laundry facilities in major apartment blocks.

MORRO JABLE

INFORMATION	
Centro Mdico Jandía	(see 11)
Cosmo Office	(see 11)
Police Station	1 D1
Post Office	2 D1
Tourist Office	(see 11)
Tourist Office	3 D3

SIGHTS & ACTIVITIES	(p110)
Centro de Buceo Félix	4 D3
Sun Car Jandía	(see 10)

SLEEPING	(p110)
Apartamentos Alberto	5 A2
Apartamentos Palm Gardens	6 D3

Apartamentos Soto	7 D2
Hostal Omahy	8 D2

EATING	(pp110-11)
Restaurante Posada San Borondón	9 D2

DRINKING	(p111)
La Cara Disco	10 D3

SHOPPING	(p111)
Cosmo Centro Comercial	11 C3
Market	12 D3

TRANSPORT	(p111)
Taxi Rank	13 D2

To Golf Club Fuerteventura (5km)

Carretera GC-640 a El Gran Tarajal

To Port (3km), Cofete (17km) & Punta de Jandía (21km)

Avenida del Faro

Calle Ntra Sra. Carmen

Carretera GC-640 a El Gran Tarajal

See Enlargement

Playa de la Cebada

Playa del Matorral

ATLANTIC OCEAN

GC-640

Calle Bentejuy

Avenida Saladar

Calle Montaña Perdida

To Stella Discoteque (450m); Costa Calma (15km); Gran Tarajal (30km); Puerto del Rosario (65km)

Calle de las Pintaderas

Avenida del Faro

Calle Senador Velázquez Cabrera

Calle Mta Sra. de Carmen

Calle Trino

Calle Matorral

Calle Laurel

Calle Buenavista

Calle Gambuesas

Avenida Jandía

Plazoleta Cirilo López

FUERTEVENTURA

MEDICAL SERVICES
Centro Medico Jandía (☎ 928 54 15 43; Cosmo Centro Comercial, Avenida Saladar; ☺ 24hr) Among several international clinics, this one is multilingual.

POST
Post office (☎ 928 54 03 73; ☺ 8.30am-2.30pm Mon-Fri, 9.30am-1pm Sat) At the northern tip of Calle Gambuesas.

TOURIST OFFICES
Tourist office (☎ 928 54 07 76; turismo@playadejandia .com; Cosmo Centro Comercial, Avenida Saladar; ☺ 8am-3pm Mon-Fri) Lots of brochures and staff who seem to be refreshingly knowledgeable about the area.

Sights & Activities
BEACHES
The magnificent **Playa del Mattoral**, stretching eastwards for over 4km from Morro Jable, is great for indulging in a variety of water sports, churning a pedalo or just lazing on the hot sand. Such a stretch rarely gets crowded but for true solitude you need to be heading for the beaches 7km further east. These are really only accessible with some kind of transport (from car via dune buggy to bicycle).

DIVING
If you're an experienced diver, you can explore the sea bottom with the **Centro de Buceo Félix** (☎ 928 54 14 18; www.tauchen-fuerventua.de in German; Avenida Saladar 27; 1/3/10 dives €32/86/259). Beginners courses are only offered in German and dives take place between 9am and 2pm. Equipment is included in the price.

BOAT TRIPS
Magic (☎ 928 73 56 56; 5hr cruises adult/child €40/20) operates a couple of smart catamarans out of the port. Sailing at 10 or 10.30am (also at 4pm from May to October), cruises include a barbecue lunch and allow plenty of time for offshore swimming and snorkelling.

If you have kids with you, you might consider **Pedra Sartaña** (☎ 670 745 51 91; tickets adult/child €36/18) which offers 'fun and games with our pirate' as an add-on – perhaps a little direly if you're beyond puberty. Sailings are Monday to Saturday.

CYCLING
Sun Car Jandía (☎ 928 54 15 84; Avenida Saladar s/n), beside La Cara disco, rents bicycles for €7/18/36 per day/three days/week, with baby seats a measly €1 extra.

GOLF
Just inland, 5km north of Morro Jable and up the Valle de Butihondo, an 18-hole golf course known as **Golf Club Fuerteventura** (☎ 928 16 00 34; fuerteventuragolf@grupoanjoca.com; Carretera de Jandía) drinks up a vast quantity of desalinated water.

Sleeping
BUDGET
Hostal Omahy (☎ 928 54 12 54; Calle Maxorata 47; d €25; Ⓟ) While you may receive a fairly gruff welcome, you won't need to complain about cleanliness or anything untoward in this eminently serviceable budget joint. It's a simple place, with the bargain prices to prove it, in a very central location.

MID-RANGE
Apartamentos Soto (☎ 928 54 14 19; fax 928 54 15 89; Calle Gambuesas; studios €39, apt €50-75) The fully equipped (kitchen, telephone, TV) studios and apartments (sleeping between two and four people) are supremely comfortable and absolutely spotless.

You can pop into the **Autos Soto car hire office** (☺ 8am-noon & 4-7pm Mon-Sat, 8am-11am Sun), on the ground floor of the building, to arrange your accommodation.

Apartamentos Alberto (☎ 928 54 51 09; Avenida del Faro 4; studios €40-48, apt €50-65; Ⓟ) A slight move up the ladder and located close to town in a quiet spot, this place offers well-maintained apartments with kitchenette, lounge room and phone, and a host of other accommodation options, from single rooms to an entire chateau. Try to snaffle a water view if possible, or spend some time in the rooftop garden.

Apartamentos Palm Gardens (☎ 928 54 10 00; fax 928 54 10 40; Avenida Saladar s/n; apt €55-76) Cascading like a ziggurat, this huge apartment complex has airy, attractive apartments that sleep between two and four people, plus helpful and friendly front desk staff who have a finger on the pulse of local events and attractions.

Eating
You can get the usual resort 'international cuisine' and fast food at innumerable places among the apartments, condos and

shopping centres along Avenida Saladar. Head into the small town proper to sample more interesting, low-key efforts that are invariably tastier.

Restaurante Posada San Borondón (☎ 928 54 14 28; Plazoleta de Cirilo López 1; mains €7.25-19.25) Somewhere a little more interesting, and offering a variety of Spanish food, is this restaurant where the grilled sole touched our soul.

The only problem here – and one that can't escape you – is that this place is trying to look like a steamship on the outside and something else (we're not sure what) on the inside.

A quartet of restaurants on the waterfront behind San Borondón serve pleasant-enough food in seaside surroundings, making them nice choices for an afternoon or early evening drink. Stick to the fresh fish and you're bound to be satisfied.

Drinking & Entertainment

The main nightlife action is along the beachfront part of the resort. A cluster of pubs is concentrated in the Cosmo Centro Comercial.

Surf Inn (☎ 928 54 22 72; ☼ 7pm-3am Mon-Sat) This place is aimed at a younger and later-arriving crowd who like to check out surfing and snowboarding videos while they sip cocktails.

You could also head for **La Cara Disco** (Avenida Saladar s/n), a block or two east from the Centro Comercial, or **Stella Discoteque** (Avenida Saladar s/n), 450m further on – look for the twin bronze lions and you are nearly there.

Shopping

Cosmo Central Comercial (Avenida Saladar) This large centre has plenty of shops selling tax-free goodies, so it's popular with visitors.

There's a small Thursday **market** (Avenida del Saladar; ☼ 9am-1.30pm) in a car park beside Avenida Saladar, a little west of the tourist office. With most stalls run by Moroccans, Africans and German dropouts, you'll be lucky to find anything that smacks particularly of the Canaries.

Getting There & Away
TO/FROM THE AIRPORT

Bus No 10 connects the town with the airport, and taxis will cost around €70.

BUS

The first No 1 bus for Puerto del Rosario (€7, two hours, at least six daily) leaves at 6am (weekdays) and the last leaves at 10.15pm. The No 10 bus via the airport (€7, 1½ hours, three daily) is faster. Bus No 5 to Costa Calma (€1.90, 40 minutes) runs frequently.

BOAT

Puerto de Morro Jable, the port, is 3km by road from the centre of town. **Trasmediterránea** (☎ 902 45 46 45; www.trasmediterranea.com) has daily jetfoils leaving for Las Palmas de Gran Canaria (€49.35, 1½ hours) and Tenerife (€68.95).

Naviera Armas (☎ 928 54 21 13; www.navieraarmas.com) ferries head for Las Palmas (€29.50, 3¾ hours) at 7pm daily.

You can get tickets for both services at the port or at the town's many travel agents.

Getting Around
TAXI

There is a taxi rank in the town centre just off Avenida Jandía. To call a taxi, ring ☎ 928 54 12 57.

AROUND MORRO JABLE
Punta de Jandía

Twenty kilometres of graded but unsealed road winds out along the southern reaches of the peninsula to a lone lighthouse at Punta de Jandía.

DETOUR

Much wilder than their leeward counterparts, the long stretches of beach on the windward side of the Peninsula de Jandía are also harder to get to. You really need a 4WD to safely negotiate the various tracks leading into the area (but once you've found a spot you like, please don't chop up the dunes with your vehicle).

The wild length of coast that is the the **Playa de Barlovento de Jandía** can get very windy – though the flying sand doesn't seem to deter the nude bathers, who are as common as the partly clothed variety. Take care swimming here: the waves and currents can often be more formidable than the usually becalmed waters on the other side of the island.

Puerto de la Cruz, a couple of kilometres east of the lighthouse, is a tiny, bedraggled fishing settlement and weekend retreat for locals. Two little restaurants, the Tenderete and Punta de Jandía, open only at lunch time, serve up the local catch to tourists passing en route to the island's westernmost point. The latter serves the freshest of fish at €7.50 but – on this visit – average coffee.

Cofete

About 10km along the same road from Morro Jable, a turn-off leads northeast over a pass and plunges to Cofete (7km from the junction), a tiny peninsula hamlet at the southern extreme of the Playa de Barlovento de Jandía (see the boxed text on p111). Sandy tracks, negotiable on foot or by 4WD, snake off to this wind-whipped strand. **Restaurante Cofete** (☎ 928 17 42 43; mains €6.20-12.20; ⊙ 11am-7pm) does drinks and excellent snacks and has a more sophisticated menu than you'd expect from a restaurant that's literally at the end of the road. They, too, do fresh fish – as well as *carne de cabra en salsa* (goat in sauce) – maybe a close relative of the semiwild creatures you pass on the journey.

Lanzarote

LANZAROTE

Lanzarote is known colloquially and in a thousand tourist brochures as the Isla de los Volcanes, with a mind-boggling 300 cones peppered about it. The fourth-largest and most northeasterly island of the Canaries, Lanzarote measures only about 60km north to south and a mere 21km at its widest point east to west. The island's name is assumed to be a corruption of Lanzarotto (or Lancelotto) Malocello, the Genoese seafarer who landed on the island in the late 13th or early 14th century.

The immediate reaction of many who come to the island is that there is nothing here. True, it's a largely arid place, but bizarrely and intriguingly so. Unesco has declared the entire island a biosphere reserve. Its largely volcanic terrain is captivating and unique; its beauty is stark, weird and very real. At times you'll think you've landed on the moon; at other times you'll wonder if you're in Africa or Hawaii. If the relentless commercialism of the other eastern islands has got you down, Lanzarote is the place to come. There are resorts here, but they're relatively low-key and easier to escape if the mood takes you.

The island's approach to tourism has in no small measure been shaped by the inspiration of the artist César Manrique. Not only has he left his personal stamp on many of the attractions around the island, but his ideas continue to inform policy on tourism development. The careful adherence to traditional building styles in the interior is largely due to the vigilance of Manrique and his successors.

HIGHLIGHTS

- **Wining**

  The LZ-30 travels through La Geria, where you can sample the local *malvasía* (Malmsey wine; p130)

- **Dining**

  The wonderful La Era restaurant in Yaiza is the spot for a long, leisurely lunch (p131)

- **Volcano Spotting**

  The heat is on in the 'Mountains of Fire' in the Parque Nacional de Timanfaya (p129)

- **Hanging Ten**

  La Caleta de Famara (p128) and Isla Graciosa (p127) offer world-class surf breaks

- **Design Delights**

  César Manrique turned his design talents to anything and everything (see the boxed text on p117), including the Cueva de los Verdes and Jameos del Agua (p126)

★ Isla Graciosa

★ Cueva de los Verdes & Jameos del Agua

★ La Caleta de Famara

Parque Nacional de Timanfaya ★

★ La Geria

★ Yaiza

■ TELEPHONE CODE: 928   ■ POPULATION: 97,000   ■ AREA: 846 SQ KM

HISTORY

Lanzarote was the first of the Canary Islands to fall to Jean de Béthencourt in 1402, marking the beginning of the Spanish conquest. Along with Fuerteventura, Lanzarote was particularly exposed to frequent raids by Moroccan pirates operating from ports along the northwest African coast, barely 100km away. The then capital Teguise was frequently sacked and many inhabitants were hauled into captivity, later to be sold as slaves. The problem was especially grave during the 16th century, and the Moroccans weren't the only source of grief. British buccaneers such as Sir Walter Raleigh, Sir John Hawkins and John Poole also visited the island, as did French bearers of the skull and crossbones such as Jean Florin and Pegleg le Clerc.

By the middle of the 17th century, misery, piracy and emigration had reduced the number of Conejeros (as the islanders are sometimes called) to just 300.

In the 1730s, massive and disastrous volcanic eruptions destroyed some of the island's most fertile land. Beyond the heartland of the great upheaval, though, islanders were to discover a rather ironic fact. The volcanic mix in the soil eventually proved a highly fertile bedrock for farming (particularly wine grapes), bringing relative prosperity to the descendants of those who had fled to Gran Canaria because of the lava flows.

Today, with tourism flourishing alongside the healthy, if small, agricultural sector, the island is home to 97,000 – not counting, of course, all the holiday blow-ins who at any given time can more than double the population.

INFORMATION
Books & Maps

Noel Rochford's *Landscapes of Lanzarote*, published by A&C Black, gives useful suggestions for drives and walks around the island of varying duration.

Michel Houellebecq's *Lanzarote* is a taut, fictionalised account of a package tour taken by a Frenchman, with some intriguing and, at times, disturbing revelations about his fellow guests at the resort in Puerto del Carmen.

Quadernos de Lanzarote, by José Saramago, is an interesting account of this Nobel Prize–winning Portuguese author's life on Lanzarote (he has lived here since the early 1990s), and mixes political opinion, memoir and a deep fondness for his new home.

Michelin map No 221, *Lanzarote & Fuerteventura*, is good to have, although any free tourist map will usually suffice for simple road trips.

A free *Map of Lanzarote*, handed out by tourist offices, hire car firms or found in hotels, is updated yearly and includes functional maps of Arrecife, Puerto del Carmen, Playa Blanca and Costa Teguise.

Newspapers & Magazines

The semiofficial quarterly *Lancelot* (often available free), published in Spanish, English and German, is available at many newsstands and tourist attractions.

Tourist Offices

There's a reasonably helpful **tourist office** (☎ 928 84 60 73; ✇ 9am-5pm Mon & Wed, 9.30am-9.30pm Tue & Thu, 9am-4pm Fri & Sat, 10am-6pm Sun) at the airport's arrivals hall.

ACTIVITIES

If lolling on the beach and dunking yourself in the ocean begins to bore, it may be time for something more active. The wilder, less visited and more rugged north coast has some of Europe's finest surfing breaks, and a surf school is based at La Caleta de Famara. The beaches of the south coast are excellent for windsurfing and diving. The sea temperature rarely drops below 18°C, and underwater visibility ranges between 6m and 20m depending on the season. Cycling, whether a gentle potter around your resort or a more strenuous outing along the lightly trafficked roads, is also possible.

ACCOMMODATION

On all of Lanzarote, there isn't a single youth hostel and only one official camp site (p134). Most accommodation is in the form of apartments and bungalows, the majority concentrated in the resorts of Puerto del Carmen, Playa Blanca and Costa Teguise. As with neighbouring Fuerteventura, the main problem for independent travellers is that the bulk of these deal with tour operators, often exclusively, and are frequently full.

Arrecife is not the world's most fascinating capital, but lone travellers without a booking might consider it as a temporary solution if nothing else turns up.

LANZAROTE

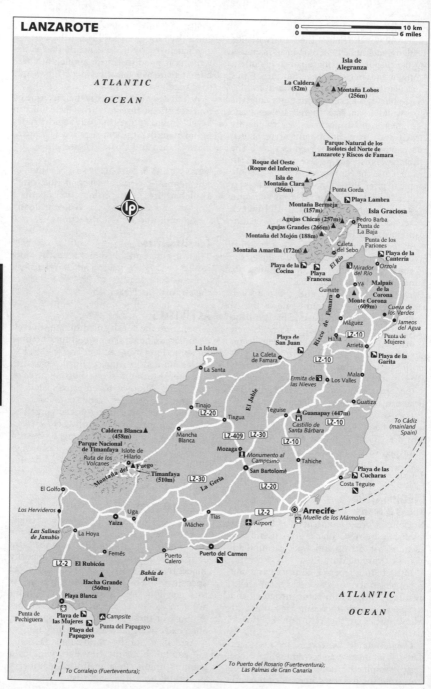

0 ____ 10 km
0 ____ 6 miles

ATLANTIC
OCEAN

Isla de
Alegranza

La Caldera
(52m)

▲ Montaña Lobos
(256m)

Parque Natural de los
Isolotes del Norte de
Lanzarote y Riscos de Famara

Roque del Oeste
(Roque del Inferno)

Isla de
Montaña Clara
(256m)

Montaña Bermeja
(157m)

Punta Gorda

Playa Lambra

Isla Graciosa

Agujas Chicas (257m) ▲

Pedro Barba

Agujas Grandes (266m) ▲

Punta de
La Baja

Montaña del Mojón (188m) ▲

Montaña Amarilla (172m) ▲

Caleta
del Sebo

Punta de los
Fariones

Playa de la
Canteria

Playa de la
Cocina

Playa
Francesa

El Río

Mirador
del Río

Orzola

Playa de la
Cocina

Guinate

Yé

Malpaís
de la
Corona

Monte Corona
(609m)

Cueva de
los Verdes

Máguez

LZ-10

Jameos
del Agua

Playa de
San Juan

Haría

Punta de
Mujeres

La Isleta

La Caleta
de Famara

LZ-10

Arrieta

Playa de la
Garita

La Santa

Ermita de
las Nieves

Mala

Los Valles

Guatiza

To Cádiz
(mainland
Spain)

Tinajo

LZ-20

Tiagua

El Jable

Teguise

Guanapay (447m) ▲

Caldera Blanca ▲
(458m)

Mancha
Blanca

LZ-409 LZ-30

Castillo de
Santa Bárbara

LZ-10

Parque Nacional
de Timanfaya

Islote de
Hilario

Mozaga

Monumento al
Campesino

LZ-10

Ruta de los
Volcanes

Fuego

Timanfaya
(510m)

LZ-30

San Bartolomé

Tahiche

Playa de las
Cucharas

La Geria

LZ-20

El Golfo

Costa Teguise

Los Hervideros

Uga

Tías

LZ-2

Arrecife

Las Salinas
de Janubio

Mácher

Airport

Muelle de los Mármoles

La Hoya

Yaiza

Femés

Puerto
Calero

Puerto del Carmen

LZ-2 El Rubicón

Bahía de
Avila

ATLANTIC
OCEAN

Hacha Grande
(560m)

Playa Blanca

Punta de
Pechiguera

Playa de
las Mujeres

Campsite

Playa del
Papagayo

Punta del Papagayo

To Corralejo (Fuerteventura);

To Puerto del Rosario (Fuerteventura);
Las Palmas de Gran Canaria

Risco de Famara

LANZAROTE

CÉSAR MANRIQUE

Born on 24 April 1919, Manrique grew up in relative tranquillity by the sea. After a stint as a volunteer with Franco's forces during the 1936–39 Civil War, he eventually followed his heart's desire and enrolled in Madrid's Academia de Bellas Artes de San Fernando in 1945, having already held his first exhibition five years earlier in his home town of Arrecife.

Influenced – but not stylistically dominated by – Picasso and Matisse, he held his first major exhibition of abstract works in 1954. In the following years, his opus toured most of Europe, and in 1964 he was invited by one of his admirers, Nelson Rockefeller, to the USA where he exhibited in New York's Guggenheim Museum. But Manrique never forgot his birthplace and returned home in 1968, after his successful US tour, brimming with ideas for enhancing what he already felt to be the incomparable beauty of Lanzarote.

He began with a campaign to preserve traditional building methods, especially in rural architecture, and another to ban the blight of advertising billboards on roadsides and across the countryside. A multifaceted artist, Manrique subsequently turned his flair and vision to a broad range of projects across the island. The whole of Lanzarote became his canvas. In all, he carried out seven major projects on the island and numerous others elsewhere in the archipelago and beyond, and at the time of his death had several more on the boil.

In Lanzarote's northeast, Manrique directed the works to make the grotto of the Jameos del Agua accessible to visitors without ruining the natural beauty of the spot. Here he also directed the construction of a music auditorium in a cavern of volcanic rock. He chose to live not just in harmony with but amid the blue-black hardened lava flows that so characterise the island, building his house in a flow in Taro de Tahiche, about 6km north of Arrecife. Since his death in a car accident on 25 September 1992, this unusual house has served as home to the Fundación César Manrique (César Manrique Foundation). Further north, the bizarre Jardín de Cactus, bristling with 10,000 cactuses of more than 1000 species, is another of Manrique's ideas. In the Montañas del Fuego, he installed the striking Restaurante del Diablo at the heart of the hostile, denuded volcanic terrain. He even thought to turn the still-surging subterranean volcanic energy to good account – the meat you eat here is grilled using its heat.

On the grand scale, it was primarily Manrique's persistent lobbying for maintaining traditional architecture and protecting the natural environment that prompted the *cabildo* (government) to pass laws restricting urban development. The growing wave of tourism development since the early 1980s has, however, threatened to sweep away all before it. But Manrique's ceaseless opposition to such unchecked urban sprawl touched a nerve with many Conejeros and led to the creation of an environmental group known as El Guincho, which has had some success in revealing – and at times even reversing – abuses by developers. Manrique was posthumously made its honorary president.

As you pass through villages across the island, you'll see how traditional stylistic features remain the norm. The standard whitewashed houses are adorned with green-painted doors, window shutters and strange onion-shaped chimney pots. Hotels beyond the resorts are sparse and the island seems to deal with the waves of tourism in a dignified and thoughtful way, weighing up the euros to be made against the quality of island life. In such ways, César Manrique's influence and spirit endure.

Otherwise, there is a smattering of alternatives at other points around the coast and a handful of inland options, including some delightful villas, and *casa rural* (country house) options.

GETTING THERE & AWAY

The following section provides a brief overview of air and boat options to and from Lanzarote. For more comprehensive information, see Getting There & Away under specific town entries.

Air

From **Guasimeta airport** (☎ 928 84 60 01), 6km southwest of Arrecife, **Binter** (☎ 902 39 13 92; www.bintercanarias.com) has at least 10 flights daily to Las Palmas de Gran Canaria (€60, 45 minutes), at least five daily to Tenerife Norte (€79, 50 minutes), two weekly to

Tenerife Sur (€79, 50 minutes) and three weekly to La Palma (€90, 50 minutes). Otherwise the traffic is made up of regular flights from the mainland by **Air Europa** (www.air-europa.com), **Iberia** (www.iberia.com) and **Spanair** (www.spanair.com) and charters from all over Europe.

For a charter flight to the UK contact **Viajes Isla Casa** (☎ 928 38 31 50; Centro Comercial Marítimo 24, Puerto del Carmen).

Boat
For details on the ferry services from Arrecife to Fuerteventura and Gran Canaria, see p122. For details on Fred Olsen ferry services between Playa Blanca and Corralejo (Fuerteventura), see p134.

GETTING AROUND
To/From the Airport
Bus No 4 connects the airport and Arrecife twice an hour between 7.20am and 10.50pm Monday to Friday. Services run between 8.50am and 10.50pm on weekends. Getting a taxi to/from the airport is easy, but will cost around €27 to, say, Playa Blanca.

Bus
Arrecife Bus (☎ 928 81 15 22) provides the public transport. The service is frequent around Arrecife, especially to Puerto del Carmen and Costa Teguise. Fairly regular runs also connect with Playa Blanca in the south and such inland towns as Teguise. Otherwise services are minimal or nonexistent.

Car
Rental places abound in all three major resorts and in the capital of Arrecife. The airport also has numerous car hire firms.

Taxi
As elsewhere, you have the option of moving around the island by **taxi** (☎ 928 52 22 11), but it is an expensive way of doing things. The fare from the airport to Playa Blanca, for example, is €27. For much the same amount, you can hire a car for the whole day.

ARRECIFE

pop 44,980
Arrecife is not Lanzarote's best advertisement, and is not a highlight of a trip here.

Aside from a couple of forts – one converted into an art gallery and stylish restaurant – it offers little of real interest. Its hotels and apartments can come in handy for those who've arrived without reservations in the popular resorts of Lanzarote. If anything, Arrecife's most notable quality is that it's actually a living, breathing town that earns its living from something other than tourism.

HISTORY
The single biggest factor behind Arrecife's blandness is probably that it only became the island's capital in 1852. Until then, Teguise ruled supreme. Although it is now marginalised, Teguise's architectural heritage shows what Arrecife missed out on by being a port for the erstwhile capital.

In 1574 the Castillo de San Gabriel first went up (it was subsequently attacked and rebuilt) to protect the port. Its sister further up the coast, the Castillo de San José, was raised in 1771.

By the close of the 18th century, a semblance of a town had taken uncertain shape around the harbour. As its commerce grew and the threat of sea raids dropped off in the 19th century, Arrecife thrived. As the defensive imperatives for keeping the capital inland receded, the move of the island's administration to Arrecife became inevitable.

ORIENTATION
Sun-blanched Arrecife presents no great navigational problems. With the notable exceptions of the Castillo de San José and the port, everything of interest is located in a tight area around the centre. If you arrive by bus, get off in the heart of Playa del Reducto and walk eastwards or hang on until you get to the bus station on the northeastern flank of central Arrecife, from where you can easily zigzag into town.

The main streets for shops and restaurants are Avenida Generalísimo Franco and the pedestrianised Avenida León y Castillo.

INFORMATION
Emergency
Bomberos (Fire Brigade; ☎ 928 81 48 58)
Cruz Roja (Red Cross; ☎ 928 81 22 22) Ring for an ambulance.
Policia Local (Police; ☎ 928 81 13 17; Avenida Coll 5)

ARRECIFE

0 — 500 m
0 — 0.3 mile

INFORMATION	
Centro Medico Lansalud	1 A1
Police Station	2 C1
Post Office	3 C1
Redes Servicios Informática	4 B1
Tourist Information Kiosk	5 C1
Viajes Insular	6 B2

SIGHTS & ACTIVITIES	(p120)
Ayuntamiento (Town Hall)	7 C1
Castillo de San Gabriel	8 C2
Castillo de San José	9 D1
Ciclo Mania	10 A2
Iglesia de San Ginés	11 C1
Museo Arqueológico	(see 8)
Museo Internacional de Arte Contemporáneo	(see 9)

SLEEPING	(pp120-1)
Apartamentos Islamar	12 B3
Hostal España	13 B3
Hotel Lancelot	14 A2
Hotel Miramar	15 C1
Pensión San Ginés	16 B3

EATING	(p121)
Covered Market	17 D1
La Tavernetta	18 B1
Mesón Asuriana	19 A1
Mesón La Tinaja	20 A1
MIAC Restaurant	(see 9)
Restaurante La Puntilla	21 B3

DRINKING	(p121)
El Convento	(see 23)
La Antigua	22 B1
La Calle Disco Pub	23 B1

TRANSPORT	(p122)
Bus Station	24 A2
Bus Stop	25 A4
Naviera Armas Office	(see 28)
Taxi Rank	26 A1
Taxi Rank	27 C1
Trasmediterránea	28 A1

Internet Access

Redes Servicios Informática (☎ 928 81 22 09; Calle Coronel Bens 17; per hour €1.50; ☺ 9am-2pm & 5-8pm Mon-Fri, 9am-2pm Sat)

Medical Services

Hospital General (☎ 928 80 16 36) To the northwest of the town centre on the highway to San Bartolomé.

Centro Medico Lansalud (☎ 928 80 50 79; Calle Coronel Ildefonso Valls de la Torre 4) Use this in town.

Money

There are dozens of banks located throughout the city that have ATMs. They are found on all the major streets and in many businesses.

American Express at Viajes Insular (☎ 928 81 31 13; Calle Doctor Rafael González Negrín 13; ⏲ 8.30am-8pm Mon-Fri, 10am-1pm Sat).

Post

Main post office (Avenida Generalísimo Franco/La Marina 8; ⏲ 8.30am-8.30pm Mon-Fri, 9am-1pm Sat) Has fax facilities too.

Tourist Offices

Tourist information kiosk (☎ 928 81 18 60; Avenida Generalísimo Franco; ⏲ 9am-1pm & 4.30-7.30pm Mon-Fri, 9am-1pm Sat) There was no sign of this being open at the time of research, but it looks as though renovations were under way, with plans of transforming the site into a band rotunda–meets–tourist office.

SIGHTS & ACTIVITIES

Converted in 1994 by the Fundación César Manrique into an attractive home for modern art, the **Museo Internacional de Arte Contemporáneo** (MIAC; ☎ 928 81 23 21; Cerretera de Puero Naos; admission free; ⏲ 11am-9pm, restaurant 1-3.45pm & 7.30-11pm, bar 11am-midnight) is in the **Castillo de San José**, which was originally raised in the 18th century to deal with pirates and, at a time of famine on the island, to provide unemployed locals with a public-works job scheme. It houses the most important collection of modern art in the Canaries (which is not saying much, granted). Aside from works by Manrique himself, artists such as Miró, Millares, Mompó, Oscar Domínguez, Gerardo Rueda, Sempere and Cárdena are on show. Both gallery and restaurant (p121) are well worth the 30-minute walk or €3.50 taxi ride from the town centre.

The city's other 'castle', **Castillo de San Gabriel** (closed for renovations at the time of writing) was the first building of any note in what was little more than a landing point for the odd caravel from Spain. This doughty fort was sorely tested on several occasions by Moroccan corsairs and European pirates in the years after its construction in 1574. Today it is home to the **Museo Arqueológico**, a grandiloquent name for a modest collection of artefacts found on the island, including many from the Cueva de los Verdes (see p126). It was all off-limits at the time of research, thanks to renovations, but with any luck it will be open by the time you read this, and more appealing than it has been in recent times.

The **Iglesia de San Ginés** (Plaza de San Ginés; ⏲ vary), an attractive church consecrated to the island's patron saint, was built in 1665 and features a statue – which originated in Cuba – of said saint. The nearby **Charco de San Ginés** is an inland lake of sorts; the surrounding area of low-key cottages and bars is being gradually gentrified.

If you fancy a dip, **Playa del Reducto** is quite a respectable beach, a spit away from Calle Doctor Rafael González Negrín. It's not the sort of place you need to psyche yourself up for – more a sheltered city-side cove that's perfectly safe for children to swim in and reasonably clean.

Taking all this in while riding a bike may appeal, so head to **Ciclo Mania** (☎ 928 81 75 35; ciclomania@nexo.es; Calle Almirante Boado Endeiza 9; mountain bikes per day for 1-2 days/week €9/7; ⏲ 9.30am-1.30pm & 5-8pm Mon-Fri, 9.30am-1.30pm Sat), which rents out different types of bicycles, with helmets and puncture repair kits included in the price. The equipment is in good shape.

ARRECIFE FOR CHILDREN

Generally, it's the resorts on the island that cater to its younger visitors. Arrecife, as the 'hub' of business on Lanzarote, is not really geared towards kids. That said, you'll have no trouble requesting cots in mid-range hotels. Restaurants don't have children's portions, and high chairs are not the norm. Smoking makes it less of an option too.

FESTIVALS & EVENTS

During February/March, **Carnaval** is celebrated here, as in the rest of the Canary Islands, with gusto – if not in quite the same style as in Las Palmas de Gran Canaria and Santa Cruz de Tenerife.

The other major fiesta is **Día de San Ginés**, which is celebrated on 25 August. Día de San Ginés is the day of the island's patron saint, and is celebrated in even the smallest *pueblo* with about a week's worth of festivities (especially on the closest Friday night). In Arrecife, the streets surrounding the Iglesia de San Ginés are home to the most boisterous celebrations.

SLEEPING

Arrecife will rarely find itself as the first port of choice for Lanzarote's visitors, but if you've arrived on the island without any accommodation prebooked and can't find anything at the resorts, this may be what you're stuck with. As the island's capital, business travellers will often base themselves here, meaning that accommodation at weekends can be cheaper than during the week.

Budget

Hostal España (☎ /fax 928 81 11 90; Calle Gran Canaria 4; s/d with shared bathroom €12/17) The cheapest deal in town, if not the entire Canary Islands, is the very basic España, where spartan rooms are often full. If you don't like cigarette smoke, look elsewhere.

Pensión San Ginés (☎ 928 81 18 63, El Molino 9; s/d €16/22) Around the corner from Hostal España, this is an avowedly local establishment that's another very cheap choice. Plain but acceptable rooms with bathroom are tidy, and the management is helpful, even if you don't speak Spanish.

Mid-range

Hotel Miramar (☎ 928 80 15 22; www.hotel-residenciamiramar.com; Avenida Coll 2; s/d/tr €44/59/76; P X ☒ ☐) Waterfront Miramar has been renovated to within an inch of its life and is the swishest, funkiest and most colourful option in town. Its 85 rooms are very comfortable and show real imagination in the décor stakes – something that's in short supply in this part of the world! It's wheelchair-accessible too.

Hotel Lancelot (☎ 928 80 50 99; hlancelot@terra.es; Avenida Mancomunidad 9; s/d €56/71; P ☒ ☒) The next best choice in town, the Lancelot has views of the city's beach and is in a good central location. Rooms are perfectly comfortable and show signs of regular updating. You'll also find live music in the piano bar.

Apartamentos Islamar (☎ 928 81 15 04, Calle Doctor Rafael González Negrín 15; s/d €40/46) Has spacious rooms/apartments (in a very drab building) with kitchen, TV and balcony, although they only represent good value if you're travelling as part of a double. At the time of writing, there was a lot of construction over the road.

EATING

MIAC Restaurant (☎ 928 81 23 21; Castillo de San José; mains €11-43; ☒ 1-4pm & 8-11.30pm) Situated in the Castillo de San José, along with the art gallery (see p120), is Arrecife's greatest

gastronomic-cum-visual experience. Glide down the spiral staircase and order some wonderful meat and fish dishes in the grooviest possible setting. Looking out over the industrial port, the décor is the usual Manrique mix of airy and inventive, while the service is bow-tied and attentive.

During the day you won't feel the need to get dressed up, but at night you may want to. Sumptuous black leather bar stools are an attraction if you're short on time and only want a tipple.

Restaurant La Puntilla (☎ 928 81 36 13; El Charco de San Ginés; mains €7-14) This is a charming lakeside addition to Arrecife's eating options. Friendly, well-kitted-out and with moreish seafood dishes taking pride of place on the menu, it's the perfect spot for an alfresco lunch on a sunny day.

Mesón Asturiana (☎ 607 54 42 75; Calle José Antonio 98; mains €7-10) If you feel like a culinary excursion to northern Spain, the Asturian dishes here could be for you.

Flavoursome chicken dishes are the house speciality, and the friendly, bustling atmosphere (with lots of plates on the walls) makes it a welcome respite from some of Arrecife's dreary back streets. Credit cards are accepted here too.

Mesón La Tinaja (Calle Guenia 2; raciones €3-12; ☒ closed Sun night) This is a pleasant Basque eating house with partly tiled walls and some wonderful *raciones* (large tapas) on offer. Pop in on Sunday for lunch and settle in for some scrumptious paella (only on Sunday).

There's a smattering of breezy outdoor cafés and eateries on Calle Cr Ruperto González Negrín and Avenida Generalísimo Franco – our pick is **La Tavernetta** (cnr Avenida Generalísimo Franco & Calle Tresguerra), which has wonderful Italian-style pizza. For lovers of local self-catering, there's a small **covered market** (Calle Liebre; ☒ 9am-1pm Mon-Sat).

DRINKING & ENTERTAINMENT

Tamer than those in mainland Spain, but still worth investigating, are the half-dozen-or-so nightspots on Calle José Antonio. Check out **La Antigua** (Calle José Antonio 62) for live music, **La Calle Disco Pub** (Calle José Antonio 74), and its neighbour **El Convento** (Calle José Antonio 76) which kicks off at about midnight and features a range of dance music styles, including UK Garage and 2-Step.

LANZAROTE

GETTING THERE & AWAY
To/From the Airport
Lanzarote's airport is 6km south of Arrecife. Arrecife Bus No 4 services run between the airport and Arrecife (€0.90, 20 minutes) every 30 minutes or so between 7.10am and 10.40pm Monday to Friday (between 8.40am and 10.40pm on weekends). A taxi for the same ride will set you back about €7.

To/From the Port
The Arrecife–Costa Teguise bus calls in at the port. A taxi costs about €3.50.

Boat
The weekly **Trasmediterránea** (☎ 902 45 46 45; www.trasmediterranea.es) ferry to Cádiz (mainland Spain) stops at Arrecife on the way from Las Palmas de Gran Canaria. It leaves at 10pm on Saturday and arrives two days later.

Trasmediterránea also has ferries at noon on Wednesday and Friday to Las Palmas (€28.10, 10 hours).

Naviera Armas (☎ 928 51 79 12; www.naviera armas.com) has four ferries on Tuesday, Thursday, Saturday and Sunday to Las Palmas (€31.90, 7¼ hours). There is a weekly ferry between Arrecife and Puerto del Rosario (€14, 1½ hours)

Puerto de los Mármoles is about 4km northeast of central Arrecife. You can get tickets at the *estación marítima* (ferry terminal) or at the **Trasmediterránea/Naviera Armas office** (☎ 928 81 10 19; Calle José Antonio 90; ☾ 8.15am-1.30pm Mon-Fri, 8.15-10.45am Sat), or one hour before embarkation.

Bus
Arrecife Bus crisscrosses the island from the bus station on Vía Medular. Many westbound buses also stop at Playa del Reducto. Bus No 2 (€1.50, 40 minutes, about every 20 minutes) runs to Puerto del Carmen while Bus No 1 serves Costa Teguise (€1.10, 20 minutes, about every 20 minutes). Up to 12 buses daily (No 6) go to Playa Blanca (€3, 1½ hours) via Puerto del Carmen and up to seven go to Teguise (€0.90, 30 minutes) via Tahiche. Three buses on weekdays (two daily on weekends) head north for Orzola (€3, 1½ hours), from where you can get a boat out to the islet of Graciosa.

Car & Motorcycle
You will find plenty of rental companies – especially around Avenida Mancomunidad and Calle Doctor Rafael González.

GETTING AROUND
Bus
A couple of *guaguas municipales* (local buses) follow circuits around town, but you're unlikely to need them.

Taxi
There's a taxi rank beside the tourist information kiosk on Avenida Generalísimo Franco and another on Calle José Antonio. Otherwise call ☎ 928 80 31 04.

AROUND ARRECIFE

COSTA TEGUISE
Only 9km northeast of Arrecife is Costa Teguise, a low-rise resort (except for some large monstrosities at its northern limits), with a series of small but happy beaches. With a few exceptions, the holiday houses, apartments and bungalows are not in overly bad taste, but the place is, like most resorts of its ilk, utterly devoid of character. There's not even a fishing village at its core to create the impression that it's anything other than a big holiday camp.

The main and most pleasant beach is Playa de las Cucharas. Those further south enjoy unfortunate views of the ports and industry near Arrecife. The Centro Comercial Las Cucharas shopping centre is the resort's focal point.

Information
Clínica Lanzarote (☎ 928 59 02 21; Avenida Islas Canarias 13) A 24-hour medical service in the Apartamentos Lanzarote Gardens complex.
Post office (☎ 928 82 72 68; Avenida Islas Canarias 12; ☾ 8.30am-2.30pm Mon-Fri, 9.30am-1pm Sat) In the Centro Comercial Las Maretas.

Sights
The Friday **craft market** (Centro Pueblo Marinero; ☾ 6-10.30pm Fri) is worth a look.

Activities
DIVING
You can sign up at long-established **Calipso Diving** (☎ 928 59 08 79; www.calipso-diving.com;

Centro Comercial Calipso) for courses and dives (€25 for one dive), and it has equipment hire for experienced divers. Calipso can also organise your diving permit, compulsory on Lanzarote (€12).

WINDSURFING

To take advantage of the steady winds in the area, get in touch with **Windsurf Paradise Lanzarote** (☎ 928 34 60 22; www.windsurflanzarote .com; Calle La Corvina 8), on Playa Las Cucharas, where you can hire equipment and book windsurfing courses (beginners from €35 for 1½ hours).

CYCLING

For bicycle hire, call by **Hot Bike** (☎ 928 59 03 04; Avenida Islas Canarias s/n), which also rents scooters (from €20 per day) and motorbikes (from €40). **Tommy's Bikes** (☎ 928 59 23 27; Calle La Goleta s/n), at Playa Galeón (the eastern continuation of Playa de las Cucharas), rents cycles and can arrange tours of the island and surrounding area.

GOLF

If you need a golfing hit, **Golf Costa Teguise** (☎ 928 59 05 12; Avenida Golf s/n) has 18 holes (from €49.50), lessons and equipment hire.

WALKING

Olita Treks (☎ 928 59 21 48; www.olita-treks.com; Centro Comercial Mareta; walks from €30) conducts excellent local walks, which cover turf such as Isla Graciosa, the island's volcanoes or various coastal stretches. Walks are either half- or full-day, and the price includes collection from your accommodation and transport. Book in advance. English is spoken.

Costa Teguise for Children

Aquapark (☎ 928 59 21 28; adult/child €19/13; ☼ 10am-6pm), just beyond the town's western limit, has the usual assortment of watery rides and slides. It's very popular with kids. Mums and dads can hire sun loungers.

Sleeping & Eating

Hotel Meliá Salinas (☎ 928 59 00 00; Avenida Islas Canarias 16; s/d €365/445; ste €650-905; villa €1680-2400; P ⊗ ⊗ ⊒ ⊜) You may not choose to stay here, but do drift in for a drink and let your breath be taken away by the magnificent central atrium – all trees, flowers and pools – designed by César Manrique.

If you are staying here, you're in for a treat. Rooms are sumptuous without being glitzy and the villas are straight from heaven. Low season reductions are available.

There's no shortage of restaurants serving whatever sort of cuisine you may want – although Spanish seems to be hard to find!

Casa Blanca (☎ 928 59 01 55; Calle Olas 4; mains €6-14.50) Has an excellent islandwide reputation, especially for grills and rice dishes. A snazzy terrace attracts alfresco diners and there's also a good wine list.

Getting There & Away

Bus No 1 connects with Arrecife (via Los Mármoles port) on a very regular basis from 7am to midnight (€0.90).

TEGUISE

Teguise, 12km north of Arrecife, is quite a surprise, an unexpected little treasure-trove amid the bare plains of central Lanzarote. The island's capital until Arrecife took the baton in 1852, it has preserved a fistful of monuments testifying to its leading role on the island over the centuries.

Maciot, the son of Jean de Béthencourt, moved in to Acatife (which was a Guanche, or indigenous Canario, settlement) and ended up living with Teguise, daughter of the one-time local chieftain. Various convents were founded and the town prospered. But with prosperity came other problems: pirates of various nationalities descended on the place several times – the only reminder of these attacks today is the ominously named Calle de la Sangre (Blood Street).

Teguise has a large Sunday morning market, which, although rather touristy, is certainly worth a browse. You'll find lots of local products, including plenty of aloe vera–based skin-care products.

Sights

Sprawling **Palacio Spínola** (Plaza de la Constitución; admission €3; ☼ 9am-3pm Mon-Fri, 10am-3pm Sat & Sun) was built between 1730 and 1780 and passed to the Spínolas, a prominent Lanzarote family, in 1895. Nowadays it serves as both museum (of sorts) and official residence of the Canary Islands Government. The house deserves a leisurely inspection, although many of the furnishings are clearly not precious period pieces from some long-forgotten era.

LANZAROTE

Across the plaza is the eclectic **Iglesia de la Virgen de Guadalupe**, which has suffered numerous remodellings (leaving it in a rather confused state) since it was first built in the 16th century.

Several monasteries dot the town, and wandering Teguise's pedestrianised lanes is a pleasure in itself. Keep your eyes peeled for the Franciscan **Convento de Miraflores**, the **Convento de Santo Domingo** and the **Palacio de Herrera y Rojas**.

The **Castillo de Santa Bárbara** (☎ 928 84 50 01; admission €3; ☼ 10am-4pm daily summer, 10am-5pm Mon-Fri, 10am-4pm Sat & Sun winter) is not only the oldest fort in the islands, but about the only castle worthy of the name. Perched up on Guanapay peak, 1.5km east of Teguise, it was erected in the 16th century by Sancho de Herrera, expanded in later years and then allowed to fall into disuse. Since being restored, it houses the relatively modest but very interesting **Museo del Emigrante Canario**, a poignant collection relating to the long history of migration from the islands to Spain's American colonies.

The castle, which offers deliriously commanding views across the plains, is worth a visit for that reason alone.

Sleeping & Eating

Acatife (☎ 928 84 50 37; Calle San Miguel 4; mains €8-26) One of a few enticing places to eat in town. The interior is all deep, dark timber and whitewash, and meals are resoundingly down-to-earth and hearty (the rabbit in red wine is a good choice), as befits the surroundings. Find it just off the town's main plaza.

El Ryad (☎ 928 84 59 31; Casa Leon, Calle Leon y Castillo s/n; mains €10-11.50; ☼ closed Mon) For a change of culinary pace, the excellent Moroccan cuisine of El Ryad might break up the Canarian diet. Dishes based on mutton and lamb feature on the menu, but it was a sublime aubergine salad that had us wishing the Canary Islands were in Moroccan hands.

Getting There & Away

Numerous buses (Nos 7 and 9) from Arrecife stop in Teguise en route to destinations such as Orzola and Haría. There are also buses, on Sunday only, which can take you to the town's market from Costa Teguise, Puerto del Carmen and Playa Blanca.

SAN BARTOLOMÉ & AROUND

Starting life as the Guanche settlement of Ajei, San Bartolomé ended up in the 18th century as the de facto private fiefdom of a militia leader, Francisco Guerra Clavijo y Perdomo, and his descendants.

A couple of kilometres northwest of town on the Tinajo road (just before the town of Mozaga), rises up the weird, white **Monumento al Campesino** (Peasants' Monument), erected in 1968 by (surprise, surprise) César Manrique to honour the unending and thankless labour that most of the islanders had endured for generations. Adjacent to that is what is called the **Museo del Campesino** (☎ 928 52 01 36; admission free; ☼ 10am to 6pm), but it's hardly a museum, rather more a scattering of craft workshops that may or may not be functioning. Most people come here to eat – ironically, at a monument dedicated to those who so often endured hunger – at the **restaurant** (☎ 928 52 01 36; mains €5-11; ☼ 12.30-4pm).

The museum's restaurant is a circular sunken architecturally-exciting affair, with a good wine and rum list and well-priced, well-prepared local cuisine, accompanied by Canarian music.

Three kilometres southwest of the aforementioned monument, along the road to pretty Yaiza and well worth a visit, is **El Grifo Museo del Vino** (☎ 928 52 40 36; www.elgrifo.com in Spanish; admission free; ☼ 10.30am-7pm Mon-Fri, 11.30am-7pm Sat & Sun).

This is a former bodega (old-style wine bar) and winery of the El Grifo company, where you can see wine-making equipment, some dating back 200 years, buy all sorts of wine-drinking requisites and indulge in a little wine tasting (€0.90 to €1.10 for a half-filled glass). We'd recommend grabbing a seat and scoffing and quaffing through the five different wines and local cheese on offer (€7.50), as long as you're not driving.

In San Bartolomé itself, the **Museo Etnográfico Tanit** (☎ 928 52 23 34; www.museotanit.com; Calle Constitución 1; admission €6; ☼ 10am-5pm Mon-Fri, 10am-3pm Sat) makes use of an 18th-century Canarian house while concentrating on the last 200 years of local life, with artefacts, equipment and exhibitions. English explanations are available – just ask for the booklet.

THE NORTH

Many of Lanzarote's northern towns and villages are pretty enough in themselves. But the principal attractions are the combined work of nature and César Manrique – his house (now a gallery), a pair of breathtaking lava caves, cactus gardens and a stunning lookout point. Stash your pockets with cash since admission to the majority costs a hefty €6.50 each. If you prefer to limit the financial damage, we recommend as a minimum Taro de Tahiche, where Manrique lived, and the Jameos del Agua cave.

TAHICHE

Fundación César Manrique (☎ 928 84 31 38; adult/child €6.50/free; ☼ 10am-7pm daily 1 Jul-31 Oct, 10am-6pm Mon-Sat, 10am-3pm Sun 1 Nov-30 Jun) is an art gallery and a centre for the island's cultural life – a visit here is an absolute must. Only 6km north of Arrecife, it was home to César Manrique who, on the island, enjoys a posthumous status akin to a mystical hero's. He built his home, Taro de Tahiche, into the lava fields just outside the town. The subterranean rooms are, in fact, huge air bubbles left behind by flowing lava. Nowadays, there's a whole gallery devoted to Manrique, plus minor works by some

---

SEEING RED

Higgledy-piggledy cactuses, their leaves green, fleshy and the shape of giant rabbits' ears, are about all that grows around the small village of Guatiza. And grow they do, in profusion, hemming in the *pueblo*. They're a last reminder of what was once a thriving trade on Tenerife and the eastern islands.

Much more than a harsh desert plant, they're home and food to *la cochinilla* (cochineal insects). To this day, these tiny insects are collected in the tens of thousands. Each one contributes a blood red droplet of the dye, cochineal, used as a colouring in food and cosmetics.

Elsewhere, the once-thriving cochineal trade has long since withered, killed off by competition from synthetic dyes. But in Guatiza a centuries-old cottage industry still just manages to persist.

---

of his contemporaries including Picasso, Chillida, Miró, Sempere and Tàpies.

At least seven buses daily stop here on their way from Arrecife to Teguise and beyond. Get off at the Cruce Manrique (Manrique Intersection) – you can't miss it, with the huge mobile sculpture by Manrique himself dominating the roundabout – and walk 200m down the San Bartolomé road.

GUATIZA

Just north of Guatiza, a small, quiet village 9km north of Tahiche, is the **Jardín de los Cactus** (☎ 928 529 397; admission €3; menú del día €10.50; ☼ 10am-5.45pm), signalled by an 8m-high spiky metal cactus, the work of – you've guessed it – César Manrique. Although it comes over as more a giant work of art than a botanical garden, it has nearly 1500 different varieties of this prickly customer, every single one labelled. A good-value restaurant operates on the premises too.

ARRIETA

Next northwards is the fishing village of Arrieta, its only attraction the modest but blue-flagged (and therefore safe and clean) **Playa de la Garita**. The village itself is a quiet, unassuming little redoubt, and you can stay in one of a few little *pensiones* (guesthouses) and apartments, which are advertised via small signs in windows.

You'll find three-storey **Apartamentos Arrieta** (☎ 928 84 82 30; Calle Garita 25; apt €30) on the main street. It's a well-maintained, plant-filled place, with good apartments that sleep two people. To see if there's a vacancy, call the owner, Rafael González Castro.

Smack-bang on Arrieta's jetty is **Restaurante El Charcón** (☎ 928 84 81 10; Muelle Arrieta; mains €6-10; ☼ noon-9pm Mon-Tue & Thu-Sat, noon-8pm Sun, closed Wed), with views of a red-and-blue house (not to mention the sea) that is easily the town's most interesting. It does mighty fine seafood dishes right through the day, and has outdoor seating if you want to take advantage of the sun.

Bus No 9 from Arrecife to Orzola, which only runs thrice daily (twice daily on weekends), calls in here.

MALPAÍS DE LA CORONA

The 'badlands of the crown' are the living (or dead) testimony to the volcanic upsurges that shook the north of the island thousands of years ago. Plant life is quietly, patiently, winning its way back, and it is here that you can visit two of the island's better-known volcanic caverns.

Cueva de los Verdes & Jameos del Agua

More obviously than on any of the other islands, lava is the hallmark of Lanzarote. So it should come as little surprise that, after the lunar wonders of the Parque Nacional de Timanfaya (p129), the flow of visitors should be strongest here, at the site of an ancient lava slide into the ocean. The cavernous **Cueva de los Verdes** and, further 'downstream', the hollows of the **Jameos del Agua** (adapted by César Manrique into a kind of New Age retreat-cum-bar) are a 1km easy walk from one another.

Cueva de los Verdes (☎ 928 17 32 20; admission €6.60; ☽ 10am-5pm) is a yawning, 1km-long chasm, which is the most spectacular segment of an almost 8km lava tube left behind by an eruption that occurred 5000 years ago. As the lava ploughed down towards the sea (a little more than 6km of tunnel is above sea level today, and another 1.5km extends below the water's surface), the top layers cooled and formed a roof, beneath which the liquid magma continued to slither until the eruption exhausted itself.

You will be guided through two chambers, one below the other. The ceiling is largely covered with what look like mini stalactites, but no water penetrates the cave. (Stalactites are formed by precipitation from continually dripping water.) The odd pointy extrusions are where bubbles of air and lava were thrown up onto the ceiling by gases released while the boiling lava flowed; as they hit the ceiling and air, they 'froze' in the process of dripping back into the lava stream.

In spite of the name 'verde', there's nothing green about this cave – some 200 years ago it was considered the property of a shepherd family, the Verdes! At other times, it served as a refuge for locals during pirate assaults on the island. All sorts of evidence of their presence, from bones to tools and ceramics, are displayed in Arrecife's underendowed Museo Arqueológico (p120).

Anyone with severe back problems might think twice about entering the cave – there are a few passages that require you to bend at 90° to get through. Similarly, it's no place for those who tend towards claustrophobia.

The visit is worthwhile in itself for a great visual gag deep inside the cave. No, we're not telling – and urge you in your turn to keep it quiet from your friends. Guided tours, lasting about 45 minutes and available in English, take place when there are 50 people waiting – and it usually doesn't take long for that to happen.

The first cavern of the **Jameos del Agua** (☎ 928 84 80 20; admission €6.60; ☽ 10am-6.30pm; bar/restaurant, 7pm-2am Tue, Fri & Sat) resembles the nave of a vast marine basilica. Molten lava seethed through here on its way to the sea, but in this case the ocean leaked in a bit, forming the startling azure lake at the heart of the Jameos. Manrique's idea of installing bars and a restaurant around the lake, adding a pool, a concert hall seating 600 (with

---

GETTING YOUR GOAT...

Until the 1960s and the advent of mass tourism, almost all the people of Lanzarote were engaged in agriculture or livestock rearing. Goats were their most versatile resource. Tougher than sheep, goats are able to survive in a more desiccated environment and can chew on spiny, hostile plants that a sheep would look at with disdain.

Alive, they provided milk, which was either mixed with *gofio* (a roasted mixture of wheat, maize or barley), drunk fresh or transformed into cheese. Once slaughtered, they were a source of meat, both fresh and as *tocineta*, which is dried and long-lasting, like jerky. Their fat, where not used for food, would be rendered down into tallow for lighting and was the basic ingredient of a number of folk remedies. Their skins were used as rugs, for making clothing – and as a marketable currency when it came to bartering. Their yarn was spun, like sheep's wool, into blankets, jackets, socks and bags.

In the 1970s, some 14,000 goats grazed the arid hills and valleys of Lanzarote. By the early 1990s, numbers had plummeted to a mere 3000 and were continuing to fall. Now, at the beginning of a new century, they're on the increase again.

wonderful acoustics) and the subtly didactic Casa de los Volcanes, was a pure brainwave. The look of the place – classic 1960s meets space age – will have you wondering why it hasn't been used as a location for a James Bond film. It would make a fantastic villain's lair!

Have a closer look into the lake's waters. The tiny white flecks at the bottom are crabs. Small ones, yes, and the only known examples of Munidopsis polymorpha (blind crabs) away from the deepest oceans. Do take notice of the signs and resist the temptation to throw coins into the water – their corrosion could kill off this unique species. Like the Cueva, access for the mobility impaired is not really possible – there are a lot of steps.

The very infrequent bus No 9 between Arrecife and Orzola stops at the turn-off for Jameos del Agua. The Cueva de los Verdes is a further (and easy) 1km walk inland. The bus timetable does not help matters, with a lot of waiting around required if you plan to use public transport. Better to have your own car or join a tour.

Orzola

Most people just pass through this northern fishing town on their way to the Isla Graciosa. Some stop for a food break in one of several restaurants flanking the port, where you can be sure that the seafood is flapping-fresh, but relatively few get wind of the **beach** a couple of kilometres west of the town – about the only one in this part of the island, which is otherwise dominated by steep, uncompromising cliffs.

MINOR CANARIES

The string of tiny islets flung out north of Lanzarote are known as the Minor Canaries, and minor they certainly are. All, except Isla Graciosa (aka La Graciosa), are part of a nature reserve, with access generally limited to researchers.

Isla Graciosa

Isla Graciosa makes for a relaxing and interesting day trip; anything longer is strictly for the keenest surfers (and the surfing here is world-class) or for those who enjoy diverging from the beaten track for its own sake.

About 620 souls live on the island, virtually all in the village of Caleta del Sebo,

where the Orzola boat docks. Behind it stretches 27.5 sq km of largely barren scrub land, interrupted by five minor volcanic peaks ranged from north to south. About a 30-minute walk southwest of Caleta del Sebo is a delightful little beach, and there's another at the northern end of the islet.

On a windy day, Caleta del Sebo can seem a cross between a bare Moroccan village and a sand-swept Wild West outpost. This place is worlds away from the tourist mainstream; the main form of transport seems to be battered old Land Rovers, and the tourist infrastructure is minimal.

There's a smattering of places to stay. **Pensión Girasol Playa** (☎ 928 84 21 18; www .graciosaonline.com in Spanish; Avenida Virgen del Mar s/n; d €15-18), about 100m left along the waterfront from where the boat docks, has basic but welcoming guest quarters upstairs with or without balcony. You'll find a breezy, casual restaurant downstairs, where good fish dishes are served (mains €7 to €9.50). Try the fresh grilled parrot fish – it's fantastic. Accommodation in nearby apartments (€36) can also be arranged.

Pensión Enriqueta (☎ 928 84 20 51; fax 928 84 21 29; Calle Mar de Barlovento 6; d €15-18) is a few blocks in from the port. It has simple, spotless doubles, with or without a bathroom, and a reasonably priced restaurant with local standards.

You may also notice that signs offering accommodation are posted up in windows throughout town. Generally, you'll get a smart little apartment for about €36 to €42 per night, sleeping up to four people.

And if too much peace and quiet has got you in a spin, you can party hard (or as close to such a thing as the island allows) at **Las Arenas** (Calle Mar de Barlovento s/n; ☯ from 12.30am Fri & Sat), a disco pub at the back of the Enriqueta that only opens for two nights of the week. Better make it count then.

Líneas Marítimas Romero (☎ 928 84 20 70; Calle García Escámez 11) runs three (four between July and September) boats daily from Orzola in the north of Lanzarote across to the islet. Tickets cost adult/child €13/6.50 return and the trip takes 20 minutes. It can get very rocky between Orzola and Punta Fariones, so you may want to pop a seasickness pill. Unless you want to be Robinson Crusoed for the night, take the outbound 10am or noon sailing, which allows time to explore before taking the last boat back at 4pm (6pm in summer).

To get around the island, it's a good idea to hire a bike. Pension Girasol Playa can help, with OK mountain bikes on offer for €6/30 per day/week, and a rudimentary map to help you find those far-off beaches.

THE NORTHWEST

In many respects, the island's northwest offers visitors the most rewards, although those seeking all-included resort-style holidays won't find much on offer. It's a place of attractive towns that still retain a local feel, some great escapes and the odd startling panorama.

MIRADOR DEL RÍO

About 2km north of Yé, the Spanish armed forces set up gun batteries at the end of the 19th century at a strategic site overlooking El Río, the straits separating Lanzarote from Isla Graciosa. Spain had gone to war with the USA over control of Cuba, and you couldn't be too careful! In 1973 the ubiquitous César Manrique left his mark, converting the gun emplacement into a spectacular lookout point.

Mirador del Río (☎ 928 17 35 36; admission €2.70; ☽ 10am-5.45pm) now has a good bar and souvenir shop. Let your heart race at the nearly 500m sheer drop and the spectacular view of Isla Graciosa, stretched taut like a leopard skin far below.

GUINATE

The main reason for visiting the village of Guinate, about 5km south of Mirador del Río, is the **Tropical Park** (adult/child €10/4; ☽ 10am-5pm), home to some 1300 rare and exotic birds that you'll certainly hear before you see. Many of them are truly beautiful, but the bird show – parrots on scooters and so on – is silly and demeaning.

Just beyond the park is another fine (and completely free) **lookout** overlooking El Río and the islets.

HARÍA

Shady Plaza León y Castillo, the centre of this village, makes a perfectly suitable resting spot and, if the time is right, a lunch or midafternoon drink stop. Haría has a good handicraft market on Saturday, which takes place between 10am and 2pm at Plaza León y Castillo.

César Manrique moved into a farmhouse outside Haría after his house, Taro de Tahiche (p125), had become untenable because of all the visitors who liked to drop by to see how he was getting on.

Restaurante Casa Kura (☎ 928 83 55 56; Calle Nueva 1; mains €7.50-12) is a vast restaurant (with plenty of windows) firmly entrenched on the tour-bus itineraries, and it can hold a cast of thousands. Despite this, you'll find a good selection of local wines and some tasty local fare – ignore the buffet table and opt for kid or rabbit fried with garlic.

If it's local atmosphere you seek, head into **Bar Ney-ya** (cnr Calle Cilla & Calle Hoya), in an old-fashioned building with high ceilings, some dark corners and an interesting selection of music.

Bus No 7 connects Haría to Arrecife via Teguise and Tahiche four times daily Monday to Friday and three times daily on weekends.

LA CALETA DE FAMARA

As a young boy, before he hit the big time, Manrique whiled away many a childhood summer on the wild beach of La Caleta de Famara. The low-key seaside hamlet of Famara doesn't seem to have changed much in many years and makes few concessions to the average tourist, apart from a couple of restaurants and the odd business devoted to surfing. It's an easy-going place, and one of the best spots to be close to a great beach without fighting for space with package-tour hordes.

Discriminating surfers, however, feel the call of Famara's excellent waves, which offer some of Europe's finest breaks. Pedro Urrastarazu at **Famara Surf** (☎ 928 52 86 76; www.famarasurf.com; Avenida Marinero 39; surf school €39; ☽ 10am-12.30pm & 1-3pm, shop 10am-8pm) rents boards (and the odd bicycle for €10 per day) and offers courses at various levels. Pedro can organise accommodation with **Apartments Famara Surf Shop** (☎ 928 52 86 76; www.famarasurf.com; Avenida Marinero 39; apt €42) in clean, well-equipped apartments with TV and fridge, whether you're there to surf or sunbathe.

Playa Famara Bungalows (☎ 928 84 51 32; www.famara.org; Urbanización Famara; bungalows €55-84;

♻ 9am-1pm & 4-7.30pm Mon-Fri, 9am-noon & 5-7pm Sat, 10am-noon & 5-7pm Sun) is 2km north of the main town, and is a smart-looking step-terraced arrangement of semi-circular holiday homes constructed with rocks and lots of white cement. It will have you thinking you're staying with Manrique himself. Bungalows sleep between two and six, and longer stays (or low season) will get you good discounts.

El Risco (☎ 928 52 85 50; Calle Montaña Blanca 30; mains €6-11.50; ♻ closed Mon) is a cheery seaside eating spot with a fishing-themed Manrique original on the walls and some very good seafood dishes on the menu. On weekends, local specialities such as rabbit dishes can be ordered. Nearby **Restaurante Bajamar** (Calle Arrufo 3; mains €6-13; ♻ closed Wed) has some of the best *langostinos a la plancha* (grilled king prawns) we've ever had, and is an airy, plant-filled and very pleasant environment. It's a popular spot for family lunches and intimate dinners.

Getting There & Away

Bus No 20 (three per day) connects Arrecife with La Caleta de Famara, Monday to Friday only. It leaves La Caleta de Famara at 7.30am, 9am and 5.30pm and sets off from the capital at 7am, 8.30am, 2pm and 5pm.

TIAGUA

About 10km south of La Caleta and 8km northwest of San Bartolomé, the ecologically aware open-air **Museo Agricola El Patio** (☎ 928 52 91 34; www.museoelpatio.com; admission €5; ♻ 10am-5.30pm Mon-Fri, 10am-2.30pm Sat) in Tiagua recreates traditional agricultural life and gives a good insight into traditional aspects of the island's culture. Signage – including some irritatingly edifying texts – is in English. You'll see loads of old equipment and furniture, a windmill, and the odd camel or donkey mooching about.

Tiagua is on the bus No 16 route from Arrecife to Tinajo. Bus No 20 to La Caleta de Famara also calls in here.

PARQUE NACIONAL DE TIMANFAYA

The eruption that began on 1 September 1730 and convulsed the southern end of the island was among the greatest volcanic cataclysms in recorded history. A staggering 48 cubic million metres of lava spurted and flowed out daily, while fusillades of molten rock were angrily rocketed out over the countryside and into the ocean. When the eruption finally ceased to rage after six long years, over 200 sq km had been devastated.

The **Montañas del Fuego** (Mountains of Fire), at the heart of this eerie 51-sq-km **national park** (☎ 928 84 00 56; admission €6.60; ♻ 9am-5.45pm, last bus tour ♻ 5pm), are appropriately named. When you reach the Manrique-designed lookout and Restaurante del Diablo (note his wonderful light fittings in the form of giant frying pans) at a rise known as the Islote de Hilario, try scrabbling around in the pebbles and see just how long you can hold them in your hands. At a depth of a few centimetres, the temperature is already 100°C; by 10m, it's up to 600°C. The cause of this phenomenon is a broiling magma chamber some 4km below the surface.

Some feeble (or rather, given the harsh environment, decidedly robust) scraps of vegetation, including 200 species of lichen, are reclaiming the earth in a few stretches of an otherwise moribund landscape of fantastic forms and shades of black, grey, maroon and red. Fine, copper-hued soil slithers down volcano cones, until it's arrested by twisted, swirling and folded mounds of solidified lava – this is one place where you really must remember to bring your camera.

The people running the show at Islote de Hilario, near the restaurant, gift shop and car park, have a series of endearing tricks. In one, they shove a clump of brushwood into a hole in the ground and within seconds it's converted by the subterranean furnace into a burning bush. A pot of water poured down another hole promptly gushes back up in explosive geyser fashion.

And the **Restaurant del Diablo** (☎ 928 84 00 56; mains €7.50-11.50; ♻ noon-3.30pm; P) is, of course, a gag in itself – whatever meat you order you can watch sizzling on the all-natural, volcano-powered BBQ out the back. The food's none too impressive but, hey, who's here for the cuisine? Vegetarians might feel a bit left out, what with all the smoking rabbit, T-bones and chicken around them. In the midst of all this carnivorous activity, there's a good list of local wines, some available by the half-bottle.

Tan-coloured buses take you along the exciting 14km **Ruta de los Volcanes**, an excursion through some of the most spectacular

LANZAROTE

FIRE WALKS

It is possible to walk within the park – but you'll need to plan in advance and you'll be part of a *very* select group. The 3.5km two-hour Tremesana guided walk (Spanish and English) leaves from the **Mancha Blanca visitor centre** (☎ 928 84 08 39; Carretera de Yaiza a Tinajo Km11.5; ☼ 9am-5pm) at 10am on Monday, Wednesday and Friday. Reserve a spot by phone or in person – at the time of research, you needed to reserve at least three weeks in advance if you wanted to walk in the summer high season! Try calling a day or two before and see if there's been a cancellation. The much more demanding Ruta del Litoral (9km, six hours) takes place once a month (no fixed date either) and you need to reserve in person and be judged fit enough to handle the pace and the terrain. Both walks are free.

volcanic country you are ever likely to see. The trilingual taped commentary can be a bit painful at times, but it is very informative. More frustrating, however, is the fact that you can't get out to simply experience the awesome silence and majesty of this stony waste.

Buses leave every hour or so and the trip takes about 40 minutes. By about 10am there can be long queues to get into the park, so you may find yourself waiting for a tour.

You can only get into the park under your own steam or on a tour bus – which you can organise through most travel agents and larger hotels.

North of the park on the same road is the much more informative **Mancha Blanca Visitor Centre** (☎ 928 84 08 39; Carretera de Yaiza a Tinajo; ☼ 9am-5pm).

INLAND & WEST COAST

The inland area and west coast of Lanzarote are within easy reach of popular tourist haunts to the south, but can seem a world away in terms of crowds, infrastructure and activities. That said, the food and wine on offer in this part of the world are reason enough to come.

LA GERIA

Nearby San Bartolomé (p124), the LZ-30 proceeds the southwest through what has to be one of the oddest-looking wine-growing regions around. The wine growers of Lanzarote have found the deep, black lava-soil, enriched by the island's shaky seismic history, perfect for the grape. The further south you go, the more common are these unique vineyards consisting of little

dugouts nurtured behind crescent-shaped stone walls, known as *zocos*, implanted in the dark earth.

The *malvasía* (Malmsey wine) produced here is a good drop and along the road you pass a good half-dozen bodegas (old-style wine bars) where you can buy the local produce at wholesale prices.

Try **Bodega La Geria** (☎ 928 17 31 78; www.lageria.com) where you can pick up bottles of dry or semi-*dulce* (sweet) *malvasía* (among others) for around €5. There's also a good little bar/café but a fairly crap gift shop attached.

One stunning little place that you may stumble upon is the boutique *finca* (farm)/ bodega **El Chupadero** (☎ 659 59 61 78; www.el-chupadero.com in German; tapas €4-8.50), which lies 4km north of Uga on the LZ-30. Great tapas can be washed down with lovely local wines from the surrounding vineyards, and the charming whitewashed décor, with beamed ceilings and black-and-white photos, is one of the most stylish in these parts.

YAIZA

Yaiza is something of a southern crossroads, so you'll probably pass through on your travels. There's no specific reason for hanging about, but if you arrive at lunch time and are feeling peckish, you'll be able to find a few pleasant-enough eateries, including one excellent restaurant (you'll need to book ahead).

It's a well-maintained town, the recipient of numerous awards for cleanliness, with a well-heeled feel. For sights, try the local church, **Nuestra Señora de los Remedios**, which was built in the 18th century and features a lovely blue, white and gold painted altarpiece and a prettily painted wooden ceiling that incorporates folkloric details.

Sleeping & Eating

Finca de las Salinas (☎ 928 83 03 25; www.finca salinas.com; Calle La Cuesta s/n; s/d €142/218, ste €266-328; P ✗ ☒) This extraordinarily beautiful 18th-century establishment is definitely worth staying in Yaiza for. Architecturally, it's like something from a film set, with Gothic and Moorish touches outside and stunningly appointed rooms inside and in the converted stables. Low season prices offer generous reductions of more than €50. Book ahead.

La Era (☎ 928 83 00 16; www.la-era.com in Spanish; Calle El Barranco 3; mains €9-15; ☺ 1pm-11pm Tue-Sun) You may as well go all out with dining too, so head here. Reservations are essential at this highly regarded restaurant, which is the best on the island. Wonderful local dishes like marinated (with local wine) pork with herbs or deboned rabbit with dates (and its own liver) compete with the traditional farmhouse décor, the pretty courtyard and the excellent wine list for your praise.

EL GOLFO & AROUND

The tour buses have just started venturing to this once-forgotten fishing village, which can still make a pleasant alternative retreat for those uninterested in the hurly burly of the international beach set.

Just south of the settlement begins a string of small black-sand (or lava, if you prefer) beaches. The one fronting the **Charco de los Clicos** is popular with sightseers. The Charco itself is a small emerald-green pond, just in from the beach and overshadowed by a rocky cliff. It is not safe to swim here though, as it can get very rough.

On the way along the coast road, which eventually leads to La Hoya, stop by **Los Hervideros**, a pair of caves through which the sea glugs and froths. After about 6km you reach the long Playa de Janubio, behind which are **Las Salinas de Janubio**, salt pans from where sea salt is extracted.

There is just one place to stay in El Golfo and it's the very charming **Hotelito del Golfo** (☎ /fax 928 17 32 72; Avenida Marítima 4; d €55; ☒), which has nine fully equipped doubles, a good restaurant and even a small swimming pool at your disposal.

You will find no shortage of eating options beyond the hotel, which is just at the entrance to the hamlet. On the waterfront, plenty of eateries compete for your attention: the **Casa Torano** (☎ 928 17 30 58; Avenida Marítima), **Lago Verde** (☎ 928 17 33 11; Avenida Marítima 46) – where you can also inquire about renting an apartment – and **Mar Azul** (☎ 928 17 31 32; Calle Mayor 42).

THE SOUTH

The island's south is home to the best resorts on offer here and attracts family groups after an easy-going, sunny time punctuated with a deep-sea fishing excursion or a night on the tiles.

PUERTO DEL CARMEN

With sunshades four lanes deep, it's the island's most popular beach. Walk the esplanade along Avenida Playas and you'll soon get a feel for the place from the signs: Ye Olde Spanish Inn, Best in British Home Cooking, Live Football…

Orientation

Lanzarote's premier resort straggles for 6km beside mostly golden sand. It's main street is the bustling Avenida Playas, which runs alongside its beach.

Information
BOOKSHOPS
Bookswop (Calle Timanfaya 4; ☺ 9.30am-6pm Mon-Fri, 9.30am-1.30pm Sat) The best source of English-language reading on the island.

EMERGENCY
Policia Local (☎ 928 84 52 52; Avenida Juan Carlos I) Directly behind the post office.

INTERNET ACCESS
Networx Xpress (☎ 928 51 52 54; Centro Comercial Marítimo; per hour €2)

MEDICAL SERVICES
Clínica Lanarote (☎ 928 51 31 71; Avenida Playas 5) A well-staffed 24-hour medical centre.

MONEY
Finding a bank in this busy resort town is no problem – the place is swarming with ATMs and exchange offices.

POST
Post office (☎ 928 51 03 81; Avenida Juan Carlos I s/n; ☺ 8.30am-2.30pm Mon-Fri, 9.30am-1pm Sat) Beside the

LANZAROTE

roundabout at the junction of Avenida Juan Carlos I and Calle Guardilama in the western part of town.

TOURIST OFFICES
Tourist office (☎ 928 51 53 37; Avenida Playas s/n; ☺ 9am-1pm & 4.30-7.30pm Mon-Fri, 9am-1pm Sat) Halfway along Playa Grande.

Activities

The main activity seems to be flaking out on the beach for its own sake or to recover from a heavy night, but there's no lack of opportunity for something less supine. Bizarrely for a large resort with such reliable wind, no-one in Puerto del Carmen seems to hire windsurfing gear or offer lessons, although you'll be able to find such things as jet ski, banana and paracraft operators.

CYCLING
For bicycle hire, contact **Renner Bikes** (☎ 629 99 07 55; Centro Comercial Marítimo).

DIVING
Among several enterprises, tried and trusted operators are **Safari Diving** (☎ 928 51 19 92; www .safaridiving.nl; Playa de la Barrilla 4), **M A Diving** (☎ 928 51 69 15; Calle Juan Carlos I 35); and **Manta Dive Centre** (☎ 928 51 68 15; www.manta-divinglanzarote.com; Calle Juan Carlos I 6).

HORSE RIDING
One- to five-hour horseback safaris are available from **Lanzarote a Caballo** (☎ 928 83 03 14; www.alturin.com; Carretera Arrecife-Yaiza; rides €25-60) for young and old alike. It's a great way to see the landscape, and hotel pick up is available.

Sleeping

At last count there were around 200 hotels, apartment blocks and bungalow complexes in Puerto del Carmen. Many deal only with tour operators but may oblige the independent blow-in – if they have a room available.

Pensión Magec (☎ /fax 928 51 38 74, Calle Hierro 11; s/d €18/27) There's just one standard *pensión* in Puerto del Carmen and it's a good one. The 14-room Magec has decent rooms with washbasin and a good track record as the cheapest place to stay in this region.

Apartamentos Isla de la Graciosa Lanzarote (☎ 928 51 33 86; Calle Reina Sofía 20; apt €51-60) These two-key apartments are located in what's known as the 'Old Town' of Puerto

del Carmen and have 16 spots that can sleep up to four people. It's kept spotlessly clean and has a 24-hour reception.

Hotel Los Fariones (☎ 928 51 01 75; www.grupofariones.com; Calle Roque del Este 1; s/d €89/134; **P** ⊠ ⊠) For a touch of luxury close to the old nucleus of town and the main happening scene along Avenida Playas, yet with the beach at your feet, indulge yourself at this four-star hotel – which has all the amenities you need and even a few you probably don't.

Eating

Among all the sauerkraut, fish and chips and other delights on offer along the Avenida Playas pleasure zone, you'll *occasionally* stumble across a place offering some local cuisine.

Restaurante La Cañada (☎ 928 51 04 15; Calle César Manrique 3; mains €7.50-24; ☺ closed Sun) Just off the Avenida Playas, this restaurant is one such rarity. You'll find lovingly prepared Canarian specialities, delightful oysters (from €3.30 each) and easy-on-the-eye décor.

For a cluster of worthwhile restaurants serving essentially Spanish cuisine, take a walk to the old port.

Puerte Viejo Grill Restaurante (☎ 928 51 52 65; Avenida Varadero s/n; mains €7.50-19) Has an attractive terrace and some breezy sea views to accompany the excellent seafood dishes. If it's meat that you're hankering for, the steaks deserve attention with a big knife.

El Asador (☎ 928 51 28 21; Avenida Varadero s/n; mains €6-18; ☺ 5-11.30pm) If you fancy mainland cuisine that will have you stretching your belt, this restaurant doles out meat dishes for appreciative diners. The décor is very traditional – a little incongruous in this flashy seaside resort, but a nice change.

Drinking & Entertainment

The bulk of the bars, discos and nightclubs in Puerto del Carmen are lined up along the waterfront Avenida Playas. If you're after maximum-density partying, try the Centro Comercial Atlántico, where you'll find such bars/disco pubs as Waikiki, Paradise or Dreams.

César's (Avenida Playas 14; www.cesars.net; ☺ 10pm-6am) A very popular nightclub that attracts a breezy, hedonistic young crowd who appreciate populist DJs, flashing lights and lots of shooters amid a faux-Roman décor.

DETOUR

If you're heading from Playa Blanca or the Papagayo beaches to any of the island's eastern resorts, take the LZ-712, a narrow winding road that will take you to new heights and a charming little town called Femés. There's little to do apart from drink in the heavenly views of the surrounding mountains and the ocean – and then drink a cold *cerveza* at the one of the town's little bars.

Biosfera Plaza (☎ 928 51 53 68; Avenida Juan Carlos I 15) This swanky, strikingly modern shopping centre also holds a few good bars and pubs, with blessed air conditioning. They open from 10am to 2am for the most part.

Cerveceria San Miguel (☎ 928 51 52 65; Avenida Varadero s/n; ☷ 10.30am-3am) A very nice spot for a cold beer, with outdoor tables, umbrellas for shade and an easy-going, cheery vibe from staff and patrons alike.

Getting There & Around

Buses run the length of Avenida Playas with frequent stops, heading for Arrecife (€1.60) about every 20 minutes from 7am to midnight.

A free **Fred Olsen** (☎ 901 10 01 07; www.fredolsen.es) bus leaves from the Varadero (the port jetty) in Puerto del Carmen at 9am and 5pm, linking with the ferry, which runs from Playa Blanca to Corralejo (Fuerteventura; one way €14.20, 35–45 minutes). In the reverse direction, free buses for Puerto del Carmen meet the 9am and 5pm ferries from Corralejo on their arrival in Playa Blanca. The morning run continues to Lanzarote's airport.

PUERTO CALERO

A few kilometres west of Puerto del Carmen and its complete antithesis, Puerto Calero is a pleasant, relatively tranquil yacht harbour with a few cafés and restaurants and a jaunty maritime vibe that sees plenty of locals in deck shoes.

Activities
SUBMARINE

The yellow sub of **Submarine Safaris** (☎ 928 51 28 98; www.submarinesafaris.com; adult/child €46/26.50) makes four one-hour dives daily, at 10am,

noon, 2pm and 4pm, reaching a depth of 27m. The less expensive (but not as good) **Aquascope** (☎ 928 51 44 81; www.lanzarote.com /aquascope; adult/child €11/free) has tours every day between 10am and 5pm, when this unusual-looking vessel makes a 40-minute trip under the sea.

DEEP-SEA FISHING

Skippered by the well-regarded Tino García, **Mizu I** (☎ 636 47 40 00, fax 928 51 43 78; fisherman/companion €60/30) will transport you to the nearby depths as you search for mako sharks and other big fish. They'll pick you up from your hotel and take you to Puerto Calero, and all equipment is included in the price.

PLAYA BLANCA

Not a bad little sweep of sand and a resort that's not yet out of control, despite the presence of an American fast-food chain at the beach. However, you're much better off crossing the ocean to Corralejo in Fuerteventura, where the beaches and dunes easily outclass Playa Blanca's. This said, the beaches at Punta del Papagayo to the east (p134) are pretty and relatively isolated, affording a glimpse of a less frantic beachside holiday. The main beach is about a 1km stroll along the waterfront, east from the port. Go beyond the tiny rock-and-sand beach you first encounter (which is safe for swimming too).

Information

Tourist office (☎ 928 51 77 94; ☷ 8.30am-12.30pm & 2-5pm Mon-Fri, 8.30am-12.30pm Sat) In the port at the rear of the ferry booking office.

Activities
BOAT TOURS

The large 33m-long **César II** (☎ 928 81 36 08; adult/child €43/23) sails to the Isla de Lobos off Fuerteventura from Monday to Friday. Tours last from 10.15am until 5.45pm and include a light lunch.

Marea Errota (☎ 928 51 76 33; www.mareaerrota .com; adult/child €42.50/24) is a handsome galleon, which looks like something straight from the swashbuckling era. It does twice-daily coastal cruises down to the Papagayo beaches. Pick-up from your accommodation is included in the price.

Blue Delfin (☎ 928 51 23 23; www.bluedelfin.com; adult/child from €40/20) has day-long tours to

Fuerteventura and Isla de Lobos, as well as shorter five-hour tours to Papagayo.

DIVING
Friendly and extremely professional **Cala Blanca** (☎ 607 30 12 30; www.calablancasub.com; Centro Comercial el Papagayo) offers individual dives, courses and a charmingly named option for absolute beginners called the 'Sea Baptism' for €50.

Sleeping
Apartamentos Gutiérrez (☎/fax 928 51 70 89; Plaza Nuestra Señora del Carmen 8; apt €30-50) Just by the town church, and one of the cheapest places to stay in this area. Tidy, attractive apartments (six in all) are available, but no English is spoken, so brush up on your Spanish or your sign language.

Apartamentos Bahía Blanca Rock (☎ 928 51 70 37; Calle Janubio s/n; apt per person €58; P ✖ ❒) For something more stylish, this place has natty, well-run Canarian-style apartments (sleeping up to four) in a complex just off Avenida Papagayo and a 100m stroll from the main beach. Prices vary hugely, according to season, but half board (one meal per day is included in the price) is a measly €4 extra, and worth considering. At New Year's Eve and Christmas you're slugged at least €60 for the compulsory 'gala'.

Villas Kamezí (☎ 928 51 86 24; Calle Mónaco s/n; apt €199-255; P ✖ ❒ ❒) A discreet, environmentally friendly complex of 33 stunning villas with two to four bedrooms each, this is a wonderful way to experience the south of the island. You can even walk to the Papagayo beaches from here, if you can be bothered tearing yourself away from your private saltwater pool. Fabulous.

Princesa Yaiza (☎ 928 51 92 22; www.princesayaiza .com; Avenida Papagayo s/n; s/d €180/250, s/d ste from €210/280; P ✖ ✖ ❒ ❒) Easily the swishest place we saw on Lanzarote, this whole complex oozes good taste, with sensitive architectural flourishes and silky-smooth service. The list of amenities makes for its own book. Low-season discounts knock about 30% off the above rates.

Eating
El Almacen de la Sal (☎ 928 51 78 85; Paseo Marítimo 12; mains €9.50-35; ☯ closed Tue) This is an excellent waterfront restaurant, with fish dishes being the pick of the bunch (although a

good vegetarian selection is also tempting). It's about halfway between the port and the main beach and is wheelchair-accessible.

Bodegón Las Tapas (☎ 928 51 83 10; Paseo Marítimo 5; tapas €5-9; ☯ closed Mon) Closer to the port, this is an inviting-looking open-plan bar with some very tempting titbits on offer. Customers were hooked by the promise of dates and bacon on skewers, *pincho moruno*-style, and stayed to work their way through quite a few of the other offerings.

Restaurante Casa Jose (Plaza de Nuestra Señora del Carmen 8; mains €5-11; ☯ closed Sunday lunch) Opposite the church, this modest restaurant is well worth visiting for fish and a number of local dishes. The vibe inside is easygoing and casual.

Getting There & Away
Bus No 6 runs at least six times daily between Playa Blanca and Arrecife via Puerto del Carmen. The journey costs €3.

Fred Olsen (☎ 902 53 50 90; www.fredolsen.es) ferries link Playa Blanca with Corralejo (Fuerteventura) four to five times daily. A one-way ticket costs €12.50 and the crossing takes 35 to 45 minutes. Competition comes from Naviera Armas, which has five to six sailings daily at €11.40 per adult.

Free Fred Olsen buses leave Puerto del Carmen (9am and 5pm) to connect with the 10am and 6pm ferry departures. A free service also meets the 9am and 5pm ferries from Corralejo. The morning run continues to Lanzarote's airport.

PUNTA DEL PAPAGAYO
The southeast coast leading up to Punta del Papagayo is peppered with a series of pretty golden-sand coves. The promontory is a Reserva Natural Protegido (Protected Nature Reserve). The road beyond the rickety toll barrier (€3 per vehicle) is dirt but quite manageable even in a small car. Or take the easy way and hop aboard the **Princess Yaiza Taxi Boat** (☎ 928 51 43 22; adult/child €12/6), which sets out four times daily from Playa Blanca.

There's a rather rudimentary **camp site** (☎ 928 17 34 52; tent site/van site €3/5; ☯ office 9.30am-7pm) that consists mostly of caravans melting under the scorching sun. As 2000 was its first, experimental year, facilities are only coming along slowly, although the bathrooms are pretty good.

Tenerife

TENERIFE

This is the archipelago's largest and highest island, with Spain's tallest peak – the Pico del Teide (3718m) – surging from its heart. The barren east coast of Tenerife contrasts starkly with the rich, green northwest, and the vertigo-inducing cliffs of the north seem worlds away from the international holiday playgrounds of Playa de las Américas and the southwest. The island's geographic and sociographic diversity provides something for everyone, from whale-watching to walking, from nightclubbing to bird-watching and from steamy cityscapes to verdant villages.

Tenerife is also the best chance you'll have of letting your hair down, shaking your booty, putting on the ritz and tripping the light fantastic – especially if you're here for Carnaval (see p138) or any other holiday festivity. This is where the famed Spanish attitude to putting pleasure before business reaches a frenzied peak in towns and cities across the island – even when the event is ostensibly religious in origin.

Most Tinerfeños, as the islanders are called, live in the north. About half occupy the city of Santa Cruz de Tenerife (the island's capital) and the university city of La Laguna, a pearl of urban elegance only 10km from Santa Cruz.

Most visitors to the island stick to the southern resorts and Puerto de la Cruz, but there are plenty of small towns and villages in Tenerife where you can get off the beaten track with a minimum of fuss.

TENERIFE

HIGHLIGHTS

■ **Party Time**
You can let your hair down and guess who's Arthur or Martha during Santa Cruz's raucous Carnaval (p138 & p142)

■ **Mountaintop Experience**
The awesome Pico del Teide (3718m) is the highest mountain in Spain (p160)

■ **In Search of Solitude**
The wild and beautiful Punta de Teno is the perfect spot for a quiet moment (p162)

■ **Lost in a Storybook**
Garachico has picture-perfect streets and natural, volcanic pools (p158)

■ **Architecture Admiration**
La Laguna and La Orotava are both full of old treasures (p145 & p155)

La Laguna ★ ★ Santa Cruz de Tenerife
Garachico ★ ★ La Orotava
Punta de Teno ★
★ Pico del Teide

| ■ TELEPHONE CODE: 922 | ■ POPULATION: 806,000 | ■ AREA: 2034 SQ KM |

HISTORY

Tenerife was the last island to fall to the Spanish (in 1496), and the indigenous inhabitants, the Guanches, did not give up without a fight. The island's name appears to have been coined by the people of La Palma, who knew it as Tinerife – White Mountain (from *tiner*, mountain, and *ife*, white) – since all they could usually see was El Teide's snow-capped peak.

Tenerife, like its neighbour and competitor Gran Canaria, soon attracted a large chunk of the settlers from Spain, Portugal, Italy, France and even Britain.

In 1821 Madrid declared Santa Cruz de Tenerife, by then the island's main port, the capital of the Canaries. The good and great of Las Palmas de Gran Canaria remained incensed about this until 1927, when Madrid finally split the archipelago into two provinces, with Santa Cruz as provincial capital of Tenerife, La Palma, La Gomera and El Hierro. Today, Santa Cruz shares the duties of regional capital of all seven islands with its long-standing rival, Las Palmas.

INFORMATION
Maps

You will find few competing small- and medium-scale maps of the island. Among the best are those by Editorial Everest costing €2.50. For Tenerife you have a choice of *Tenerife Costa Sur* and *Tenerife Costa Norte*.

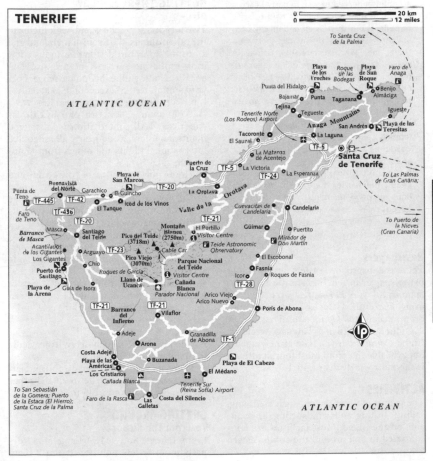

CARNAVAL CAPERS

Only Rio de Janeiro does it better, and even *that* party does not overshadow Santa Cruz's efforts to make **Carnaval** (www.carnavaltenerife.com) a nonstop 24-hour party orgy. The fun begins in early February and lasts about three weeks. Many of the gala performances and fancy-dress competitions take place in the Recinto Ferial (fairgrounds), but the streets, especially around Plaza España, burst into a frenzy of outlandish activity as the whole island seems to participate in masked balls and an almost permanent state of good-natured frivolity.

Don't be fooled into thinking this is just a sequin-bedecked excuse to party hearty though. It may sometimes be hard to see or believe, but there is an underlying political 'message' to the whole shebang. Under the Franco dictatorship, Carnaval ground to a halt and there didn't seem to be too much to celebrate. The Catholic Church's cosy relationship with the fascists was another source of frustration, so when Carnaval was relaunched after the death of General Franco it was front-page news (literally) and the citizens of Santa Cruz wasted no time in lampooning the sexual and moral hypocrisy of the church and the fascists. Today, you will still see a lot of people dressed for the event as naughty nuns and perverted priests, and more drag queens than you can poke a stick at. And all in the name of good, clean fun.

Newspapers

There is a disproportionately large number of newspapers in Tenerife. The most popular Spanish titles are *El Día, La Gaceta de Canarias, Diario de Avisos* and – a newcomer on the scene – *La Opinión de Tenerife*.

Of the several English-language weeklies, *Island Connections* (for sale at newsagents but available free from most tourist offices) is the most widely distributed.

ACTIVITIES

The gamut of water sports, such as diving, sailing, fishing and windsurfing, is available on the island. Most facilities are concentrated in and around the southwestern resort areas.

There's good scope for walking. You can follow 11 trails within the Parque Nacional del Teide, whose rangers lead guided walks daily. Other attractive areas are the Anaga mountains in the northeast and around the Valle de la Orotava. Ask at any tourist office for details.

ACCOMMODATION

While finding a room is generally not a problem in Santa Cruz and on the northern half of the island, the same cannot be said for the resort areas of the south, particularly around Costa Adeje, Los Cristianos and Playa de las Américas. Arriving here at night without a reservation can be a dodgy business.

GETTING THERE & AWAY
Air

Two airports serve the island, with flights to the other islands, the Spanish mainland and a host of European destinations, plus a few more exotic ones such as Venezuela and Havana. Facilitating nine million passengers per year – often well in excess of 25,000 daily – is modern **Tenerife Sur airport** (Reina Sofía; ☎ 922 75 95 10), about 20km east of Playa de las Américas. All international chartered flights land here, as do nearly all scheduled international flights and others from mainland Spain.

The airport functions 24 hours a day and has half a dozen car-rental offices, a post office, several banks, ATMs and exchange booths, and knowledgeable staff at its **tourist information office** (☎ 922 39 20 37).

Almost all interisland flights, plus a few scheduled international and mainland services, use the older and smaller **Tenerife Norte airport** (Los Rodeos; ☎ 922 63 56 35). Here you'll find an exchange booth, some car-rental reps, a bar and an information desk where you can get a map of Santa Cruz, but little else.

Boat

For details of the weekly ferry from Cádiz in mainland Spain, see p249.

There are regular ferry, hydrofoil and jetfoil services from Tenerife to all the other islands. See p250 and p145 for details.

GETTING AROUND
To/From the Airport

From Tenerife Sur, TITSA bus No 487 departs more or less hourly between 8.10am

and 10pm for Los Cristianos (€1.50) and
Playa de las Américas (€1.85). It's less than
a half-hour ride to both destinations. No 341
departs at least hourly from 6.50am for Santa
Cruz (€5, about 1½ hours). There are four
buses (No 340) daily to Puerto de la Cruz
(€7.85) via Tenerife Norte airport (€5).

Call ☎ 922 39 21 19 for a taxi. Approximate
fares from Tenerife Sur to the following
destinations are:

Los Cristianos €17.50
Playa de las Américas €20
Los Gigantes €44
Puerto de la Cruz €95
Santa Cruz €61.50
El Médano €8

From Tenerife Norte, frequent TITSA buses
go to Santa Cruz (€1.10, 20 minutes). No
102 goes to Puerto de la Cruz (€3) via La
Laguna, only 3km from the airport. Bus No
340 calls by the airport on its way between
Puerto de la Cruz and Tenerife Sur airport
(four daily).

A taxi into Santa Cruz from Tenerife
Norte costs around €15. The fare to Puerto
de la Cruz is around €25.

Bus

TITSA (Transportes Interurbanos de Tenerife SA; ☎ 922
53 13 00; www.titsa.com) runs a spider's web of
services all over the island, as well as within
Santa Cruz and other biggish towns.

Car

If you want to get past the crowds at the
resorts and set off on your own, you'll likely

BONOBUS

If you intend to use the bus a lot, get a
Bonobus card. It costs €12 and is used
instead of normal single-journey tickets.
It represents a big saving – at least 30%,
and up to 50% on longer journeys. Insert
the card in the machine on the bus, tell
the driver where you are going and the
amount is subtracted from the card. The
Bonobus card is good for any trip, inter-
city or local, throughout the island. It also
gives you half-price admission into some
of the island's museums, such as the
Museo de la Naturaleza y El Hombre in
Santa Cruz (p141).

---

need a rental car. Rental agencies are almost
as plentiful on the island as English pubs,
so you shouldn't have a problem finding a
car, even if you want same-day rental. The
generally reliable international chains (see
p252 for listings) are present in all major
resort areas. Expect a car to cost between
€25 and €40 a day. You'll also find a generous sprinkling of small businesses offering
older, usually cheaper cars for as low as
€15 a day.

Taxi

You can take a taxi anywhere on the island –
but it is an expensive way to get around.
You are much better off hiring a car. See
p252 for details.

SANTA CRUZ DE TENERIFE

pop 188,450
This bustling port city is one of the busiest
in Spain. If you're not expecting much from
the city, you're in for a real surprise – Santa
Cruz is friendly and fun loving, with a
tropical feel. As you stroll along its sunny
streets, you'll find attractive shady plazas,
brightly painted buildings from past and
present and some excellent shopping.
While it's somewhat short on significant
'sights', it's certainly not short on charm.
With very good bus transport, it makes a
sensible base for exploring the northeast of
the island – and here you feel you are truly
in Canario territory, with a surprising lack
of tourist crowds.

ORIENTATION

Taking Plaza España as a hub, everything
of interest lies within a kilometre or less.
At the southwestern edge is the bus station, while to the northeast is the terminal
for jetfoils to/from Las Palmas de Gran
Canaria. With the exception of the Museo
Militar de Almeyda (near Muelle Ribera),
most of the handful of sights and good
shops lie within the central grid of streets
leading inland from Plaza España.

Maps

The small, in-your-palm town map handed
out by the tourist office is refreshingly

accurate and helpful. If you would like even
more, you could purchase a copy of Editorial Everest's map of Santa Cruz de Tenerife
(€2.50), a street map with details of tourist
attractions.

INFORMATION
Bookshops
La Isla Bookshop (☎ 922 28 54 81; Calle Robayna 2;
🕙 9.30am-1.15pm & 5-8.15pm Mon-Fri, 9.30am-1.15pm
Sat) This shop has titles in English, including novels, a
few Canaries guidebooks and a selection of Lonely Planet
guides.

Emergency
Police Station (☎ 922 22 24 47; Avenida Tres de
Mayo 32)

Internet Access
Yakiciber (☎ 922 27 52 08; Calle Ramón y Cajal 23;
per hr €1.80; 🕙 10.30am-2.30am Mon-Sat,
3.30pm-2.30am Sun)

Medical Services
Hospital Rambla (☎ 922 29 16 00; Rambla General
Franco 115)

NAMING NAMES

The townsfolk of Santa Cruz de Tenerife
are known in the local slang as Chichar-
reros after the *chicharros* (horse mackerel)
that was once favoured by the fishermen
of the island.

Post

Main Post Office (☎ 922 24 51 16; Plaza España 2; ⏰ 8.30am-8.30pm Mon-Fri, 9.30am-2pm Sat) Allows you to send faxes.

Telephone

Street phones abound in Santa Cruz.

Telephone Office (☎ 922 24 72 74; Paseo de las Milí- cias de Garachico 3; Internet per hr €1.80; ⏰ 9am-10pm Mon-Fri, 9.30am-2pm & 5-9pm Sat & Sun) This is a good, efficient office, with Internet access.

Tourist Offices

Scattered about the city you'll find some computer terminals in public spaces, with touch-screen information about Santa Cruz attractions.

Tourist Office (☎ 922 23 95 92; Plaza España s/n; ⏰ 8am-6pm Mon-Fri, 9am-1pm Sat) This is located in the Cabildo Insular de Tenerife building. Don't confuse it with the fairly uninformed tourist information kiosk in front of the adjacent post office.

SIGHTS

The majority of Santa Cruz's sights are within easy walking distance of Plaza Es- paña. While the city is not packed with at- tractions like other European capitals, there are some attractive buildings and well-run exhibitions to distract you.

Museums

Museo de la Naturaleza y El Hombre (☎ 922 20 93 20; www.museosdetenerife.org in Spanish; Calle Fuente Mo- rales s/n; adult/child €3/1.50; ⏰ 9am-7pm Tue-Sun) is a multimedia, multiscreen, multistorey edifice dedicated to volcanoes, the flora and fauna of the islands and Tenerife's ancient culture. It has several fascinating Guanche mummies and skulls, a handful of artefacts, including pottery, and a well-presented natural sci- ences section.

The museum, which occupies a former hospital, has excellent wheelchair access and a wonderful shop, where very good souvenirs and books relating to the islands can be found.

Museo de Bellas Artes (☎ 922 24 43 58; Calle José Murphy 12; admission free; ⏰ 10am-8pm Mon-Fri), bor- dering Plaza Príncipe de Asturias, is home to an eclectic mix of paintings by Canarian and Flemish artists (including Bruegel), as well as sculpture, a weapons collection and old coins. Spanish artists to look out for include Ribera and Sorolla.

SANTA CRUZ VS LA LAGUNA

Alonso Fernández de Lugo landed on Ten- erife in 1494 to embark on the conquest of the final and most-resistant island in the archipelago. But it was La Laguna, a few kilometres inland, that blossomed as the island's capital at first. Santa Cruz de Santiago, as Santa Cruz de Tenerife was then known, remained a backwater until its port began to flourish in the 18th and 19th centuries. Only in 1803 was Santa Cruz 'liberated' by Spanish royal decree from the municipal control of La Laguna, and in 1859 it was declared a city. From then on it has never looked back, its port giving it an advantage La Laguna could never match.

TENERIFE

War buffs might want to check out the martial museum, **Museo Militar de Almeyda** (☎ 922 84 35 00; Calle San Isidro 1; admission free; ☺ 10am-2pm Tue-Sat). The most famous item here is *El Tigre* (The Tiger), the cannon that reputedly blew off Admiral Nelson's arm when he attacked Santa Cruz in 1797. Much of the museum is devoted to the successful defence of the city and the capture of the invading force.

Around the Centre

Santa Cruz is a busy port city and simply meandering around is a pleasant way to while away the day. Starting a wander from the waterfront Plaza España, whose centrepiece is a somewhat controversial memorial to the fallen of the 1936–39 civil war, you could head inland along Plaza Candelaria and the pedestrianised shopping strip of Calle Castillo. A right turn along Calle José Murphy will, after a couple of blocks, bring you to the **Iglesia de San Francisco**, a Baroque church built in the 17th and 18th centuries.

Three small blocks southwest of Calle Castillo is the city's 19th-century **Teatro Guimerá** (see p144), whose austere facade belies a rather sumptuous interior reminiscent of Madrid's Teatro Real, with semicircular balconied seating and plenty of gilt. Nearby, **Centro de Fotografía** (☎ 922 29 07 35; Plaza Isla de la Madera s/n; admission free; ☺ 11am-1pm & 6-9pm Mon-Fri) is a pretty interesting photographic gallery that often has very good exhibitions and some cutting-edge displays of digital and video art. If you're in town for the FotoNoviembre exhibition, held in November, make a point of dropping by.

Plaza Iglesia shows signs of gentrification, with some brightly painted buildings adding some charm to what has been a grotty part of town. Here you'll see the striking bell tower of the city's oldest church, the **Iglesia de Nuestra Señora de la Concepción** (Plaza Iglesia; ☺ mass 9am & 7.30pm), which has a tiled roof and some traditional *mudéjar* (Islamic-style architecture) ceiling work. The present church was built in the 17th and 18th centuries, but the original building went up in 1498 just after the island was conquered. At the heart of the shimmering silver altar is the Santa Cruz de la Conquista (Holy Cross of the Conquest), which gives the city its name. Tradition has it that Alonso Fernández de Lugo, the Spanish commander, planted it in his camp to give thanks for his 1494 victory over the Guanches.

Check out too the anteroom to the sacristy (to the right of the altar). The altarpiece in the chapel beside it was carved from cedar on the orders of Don Matías Carta, a prominent personage who died before it was completed. He lies buried here and the pallid portrait on the wall was done *after* his death (hence the closed eyes and crossed arms). There's also a fine painting of *La Adoración de los Pastores* (The Adoration of the Shepherds) by Juan de Miranda.

A five- to 10-minute walk southwest along the waterfront brings you to the 17th-century **Castillo de San Juan**. In the shadow of this protective fort there used to be a lively trade in African slaves. Nowadays its squat, rectangular basalt form is overshadowed by the magnificent, soaring, white auditorium of **Auditorio de Tenerife** (see p144), designed by the internationally renowned Spanish architect Santiago Calatrava and possessing superb acoustics.

Just beyond this contrasting pair is the **Parque Marítimo César Manrique** (Avenida Constitución s/n; adult/senior/child €2.50/1/1.20; ☺ 10am-7pm), where you can have a dip in one of the wonderful designer pools or just lie back on the sun loungers (available for hire for €2) and drink in the beautiful view and something refreshing. It's suitable for all ages, but particularly so for children. For more information about César Manrique, see p117.

FESTIVALS & EVENTS

Santa Cruz's **Carnaval** – the Canarian fiesta *par excellence* – is *the* event on Tenerife. Needless to say, finding a place to stay on the island at this time (February) – if you don't have an advance booking – is a rather tall order. See p138 for more information.

The founding of the city is celebrated on 3 May, **Día de la Cruz**, but this is a sober affair in comparison to Carnaval.

The biggest event on the serious music calendar is the **Festival de Música de Canarias**, held annually in January and February in Santa Cruz de Tenerife and Las Palmas de Gran Canaria (on the island of Gran Canaria). For more information, visit the website at www.socaem.com.

FotoNoviembre (www.fotonoviembre.com in Spanish), held in early November to early December, is a wide-ranging photography festival.

SLEEPING
Budget
For a city this size, there are few budget places and some are less than inviting. That doesn't stop them filling up at Carnaval time, though... We've selected the best of the budget bunch.

Pensión Casablanca (☎ 922 27 85 99; Calle Viera y Clavijo 15; s/d €15/21) This place had a nifty face-lift a few years ago and is brimming with cute charm and some interesting decorative paint finishes, not to mention the sweet service. The rooms are tiny but good value. The corridor bathrooms have been updated and are better than many shared facilities.

Pensión Mova (☎ 922 28 32 61; Calle San Martín 33; s/d €12/24) A long-standing budget option, guarded by a large Alsatian in one of the city's scruffier (but not scary) streets. Plain rooms are tidy and reasonably welcoming, and have functional (albeit minimal) facilities at a bargain price.

Mid-Range
Hotel Contemporáneo (☎ 922 27 15 71; www.hotelcontemporaneo.com in Spanish; Rambla General Franco 116; s/d €60/88; P 🗙 🖳 🖳) A great peach-coloured layer cake of a place to stay on this elegant street. Very large rooms have all the amenities a business traveller could want (including satellite TV) and it's no hassle to organise baby-sitting if you're a family traveller. Nab a room with a balcony, if you can.

Hotel Taburiente (☎ 922 27 60 00; fax 922 27 05 62; www.hoteltaburiente.com; Calle Dr José Naveiras 24a; s/d/tr €53/64/84; P 🗙 🖳) Fully equipped rooms at this hotel represent excellent value. It's located in a nice part of town, and has attractive rooms and communal areas. With a rooftop swimming pool, sauna and dedicated garage, it has a lot going for it. Even the foyer, with a bit of gilt and some nice old furniture, has charm.

Hotel Atlántico (☎ 922 24 63 75; fax 922 24 63 78; Calle Castillo 12; s/d incl breakfast €38/57) This is a central, multistorey hotel with a clued-in management team offering great service and well-kitted-out rooms. If you're a light sleeper, you might want to avoid balcony rooms, which can get noisy.

Hotel Anaga (☎ 922 24 50 90; fax 922 24 56 44; Calle Imeldo Serís 19; s/d/tr €32/53/71) The Anaga is a simple spot, where old-fashioned rooms from the 1930s feature creaky beds, lino

floors and big bathtubs. The management's friendly and the location is very handy.

Top End
Hotel Mencey (☎ 922 60 99 00; mencey@starwood.com; Calle Dr José Naveiras 38; s/d from €215/295; P 🗙 🖳 🖳) Prestigious Hotel Mencey is where the jet set stay when they're in town. Rooms are sumptuous, facilities are top-notch and the grandeur never fades. We could lie by the tree-fringed poolside and sip cocktails for the rest of our days if our schedule permitted. In the low season, you can expect prices to drop by about 20%, although the price of the Royal Suite (€980) does not change.

EATING
Restaurants
La Fundación (☎ 922 28 39 72; Calle Imeldo Seris 25; mains €7.50-14.50; 🕑 closed Sun) This place is where Santa Cruz's movers and shakers wine and dine on market cuisine. In an old Canarian mansion, wonderfully restored to blend modern and traditional elements, a smart crowd chows down on winners such as *ensaladas de quesos Canarios con membrillo y miel de retama* (salad of Canarian cheeses with quince and honey), all washed down with excellent wines. Reservations are a good idea, as is trying to grab a table in the plant-filled central courtyard.

La Taberna de Wally (☎ 922 27 34 13; Calle Viera y Clavijo 44; mains €7.50-9; 🕑 closed Mon) A delight. Try freshly prepared salads in a gorgeous garden courtyard overlooking the street, with an operatic soundtrack in the background. At night, the friendly owner turns the place over to a DJ who spins great chill-out music and attracts a good-looking crowd.

Mesón Treinta y Ocho (☎ 922 27 10 65; Calle Viera y Clavijo 38; mains €8.50-18.50; 🕑 closed Mon) A supremely elegant and quite romantic place, where fine Canarian and Basque food is complemented by a very good wine list and silky – ahem, and good-looking – service.

Rincón de la Piedra (☎ 922 24 97 78; Calle Benavides 32; mains €6.50-11.50; 🕑 closed Sun) A down-to-earth yet commendable restaurant in an attractively decorated old Canarian house. There are plenty of exposed wood beams, and a church-like feel. Service is incredibly helpful and great wines by the glass are available. We went crazy for the *ventresca* (a milder cut of tuna), but fellow

TENERIFE

diners were generally opting for the snazzy hot-stone meat offerings that are cooked at your table.

La Cazuela (☎ 922 27 23 00; Calle Robayna 34; mains €7.50-14.50) Drenched in Canary yellow, this place is heartily recommended by locals for truly tasty local dishes. Settle in for a long, filling lunch and try the *cazuela* (a casserole made with fresh or salted fish).

Cafés & Terrazas
Cafés abound here, probably because of the friendly, gregarious nature of many of the locals, and the agreeable climate, which makes outside tables a standard feature.

Bar Zumería Doña Papaya (Lady Papaya Juice Bar; ☎ 922 29 06 79; Calle Callao de Lima 3; juices €1.35; ☽ closed Sun) This place has a lot to answer for – namely our raging addiction to fresh strawberry juice, which started here and can never be assuaged by any other juice bar. A wonderful selection of fresh fruits sits waiting to be pulped amid the cigarette smoke and chatty customers. There's no cheaper, more enjoyable way to get a vitamin C hit.

Café del Príncipe (☎ 922 24 26 75; Plaza Príncipe de Asturias s/n) Within the leafy plaza in the centre of town, this is a great setting for a coffee or cocktail.

Pleasant café *terrazas* (terraces) to while away your time include those on Plaza Candelaria and the shady number on the fringe of Parque García Sanabria, where you can let the kids romp in the adjacent playground.

Self-Catering
Mercado de Nuestra Señora de África (Calle San Sebastián; ☽ 11am-11.30pm Mon-Sat) This rather claustrophobic covered market is a little disappointing by mainland Spanish standards, although there are 300 stalls to check out. All the same, it's worth a visit if only to marvel at the variety of fish pulled from the ocean.

DRINKING & ENTERTAINMENT
Condal y Peñamil (☎ 922 24 49 76; Callejón Combate 11; ☽ closed Mon) The best place in town to savour a drink and a morsel of tapas is this old-fashioned–looking place with blood-red décor and smooth service. It's on a narrow, pedestrianised street in the centre of the city. The *pan con tomate y jamón* (tomato bread and ham) is nothing less than heavenly.

Nightclubs
Nightlife really takes off from about 2am at the northern end of Avenida Anaga – work your way from the Arco to the nearby Fool Company.

Arco Pub (Avenida Anaga 31; ☽ 6pm-3.30am Mon-Sat) Live music, good cocktails and plenty of sociable young yuppies.

Fool Company (Avenida Anaga 25; admission €10; ☽ midnight-6am Wed-Sat) Also has live music, but mostly funk and R&B DJs. It can get packed with a party-loving crowd. Look for the plastic bamboo out the front.

Theatre & Classical Music
Auditorio de Tenerife (☎ 922 27 06 11; www.auditoriodetenerife.com; Avenida Constitución s/n). Tenerife's newest and flashest entertainment option resembles a cross between a ship's sails and the Sydney Opera House, and hosts opera, dance and classical-music performances, among others.

Teatro Guimerá (box office ☎ 902 33 33 38; Plaza Isla de la Madera s/n; tickets €12-18; ☽ 11am-1pm & 5-8pm). The other venue for highbrow entertainment, whether music or theatre.

SPECTATOR SPORTS
Football
Santa Cruz is home to CD Tenerife, who currently play in the second division. You can buy tickets at the *taquilla* (box office) of their stadium, Estadio Heliodoro Rodríguez López, or call into the club's **HQ** (☎ 922 29 81 00; www.cdtenerife.com in Spanish; Callejón Combate 1).

SHOPPING
The main shopping strip is the pedestrianised Calle Castillo and surrounding streets, including Calle Pilar, Calle Béthencourt Alfonso, Calle Teobaldo Power and Calle Viera y Cavijo. Some promising deals are available on electronics and watches, but there are also some great little boutiques, stocked with clothes from Spanish and international designers.

El Corte Inglés (☎ 922 84 94 00; Avenida Tres de Mayo 7; ☽ 10am-10pm Mon-Sat) Monster-sized, and will keep you stocked in whatever your heart desires. It also has a fantastic supermarket.

Handicrafts kiosk (Plaza España s/n; ☽ 9.30am-2pm & 5-8pm Mon-Sat) If you're after something typical of the island, browse around the rectangular government-sponsored kiosk opposite the main post office. All items are for sale.

Rastro (flea market; Calle José Manuel Guimerá; ☾ Sun) This flea market is held along the street leading up to the covered market. The action is all but over by the early afternoon, so get here early-ish to savour the scruffy-but-harmless atmosphere.

GETTING THERE & AWAY
Air
Tenerife Norte is the nearest airport to Santa Cruz. It handles nearly all flights between the islands, and very few others. See p138 for details.

Boat
The **Trasmediterránea** (☎ 922 84 22 44; www.trasmediterranea.com; Estación Marítima, Muelle Ribera) ferry to Cádiz, via Las Palmas de Gran Canaria and Arrecife on Lanzarote (see p249), leaves weekly at 10am on Saturday (€22.39, car €27.60).

Trasmediterránea runs three jetfoils per day to Las Palmas (€49.35). The 8am sailing (10am on Sunday) continues on to Morro Jable in Fuerteventura (€68.90). It also has a weekly boat to Santa Cruz de la Palma (€28.10, eight hours), which leaves at 11.59pm on Thursday.

Naviera Armas (☎ 922 53 40 52) runs a fast ferry to Las Palmas twice daily (€15.40) – once daily on weekends – and to Puerto del Rosario (Fuerteventura) once weekly (€37.40). It also has a boat to La Palma (€17.60) four times a week and one per week to Arrecife on Lanzarote (€37.40).

Fred Olsen (☎ 922 62 82 00; www.fredolsen.es) has six high-speed ferries daily to Agaete (€27, 1¼ hours) in the northwest of Gran Canaria, from where you can take its free bus onwards to Las Palmas (35 minutes).

You can buy tickets for all three companies from travel agents or from the main Estación Marítima Muelle de Ribera building (which is where the Fred Olsen boats leave from). Naviera Armas has its base further to the south.

Bus
TITSA buses radiate out from the **bus station** (☎ 922 21 56 99), beside Avenida Constitución, to pretty much every place of interest around the island. Major routes include:

No 102 Puerto de la Cruz via La Laguna & Tenerife Norte (€3.50, 55 minutes, every 30 minutes)
No 103 Puerto de la Cruz direct (€3.50, 40 minutes, over 15 daily)
Nos 106 & 108 Icod de los Vinos (€5, 1¼ hours, over 15 daily)
No 110 Los Cristianos & Playa de las Américas direct (€6.40, one hour, every 30 minutes)
No 111 Los Cristianos & Playa de las Américas via Candelaria & Güímar (€6.40, one hour 20 minutes, every 30 minutes)
No 341 Tenerife Sur (€5, 50 minutes, 20 daily)
Nos 014 & 015 La Laguna (€1, 20 minutes, every 10 minutes or so)

Car & Motorcycle
Car-rental companies are scattered all over the city centre. Major operators also have booths at the *estación marítima* (ferry terminal). Paid parking stations can be found underneath Plaza España and in the Mercado de Nuestra Señora de Africa market.

GETTING AROUND
To/From the Airport
See p138 for details of the regular buses serving both airports.

A taxi to Tenerife Norte will cost about €15 and for Tenerife Sur, the fare will be around €60.

Bus
TITSA buses provide the city service in Santa Cruz. No 914 runs from the bus station to the centre (Plaza General Weyler and Plaza España) about every 15 minutes (every half-hour on weekends). Other local services include the circular routes Nos 920 and 921. A local trip costs €0.85.

Taxi
The major taxi stands are on Plaza España and at the bus station. Call **Radio-Taxi San Pedro** (☎ 922 31 00 00) for bookings.

THE NORTHEAST

LA LAGUNA
pop 128,800
An easy day trip from Santa Cruz or Puerto de la Cruz, San Cristóbal de la Laguna is a lively student town and should not be missed – thanks to its youthful energy, well-preserved architectural highlights and what

TENERIFE

LA LAGUNA

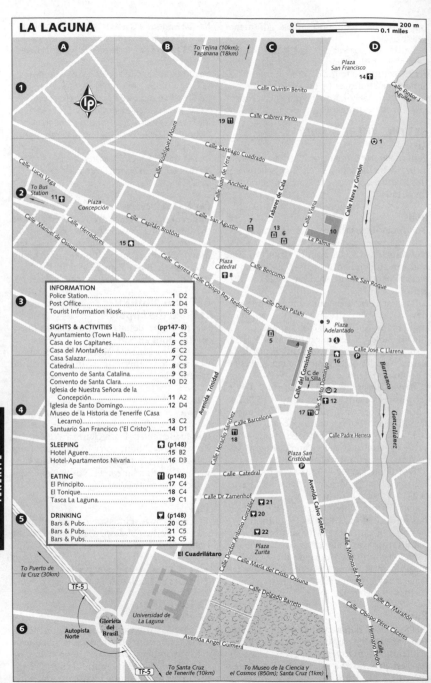

0 — 200 m
0 — 0.1 miles

To Tejina (10km);
Taganana (18km)

Plaza
San Francisco
14

Calle Pintor J
Aguilar

Calle Quintín Benito

19

Calle Cabrera Pinto

Calle Santiago Cuadrado

Calle Rodríguez Moure

Calle Juan de Vera

Calle Nava y Grimón

Calle Lucas Vega

To Bus
Station
11

Plaza
Concepción

Calle Manuel de Ossuna

Calle Herradores

Calle Capitán Brotóns

Calle Juan Anchieta

Calle San Agustín

Tabares de Cala

Calle Viana

7

13   6

10

La Palma

15

Calle Carrera (Calle Obispo Rey Redondo)

Plaza
Catedral
8

Calle Bencomo

Calle San Roque

Calle Deán Palahí

9 Plaza
Adelantado

5

Calle José C Llarena

3

16

Barranco

Gonzáliñez

4

C de
la Silla

2

17   12

Calle Santo Domingo

Calle del Consistorio

Avenida Trinidad

Calle Heraclio Sánchez

Calle Barcelona

18

Calle Padre Herrera

Plaza San
Cristóbal

Calle Catedral

Avenida Calvo Sotelo

Calle Molinos de Agua

Calle Dr Zamenhof

21

20

22

Plaza
Zurita

Calle Doctor Antonio González

El Cuadrilátaro

Calle María del Cristo Ossuna

Calle Delgado Barreto

Calle Obispo Pérez Cáceres

Calle Dr Marañón

Calle Hermano Pedro

To Puerto de
la Cruz (30km)

TF-5

Glorieta
del
Brasil

Autopista
Norte

Universidad de
La Laguna

Avenida Ángel Guimerá

TF-5

To Santa Cruz
de Tenerife (10km)

To Museo de la Ciencia y
el Cosmos (850m); Santa Cruz (1km)

INFORMATION	
Police Station..1	D2
Post Office...2	D4
Tourist Information Kiosk.....................(pp3)	D3

SIGHTS & ACTIVITIES	(pp147-8)
Ayuntamiento (Town Hall)......................4	C3
Casa de los Capitanes.............................5	C3
Casa del Montañés..................................6	C2
Casa Salazar...7	C2
Catedral...8	C3
Convento de Santa Catalina....................9	C3
Convento de Santa Clara.......................10	D2
Iglesia de Nuestra Señora de la Concepción...11	A2
Iglesia de Santo Domingo......................12	D4
Museo de la Historia de Tenerife (Casa Lecarno)...13	C2
Santuario San Francisco ('El Cristo')......14	D1

SLEEPING	(p148)
Hotel Aguere..15	B2
Hotel-Apartamentos Nivaria..................16	D3

EATING	(p148)
El Principito..17	C4
El Tonique..18	C4
Tasca La Laguna...................................19	C1

DRINKING	(p148)
Bars & Pubs...20	C5
Bars & Pubs...21	C5
Bars & Pubs...22	C5

TENERIFE

may well be the island's most determined *marcha* (nightlife).

History
Alonso Fernández de Lugo's troops ended up making a permanent camp in what is now known as La Laguna (the lagoon from which the name comes was drained only in 1837).

By the end of the 15th century the old town as it is today was pretty much complete, and La Laguna was a bustling city of merchants, soldiers, bureaucrats and the pious. In 1701 the university was established.

Orientation
The bus station is about a 10-minute walk to the northwest of the old centre. The university, where you'll find the bulk of the bars and plenty of simple eateries, lies to the south of the old centre. The little accommodation available is in the historic area, as are some nice restaurants, banks, the post office and the tourist offices.

Information
EMERGENCY
Police Station (☎ 922 25 04 52; Calle Nava y Grimón 66)

POST
Post Office (☎ 922 61 43 04; Calle Santo Domingo; ✆ 8.30am-2.30pm Mon-Fri, 9.30am-1pm Sat)

TOURIST OFFICES
Tourist Kiosk (☎ 922 63 11 94; Plaza Adelanto s/n; ✆ 8am-8pm Mon-Sat) If you're interested in historical buildings, ask for an English version of the *San Cristóbal de La Laguna, World Heritage Site* brochure.

Sights
CANARIAN MANSIONS
La Laguna allows you to fully appreciate the beauty and eccentricity of Canarian urban architecture – bright facades graced with ponderous, wooden double doors and pretty balconies, and corners embellished with grey stone. Broad, elegant, wood-shuttered windows conceal cool, shady patios, in the best cases surrounded by first-storey verandas propped up by slender timber columns. Whenever you see an open door, look inside – with luck the inner sanctum will also be open.

The documents, maps, artefacts and descriptions are interesting enough at **Museo**

de la Historia de Tenerife (Casa Lecarno; ☎ 922 63 01 03; Calle San Agustín 22; adult/student €3/1.50, admission free Sun; ✆ 10am-8pm Tue-Sun), but the 16th-century mansion itself is well worth looking over, with its extremely effective and tasteful renovation. Note the brickwork, which features Renaissance designs, on either side of the stone portico at the museum's entrance.

Calle San Agustín and the surrounding streets are lined with fine old houses. Take a look inside **Casa del Montañés** at No 16. Peek too into the tranquil patio of No 28, the **Casa Salazar**, nowadays home to the bishop of La Laguna. The imposing **Casa de los Capitanes** is beside the *ayuntamiento* (town hall) on Calle Carrera (aka Calle Obispo Rey Redondo). You'll see others as you wander, so keep your eyes peeled.

CHURCHES & CONVENTS
It's also worth checking out La Laguna's contributions to religious architecture.

Iglesia de Nuestra Señora de la Concepción (Plaza Concepción; ✆ 10am-12.15pm & 5-7.15pm Tue-Sun) was the island's first church – constructed in 1502 – and has undergone many changes since. Elements of Gothic and plateresque styles can still be distinguished, and the finely wrought wooden *mudéjar* ceilings are a delight.

A few minutes' walk east, the **Catedral** (Plaza Catedral) was completely rebuilt in 1913 and seemed to be undergoing a similar makeover when we visited, with a hell of a lot of scaffolding going on. Inside is a fine Baroque retable in the chapel dedicated to the Virgen de los Remedios. It also hosts some fine paintings by Cristóbal Hernández de Quintana, one of the islands' premier 18th-century artists.

The **Iglesia de Santo Domingo** (Calle Santo Domingo), originally a hermitage and expanded in the 17th century, also contains some good examples of De Quintana's work. You'll probably notice the vivid murals painted by Mariano Cossío and Antonio González Suárez too – from the 20th century, for a change!

At the very northern end of the old quarter, the **Santuario San Francisco** (Plaza San Francisco s/n; admission free; ✆ 10.30am-1pm & 4-9pm), or the Santuario del Santísimo Cristo de La Laguna, to give it its full name (although the locals call it El Cristo), contains a blackened wooden sculpture of Christ – the most venerated crucifix on the island. That said, it's a good idea to be as respectful as possible inside, as most of the people here are praying – not sightseeing.

Of the convents, the most interesting is **Convento de Santa Clara** (cnr Calles Anchieta & Viana; 9.30am-1pm & 3-5.30pm). You can also visit its fine 16th-century chapel. The Santa Clara chapel and the closed order in **Convento de Santa Catalina** (Plaza Adelantado; 7-11.45am Mon-Sat, 6.30-8pm Sun) are still active.

OTHER SIGHTS

Museo de la Ciencia y el Cosmos (☎ 922 31 52 65; www.museosdetenerife.org; Calle Vía Láctea s/n; adult/child/student €3/free/1.50; 9am-7pm Tue-Sun) If you enjoy pushing buttons, watching balls and things jiggling around (away from the crowded beaches), and musing on the forces of nature, you can have fun here, even if you don't speak Spanish. About 1.5km south of Plaza Adelantado, it also has a planetarium, so you can stargaze during the day. It's a good choice for those wanting to have their children stimulated by something other than cheap electrical goods.

Language Courses

The **Universidad de La Laguna** (☎ 922 60 33 45; www.ull.es/sidiomas) offers four-month Spanish classes at all levels.

Festivals & Events

The most important fiestas in La Laguna are the **Romería de San Benito Abad** on the first Sunday of July and the **Fiesta del Santísimo Cristo** from 7 to 15 September. **Carnaval** (February/March) and **Corpus Christi** (June) are also celebrated with gusto.

Sleeping

Unfortunately, sleeping possibilities are extremely limited, but are of a very high standard.

Hotel Aguere (☎ 922 25 94 90; haquere@infonegocio .com; Calle Carrera 55; s/d €49/63) This stylish 22-room hotel sits opposite the Teatro Leal. Constructed in 1760, it has a delightful glass-roofed patio and gorgeous, old-fashioned rooms with wooden floors. It's not laden with up-to-date amenities, but still represents excellent value in terms of ambience.

Hotel-Apartamentos Nivaria (☎ 922 26 42 98; www.hotelnivaria.com; Plaza Adelantado 11; studio €71-78, apt €96; P 🐾) While Nivaria occupies a much-altered 18th-century building, it has retained its own gracious patio and many Canarian features. Its three-star studios and apartments are mighty attractive (with fridge, phone, bathtub etc), with solid wooden furniture and lots of light. Studios sleep one or two persons, while the apartments can accommodate three people.

Eating

El Príncipito (☎ 922 63 39 16; Calle Santo Domingo 26; mains €8-16.50; closed Mon) One of La Laguna's swishest restaurants. You'll swear you're in France, as both the food and décor have a decidedly Gallic twist. It's good value, and reservations are recommended at lunch time.

El Tonique (☎ 922 26 15 29; Calle Heraclio Sánchez 23; mains €7.20-15; closed Mon lunch & Sun) Head down the stairs for this wonderful, friendly eating spot with its walls lined with bottles of fine wine. These are but a sample of more than 250 different varieties quietly maturing in Tonique's cellars. And the food? Very, very good – we'd gladly wait for a table (it's popular for lunch) for another serve of *pimientos del piquillo rellenos de merluza* (small peppers stuffed with hake).

Tasca La Laguna (☎ 922 63 33 30; Calle Juan de Vera 53; tapas/raciones €2.40-9.50; 5pm-2am Wed-Mon) A great, lively night-time haunt, where the so-called tapas are actually sizable portions of mouth-watering delight. Try the *salchichas* (pork sausages) with three different sauces.

Drinking & Entertainment

Students provide the nightlife, and the bulk of the bars are concentrated in a tight rectangle northeast of the university, known as El Cuadrilátero. At its heart, pedestrianised Plaza Zurita is simply two parallel lines of bars and pubs. It would be invidious to single out a handful from so many – just set off bar-hopping and find what suits your tastes.

Getting There & Around
BUS

There is a stream of buses to Santa Cruz (No 015 is best, as it takes straight you to Plaza España for €1) and a regular service to Puerto de la Cruz (Nos 101 and 102), La Orotava (No 062) and beyond.

Car street parking is a minor hell. There's a paying underground car park beneath Plaza San Cristóbal.

SAN ANDRÉS & AROUND

The village of San Andrés, all narrow, shady streets, is 6km northeast of Santa Cruz. It is distinguished by the now-crumbled round tower, which once protected the town, and some good little fish restaurants, which alone justify the short journey. Bustling **Marisquería Ramon** (Calle El Dique 23; mains €7-36; ⓥ closed Mon) is a polished, popular eating house just southwest of the tower. It gets packed to its fishy gills at lunch time, which is all handled with aplomb by the bustling waiters. Pick your fish from the glass-fronted fridge and go for the giant house salad as an accompaniment.

It matters not one jot that the golden sands for the **Playa de las Teresitas**, just beyond the village, were imported from the Sahara. It's an extremely pleasant beach where the sunbathers are almost exclusively Spanish, whether local or from the mainland. Parking is available (although quite limited) and it's perfectly safe for children to swim here.

There are frequent buses (No 910) from Santa Cruz to San Andrés, continuing on to Playa de las Teresitas. Bus No 245 goes northeast from San Andrés to the end of the road at Igueste, following another 6km of beautiful coastline.

TAGANANA & THE ANAGA MOUNTAINS

A spectacular trip leads up the Barranco de las Huertas to cross the Anaga range (geologically the oldest part of the island) and plummet down on the other side to the little hamlet of Taganana. The views to the craggy coast from above it are breathtaking.

Bus No 246 comes to Taganana at least six times daily from Santa Cruz.

There's little to see or do in Taganana, but it's only a few more kilometres to the coast and **Roque de las Bodegas**, which has a number of small restaurants and drink stands. Local windsurfers, surfers and boogie boarders savour its beach – and, even more so, the rocky strand of **Almáciga**, 1.25km eastwards.

If you have your own wheels, backtracking up and into the Anaga mountain range and heading west at the intersection (follow signs for La Laguna) continues a spectacular excursion. It's a ridge ride with views of the ocean to both north and south and of the islands of Gran Canaria and El Hierro rearing from the seas, if the air's clear. Take time to pause at the numerous *miradores* (lookouts) along the way.

Festivals & Events

Taganana hosts an odd celebration in March or April (the date changes), in which an effigy of Judas Iscariot is burned in a kind of collective purging of the villagers' sins and guilty consciences!

BAJAMAR & PUNTA DEL HIDALGO

You might want to allow for a side trip to this part of the coast as you head towards La Laguna from Taganana. Once the mountain road has dropped to the plain, turn west for Tegueste. About 10km beyond the junction, you reach the local seaside resort of Bajamar (via Tejina). The only real swimming is in large man-made rock pools awash with Atlantic rollers, but it is popular with Canarios and mainland Spaniards.

As resorts go, it's pretty low-key, which can be an attraction in itself. Three kilometres northeast, Punta del Hidalgo is an extension of Bajamar. Locals try their luck on boogie boards in the surf of Playa de los Troches.

If you want to stay in Bajamar, try the amiable **Hotel Delfín** (☎ 922 54 02 00; hotel delfin@rthsl.es; Avenida el Sol 39; s/d/tr €31/46/66.50; Ⓟ Ⓧ ⓓ), which has some lovely sea views and well-appointed rooms (breakfast included). Reception is open 24 hours and wheelchair access is good.

Bus No 105 runs here every 30 minutes from Santa Cruz via La Laguna. It costs €2 to Bajamar and €2.30 to Punta del Hidalgo.

TACORONTE & EL SAUZAL

In keeping with its role as one of the island's most important wine regions, the town of Tacoronte celebrates its fiesta of **Cristo de los Dolores** with harvest festivities on the first Sunday after 15 September. It's a good time to be here as much wine tasting is done.

Downhill from the modern town centre is the **Iglesia de Santa Catalina** (signposted) – a bright little whitewashed church built in the Canaries' colonial style. You'll also see a handful of traditional old houses, but otherwise there really isn't a lot to the place.

Just beside the El Sauzal exit from the motorway is **Casa del Vino La Baranda** (☎ 922 57 25 35; Autopista del Norte; admission free; ⓥ 11am-10pm

---

LA MATANZA DE ACENTEJO & LA VICTORIA

At the spot now called La Matanza de Acentejo (The Slaughter of Acentejo), Bencomo's Guanches inflicted a nasty defeat on Alonso Fernández de Lugo's Spaniards in 1494. Two years later, though, de Lugo was back and this time he had better luck, winning a decisive victory over the Guanches 3km south of the scene of his earlier defeat. Predictably, the village that eventually sprang up here was known as La Victoria.

Bus No 101 links these towns to Puerto de la Cruz and Santa Cruz.

Tue-Sat, 11am-6pm Sun), a museum devoted to wine and its production, located in a traditional Canarian country house. It's a charming place, with some beautiful views of El Teide on a clear day. It also has a well-regarded restaurant.

In summer, classical-music concerts are held here as part of the Classical Music at Casa del Vino programme (call the Casa del Vino for more information if you're here in August).

Bus No 101 links these towns to Puerto de la Cruz and Santa Cruz every 30 minutes or hourly (according to the time of day).

THE NORTH

PUERTO DE LA CRUZ

pop 30,500

Without a doubt, Puerto de la Cruz is the major tourist engine of northern Tenerife, yet it's managed to cling to its small-town personality. The result is a pretty coastal town, with palm trees swaying along a seaside promenade, that's also a real, working town, where locals come to chat in the central plaza. It's a good deal calmer than the resorts of the south, though there is still a lot to keep you busy and the nightlife has something for everyone.

History

Until it was declared an independent town in the early 20th century, Puerto de la Cruz was just the port of the wealthier area of La Orotava. Bananas, wine, sugar and cochineals (dye-producing insects) were

exported out of the merchant ports here, and a substantial bourgeoisie class developed in the 1700s. In the 1800s, the English arrived, first as merchants and later as sun-seeking tourists, marking the beginning of the tourist transformation that characterises the town today.

Orientation

The heart of Puerto de la Cruz is the busy square Plaza Charco. The historic buildings are huddled around the plaza, while to its east, a long coastal promenade marks the site of major tourist developments (such as high-rise hotels and the Costa Martiánez saltwater pool complex). To the west of Plaza Charco is a maze of pedestrian streets, though the further west you go the less well kept the town becomes. The Playa Jardín at the western edge of town is a good 25 minutes walk from the centre.

Information

BOOKSHOPS

The Bookshop (☎ 922 37 40 37; Calle Iriarte 42; ☽ 10am-1.30pm & 5-7pm Mon, Wed & Fri, 10am-1.30pm Tue, Thu & Sat) New and used books, CDs and videos in English, Spanish and a handful of other languages.

EMERGENCY & MEDICAL SERVICES

Hospital Tamaragua (☎ 922 38 05 12; cnr Calles Agustín de Béthencourt & Valois; ☽ 24hr) Private clinic in the centre of town.
Le Ro (☎ 922 37 33 01; Edificio Martina, Avenida Generalísimo; ☽ 9am-noon Mon-Fri, closed summer) Specialist shop for disabled and elderly travellers, offering wheelchair rental and travel assistance.
Police Station (☎ 922 37 84 48; Plaza Europa)

INTERNET ACCESS

Internet Café Pl@za (☎ 922 37 66 78; www.plazadelcharco.com; Plaza Charco, Centro Comercial Olimpia; per 30 mins €2.40; ☽ 10am-2pm & 4-10pm)

LAUNDRY

Lavandería Minosa (☎ 922 38 32 58; Calle Mazaroco 26; wash & dry up to 4k €6; ☽ 9am-1pm & 4-7.30pm Mon-Fri, 9am-1pm Sat)

POST

Main Post Office (Calle Pozo)

TOURIST OFFICES

Tourist Office (☎ 922 38 60 00; www.puertodelacruz.org; Plaza Europa; ☽ 9am-7pm Mon-Fri, 9am-noon Sat)

PUERTO DE LA CRUZ

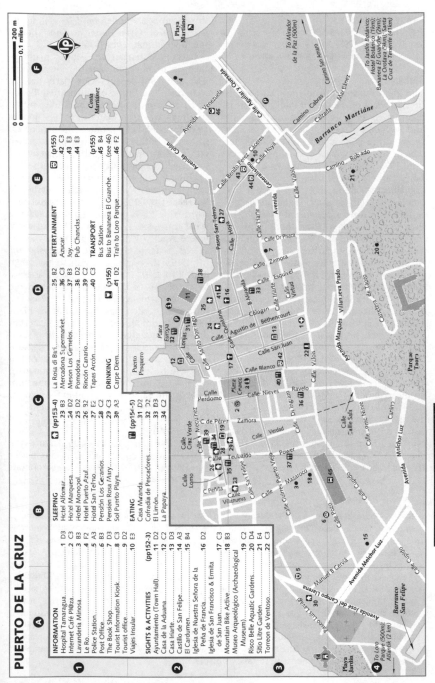

INFORMATION

Hospital Tamaragua	**1** D3
Internet Café Pl@za	**2** C3
Lavandería Minosa	**3** B3
Le Ro	**4** F2
Police Station	**5** A3
Post Office	**6** B3
The Book Shop	**7** D3
Tourist Information Kiosk	**8** C3
Tourist office	**9** D2
Viajes Insular	**10** E3

SIGHTS & ACTIVITIES (pp152-3)

Ayuntamiento (Town Hall)	**11** D2
Casa de la Aduana	**12** C2
Casa Iriarte	**13** D3
Castillo de San Felipe	**14** A3
El Cardumen	**15** B4
Iglesia de Nuestra Señora de la Peña de Francia	**16** D2
Iglesia de San Francisco & Ermita de San Juan	**17** C3
Mountain Bike Active	**18** B3
Museo Arqueológico (Archaeological Museum)	**19** C2
Risco Belle Aquatic Gardens	**20** D4
Sitio Litre Garden	**21** E4
Torreon de Ventoso	**22** C3

SLEEPING 🛏 (pp153-4)

Hotel Alfomar	**23** B3
Hotel Marquesa	**24** D2
Hotel Monopol	**25** B3
Hotel Puerto Azul	**26** B2
Hotel San Telmo	**27** E2
Pensión Los Geranios	**28** C2
Pensión Rosa Mary	**29** C3
Sol Puerto Playa	**30** A3

EATING 🍴 (pp154-5)

Casa Miranda	**31** D2
Cofradía de Pescadores	**32** D2
El Limón	**33** D3
La Papaya	**34** C2
La Rosa di Bari	**25** B2
Mercadona Supermarket	**36** C3
Meson Los Gemelos	**37** B3
Pomodora	**38** D2
Rincón Canario	**39** C2
Tapas Arcón	**40** C3

DRINKING 🍷 (p155)

Carpe Diem	**41** D2

ENTERTAINMENT 🎭 (p155)

Azucar	**42** C3
Joy	**43** E3
Pub Chanclas	**44** E3

TRANSPORT (p155)

Bus Station	**45** B4
Bus to Bananera El Guanche	(see 46)
Train to Loro Parque	**46** F2

TRAVEL AGENCIES

Viajes Insular (☎ 922 38 02 62; www.viajesinsular.es; Avenida Generalísimo 20) This is the best local travel agency and can help with air fares, ferry travel, car rental etc.

Sights

The Plaza Europa, a balcony of sorts built in 1992, may be a modern addition, but it blends well with its historic surroundings and is a good place to start your visit. The tourist office is here, as is the **ayuntamiento**, which was a banana-packaging factory until 1973. From here head down the Calle Lonjas, where on the corner you'll find the **Casa Miranda**, one of the town's better examples of 18th-century Canarian architecture. It's now a restaurant (see p154). Beyond it is **Casa de la Aduana** (built in 1620), the old customs house, where now you can find some of the best artisan shops in town. A short walk away is **Museo Arqueológico** (Archaeological Museum; ☎ 922 53 58 16; Calle Lomo 9; admission adults/children under 8/children & students €3/free/1.50; ⊙ 10am-1pm & 5-8pm, Tue-Sat, closed Aug), with its collection of ceramics, maps and Guanche memorabilia.

Next head southeast to the **Plaza Charco** (Puddle Plaza), so named because it used to fill up with water every time a storm sent waves over the port walls and into town. The plaza (raised a few years ago, so there are no more puddles) is the centre of town life, and it's full of activity day and night. Just off the plaza is **Iglesia de San Francisco**, which was tacked on to tiny **Ermita de San Juan**, the oldest structure in the town (built in 1599). Three blocks away is **Iglesia de Nuestra Señora de la Peña de Francia**, a 17th-century church with three knaves, a wooden *mudéjar* ceiling and the image of 'Gran Poder de Dios', one of the town's most revered saints.

Several Canarian mansions, many of them in poor repair, dot the town centre. The mid-18th-century **Casa Iriarte** (Calle San Juan), once the home of intellectual Tomás de Iriarte and the site of clandestine political meetings, has seen better days. The **Torreon de Ventoso** (Calle Valois) is one of the better-kept historic buildings. The tower once formed part of the town's Augustine convent and was used to keep watch over the port.

Outside the town centre there are also some noteworthy spots, such as **Castillo de San Felipe** (☎ 922 38 36 63; ⊙ open for special events only) beside Playa Jardín, and the **Mirador de la Paz** above town, a square with great views where Agatha Christie supposedly was inspired to write the novel *The Mysterious Mr Quin*. Don't miss a visit to the **Jardín Botánico** (☎ 922 38 35 72; Calle Retama 2; admission €3; ⊙ 9am-6pm Oct-Mar, 9am-7pm May-Sep) on the road out of town. Established in 1788, the botanical garden has thousands of plant varieties from all over the planet. Just 1km down the road, the **Sitio Litre garden** (☎ 922 38 24 17; Carretera del Botánico; admission €4.50; ⊙ 9.30am-2.30pm) boasts a luscious orchid collection and the town's oldest *drago* (dragon tree; see p37). Another tropical oasis is the **Risco Belle Aquatic Gardens**, which sit in the heart of the **Parque Taoro** south of the town centre.

LORO PARQUE

Where else can you see 3000 parrots (the world's largest collection) all in one place? **Loro Parque** (☎ 922 37 38 41; www.loroparque.com; Calle

---

GOING BANANAS

Bananas have been grown in the Canary Islands for centuries, though they only really came into their own as *the* export cash crop around the 1870s. Today they are still the single most important crop in the islands and the most important foreign-currency earner after tourism.

Easily grown in tropical and subtropical environments, bananas brim with vitamins A and C, potassium and carbohydrates. People have been raving about them since ancient times – Alexander the Great encountered them during his conquests in India, 300 years before Christ.

The banana plant is, in fact, an outlandishly large herb. After the first planting, it can take up to 15 months for fruit to appear. From its underground stem (or rhizome) springs a false trunk, all sappy and bendy (like rolled-up newspaper) that can grow up to 6m. The false trunk gives forth a huge, spear-shaped, mauve flower, from which will grow a bunch of up to 150 bananas, the whole divided into 'hands' of 10 to 20 'fingers' (pieces of fruit). As each plant bears only one bunch, the false trunk is pruned away to make way for new ones, sprouting from the same underground stem, to take its place.

The winding road to Taganana across the Anaga range (p149)

Tenerife's Pico del Teide at sunset (p160), seen from Alto de Garajonay, La Gomera (p188)

DAMIEN SIMONIS

The Saharan sands of Playa de las Teresitas, San Andrés, Tenerife (p149)

DAMIEN SIMONIS

Terraced hillside of Valle Gran Rey,
La Gomera (p192)

INGRID RODDIS

DAMIEN SIMOI

Gomeran honey for sale at Plaza
Américas, San Sebastián de la Gomera
(p180)

INGRID RODD

Casas rurales (country houses) in
Benchijigua, La Gomera (p191)

View of San Sebastián de la Gomera from the water (p180)

DAVID EI

Avenida Loro Parque; adult/child €21/10.50; ⓨ 8.30am-6.45pm), the self-declared 'must' of the Canaries, is home to 340 species of parrots along with other exotic animals, all considered 'ambassadors of their species' by the park's ownership. Unless you object in principle to wild animals in captivity, the park is really quite impressive. Clean and well laid out, it's a fun family outing. Don't miss the dolphin and parrot shows, the aquarium with 15,000 aquatic animals, and the world's largest 'penguinarium'.

You could walk here, but much easier is hopping on the free train that leaves every 20 minutes from Avenida Venezuela.

BANANERA EL GUANCHE
Take a look around the **Valle de la Orotava** (Orotava Valley) and you can't miss the importance banana plantations have in the area. See a working plantation up close and learn everything you ever didn't need to know about cultivating, trading and eating bananas at **Bananera El Guanche** (☎ 922 33 00 17; www.bananaelguanche.com; Carretera del Botánico; adult/child 8-12 €6.75/3.40; ⓨ 9am-6pm). The Bananera is about 2km out of Puerto de la Cruz on the road leading to La Orotava, but if you don't have a car, take the free bus that leaves every half-hour from Avenida Venezuela.

Activities
COSTA MARTIÁNEZ
Designed by Canario César Manrique (see p117), the watery playground of **Costa Martiánez** (☎ 922 38 59 55; Avenida Colón; adult/child €3.50/1.10; ⓨ 10am-sunset, last entry 5pm Oct-Apr, 6pm May-Sep), northeast of the centre, has four saltwater pools and a big 'lake' in the centre. It can get crowded, but the small volcanic beaches around are probably even more so. Swim, sunbathe, or grab a bite at one of the many restaurants and bars.

ADVENTURE SPORTS & DIVING
Offering a hodgepodge of adventure-sport rental, excursions and courses, **El Cardumen** (☎ 922 36 84 68; Avenida Melchor Luz 3; ⓨ 9.30am-1.30pm & 5-8pm Mon-Fri, opens 10am Sat) is the place to go if you're looking for action.

Mountain Bike Active (☎ 922 37 60 81; www.mtb-active.com; Edificio Daniela 26, Calle Mazaroco; bike rental from €36 per day; ⓨ 5-7pm), just across from the bus station, organises trips to El Teide and around.

Divers should ring **Atlantik** (☎ 922 36 28 01; ⓨ 9am-6.30pm Mon-Fri, 12.30-2pm Sat), a scuba outfitter based in the Hotel Maritim, 2km west of the town centre.

Organised Tours
The **tourist office** (☎ 922 38 60 00) offers five different guided routes through town. Contact the office or meet up with the guides at the information kiosk on Plaza Charco.

For nature hikes, contact local guide **Gregorio** (☎ 922 38 40 55; fax 922 33 09 10; Hotel Tigaiga, Parque Taoro 28; trips per person €30-40). Trips include a picnic lunch and transport.

Festivals & Events
Puerto de la Cruz is big on fiestas. In February, the town pitches into **Carnaval** with a gusto approaching Santa Cruz's Carnaval festivities (see p138 and p142). On 3 May, crosses and chapels are decorated with flowers in a simultaneous celebration of the city's foundation and the **Exaltation of the Cross**. On the eve of the saint's day of San Juan, 23 June, grafted on to the pre-Christian celebration of midsummer's day, bonfires light the sky and, in a throwback to Guanche times, goats are driven for a dip in the sea off Playa Jardín. The town's main celebrations are in July, when there's a whole programme of events, such as concerts, parades and public dinners. The most rambunctious celebration, at least for the kids, is the 29 November **Fiesta de Los Cacharros**, when children rush through the streets, dragging behind them a string of old pots, kettles, pans, car spares, tin cans – just about anything that will make a racket.

Sleeping
You will not be at a loss for good accommodation in Puerto de la Cruz, in all price ranges.

BUDGET
Pensión Rosa Mary (☎ 922 38 32 53; Calle San Felipe 14; s €15-18, d €20-25) The décor at this place is a bit out of date but the friendly owner is rightly proud of this welcoming *pensión*, which has a sunny rooftop terrace and clean rooms.

Pensión Los Geranios (☎ 922 38 28 10; Calle Lomo 14; d €24) The comfy, double-only rooms are small but well decorated, and some have balconies for the same price. The *pensión* is on a quiet side street.

Hotel Puerto Azul (☎ 922 38 32 13; www.hotel -puertoazul.com; Calle Lomo 24; s €15-18, d €23-33) Down the street from Los Geranios, rooms here are tiny and have an institutional air, but each has a newish, clean bathroom.

Hotel Alfomar (☎ /fax 922 38 06 82; Calle Peñita 6; s/d/tr €15/21/30) A poster of the Spanish king and queen sits above the elevator, welcoming you to this basic but friendly one-star hotel. Rooms smell a little stale, but have adequate private bathrooms and nice balconies.

MID-RANGE

Hotel Marquesa (☎ 922 38 31 51; www.hotelmarquesa.com; Calle Quintana 11-13; s €33-42, d €48-67; ⚑) Built in 1712, this was one of the town's original hotels. Rooms are simple, but most have balconies, and the hotel's interior, built around a central patio, is truly lovely. The hotel's Tasca restaurant is a nice place for an informal seafood dinner.

Hotel Monopol (☎ 922 37 03 10; Calle Quintana 15; s €37-59, d €70-120 incl breakfast & dinner; ⚑) Just down the street from Hotel Marquesa is another original hotel, this one built in 1742. Canary-type balconies give it charm and the interior is somewhat kitsch, with tropical flowers strewn everywhere. Rooms are small but well equipped.

Hotel San Telmo (☎ 922 38 58 53; hotelsantelmo @hotelsantelmo.com; Paseo San Telmo 18; s €34-37, d €60-66; ⚑) Like the reception, rooms look as though they haven't been refurbished since 1969. They're comfortable and clean, though, and the hotel couldn't be more central.

TOP END

Hotel Botánico (☎ 922 38 14 00; www.hotelbotanico .com; Avenida Richard J Yeoward 1; s/d incl breakfast €193/ 276; P ✗ ⚑ ⚑ ⚑) The most exclusive hotel on this part of the island, the Botánico has beautiful gardens, a great pool area and a new spa centre (see the boxed text on p172). Rooms are comfortable though not luxurious, with big balconies and all standard amenities.

Sol Puerto Playa (☎ 922 38 41 51; www.solmelia .com; Avenida José del Campo Llanera 2; s/d €92/114; P ✗ ⚑ ⚑) It's one of those giant, towering hotels that could be anywhere in the world, but the service is good, the location convenient and the rooms clean (though tiny!).

Eating
BUDGET

Cofradía de Pescadores 'Gran Poder de Dios' (☎ 676 87 38 56; Calle Santo Domingo; mains €10; ☺ noon-midnight) You may be put off by the somewhat grubby doorway of this humble restaurant and fishermen's union, but you should enter anyway. The reward is the freshest fish in town, cheaper than it's sold anywhere else (though admittedly the patio dining room could use a thorough cleaning).

Tapa Arcón (☎ 922 37 19 88; Calle Blanco 8; tapas about €4) *Papas arrugadas* (wrinkly potatoes) with *mojo* (spicy salsa sauce), mussels and fried squid are just a few of the tapas you can nibble while sitting out on the bar's pavement café.

El Limón (☎ 922 38 16 19; cnr Calles Esquivel & B Miranda; daily special €6) A fun vegetarian café and juice bar where you can get veggie dishes, coffee and hard drinks, too.

Mercadona Supermarket (Calle Nieves Ravelo 6) Groceries for self-caterers.

MID-RANGE

Rincón Canario (☎ 922 38 12 83; Calle Cruz Verde 2; mains €6-12) One of several good eateries on this street, dishes here range from traditional seafood plates to internationalised chicken curries. The downstairs Canary-style patio is cheerful.

Meson Los Gemelos (☎ 922 37 01 33; Calle El Peñón 4; mains €5-8) The house specialities are grilled meats and friendly service. There's a covered interior patio and lots of locals.

La Papaya (☎ 922 38 28 11; Calle Lomo 10; mains €6-8) A series of small dining rooms with rock walls, this is a charming place that serves sole cooked seven ways. There are Canarian touches on a largely international menu.

La Rosa di Bari (☎ 922 36 85 23; Calle Lomo 23; mains €6-10) Pastas and other Italian specialities are served in an elegant dining room.

Pomodora (☎ 922 38 13 28; Punta Viento; mains €5-10) The location, in a cave under the seaside promenade, is the main draw at this restaurant and pizzeria. Diners get a fantastic view of the rocky coast.

TOP END

Casa Miranda (☎ 922 37 38 71; Calle Santo Domingo 13; mains €9-13) A three-storey Canarian mansion built in 1730, this was the family home of 18th-century Venezuelan president Francisco de Miranda. Nowadays you can get seafood and grilled meats in the fine dining room, or order tapas out on the pavement café.

Drinking & Entertainment

Most nightspots are in the town centre (Plaza Charco and around) or along Avenida Generalísimo.

Azucar (☎ 922 38 70 14; Calle Iriarte 1; ☺ 8.30pm-2.30am) A good place to start the night off, with tasty tapas and the gamut of Caribbean cocktails. Dancing starts around midnight.

Pub Chanclas (Calle Hoya 62) After Azucar, head here for upbeat Spanish pop.

Joy (☎ 922 37 39 85; Calle Obispo Perez Cáceres; admission free before 2am, €6 with drink after 2am) A dark disco pumping a mix of techno, pop and house. It's popular with the local 20-something crowd.

Carpe Diem (☎ 600 68 98 87; Calle Quintana) For something a little quieter, this is a refined wine and cocktail bar with ocean views.

Getting There & Away

The bus station is on Calle Pozo in the west of town. There are frequent departures for Santa Cruz (about 45 minutes). Prices range from €1.20 for a short ride up to €12 or more for a trip across the island. No 103 is direct while No 102 calls by Tenerife Norte airport and La Laguna. Nos 325, 354 and 363 offer a regular service to Icod de los Vinos. No 340 passes by both island airports four times daily and No 343 has four daily services to Playa de las Américas. A number of routes pass through La Orotava.

Getting Around

For information about bike rental, see p153. For details about car hire, see p252.

The long-distance bus routes starting in or passing through Puerto de la Cruz often do double duty as local buses.

Taxis are widely available and are an easy and relatively inexpensive way to jet across town (a 15-minute ride should cost less than €5).

LA OROTAVA

pop 39,095

It doesn't get more postcard-perfect than this colonial town, where you'll find cobblestoned streets, flower-filled plazas and more noteworthy wooden balconies than in the rest of the island put together. La Orotava is probably the prettiest town on Tenerife, and is one of the most truly 'Canarian' places in all the Canary Islands.

The lush valley surrounding 'la villa' (the village, as the town is known) has been one of the island's most prosperous areas since the days of the Guanches. As early as the 16thcentury, well-to-do Spaniards were building churches and manor houses here. The valley is a major cultivator of bananas, potatoes and vineyards, and the area is also known for embroidery.

Information

EMERGENCY

Police Station (☎ 922 33 01 14; Calle Cólogan 2)

TOURIST OFFICES

Tourist Office (☎ 922 32 30 41; www.villadelaorotava .com in Spanish; Carrera Escultor Estevez 2; ☺ 8.30am-6pm) A well-marked tourist route of the town's major monuments starts from this office.

Sights

More than any other Tenerife town, La Orotava has been able to preserve the beauty of its past. Colonial mansions and old stone churches stand proudly, surrounded by manicured gardens. The centre is easy to cover on foot, though you'll need at least half a day to appreciate it.

Plaza Constitución, a large, shady plaza just a block from the tourist office, is a good place to start. On the plaza's northeastern side is the **Iglesia de San Agustín**, a simple church with a pretty wooden ceiling. Next door, the stately **Liceo de Taoro** building (1928) is a huge, pink monument to the finer things in life. An English-style garden separates the mansion from the street, and though it looks standoffish you can walk inside and have a drink at the café. The Liceo is a private cultural society, but you can pay a nominal fee of around €1.50 to be a member for a day.

Also on the plaza are the 19th-century **Jardínes del Marquesado de la Quinta Roja** (☺ 9am-6pm), a series of orderly flower gardens cascading down the hillside. The gardens are worth a visit, but be warned that it's a real hike to get to the top of them!

If plant life is your thing, also visit the sweet-smelling **Hijuela del Botánico** (☺ 9am-2pm Mon-Fri) just across Calle León. This small botanic garden was created as a 'branch' of the

TENERIFE

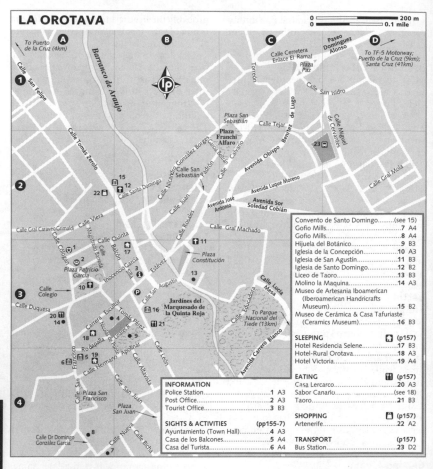

LA OROTAVA

INFORMATION
Police Station..................................1	A3
Post Office....................................2	A3
Tourist Office.................................3	B3

SIGHTS & ACTIVITIES   (pp155-7)
Ayuntamiento (Town Hall)...............4	A3
Casa de los Balcones.......................5	A4
Casa del Turista.............................6	A4
Convento de Santo Domingo........(see 15)	
Gofio Mills...................................7	A4
Gofio Mills...................................8	A4
Hijuela del Botánico.......................9	B3
Iglesia de la Concepción.................10	A3
Iglesia de San Agustín....................11	B3
Iglesia de Santo Domingo...............12	B2
Liceo de Taoro..............................13	B3
Molino la Maquina.........................14	A3
Museo de Artesania Iboamerican	
(Iberoamerican Handricrafts	
Museum)....................................15	B2
Museo de Cerámica & Casa Tafuriaste	
(Ceramics Museum)......................16	B3

SLEEPING   (p157)
Hotel Residencia Selene.................17	B3
Hotel-Rural Orotava.......................18	A3
Hotel Victoria..............................19	A4

EATING   (p157)
Casa Lercaro................................20	A3
Sabor Canario.........................(see 18)	
Taoro......................................21	B3

SHOPPING   (p157)
Artenerife...................................22	A2

TRANSPORT   (p157)
Bus Station.................................23	D2

larger Jardín Botánico in Puerto de la Cruz. Around 3000 plant varieties are gathered here, and there are birds and butterflies too.

Also on Calle León is **Museo de Cerámica** (Ceramics Museum; ☎ 922 32 14 47; Calle León 3; admission €2; ☼ 10am-6pm Mon-Sat, 10am-2pm Sun), boasting the largest clay-pot collection in Spain. The museum is well laid out, and there are detailed explanations in several languages – but these are just pots, after all, and after a few dozen they all begin to look the same.

Head down Calle Tomás Zerolo to visit **Museo de Artesania Iberoamericana** (Iberoamerican Handicrafts Museum; ☎ 922 32 17 46; Calle Tomás Zerolo 34; admission €2.10; ☼ 9.30am-6pm Mon-Fri, 9.30am-2pm Sat), housed in the former Convento de Santo Domingo. Exploring the cultural

relationship between the Canaries and the Americas, the museum exhibits musical instruments, ceramics and other titbits. The **Iglesia de Santo Domingo** next door has beautiful carved doors and a rich *mudéjar* ceiling.

Back in the centre of town, the **Iglesia de la Concepción** (☼ 11am-1pm & 5-8pm) is worth a look; this is one of the finest examples of Baroque architecture in all the archipelago. Follow Calle Colegio (which becomes San Francisco) uphill from behind the church. This street is home to several of the **Doce Casas**, 12 historic Canary mansions that are one of La Orotava's most distinguishing features. At Colegio No 5-7 is the 17th-century **Casa Lercaro** (☼ 10.30am-8.30pm), now a home-furnishings shop and a café (see Sleeping & Eating, below).

Down the street at San Francisco 3 is the **Casa de los Balcones** (Casa Fonesca; ☿ 8.30am-6.30pm Mon-Fri, 8.30am-5pm Sat, 8.30am-1pm Sun). Built in 1692, the interior and exterior balconies feature ornate carvings. Across the street is **Casa del Turista**, or Casa de la Familia Molina, which has similar features but is less outstanding. Its opening hours are the same and in both Casas local handicrafts are for sale.

On your way up Calle Colegio, stop at No 5–7, where **Molino La Maquina** (☿ 8am-1pm, 2.30-6pm) makes *gofio*, a bland powder made from corn or wheat. The pretty, white stone towers were the old water mills used to grind corn. Now they're just for show and everything is done electronically. There is another historic **gofio mill** further along the road (see the La Orotava map or follow your nose). At both you can buy *gofio* for around €1.30/kg.

Festivals & Events

Corpus Christi takes on special meaning in La Orotava. Each June, mammoth floral carpets using tons of volcanic dirt, flower petals, leaves, branches and any other organic material at hand are painstakingly designed in the streets and plazas.

Sleeping & Eating

Hotel-Residencia Silene (☎ 922 33 01 99; Calle Tomás Zerolo 9; s/d €25/38) At this tiny place all rooms look like your grandmother's guest room: welcoming and old-fashioned, if a bit stuffy. The enormous balconies and €1 breakfast are nice perks.

Hotel Rural Orotava (☎ 922 32 27 93; www.hotel orotava.com; Calle Carrera 17, s €50, d incl breakfast €65-75) Cosy and with character, this is one of the town's best options. A 16th-century manor house, its original details such as wooden ceilings and floors have been well preserved, and antique furniture and white linens in the rooms show it off well.

Hotel Victoria (☎ 922 33 16 83; www.victoria.tene riffa.com; Calle Hermano Apolinar 8; s €53-77, d incl breakfast €71-96) Another converted 16th-century house, though the interior here looks and feels modern. The hotel restaurant is open Tuesday to Sunday for lunch and dinner.

Sabor Canario (☎ 922 32 27 93; www.hotelorotava .com; Calle Carrera 17; mains €5 to €8) You'll find tasty local fare at this friendly place (located in Hotel Rural Orotava), which also has a pleasant patio.

Casa Lercarco (☎ 922 32 62 04; Calle Colegio 5-7; tapas around €6) This home-interiors shop serves tapas-style plates of local and peninsular cheeses and cured meats in a privileged spot overlooking the valley.

Taoro (☎ 922 33 00 87; Calle León 5; menú €8) has great pastries and a cheap restaurant in the interior patio.

Shopping

Artenerife (☎ 922 32 22 85; Calle Tomás Zerolo 27; ☿ 10am-5pm Mon-Fri, 10am-1pm Sat) Located in the Casa Torrehermosa, Artenerife sells high-quality (and high-priced) island crafts.

Getting There & Away

La Orotava is 9km inland from Puerto de la Cruz, and it's well connected to the town by bus Nos 345, 348, 350, 352 and 353. Bus No 63 (and others) comes from Santa Cruz. Call the **bus station** (☎ 922 33 27 02) for more information.

ICOD DE LOS VINOS

pop 21,803

An umbrella-shaped tree called the *drago* is the cause of a lot of fuss in this town. Indeed, it's worth a look and a read-up (see p37), but there is more to Icod than its revered plant life. The shady main square, Plaza San Marcos, is a lovely, leafy spot to rest and enjoy the town's white-walled church, and the town itself is a maze of hilly streets where you'll find quiet squares, and shops selling local wines.

Information

Tourist Office (☎ 922 86 96 00; Calle San Sebastián 6) Just off the main plaza.

Sights

The most promoted sight and the pride of the town is the world's largest and oldest **drago tree**, which supposedly has been here for more than 1000 years. Past **Plaza Constitución** (aka Plaza Pila), a square with historic Canary homes, is **Drago Park** (fax 922 81 44 36; admission €4; ☿ 9am-6.30pm, fax ahead to request a guided tour), where you can pay to get up close to the famous tree. The best view, however, is the free one from **Plaza San Marcos** in the centre of town. Here you

TENERIFE

can also see the **Iglesia de San Marcos**, which has an ornate silver high altar and a sacred **museum** (admission €0.60).

The second major sight here is the **Mariposario del Drago** (☎ 922 81 51 67; Avenida Canarias; adult/child €6.50/4; ☯ 9am-6pm Mon-Sat, 9.30am-6pm Sun summer, 9am-6pm Mon-Sat, 9.30am-7.30pm winter), a hot and sticky greenhouse full of exotic butterflies. There are so many that they'll land right on you! The price seems high for such a tiny place, but the visit is interesting and educational.

Eating

Enjoy good local dishes at **Restaurante Carmen** (☎ 922 12 24 32; Calle Hércules 2; mains €6-12). The restaurant has a homespun feel, with square wooden tables and yellow walls full of decorations. Another place for Canary fare is the simple and sunny **Agustín y Rosa** (☎ 922 81 07 92; Calle San Sebastián 15; menú del día €9).

Getting There & Away

If you're driving, you'll find that parking here can be difficult. Save yourself a headache and follow the signs towards the paid car park near the Mariposario. Arriving by bus is easy: No 106 comes directly from Santa Cruz, No 354 comes from Puerto de la Cruz, and No 460 makes the trip up from Playa de las Américas. The **bus station** (☎ 922 81 13 04) is to the northeast of the town centre.

GARACHICO

pop 5700

Really just a cluster of low houses around a lively central plaza, Garachico is one of the few coastal towns that has kept its Canarian identity in the face of tourism. There are no big hotels, probably because there is no real beach, though swimming in the natural, volcanic coves along the rocky coast is a joy.

Named for the rock outcropping off its shore (*gara* is Guanche for 'island', and *chico* is Spanish for 'small'), Garachico is a peaceful place. You'd never guess the history of calamities that lies behind its whitewashed houses and narrow, cobblestoned streets perfect for strolling. Garachico was once an important commerical port, but its unlucky inhabitants suffered a series of disasters that all but finished off the hamlet. Freak storms, floods, fires, epidemics and in 1706 a major volcanic eruption that destroyed the port and buried half the town in lava, reduced the once-thriving town to a poor shadow of its former self.

Just outside town you can hike trails that follow the path of the disastrous lava flow.

Information

Tourist Office (☎ 922 13 34 61; Calle Esteban de Ponte 5; ☯ 9am-2pm & 3-7pm Mon-Fri, 10am-3pm Sat) Stocks maps of the town.

Sights & Activities

The heart and soul of Garachico is the main plaza, dotted with palm trees and café tables. At night adults play cards while children run around, and the plaza becomes *the* place to see and be seen. Here is the **Iglesia** and former **Convento de San Francisco** (1524). The latter houses a small **museum** (☎ 922 83 00 00; admission €0.60; ☯ 10am-6pm Mon-Fri) about the town's history. Just off the plaza is the **Iglesia de Santa Ana**, with a dominating white bell tower.

Down Calle San Roque, a simple **art museum** (admission €0.60; ☯ 10am-6pm Mon-Fri) is

---

HOW TENERIFE MISSED THE EVOLUTIONARY BOAT

The Galápagos Islands, at the other end of the world, far off the Pacific coast of South America, are famous for having inspired Charles Darwin's theory of evolution.

Less well known is that the first port of call for Darwin's ship, the *Beagle*, was to have been Tenerife. But just as the crew were preparing to land, the island authorities told them they would have to spend a couple of weeks in quarantine. So the captain turned the nose of his boat and headed for the deep Atlantic.

Who knows? Had they landed, Tenerife's wealth of endemic plants, trees and animals, evolved over thousands of millennia in this island microcosm, might well have contributed to the development of Darwin's ideas. As he wrote regretfully in his journal, 'We have just left perhaps one of the most interesting places in the world, just at the moment when we were near enough for every object to create, without satisfying, our utmost curiosity.'

located in the former Convento de Santo Domingo. A less conventional sight in the other direction, in the Plaza Juan González (aka Plaza Pila), is the **Puerta de Tierra** (Land Gate), all that's left of Garachico's once-thriving port. It was once right on the water but thanks to the volcanic eruption is now in the centre of town.

On the water you can visit **Castillo de San Miguel** (admission €0.60; 10am-8pm Mon-Fri, 10am-6pm Sat & Sun), a squat stone fortress built in the 16th century. Sometimes cultural expositions are held inside.

Divers will want to check out the **scuba centre** in the *pensión* El Jardín (922 83 02 45; www.argonautas.org; Calle Esteban de Ponte 8; dives with equipment rental €30).

Festivals & Events

The **Romería de San Roque**, held each August, is Garachico's most important annual festival, and the town fills with pilgrims (and partiers) from throughout the island. San Roque (St Roch), the town's patron, was credited with saving the town from the Black Death, which arrived in 1601.

Sleeping

Garachico is a great place to stay if you're looking for a small-town feel with easy access to northern Tenerife.

El Jardín (922 83 02 45; www.argonautas.org; Calle Esteban de Ponte 8; s €18, d €18-45) The only place in town that can qualify as 'budget'. It varies as much in room quality as it does in price – while the €45-per-night room is spacious and almost elegant, the cheaper rooms seem to be decorated with the leftovers of a 1970s flea market. If possible, see your room before booking.

Hotel La Quinta Roja (922 13 33 77; www.quinta roja.com; Glorieta de San Francisco; s €73-85, d incl breakfast €84-120;) For more class and comfort, head to this infinitely charming hotel. A restored 16th-century manor house set on the main plaza, it has spacious rooms with wooden floors and ceilings and cheery tiled bathrooms. The breakfast is exquisite, and the friendly staff can arrange day trips or excursions.

Hotel San Roque (922 13 34 35; www.hotelsan roque.com; Calle Esteban de Ponte 32; s €158-185, d incl breakfast €185-230;) The exclusive, stylish San Roque blends the old (the hotel is a restored 17th-century mansion) and the

new (the French owners have a passion for modern art). All rooms have spa baths, CD players and contemporary furniture.

Hotel Rural El Patio (922 13 32 80; www.hotel patio.com; Finca Malpaís 11; s €50-87, d €63-114) Just west of town in El Guincho is this tranquil, white-walled place tucked among plantains. The house was built in 1563, and rooms are spread throughout a series of small buildings set around a stone patio.

Eating

Casa Gaspar (922 13 31 06; Avenida República de Venezuela 2; mains €10) This classy place is everybody's favourite restaurant, serving the freshest seafood in town with a smile.

There are several other restaurants along the Avenida. For a cold beer and a chat with the locals, head to the **kiosk bar** in the Plaza Libertad.

Getting There & Away

Bus No 107 connects the town with Santa Cruz, La Laguna, La Orotava and Icod de los Vinos, while No 363 comes and goes from Puerto de La Cruz.

THE CENTRE

PARQUE NACIONAL DEL TEIDE

Covering 18,990 hectares, the Teide is not Spain's largest national park, but it is the most popular, with a whopping four million visitors a year. Most of these come by bus and don't wander far off the highway that snakes through the middle of the park, but that just means that the rest of us have more elbow room to explore. There are currently 21 walking tracks crisscrossing the park (30 more tracks will soon be signposted), marking the way through volcanic terrain, beside unique rock formations, and up to the peak of El Teide, which at 3718m is the highest mountain in Spain.

This area was declared a national park in 1954, with the goal of protecting the landscape and the wildlife here, which includes 14 plants not found anywhere else on earth. The landscape, while not beautiful in a traditional sense, is fascinating; more than 80% of the world's volcanic formations are here in the park, including rough badlands (deeply eroded barren areas), smooth *pahoehoe* or *lajial* lava (rock that looks like twisted taffy) and pebble-like lapilli. There are also complex formations such as volcanic pipes and cones. The park protects nearly 1000 Guanche archaeological sites, many of which are still unexplored and all of which are unmarked, preventing curious visitors from altering the sites.

El Teide itself, which is visible from many parts of the island and on clear days can be seen from the other islands, dominates the northern end of the park. If you don't want to make the four-hour climb to the top, take the cable car (below). Surrounding the peak are the *cañadas*, flat depressions likely caused by a massive landslide 180,000 years ago.

Information

The park has two excellent visitors centres, **El Portillo** (☎ 922 35 60 00; www.mma.es; Carretera La Orotava-Granadilla; ☉ 9am-4pm) in the northeast and **Cañada Blanca** (☎ 922 37 33 91; Carretera La Orotava-Granadilla; ☉ 9am-4pm) in the south. At either you can pick up maps and hiking information as well as an incredibly informative little guidebook to the park (€8). Take time to see the exhibits about the park's volcano and wildlife and, at El Portillo, stroll around the centre's botanic garden.

Pico del Teide

elevation 3718m

The **cable car** (☎ 922 69 40 38; adult/child under 14 €20/14; ☉ 9am-4pm) provides the easiest, most popular and most expensive way to get up to the peak of El Teide. If you don't mind paying €20 per person to say you've been to the top of Spain (well, almost the top, as you land 200m below the summit), the views are great – unless a big cloud is covering the peak, in which case you won't see a thing. On clear days the volcanic valley spreads out majestically below, and you can see the islands of La Gomera, La Palma and El Hierro peeking up from the Atlantic. It takes just eight minutes to zip up 1200m.

A few words of warning: those with heart or lung problems should stay on the ground, as oxygen is short up here in the clouds. It's chilly, too, so no matter what the weather's like below, bring a jacket. The cable cars, which each hold around 35 passengers, leave every 10 minutes, but get here early (before noon) because at peak times you could be queuing for two hours! The last ride down is at 5pm.

See p161 if you want to tackle the mountain on foot or just want to hike the final 200m.

Roques de García

A few kilometres south of the peak, a bizarre set of rocks pokes up in an unlikely fashion from the plains around the *parador* hotel. Known as the Roques de García, they are the result of erosion of old volcanic dykes, or vertical streams of magma. The hard rock of the dykes has been bared while

THE DAY EL TEIDE SWALLOWED THE SUN

These days scientists can explain exactly how a volcano erupts: magma from the earth's core explodes through the crust and spews ash, rock and molten lava over the land. But the Guanches living in pre-Hispanic Tenerife had a more romantic version. According to a legend which almost surely refers to the last eruption of El Teide in the 13th century, the so-called eruption was caused when El Teide swallowed the sun. The people believed that the devil, 'Guyota', lived inside 'El Cheide', as El Teide was then known. One day he came out of his underground lair and saw the sun. Jealous of its light, he stole it and hid it inside his lair, causing death, destruction and darkness all over the island. The Guanches begged Chaman, the sky god, for help, and the god battled Guyota inside the volcano. The Guanches knew Chaman had triumphed when one morning they awoke to see the sun back in the sky and the volcano plugged with rock, trapping the evil Guyota inside forever.

The legend coincides perfectly with what happened following the medieval eruption. An ash cloud covered the sun, and the only light the Guanches saw came from the mouth of the active volcano, leading them to believe the sun was trapped there. The volcano's toxic ash would have killed many plants and animals, and the 'battle' going on inside the volcano was probably the rumblings following the eruption. The 'plug' that safely trapped Guyota in El Cheide was new volcanic rock.

surrounding earth and rock has been gradually swept away. The weirdest of the rocks, the Roque Cinchado, is wearing away faster at the base than above, and one of these days is destined to topple over (so maybe you shouldn't get up too close). Spreading out to the west are the bald plains of the Llano de Ucanca. The road out to Los Cristianos is to the southwest and the road to Santiago del Teide is to the northwest.

This is the most popular spot in the park and is viewed by nearly 90% of its visitors. The car park is always crowded, but most people just leave their cars or tour buses for a 15-minute glance. If you plan to hike the relatively easy trail that circles the rocks, you'll most likely be alone.

Pico Viejo

With a name meaning 'old peak', this is the last of Tenerife's volcanoes to have erupted on a grand scale. In 1798, its southwestern flank tore open, leaving a 700m gash. Today you can clearly see where fragments of magma shot over 1000m into the air and fell pell-mell. Torrents of lava gushed from a secondary, lower wound to congeal on the slopes. To this day, not a blade of grass or a stain of lichen has dared return to the arid slope.

Walking

Few of El Teide's visitors venture far off the paved highway that slices through the park, but it's worth being one of them.

GUIDED WALKS

Park rangers host guided walks up the mountain in both Spanish and English. The pace is gentle and there are frequent information pauses. Even though you'll huff and puff rather more than usual because of the high altitude, the walks are suitable for anyone of reasonable fitness (including children aged over 10).

Groups leave at 9.15am and 1.30pm from the visitors centre at El Portillo, and at 9.30am and 1pm from the visitors centre at Cañada Blanca. Walks last about two hours.

Groups are small, so it is essential to call ahead and reserve a spot (☎ 922 29 01 29).

SELF-GUIDED WALKS

The general park visitors' guide lists 12 walks, ranging in length from 600m to 17.6km, some of which are signed. Each walk is graded according to its level of difficulty (ranging from 'low' – the most frequent – to 'extreme'!). You're not allowed to stray from the marked trails, a sensible restriction in an environment where every tuft of plant life has to fight for survival.

Of these, among the most popular is the 16km **Las Siete Cañadas** day walk between the two visitors centres; longish, yes, but almost entirely flat and utterly without shade, so wear a wide-brimmed hat. Set out along the broad track that begins just across the road from the El Portillo visitors centre. In a little over five minutes, cross a barrier that heralds the entrance to the park, and you're away. Within half an hour, you're amid whorls, hanks and twists of lava, looking like melted chocolate that might have congealed only yesterday. You'll see lots of the 'Teide Broom' shrubs (see p36) that fill so much of the park, and if you're here in early summer you'll likely see the spectacular 'Teide Bugloss' (see p36) in bloom. Allow four to five hours and remember to take plenty of water with you.

If you have a vehicle, drive it to the far end of the walk and take the morning bus (see p162) back to the start. This way, you're not dependent upon catching the afternoon bus back to your vehicle and can time the walk the way you want to.

You don't have to be a masochist to enjoy the challenge of walking from road level up to **La Rambleta** at the top of the cable car, followed by a zoom down in the lift. Get off the bus (ask the driver to stop for you) or leave your car at the small roadside parking area (signed 'Montaña Blanca' and 'Refugio de Altavista') 8km south of the El Portillo visitors centre and set off along the 4WD track that leads uphill. En route, you can make a short (half-hour, at the most), almost level detour along a clear path to the rounded summit of **Montaña Blanca** (2750m), from where there are splendid views of Las Cañadas and the sierra beyond. Alternatively, make the Montaña Blanca your more modest goal for the day and head back down again (about 2½ hours for the round trip).

For the full ascent to La Rambleta, allow about four hours. Although, of course, you can make it easy by taking the cable car up and walking back down!

TENERIFE

ON LOCATION IN TENERIFE

Tourists aren't the only ones awed by the lunar landscapes of volcanic Tenerife. Many film-makers, looking for arid backdrops for spaghetti westerns or otherworldly landscapes for alien movies, have come here to shoot. Parts of *Star Wars, The Ten Commandments* and the original *Planet of the Apes* were filmed here. The lands around El Teide are especially popular, particularly along the 'Siete Cañandas' trail.

THE SUMMIT AWAITS

Even though the steep there-and-back walk between the top of the cable car and the summit takes only around 20 minutes, it isn't easy. The difficulty resides not in the climb but in the hoops you have to jump through before you set out.

There's a permit scheme in force that restricts, to 50 at one time, the number of visitors who can pass on to the summit.

That's fair enough, and understandable, given that you're entering a fragile, unique ecosystem that's fighting to survive. But you can't just pick up a permit from the visitors centre. You need to go to the national park's **Servicio de Uso Público office** (☎ 922 29 01 29; 4th fl, Calle Emilio Calzadilla 5; 9am-2pm Mon-Fri) in Santa Cruz. Take a photocopy of the personal details pages of your passport or ID. Permits, which are free, specify both the date and the two-hour window during which you're allowed beyond the barrier. In addition to the permit, take your passport or ID with you on the walk, as you'll probably be asked to produce it.

And enjoy the view – you will have deserved it!

IT'S ASTRONOMICAL

One of the best places in the northern hemisphere to stargaze is the **Teide Astronomical Observatory** (☎ 922 60 52 00), set just off the TF-24 highway that runs between La Laguna and the El Portillo visitors centre. Scientists from all over the world come to study here and at its sister observatory in La Palma (see the boxed text on p198). You can add your name to the list of those who've seen the insides of the mammoth telescopes scattered here if you stop by any Friday morning between 10am and 12pm, December to March. You'll need to make an appointment first. For more information, see www.iac.es.

Sleeping & Eating

Parador Nacional (☎ 922 37 48 41; canadas@parador.es; s/d €78/97; Ⓟ) Camping isn't allowed inside the park, but you can stay here. Rooms are comfortable if far from stylish, and the cosy restaurant serves excellent local dishes. However, we think the best thing about the Parador is its tranquil mountain views.

North of the El Portillo visitors centre are several restaurants offering sandwiches and simple fare.

Getting There & Away

Surprisingly, only two public buses arrive at the park daily: the No 348 from Puerto de la Cruz and the No 342 from Playa de las Américas. Both head to the park at 9.15am, arriving at the *parador*, and leave again at 4pm. That's good news for the countless tour companies that organise bus excursions to and around the park, though not so encouraging for the independent traveller. The best way to visit is with your own car. There are four well-marked approaches to the park, the prettiest being the TF-24 coming from La Laguna, which meets up with the TF-21 at El Portillo visitors centre. The TF-21 is the only road that runs through the park, and the *parador*, the cable car and the visitors centres are all off this highway. To see anything else, you have to walk. From the south, the TF-21 and TF-38 highways come up from Vilaflor and Chío, respectively.

THE NORTHWEST

PUNTA DE TENO

When ancient explorers mistook the Canary Islands for Atlantis (see p19), it must have been because of places like Punta de Teno. It's what daydreams are made of – waves crashing against a black, volcanic beach, solitary mountains rising like giants in the background, the constant whisper of lizards scurrying in the brush... This beautiful spot, the most northwestern of the island, is no secret. But it still has a wild charm that the dozen or so cars parked around here can't take away. You can fish off the point, splash along the rocky coast or just absorb the view.

Think twice about heading out here if there have been recent heavy rains, as mud and rockslides are not uncommon.

Take the highway towards Buenavista del Norte and keep following the signs to the Punta, some 7km further on the highway TF-445. Bus Nos 107 and 363 come and go to Buenavista from Santa Cruz and Puerto de la Cruz, respectively, but to get out to the Punta you need your own car.

MASCA

If you arrive before, say, 10am, you could be tricked into thinking that you're the one who discovered this little mountain town. It wouldn't be true, of course – plenty of tourists and tour buses arrive daily – but nevertheless Masca feels like an oasis lost in the harsh landscape.

For the **Fiesta de la Consolación** in the first week of December, many of the villagers wear traditional dress and bring out their *timples* (string instruments resembling a ukelele) and other instruments for an evening of Canarian music.

A popular but demanding trek is down Barranco de Masca to the sea. Allow six hours to hike there and back or do it the smart way – ring the Nashira Uno office (see p164) the day before to reserve a place on the afternoon boat from the beach at the bottom of the ravine to Los Gigantes.

The boat leaves at 3.30pm, assuming the ocean is calm, and sometimes there's a later

one too but you have to call to confirm times.

There are two No 355 buses per day to/from Santiago del Teide.

LOS GIGANTES & PUERTO DE SANTIAGO
pop 5600

Two towns, one heart. It's hard to tell where one beach town starts and the other ends, but that doesn't really matter because both are tourist hot spots boasting sun and sand, high-rise hotels, and restaurants galore. Don't miss the **Acantilados de los Gigantes** (Cliffs of the Giants), imposing rock walls that soar up to 600m out of the ocean along the town's northern coast. The submerged base of these cliffs is a haven for marine life, making this one of the island's supreme diving areas.

The best views of the cliffs are from out at sea (there's no shortage of excursion companies offering short cruises) and from Playa de los Gigantes, a tiny volcanic beach beside Los Gigantes' port that offers little more than a breathtaking view. A far nicer beach is Playa de la Arena in Puerto de Santiago. Though there are no cliff views, you can see across to La Gomera on a clear day.

Information
Tourist Office (☎ 922 86 03 48; Calle Manuel Ravelo 20, local 35; ⏰ 9am-3.30pm Mon-Fri, 9am-12.30pm Sat) On the 2nd floor of the shopping centre across from Playa de la Arena.
WP Perceptions Internet Center (☎ 922 86 80 60; Calle Lajial, local 7; per 30 mins €3; ⏰ 10am-4.30pm Mon-Fri) In the same building as Hotel Playa La Arena (see p164).

DETOUR

The northwest corner of Tenerife offers some of the most unspoilt and least-visited terrain on all the island. From Garachico, head west on the TF-42 highway past Buenavista and down the TF-445 to the lonely, solitary **Punta de Teno** (p162).

You'll have to return to Buenavista to catch the TF-436 mountain highway to Santiago del Teide. Curve after hairpin curve obligates you to slow down and enjoy the view. Terraced valleys appear behind rugged mountains, and **Masca** (p163) makes the perfect pit stop. When the highway reaches Santiago, you can head either north on the TF-28, towards Garachico, or south towards Los Gigantes, where signs point the way down to **Playa de la Arena** (p163), a sandless beach that's nearly as pretty as Punta de Teno, though much more developed.

You'll need a full morning to complete the route, or longer if you plan to stay a while at the coast or in Masca.

TENERIFE

TRAGEDY AT LOS RODEOS

Behind Tenerife's fun-and-sun reputation lies a dark episode in the island's past. In 1977 it was the site of one of the worst air disasters of all time when two 747s loaded with holiday-makers from the Netherlands and the United States collided on the runway, killing all 583 people on board.

Ironically, neither plane was scheduled to be at Tenerife Norte (Los Rodeos) airport that fateful March day. Both had been rerouted there when the Canary Island's only other airport, Las Palmas, was closed because of a bomb threat (Tenerife Sur was built later). Foggy weather and misunderstood instructions from air traffic control contributed to the tragedy.

Activities

If you're only going to dive in one spot on Tenerife, do it here. Marine life is abundant, with stingrays among the most frequently spotted creatures. **Los Gigantes Diving Centre** (☎ 922 86 04 31; www.divingtenerife.co.uk; Los Gigantes Marina; dive with equipment rental €41; ☷ 9.30am-5pm Mon-Fri), an English-owned outfit, has been diving here for more than a decade. Dive excursions are run at 10am and 2pm. You could also try **Marina Los Gigantes** (☎ 922 86 80 95; www.tenerifeafondo.org; Los Gigantes Marina; ☷ 9.30am-4.30pm), which makes four dives daily and also runs whale and dolphin trips. Both outfits can help arrange accommodation.

Equally as popular are whale and dolphin trips. The waters between western Tenerife and La Gomera are among the world's best for spotting these amazing creatures, and numerous boats search for them. One reputable outfit is **Nashira Uno** (☎ 922 86 19 18; www.losgigantes.com/nashira.htm; Edificio Florencia, Avendia Jose Gonzalez Fortes; 3hr safari adult/child aged 5-12 €30/15; ☷ 9.30am-2.30pm Mon-Fri & 5-7pm Sat), which makes three trips daily, and also offers jet ski rentals and parascending.

Flipper Uno (☎ 922 86 21 20; Avenida Marítima 15; 3hr excursion adult/child €32/16; ☷ 9am-1.30pm & 4-7pm), located behind Renate restaurant, is a replica of an 18th-century galleon. It sails twice daily and most trips include food and a swim beside the cliffs.

Sleeping & Eating

Apartamentos Marinero (☎ 922 86 09 66; poblado marinero@cajacanarias.net; Acantilados de los Gigantes; 2-person apt €66, 4-person apt €75-91) Looking out over the marina in Los Gigantes, the flats here aren't luxurious. But they are clean and spacious, with cool tile floors and balconies with views of either the cliffs or an interior patio.

Hotel Playa la Arena (☎ 922 79 51 58; www.spring hoteles.com; Calle Lajial 4, Playa de la Arena; s €62-86,

d €84-120 ; (P) ☒ ☐ ☒) Upscale, and one of the better-value places. The sprawling foyer is impressive, and the 432 rooms have marbled bathrooms, balconies and tasteful décor with rich wooden furniture. Includes breakfast.

You won't be hard-pressed to find a restaurant (most are by Los Gigantes Marina or along the Avenida Marítima), but there are slim pickings for truly good ones.

Restaurante Marinero Jesse (☎ 922 86 19 55; Playa de Los Gigantes; mains €12-18; ☷ 11am-11pm) Right off the beach, Jesse specialises in paella, fresh seafood and fantastic views. There is also an impressive list of local wines. The atmosphere is casual by day and dressier in the evening, when reservations are usually necessary.

El Rincón de Juan Carlos (☎ 922 86 80 40; Pasaje de Jacaranda 2; mains €11-27, menú del día €39; ☷ dinner only) A bit fancier (and pricier), this is just off the main plaza in Los Gigantes. Try the baked *cherne* (stone bass fish) with almond sauce.

La Vela (☎ 637 21 76 42; Calle Los Guíos, Poblado Marinero; ☷ 10.30am-11pm summer, 10.30am-8pm winter) Head here for dessert, where amazingly rich, Italian-style ice cream is made on the premises.

Getting There & Around

Bus No 473 comes and goes from Los Cristianos, and bus No 325 links the town with Puerto de la Cruz. For those with wheels, it's a well-marked 40km drive from Los Cristianos.

If you're in a rush, call a taxi on ☎ 922 86 16 27.

THE EAST

A modern motorway (the TF-1) cruises down Tenerife's eastern coast, linking Santa Cruz to the resorts of the south in an easy

40-minute drive. The lunar-like landscape of the east is dry, dusty and sterile, and bright little villages scattered around contrast sharply with harsh rocks and treeless hills. If you're in a hurry the motorway is fine, but to really get the feel of this volcanic terrain, brave the winding TF-28 highway, formerly the principal thoroughfare, which crawls along the mountain ridge above the coast.

CANDELARIA
pop 16,000

Just 18km south of Santa Cruz is Candelaria, a busy little village whose only real claim to fame is its basilica, home to the patron saint of the entire Canary archipelago, Our Lady of Candelaria (see below for details about her mysterious arrival on the island). The ornate 1950s **Basílica de Nuestra Señora de Candelaria** (☎ 922 50 01 00; ☯ 7.30am-1pm & 3-7.30pm) sits at the edge of the town centre, overlooking a rocky beach and flanked by a plaza where nine huge statues of Guanche warriors stand guard. During the official festivities for the **Virgin de la Candelaria** celebration on 15 August (see the boxed text below), this plaza fills with pilgrims and partiers from all over the islands.

On the northern edge of town, two hotels and the best swimming beach in the area form Las Caletillas, which is technically a separate town, although you would never know it.

Information
Tourist Office (☎ 922 50 04 15; fax 922 50 26 83; Plaza CIT; ☯ 9am-2pm & 4.30-7pm Mon-Fri) Located at the northern end of town, beside Hotel Tenerife Tour.

Sleeping, Eating & Drinking
Hotel Tenerife Tour (☎ 922 50 02 00; www.tenerife tour.com; Avenida Generalísimo 170; s €41-53, d €52-76; P ⬜ ⬜) Right on the water, this place has comfy rooms with balconies. Views are either of the large pool complex and ocean beyond, or of the hotel's tropical garden.

Gran Hotel Punta del Rey (☎ 922 50 18 99; www.hoteles-catalonia.es; Avenida Generalísimo 165; s/d €54/60; ⬜ ⬜) This isn't on the beach, but it has a beautiful saltwater pool designed by César Manrique (see the boxed text on p117).

You'll find several informal bars around the church plaza (Plaza Patronata de las Canarias).

Getting There & Away
If you're driving, take exit 9 of the TF-1 motorway. Bus Nos 122, 123, 124 and 131 connect the town with Santa Cruz.

GÜIMAR & AROUND
pop 16,000

A rural village with views of a gauzy blue ocean in the distance, Güimar is the first important town you'll come to on the TF-28 (if coming from Candelaria). Though the town centre is well kept and is nice for a stroll, most people come to see the **Pirámides de Güimar** (☎ 922 51 45 10; www.piramidesdeguimar.net; Calle Chacona; adult/child aged 9-12/child under 8 €9.75/5/ free; ☯ 9.30am-6pm), a centre featuring much-restored pyramid ruins that explores an intriguing question: could the Canarios have had contact with America before Columbus famously sailed the ocean blue? The theory that they did was developed by renowned Norwegian scientist Thor Heyerdahl, who

---

THE VIRGIN OF CANDELARIA

In 1392, a century before Tenerife was conquered and Christianised, a statue of the Virgin Mary holding a *candela* (candlestick) washed up on the shore near modern-day Candelaria. The Guanche shepherds who found the statue took it to their king and, according to legend, the people worshipped it. When the Spanish conquered the island a century later, they deemed the statue miraculous, and in 1526 commander Pedro Fernández de Lugo ordered that a sanctuary be built for it. The logical explanation of the 'miracle' is that the statue was either the figurehead from a wrecked ship, or a Virgin brought by French or Portuguese sailors, who had been on the island before the Spanish conquest. In either case, the statue was swept away by a violent storm in 1826 and was never found. The ornate statue that is today swathed in robes in the Basilica of Our Lady of Candelaria was carved soon after by local artist Fernando Estévenez. On 15 August, the day she was supposedly found by the Guanches, the Virgin is honoured by processions, numerous masses and a kitschy re-enactment of costumed 'Guanches' worshipping her.

lived on Tenerife until his recent death and based his ideas on the Mayan-like pyramids discovered in Güímar.

Bus Nos 120, 121, 124 and 127 from Santa Cruz stop at the Güímar bus station, a few blocks from the pyramids.

On the TF-61 highway linking Güímar with **Puertito**, a tiny coastal town where you can have a swim, is the rural hotel and restaurant **Finca Salamanca** (☎ 922 51 45 30; www.hotel-fincasalamanca.com; Carretera Güímar-Puertito; s incl breakfast €46-62, d incl breakfast €63-96; P ☲). Set in a peaceful spot surrounded by mountains, rooms are in cheery bungalow-like buildings. The restaurant, an old tobacco barn where local products are served with pride, has mains costing from €9 to €20.

About 12km further south is **El Escobonal**, where the **Archeological & Ethnographical Museum of Agache** (☎ 922 53 04 95; Plaza El Escobonal; ☹ 5-8pm Mon-Fri) displays all kinds of odds and ends related to Guanche and island culture. Continue on to **Fasnia** and the tiny **Ermita de la Virgin de los Dolores**, a chapel perched on a hill at the edge of town (off the TF-620 highway). It's usually closed, but is worth the short drive up for the panoramic views of the harsh, dry landscape.

Keep on the TF-620 past the *ermita* to reach **Roques de Fasnia**, a little town carved into the volcanic cliff. There's a tranquil, volcanic, black-sand beach that's rarely crowded. Eat cheap at **Maracay** (☎ 922 53 04 01; Cruce de los Roques), a bar and restaurant on the highway. It's low on atmosphere but has tasty grilled meats for around €6.

A bit further south is **Porís de Abona**, a charming little fishing village built around a small harbour. There's a pool-like area where you can take a dip in the ocean, and a boardwalk that gives great views of the rugged coast.

EL MÉDANO
Better brush up on your surfing jargon. Thanks to the unceasing breezes along the coast here, El Médano is a world-class spot for windsurfers, and enthusiasts from the world over flock to the town's long, flat beaches. The laid-back atmosphere they bring with them gives the resort a bohemian air, a refreshing change from the touristy feel elsewhere. A long wooden boardwalk lines the main beach, and it's perfect for evening strolls, though the

sandy beach itself (not a rock in sight!) is also great for walking.

Information
Tourist Office (☎ 922 17 60 02; www.granadilla.com; Plaza los Príncipes de España; ☹ 9am-3pm Mon-Fri, 9am-noon Sat)
Cyber Corner (☎ 922 17 83 59; Paseo Nuestra Señora Mercedes de Roja 26, local 2; ☹ 10am-2.30pm & 5-11pm) Connect to the Internet at this spacious and friendly place right off the beach.

Activities
Without a doubt, windsurfing is the main activity here. At any time of the day the water is dotted with dozens of surfers showing off their skills. Many centres offer classes and equipment rental, but novices should be aware that the winds here are very strong and challenge even the pros! If you decide to give it a go, head to the **Surf & Kite Center** (☎ 922 17 66 88; www.surfcenter.info; ☹ 10.30am-7pm), where you can rent equipment or sign up for courses. It's on the beach past Hotel Playa Sur Tenerife.

For true thrill-seekers, kitesurfing (surfing on a short board while a huge kite pulls you along) is the newest way to end up in hospital. Get information at the Surf & Kite Center's **Azul Kite School** (☎ 922 17 83 14; Paseo Mercedes de la Roja 26; 12hr course €200; ☹ 1am-1pm & 4-7pm Tue-Sat, 11am-8pm Tue-Sat in summer).

Sleeping & Eating
Hotel Playa Sur Tenerife (☎ 922 17 61 20; www.hotel playasurtenerife.ws; Playa El Médano; s/d €50/78; ☲ P) If the sound of the waves puts you to sleep, you'll like it here. It sits on a quiet spot by the beach at the edge of town. Rooms have attractive pale wooden furniture, small balconies and incredible ocean views.

Senderos de Abono (☎ 922 77 02 00; Calle Peatonal de la Iglesia 5; s/d incl breakfast €40/60; ☒ ☲) This rural hotel is to the northwest of El Médano in Granadilla de Abona, a town just off the TF-28 with a lovely stone church. A converted post office, its rooms are in a series of old stone buildings and are packed with local flavour and charm. The hotel's restaurant is decorated with antique farm equipment and offers delicious entrées for €6 to €9.

Tasca Frontos (☎ 922 77 72 54; Granadilla; mains €9-11; ☹ 1-10.30pm Tue-Sat) Just a few kilometres further north of Senderos de Abono is this restaurant serving both traditional and creative Canary cuisine on a terrace with amazing mountain views. During working hours, you can also visit Tasca's winery.

Casa Fito (☎ 922 77 71 79; Carretera General Chimiche 4; mains €12-13) Keep on the TF-28 for another excellent rural restaurant. A former tomato factory, Casa Fito is a homespun, stone-walled restaurant serving simple dishes made with fresh, local ingredients.

There are several good restaurants on the pedestrian thoroughfare that runs through El Médano's town centre. Try **El Astillero** (☎ 922 17 82 20; Paseo Marcial García 2; mains €6-10) for local dishes and a homy feel. Afterwards, head down the street for home-made ice cream at the **Heladería Picacho** (Paseo el Picacho 2).

Getting There & Away
El Médano is just east of the Tenerife Sur airport, off exit 22 of the TF-1. Bus No 470 leaves hourly from Los Cristianos, and No 116 leaves every two hours from Santa Cruz.

THE SOUTH

LOS CRISTIANOS, PLAYA DE LAS AMÉRICAS & COSTA ADEJE
pop around 150,000
Bring the extra-large tub of sunscreen, because you're going to need it. 'Beach and sun and beach and sun' is the mantra of this lively resort area on the southwestern tip of the island. Large multipool resorts with all-you-can-eat buffets have turned what was a sleepy fishermen's coast into one of the most important economic engines of Tenerife. The beaches (artificially made with Saharan sand, but nice just the same) draw a mixed crowd. You're as likely to see toddlers with their exasperated parents as you are a retired couple or a group of 20-somethings out for a good time.

The nightlife, which comes in every shape and size of neon lights, is a draw too. And don't forget the dizzying array of restaurants. Where else can you eat in an 'authentic Mexican Cantina' for lunch, a 'real Parisian café' for dinner and have a drink in a familiar-feeling Irish pub afterwards? Of course, all that variety leaves little room for Spanish culture to shine through. You can find places to sample local dishes and have a look

at some Canary crafts, but to see the true Spain, head inland or use Los Cristianos' commercial port to hop over to one of the small western islands. Here in the south, golden tans and golden beaches reign.

Orientation
Although they are three different resort areas, each with their own personality, though they're often lumped together and referred to as one. Furthest south is Los Cristianos, whose maze of a town centre still retains – barely – the feel of the fishing village it was until tourism arrived in the 1970s. Just beyond it is Playa de las Américas. Technically both are in the same municipality of Arona, but Playa de las Américas has evolved into an altogether flashier place, with high-rise hotels and scarcely a corner left without a shopping centre. Parts of it are like Las Vegas in their deliberate glamour (complete with a pyramid and fake Roman statues!), while the northern end of town, Las Verónicas, is downright seedy. The Costa Adeje flows seamlessly from the northern border of Playa de las Américas and is home to posh hotels and some of the better beaches. It's quieter and has the best reputation of the bunch, though like the rest of the coast here, it is one long strip of shopping centres and international restaurants.

The area is still building itself and roads are being constantly constructed and renamed, so finding your way around can be tough. Some streets go by more than one name, like the central avenue in Los Cristianos that's currently referred to as Prolongación General Franco, Carretera Accesso Cristianos and Bulevar Cajofe (the last seems to be the official one). The free tourist office map is helpful, but if you're still confused ask around and do what the locals do – orient yourself by the hotels and large buildings, all of which are named.

Information
BOOKSHOPS & LIBRARIES
Librería Barbara (Calle Pablo Abril 5, Los Cristianos) English, German and French titles plus maps and guidebooks.
Public Library (☎ 922 75 70 06; Centro Cultural, Plaza Pescador 1, Los Cristianos; ☺ 9am-2pm & 4-6pm Mon-Fri, 10am-12.30pm Sat) Great resource for island-related material, and some foreign-language titles.

LOS CRISTIANOS, PLAYA DE LAS AMÉRICAS & COSTA ADEJE

0 — 500 m
0 — 0.3 miles

Ⓐ   **Ⓑ**   **Ⓒ**   **Ⓓ**

INFORMATION
Hospital Las Américas.........................1 B5
Lasseter Sistemas.............................2 C5
Librería Barbara................................3 C4
Orange Badge...................................4 D6
Police Station (Las Américas)..............5 B5
Police Station (Costa Adeje)................6 B4
Police Station (Los Cristianos).............7 D4
Post Office (Costa Adeje)....................8 A3
Post Office (Los Christianos)................9 C5
Primary Care Centre.........................10 C6
Public Library.............................(see 17)
Salon Recreativo Montecarlo..............11 C5
Tourist Office.................................12 A4
Tourist Office.................................13 A5
Tourist Office.............................(see 16)
Tourist Office.............................(see 17)
Washtub Laundry............................14 B5
Whirly Wash..................................15 B6

SIGHTS & ACTIVITIES (pp169-70)
Centro Comercial San Telmo............16 B6
Centro Cultural...............................17 D4
Club de Buceo Rincón de Arona........18 B5
Le Ro.....................................(see 24)

Neptuno, Travelin' Lady & Other
  Whale Watching Excursions........19 C5
Ocean Trek..................................20 B4

SLEEPING (pp170-1)
Anyka Sur....................................21 B5
Apartamentos Mar y Sol..................22 D6
Bungalows Altamar.........................23 B4
H10 Oasis Moreque.........................24 C6
Hotel Andrea's..............................25 D4
Marcus Management.......................26 B5
Mediterranean Palace Hotel.............27 B6
Pensión La Paloma.........................28 C4
Pensión La Playa............................29 C5
Pensión Lela.................................30 C4
Playazul......................................31 B4
Tenerife Holiday Rent......................32 B6

EATING (pp172-3)
Bar El Cine...................................33 B5
Capricho.....................................34 C4
Casa del Mar................................35 B5
El Faro..36 A5
Garibaldi.....................................37 A5
Mesón Mojo Picón..........................38 B5

Punta Veró...................................39 B5
Rincón del Marinero........................40 B5
Supermercado Carolina....................41 D4

DRINKING (p173)
Caribe....................................(see 16)
Casablanca..............................(see 16)
Las Verónicas...............................42 A4
Piano Bar Safari............................43 C5

ENTERTAINMENT (p173)
La Pirámide de Arona......................44 A5
Metrópolis...................................45 A5

SHOPPING (p173)
Art Tenerife Kiosk..........................46 A4
Azulito.......................................47 C4
Rosa Rosa....................................48 C4

TRANSPORT (p173)
Bus Station (Los Cristianos)..............49 D6
Bus Station (Playa de Las Américas).50 B3
Temporary Bus Station Los
  Cristianos.................................51 C6
Touristic Tour Bus Stop...................52 A5

TENERIFE

To Puerto Colón (2km);
Water Sports Club (2km);
Excursion Shop (2km)

Costa Adeje
TF-1

To Hospital Costa Adeje; Diversity;
Aquapark Tenerife (2km); Skypark
Waterpark (4km); Aqua Club
Termal (4km); Vitanora Spa (4km);
Grand Hotel Bahía del Duque (4km);
Karting Klub Tenerife (5km);
Tropicana (6km)

To Parque Nacional
del Teide (26km)

Avenida Rafael Puig Lluvina
Avenida Pueblos
Autopista Sur

Playa del Bobo

Avenida Centenario

Barranco del Rey

To
Golf Las Américas (400m);
Las Galletas (15km);
Tenerife Surn Airport (18km)

0 — 400 m
0 — 0.2 miles

Bulevar Chajofe

Montaña Chica

Avenida Aquitecto
Gómez Cuesta

Edificio Altamar

Playas de Troya

Paseo Marítimo

Avenida Santiago Puig

Paseo Eldorado

La Montañeta

Avenida Franco Andrade Fumero
Avenida Rafael Puig Lluvina

Playa de las Américas

Avenida Antonio Domingues Alfonso
Avenida Noelia Alfonso Cabrera
Siete Islas
Gómez Cuesta

El Guincho

Avenida Aquitecto
Avenida Américas

El Cabezo Grande

Punta del Camisón

La Montaña
El Nido
Calle Ramón Pino
Calle Noruega
Avenida Suecia
Avenida Juan XXIII
Plaza Carmen
Cristobal Colón
Calle General Franco
Amellia Alayón
Calle Valle Menéndez
Caldera
Dr Sabina
Montaña Chica
Barranquillo

Calle General Franco
Calle Palom...
Avenida Juan Alfonso Franco
Calle Berlin
Calle Madrid
María Amalia Frias
Paseo Marítimo

Jesús Domínguez
Calle Espín

Los Cristianos

Los Arenales

Bulevar Chajofe

Avenida Chayofita

Calle Finlandia
Avenida
Calle Noruega
Calle Habana

Playa de las Vitas

Bridge

See Enlargement

To Arona;
Autopista TF-1 (600m);
Parque Ecológico Las
Águilas del Teide (3km);
Tenerife Sur Airport
(15km)

Carretera Autopista
Hermano Pedro Bethencourt

To Las
Galletas
(12km)

Avenida San Francisco
Amsterdam

Calle Berna
Avenida Juan Carlos
Avenida Londres
Tamesi
Asomada
Mentoco
Chalana

Paseo Marítimo

Playa de
Los Cristianos

Puerto de
Los Cristianos

Ferry
Terminal

ATLANTIC OCEAN

EMERGENCY
Police Stations Los Cristianos (☎ 922 75 71 33; Calle Valle Menéndez 5); Playa de las Américas (☎ 922 78 80 22; Avenida Noelia Alfonso Cabrera 5); Costa Adeje (☎ 922 79 78 11; Sector Las Terrazas) The Costa Adeje station is beside the Palacio de Congresos.

INTERNET ACCESS
Lasseter Sistemas (☎ 922 79 65 04; Bulevar Chajofe 8, Los Cristianos; ☼ 9am-11pm, closed Sun) It's hidden behind a stairwell, so watch out for the sign on the pavement.
Salon Recreativo Montecarlo (☎ 922 79 63 20; Calle Peatonal Berlin 2, Los Cristianos; per hr €2; ☼ 9am-1am)
The Pool Center (Centro Comercial Puerto Colón, Costa Adeje; per 30 min €2)

LAUNDRY
Washing a load costs about €6, more if you also want your clothes dried.
Washtub Laundry (☎ 922 79 44 90; Edificio Altemar, Avenida Noelia Alfonso Cabrera, Playa de las Américas) Bring in laundry by 1pm to get it back the same day.
Whirly Wash (☎ 922 79 02 99; Edificio Los Cristianos, Avenida Habana, Los Cristianos) Free pick-up and delivery.

MEDICAL SERVICES
Disabled Needs Le Ro (☎ 922 75 02 89; Calle Amsterdam 8, Edificio Mar y Sol, Los Cristianos); Orange Badge (☎ 922 79 73 55; www.orangebadge.com; Cristian Sur Apartments, Avenida Amsterdam 9, Los Cristianos) Both companies offer wheelchair rentals and Le Ro also provides specialised medical attention.
Hospital Costa Adeje (☎ 922 79 10 00; Urbanización San Eugenio, Costa Adeje)
Hospital Las Américas (☎ 922 79 24 00; Calle Arquitecto Gómez Cuesta, Playa de las Américas)
Primary Care Center (Centro de Salud Los Cristianos; ☎ 922 78 78 47; Valdés Center, Avenida Juan Carlos I, Los Cristianos)

POST
Post Office (Paseo Valero)

TOURIST OFFICES
Tourist Offices Los Cristianos (☎ 922 75 71 37; www.arona.org in Spanish; Centro Cultural, Plaza Pescador 1); Playa de las Vistas (☎ 922 78 70 11; Centro Comercial San Telmo); Playa de las Américas (☎ 922 79 76 68; Centro Comercial City Center, Avenida Rafael Puig Lluvina); Costa Adeje (☎ 922 75 06 33; Avenida Litoral) The Costa Adeje office is by the Barranco del Rey.

Activities
The 2800 average hours of yearly sunshine means that beaches are the star attraction

here, but if you just can't take another day in the sun there are plenty of other things to do to stay busy.

Most activity firms rely heavily on their 'public relations' agents to bring in tourists. Some are quite helpful; others can be bothersome. But without a doubt you'll have plenty of information at your fingertips should you choose to book a day trip or participate in one of the activities listed below.

DIVING
The volcanic coast here makes for excellent diving, and calm waters means that even a first-timer can have a thrilling 'try-dive' in the ocean. A standard dive runs upwards of €30, though the per-dive rate drops if you're planning several days of diving. **Ocean Trek** (☎ 922 75 34 72; www.tenerife-diving.com; Avenida Rafael Puig Lluvina; ☼ 9am-9pm), just beside Hotel Tenerife Sol in Playa de las Américas, offers the standard array of boat dives, courses and speciality night dives or wreck dives. Somewhat more informal is **Club de Buceo Rincón de Arona** (☎ 922 79 35 50; www.nivarnet.com /rincondearona; Muelle de los Cristianos; ☼ 8.30am-6pm), a friendly little place hidden in a shack behind the Casa del Mar. In Costa Adeje, try **Diver-sity** (☎ 922 71 71 29; www.diver-sity.com; Centro Comercial Central Playa, local 1; ☼ 9am-6pm), where nondivers can take a 'snorkelling safari'.

SAILING, WINDSURFING & BOATING
If getting packed onto a huge catamaran with dozens of strangers is your idea of a relaxing day at sea, you'll have plenty of offers from which to choose. But to find something a bit more intimate, you'll have to dig a little deeper (and pay a little more).

If money is unlimited, **Water Sport Club** (WSC; ☎ 922 71 54 04; www.tenerife.com/wsc; Puerto Colón, Costa Adeje; ☼ 9am-7pm) will set you up with a 12m sailboat, including crew and food, for a measly €550. On a more modest scale, WSC rents out jet skis for €35 for a 20-minute ride, and kayaks for €12 per hour, and offers parascending (getting tied to a parachute and pulled behind a ski boat) starting at €25.

Right beside WSC is **Excursion Shop** (☎ 922 71 41 72; www.tenerife-direct.com; Puerto Colón, Costa Adeje; ☼ 9.30am-5pm), which offers many of the same activities as WSC and sometimes at better prices. If you just want a few hours

TENERIFE

out on the water, try one of the whale-watching trips (see below).

GOLF

Constant mild weather means that Tenerife is one of the few places in the world where golfers can play year-round. It's not the most ecologically sound activity on the island (water is a constant problem, and green courses need plenty of it) but that hasn't stopped sprawling courses from popping up all around Playa de las Américas. Some of the best courses here are found at the following:

Golf Costa Adeje (☎ 922 71 00 00;www.golfcosta adeje.com; Finca Los Olivos; 18 holes €45-78; ☾ 7.30am-7pm)

Golf Las Américas (☎ 922 75 20 05; www.golf -tenerife.com; Playa de las Américas, 18 holes €50-85; ☾ 7am-7pm)

Golf del Sur (☎ 922 73 81 70; www.golfdelsur.net; Ur-banizacíon Golf del Sur; 18 holes €50-70; ☾ 7.30am-7pm)

WHALE-WATCHING

Companies offering two-, three- and five-hour boat cruises to spy on whales and dolphins are set up at the end of Playa de Los Cristianos, near the port, and in Puerto Colón in Costa Adeje. Most trips include food, drink and a quick swim. Though all are basically the same, with a three-hour trip costing upwards of €25, we especially recommend two smaller companies, **Neptuno** (☎ 922 79 80 44; ☾ 9am-7pm) and **Travelin' Lady** (☎ 609 42 98 87; child under 10 free; ☾ 9.30am-8pm Sun-Fri, noon-3pm Sat). Both offer personal service, small boats, and lower prices than many other outfits in the area.

FISHING

Deep-sea fishing jaunts range from about €36 for a three-hour trip to €70 for a day on the water. Get information from the kiosks set up at the western end of Playa de Los Cristianos or from Water Sport Club (see p169) in Costa Adeje.

Los Cristianos & Playa de las Américas for Children

This is a great area to travel with children, and there are plenty of things to keep them busy. Along the beaches, carnival-like attractions, such as bumper cars and mini bungee-jumping setups, are popular with older kids, while playgrounds on Playa

de Los Cristianos and behind the Centro Comercial in Los Cristianos can keep the little ones entertained.

Away from the beaches are several theme parks, such as **Skypark Waterpark** (☎ 922 71 63 95; Torviscas; ☾ 10am-9pm summer, 10am-6pm winter) and **Aquapark Tenerife** (☎ 922 71 52 66; San Eugenio Alto; ☾ 10am-6pm). For older kids, **Karting Klub Tenerife** (☎ 922 73 07 03; Carretera del Cho, Arona; ☾ 10am-8pm) offers go-karts and video games. All parks have free bus services. If you want a break from the children, baby-sitting services can often be found through hotel receptions.

Tours

The **Touristic Tour** train leaves every hour on the hour from 10am until 10pm just in front of the Colon Apartments on Avenida Rafael Puig Lluvina. The trip around Las Américas and Los Cristianos costs €9 for adults. Children ride for free.

Festivals & Events

The **Centro Cultural** (☎ 922 75 70 06; Plaza Pescador 1, Los Cristianos; tickets €3) offers a variety of cultural events, such as **Cine de Verano**, a summer festival of open-air movies offered (in Spanish) nightly except Wednesdays. The latest big show to hit the area is **Tropicana** (☎ 902 33 12 34; www.indigocio.com; Cruce de los Olivos, Costa Adeje), a Cuban variety show with fabulous costumes, and music that will get you moving. At the **Fuego y Danza** (☎ 922 75 75 49; La Pirámide de Arona, Avenida Américas, Playa de las Américas), Carmen Mota's Spanish ballet performs a modern interpretation of the opera *Carmen*. Tickets for all cultural events are often cheaper if organised through your hotel rather than by calling the venues.

The **Festival Son Latino** is one of the most exciting events of the year for the Latin music scene. In late August, dozens of top-name performers descend on the beaches around Playa de las Américas, playing until dawn for a giddy young crowd. The festival may have its days numbered though, as residents have had enough of the rowdy drunk crowds and are trying to convince the town council to cancel it.

Sleeping

For the die-hard independent traveller this will sound like a travesty, but the best accommodation in this hotel jungle is found

TENERIFE

with the big tour operators, whose rock-bottom prices on package deals may work out to be cheaper than a week's shopping bill back home. Some of the most popular and reputable agencies are Thomas Cook-JMC, Thompson, My Travel, First Choice and Cosmos, all of which are brimming with deals. If you decide to stake out on your own anyway, try apartment agencies first. A pleasant flat for two, with kitchen, TV and living area, starts at around €55 per night. Contact the tourist office for a full listing of agencies, or start with these: **Anyka Sur** (☎ 922 79 13 77; anykasursl@interbook.net; Apartamentos Azahara, local 5 & 6, Los Cristianos), **Marcus Management** (☎ 922 75 10 64; fax 922 75 37 25; Apartamentos Portosin, local 3, Playa de las Américas) and **Tenerife Holiday Rent** (☎ 922 79 02 11; fax 922 79 58 18; Edificio Tenerife Garden, local 4, Playa de las Américas).

BUDGET

If you're hunting for a hostal or *pensión*, look no further than Los Cristianos. That's because it's the only area hereabouts with truly budget accommodation, although the package deals mentioned previously may work out to be even cheaper. Expect a decent room for two to cost around €25 a night, and remember to book ahead, as the limited number of *pensiones* means they're often full.

Pensión La Playa (☎ 922 79 22 64; Calle Paloma 9, Los Cristianos; d/tr €24/30) The dormitory-style rooms face a lively pedestrian side street, so bring earplugs if you plan to sleep at night. A warning: La Playa is not for those with claustrophobia (or fat suitcases), as stairwells are painfully thin. The communal bathrooms are smallish but clean.

Pensión La Paloma (☎ 922 79 01 98; Calle Paloma 7, Los Cristianos; s/d/tr €18/24/30) Just across the street from La Playa, rooms here boast private bathrooms and more charm than those of its neighbours. The interior is newly refurbished.

Pensión Lela (☎ 922 79 13 19; Calle Juan XXIII 34, Los Cristianos; s/d €18/24) A little worn around the edges but clean enough, the best Lela has to offer are the wide balconies outside some rooms. The communal bathroom is kiddie-sized.

MID-RANGE

Hotel Andrea's (☎ 922 79 00 12/24; www.hotelesreveron .com; Calle General Franco 23, Los Cristianos; s/d €35/53) Some guests complain that it gets hot and noisy, but newly renovated rooms are clean, private bathrooms are more than adequate, and a small personal balcony lets in the Tenerife breeze.

H10 Oasis Moreque (☎ 922 79 03 66; www.h10.es; Avenida Juan Carlos I 28, Los Cristianos; s €45-63.50, d €60-97; ⊠ ⍑) One of the few hotels in Los Cristianos that's actually on the beach. You won't be enchanted by the bland décor, but rooms have wide balconies, with more than half of the rooms looking out to the ocean, and ceiling fans make rooms comfortable, even in summer heat. The small pool has a garden feel to it.

Apartamentos Mar y Sol (☎ 922 75 05 40; fax 922 79 54 73; Avenida Amsterdam 8, Los Cristianos; studio/1-bedroom apt €76/96; ⍑) These spacious apartments are modern and fully equipped for disabled guests, with room for wheelchairs and specially adapted bathrooms.

Bungalows Altamar (☎ 922 79 00 00; fax 922 79 25 13; Edificio Altamar, Avenida Aquitecto Gómez Cuesta, Playa de las Américas; 2-/3-person apt €45/51; ⍑) Good value, with a nice pool area and comfy apartment-like bungalows. All have balconies and kitchenettes.

Playazul (☎ 922 79 19 19; fax 922 79 16 14; Edificio Playazul, Avenida Aquitecto Gómez Cuesta, Playa de las Américas; 2-/3-/5-person apt €53/62/81; ⍑) A small step up the comfort scale from Bungalows Altamar, with the same amenities.

TOP END

Mediterranean Palace Hotel (☎ 922 79 40 11; www.marenostrumresort.es in Spanish; Avenida Américas, Playa de las Américas; s/d €132/144; Ⓟ ⊠ 🍽 💻 ⍑) Ideally located on the Los Cristianos (that is, quiet) side of Playa de las Américas, the Palace is one of four resorts in a complex on the same site, and you have access to the other hotels' pools and restaurants. Service is top-notch, and rooms are comfortable though not as grand as you'd expect from a five-star hotel.

Gran Hotel Bahía del Duque (☎ 922 71 30 00; www .bahia-duque.com; Calle Alcalde Walter Paetzmann, Costa Adeje; s/d incl breakfast €284/302; Ⓟ ⊠ 🍽 💻 ⍑) Prepare to be pampered, and to pay for it. Considered the island's top hotel, the five-star Bahía del Duque is built to look like a Canary village. Rooms are large, sunny and luxurious, and the hotel's 11 restaurants are guaranteed to help you put on a few pounds.

TENERIFE

Eating

There are so many restaurants here, and so many with short life spans, that it's impossible to give a solid overview of the dining variety on offer. From €5 Chinese buffets (most of which seem to be named 'Slow Boat') to elegant dinner shows, you'll find them all here. Some restaurants on the main drags are almost theatrical in their atmospheric depictions of Mexico, the Italian Riviera or a Parisian café, but there are hidden corners where you'll find Spanish and Canarian food too. Entrées are around €10.

BUDGET

Bar El Cine (☎ 609 10 77 58; Calle Juan Bariajo 8, Los Cristianos; mains under €6) The locals' favourite for cheap eats, El Cine is hidden on a side street behind Plaza Moncloa. The place is nothing to look at, but its fresh grilled sardines, grilled prawns and trademark chicken wings are something special.

Capricho (cnr Juan XXIII & Peatonal Roma, Los Cristianos; shakes about €3) This place has lots of fresh fruity shakes and juices.

Casa del Mar (☎ 922 79 32 75; Esplanada del Muelle, Los Cristianos; mains €6-8) Enjoy views of the sea (and the decidedly unappealing commercial port in front of it) as you savour the freshly caught *lubina* (sea bass), *dorada* (sea bream) and *merluza* (hake). On the roof is a sunny terrace bar selling drinks and ice cream.

Supermercado Carolina (☎ 922 79 30 69; Calle General Franco 8, Los Cristianos) One of the better supermarkets around.

MID-RANGE

Rincón del Marinero (☎ 922 793 553; Muelle Los Cristianos; mains €9-13) Specialising in local seafood, this place has a blue-and-white boat marking the entrance, and all tables sit under a covered terrace (proof that there's never bad weather here – there is no inside to escape into!).

Mesón Mojo Picón (☎ 922 75 02 73; Residencial Las Viñas, Playa de las Américas; mains €9-14) This place features Spanish specialities from all over the mainland, such as Andalucian gazpacho, Catalan bread with tomato, and Iberian cured sausages, and they're served to you on the informal patio.

Punta Veró (☎ 922 79 72 63; Edificio Viste Marino, Calle Jesus Dominguez 'Grillo', local 6, Los Cristianos; mains €6-15) Perfect for the indecisive – pizza, salad, home-made paella, grilled meats and seafood all share a spot on the menu, but the Gomeran owner makes sure nothing strays too far from island fare.

TOP END

El Faro (☎ 922 75 08 12; Avenida Américas, Parque Santiago V, Playa de las Américas; mains €10-17) For a couple's night out, El Faro fits the bill perfectly. Watch the world go by from the 2nd-storey terrace as you savour the international meat, fish and pasta dishes.

Garibaldi (☎ 922 75 70 60; Avenida Rafael Puig Lluvina, Playa de las Américas; mains €9-18) This fine Italian restaurant serves its meats and pastas on a romantic patio with a fountain at its centre.

GETTING AWAY FROM IT ALL – TENERIFE SPAS

Holidaying can be tough, especially when there's so darn much to see and do. Thank goodness for day spas.

Around Costa Adeje, escape to **Aqua Club Termal** (☎ 922 71 65 55; www.aquaclubtermal.com), which, according to itself, is the most comprehensive thermal and sports complex in Europe. It has 6000 sq m of floor space, all dedicated to pampering. Don't miss the Turkish bath or the 'mineral dew'.

Vitanova Spa (☎ 922 79 56 86; www.vitanovatenerife.com; Calle Alcalde Walter Paetzman s/n, Playa del Duque), also in Costa Adeje, offers massages and facials as well as things you've probably never even heard of.

The **Mare Nostrum** (☎ 922 75 75 40; www.expogrupo.com) resort, in Playa de las Américas, is also sure to spoil. There are fungal wraps (hmmm, sounds enticing) and electrotherapy for serious spa-goers, and massages and steam baths for those looking to unwind.

In Puerto de la Cruz, the new Oriental Spa Garden of **Hotel Botánico** (☎ 922 38 14 00; www.hotelbotanico.com; Avenida Richard J Yeoward 1) was preparing for its grand inauguration at the time of publication (see p154). With Thai décor throughout, here you'll be able to get an underwater massage, couple massages and seaweed wraps.

La Pirámide (☎ 922 79 63 60; Avenida Américas, Playa de las Américas; mains €9-20) The dinner theatre at the restaurant inside Arona's pyramid-shaped congress hall is a fun alternative to regular dining. The atmosphere is a cross between a cruise-boat dinner show and a 1970s red-leathered lounge.

Drinking & Entertainment

Los Cristianos' city centre pretty much shuts down after the clock strikes twelve. All the action moves down to the Centro Comercial San Telmo, the shopping centre behind Playa de las Vistas. After midnight the dull little strip is transformed into a string of nightclubs pumping out music late into the night.

In Las Américas, where having a neon sign seems to be a requirement, the number of bars will make your head spin.

Piano Bar Safari (☎ 922 75 10 65; Calle Paloma, Los Cristianos) This new bar claims to have the cheapest beer in town and without a doubt offers some of the best live music. Jazz and easy listening are the staples here – making a pleasant respite from the techno music played in many bars – and regular acts include Kenny G (he of ringlets and sax fame).

Caribe (Centro Comercial San Telmo, local 7C) This light-hearted salsa club is one of the most popular.

Casablanca (Centro Comercial San Telmo, local 17) A club with plenty of Spanish pop music.

Metrópolis (Avenida Rafael Puig Lluvina, Playa de las Américas) For the serious partier, there's no substitute for this megadisco near the Hotel Conquistador. It's considered the best dance spot in the area.

Las Verónicas on Playa de las Américas' border with Costa Adeje, is an area packed with nocturnal activity and is popular with the under-30 crowd. Unfortunately, it has a reputation for drawing troublemakers as well as the hordes out for a good time.

Shopping

Modern shopping centres are popping up on every corner, but for traditional Canary textiles, such as pretty floral-themed tablecloths and napkin sets, head to either **Azulito** (cnr Calles General Franco & Pablo Abril, Los Cristianos) or **Rosa Rosa** (cnr Calles General Franco & Pablo Abril, Los Cristianos). Though some items come from China, many are made here on the islands.

Ask to be sure. For more variety, check out one of the **Art Tenerife** (☎ 902 32 04 20) kiosks. There are several kiosks spread throughout the area, each selling artisan products from the island.

Getting There & Away

AIR

Hopping over to Playa de las Américas is easy from mainland Europe. The Tenerife Sur airport is just 30km away and daily flights from Spain, the UK, Germany and other destinations give you plenty of flying options (see p138 for details and for information on getting to/from the Tenerife Sur airport).

BOAT

Ferries come in and out of the Los Cristianos port day and night. See p250 for details.

BUS

Plenty of Tenerife's bright green TITSA buses come through the area, stopping at stations in Los Cristianos and Playa de las Américas. Bus Nos 110 (direct, €6.10, one hour) and 111 (indirect) come and go from Santa Cruz. Bus No 487 (€1.90, 45 minutes) goes to Tenerife Sur airport, but to get to Tenerife Norte airport you have to pass through Santa Cruz. Plenty of other buses run between the two resorts, en route to destinations such as Arona (No 480), Los Gigantes (No 473), Puerto de la Cruz (No 343), El Médano (No 470) and Las Galletas (No 467). At the time of writing, the Los Cristianos bus station was being renovated, so all buses were stopping on Avenida Juan Carlos I, just below the Valdés Center. For 24-hour bus information call ☎ 922 53 13 00.

Getting Around

Most of the long-distance bus routes do double duty as local routes, stopping along the major avenues of Los Cristianos and Playa de las Américas before heading out of town.

There are taxi stands outside most shopping centres; taxis also pass regularly along the larger boulevards. Getting a taxi at night usually isn't a problem, as most people choose to walk. A ride across town should cost between €5 and €7.

TENERIFE

AROUND LOS CRISTIANOS, PLAYA DE LAS AMÉRICAS & COSTA ADEJE

Exotic Parks

What strikes your fancy? Birds? Cacti? Camels? They're all here near the coast, most of them just a hop, skip and a free bus ride away (all parks below offer free bus transportation from various hotels). About 3km outside of Los Cristianos towards Arona is the **Parque Ecológico Las Aguilas del Teide** (☎ 922 72 90 10; Arona; adult/child 6-12 €17/8; ☺ 10am-6pm), a theme park whose main show stars eagles that swoop dramatically over the crowd. You can also see hippos, crocodiles and other wild beasts here.

In Guaza, the **Exotic Park** (☎ 922 79 54 24; Autopista del Sur exit 26; adult/child 6-14 €10/5; ☺ 10am-7pm) offers a chance to do things you never knew you wanted to do – like go inside a bat cave and see a 'reptilarium' up close. There are also monkeys, exotic plants, birds, and supposedly the world's largest cactus collection. At the calmer end of the spectrum is **Camel Park** (☎ 922 72 11 21; La Camella; ☺ 10am-5pm; adult €9-30, child €4.50-15), a camel-breeding and riding centre with a few traditional farm animals.

Las Galletas

If Playa de las Américas is a large pizza with all the toppings, Las Galletas is a small cheese and pepperoni. Not as big, not as flashy, but sometimes all you need. The volcanic beach is rocky and the colour of pencil lead, and dozens of tiny fishing boats lie belly-up on the sand, proof that this growing town is still just a fishing village at heart. The town centre is rather drab, but it's easy to navigate and caters well to travellers.

INFORMATION

The **tourist office** (☎ 922 73 01 33; info-galletas@ arona.org; La Rambla; ☺ 9am-3.30pm Mon-Fri) is at the western end of La Rambla, the tranquil tree-lined walkway that runs parallel to the Paseo Marítimo. To get your Internet fix, head across the Rambla to **La Vava Pipi** (☎ 922 78 41 65; Calle Carmen García 1; per hr €2.60).

SIGHTS & ACTIVITIES

Wind and water have carved the beautiful rock formations of **Montaña Amarilla** (Yellow Mountain), a volcanic mound on the coast outside town. To get here take Avenida Jose Antonio Tavio (beside the Ten Bel complex) down to Calle Chasna. At the end of the street is a small car park and a path leading you down to the water. You can ramble on the rocks, enjoying a gorgeous and building-free view of the coast, or hike around the *montaña*.

Las Galletas is considered one of the best diving spots in the south, together with Los Cristianos and Los Gigantes. For courses, try-dives and excursions, head to **Buceo Tenerife Diving Center** (☎ 922 73 10 15; www.buceotenerife.com; Calle María del Carmen García 22; ☺ 9am-6pm). One dive plus equipment rental costs €25 to €30 and a try-dive costs €37. Dives are at 9am, noon and 3pm.

Rent sailboats and windsurfers, or take classes, at the **Escuela de Vela las Galletas** (☎ 629 87 81 02; Playa Las Galletas; ☺ 10am-6pm Tue-Sun). Windsurfer rental costs €15 per hour, and catamaran rental €30 per hour.

SLEEPING

Geared towards budget and mid-range travellers, accommodation options here are few but sufficient.

Camping Nauta (☎ 922 78 51 18; Carretera 6225, Cañada Blanca; per person €3.60 & per tent €3.60) This is the only fully equipped camp site on Tenerife. Nauta is not known for the cleanest facilities, but it's cheap and is the only place on the island that has hook-ups for caravans.

Pensión Los Vinitos (☎ 922 78 58 03; Calle Venezuela 4; d €18.25). Management may not always be friendly, but the pension is an easy walk to the beach from the town centre, and all rooms have private bathrooms. For a bit extra you can also get a small terrace.

Pensión La Estrella (☎ 922 73 15 62; Carretera General; d with hall bathroom/toilet only/full bathroom €14/20/25) This place is relatively cheery but far from the action. It's also somewhat aged – the mattresses were probably a lot more comfortable 15 years ago than they are today.

Ten Bel (☎ 922 73 07 21; www.tenbel.com; Urbanizacíon Tenbel; 1–2-person apt €33.80-54.40, 3-person apt €50-63.50) The nicest place in town. This 'holiday village' is a complex of four separate apartment buildings that has private coast access (it's on a big cliff beside the water, but you can swim in the coves) and several pools. Apartments vary widely but in general they're simple and clean, if low on charm.

EATING

A string of waterfront restaurants lines Paseo Marímo, most serving that vague international mix of seafood, pizza and paella.

Via Moana (☎ 922 73 25 40; Playa de las Galletas; mains €10-18; ✆ noon-3am summer only; Ⓟ) Get away from the crowds at this laid-back café and restaurant that's right on the water. On summer nights live music or a DJ turns the place into the town's main nightspot, with an eclectic mix of jazz, folk, Celtic and rock music.

GETTING THERE & AWAY

Las Galletas is a few kilometres off the TF-1, exit 26. Bus route Nos 467, 470 and 473 connect it with Los Cristianos, and route Nos 112 and 115 come and go from Santa Cruz.

TENERIFE

La Gomera

There is no one way to describe this little round island, dubbed Isla Columbina (Columbus Island) because of its ties to the explorer. Though just 25km across at its widest, there are enough microclimates here to fill an entire continent, ranging from the dry, sun-soaked south to the green valleys of the west and the ever-cloudy, verdant centre, where trees trap the mist and moisture. Deep gorges are carved into the land, radiating from the island's centre like the spokes of a wheel and making it impossible to get anywhere as the crow flies.

From the ocean, La Gomera looks like an impenetrable fortress, with precipitous cliffs that crash headfirst into the water. The island is the most dormant of the Canaries, and you'll notice the absence of cones and craters, proof there's been no volcanic activity here for millions of years. The most visible remains of lava fills are the *roques* – odd rock formations that were gradually exposed as the volcanic fissures eroded.

La Gomera has long been a haven for independent travellers and trekkers, and the island is well equipped to handle hikers and nature-lovers. In recent years a few chain hotels have also popped up, drawing an increasing number of package tourists. Yet the majority of those who arrive on La Gomera come on short day trips from Tenerife and get just a superficial glimpse of this beautiful and varied island.

Tourism is now the heavyweight of the Gomeran economy, but agriculture remains important. Bananas, vines, potatoes and corn are all cultivated on the steep slopes of the ravines.

HIGHLIGHTS

★ Los Órganos

★ Las Rosas

★ Parque Nacional de Garajonay

Valle Gran Rey ★

San Sebastián de la Gomera ★

■ **Walking**

A stroll among the ancient laurels of the Parque Nacional de Garajonay is a must (p188)

■ **Driving**

A four-wheeled cruise through the terraced slopes of the Valle Gran Rey provides a lesson in green (p192)

■ **Hearing**

You won't believe your ears – a conversation in the Silbo whistle in Las Rosas (p179)

■ **Dining**

The elegant Parador Nacional in San Sebastián de la Gomera is La Gomera's top restaurant (p185)

■ **Seeing**

Wind in your hair, spray on your face...the majestic Los Órganos need to be viewed from the water (p188)

■ TELEPHONE CODE: 922	■ POPULATION: 19,098	■ AREA: 378 KM

HISTORY

Throughout the 1400s the Spaniards tried unsuccessfully to conquer La Gomera. When they finally managed to establish a presence on the island in the middle of the century, it was due to a slow and fairly peaceful infiltration of Christianity and European culture rather than the result of a battle. Early on, the aborigines were permitted to keep much of their culture and self-rule, but that changed when the brutal Hernán Peraza the younger became governor. The Gomeros rebelled against him (see p183), unleashing a blood bath that killed hundreds of islanders.

After the activity of those first years, and the excitement that accompanied Christopher Columbus in his stopovers on the island (see p184), there followed a long period of isolation. La Gomera was totally self-sufficient and had little contact with the outside world until the 1950s, when a small pier was built in San Sebastián, opening the way for ferry travel and trade.

Even so, it was difficult to eke out a living by farming on the island's steep slopes, and much of the population emigrated to Tenerife or South America. Even today, there are more Gomeros living on Tenerife than on their own island.

INFORMATION
Maps

La Gomera Tour and Trail (1:40,000) is a fairly good walking map with 70 routes

LA GOMERA

WHISTLE WHILE YOU WORK

One look at the deep ravines and rugged terrain of La Gomera is enough to understand that there's a need here for creative communication. Before the age of paved roads and mountain tunnels, rambling up and down the steep slopes of the island must have become tiring. The aborigines' solution was a whistling language, called Silbo Gomero, that helped them communicate despite the uncooperative landscape.

Silbo Gomero probably began as a greeting or danger signal, but it has grown into a fully functioning language with more than 4000 words. By placing a finger in the mouth and moulding the tongue in various ways, a whistler can create any number of sounds that combine to form words. The other hand is used like a megaphone to project the whistle, which can be heard up to 4km away.

Gomero Juan Cabello uses Silbo every day. 'It's my mobile phone, my fax machine and my Internet,' says the 50-year-old whistling expert. He points out that even in today's age of super telecommunications, whistling has its uses: 'When I got separated from my family in a huge flea market on the peninsula, I just whistled out, "Over here! I'm ready to go!" and we found each other in no time.'

Historically, Silbo was used to spread important news and to call doctors and priests in cases of emergency. However, in the late 20th century it came close to extinction, nearly killed off by the use of cars and telephones. Cabello is one of the few islanders who uses Silbo regularly – 'I talk to everyone with it, my wife, my kids and my colleagues at work,' he says. Silbo is now a mandatory school subject for primary students, and lots of Gomero kids use bits and pieces of Silbo to call out to each other or to send a quick message across the village square. The locals are confident that a new generation of whistlers is a guarantee of the language's survival.

After all, Silbo is useful for just about everything, Cabello says. 'The only time you can't use the Silbo Gomero is when you're trying to flirt with a girl: the whole island would find out!'

You can hear Cabello give a Silbo demonstration daily at Restaurante Las Rosas (see p187).

described briefly in English (around €7). For even more detail, try *La Gomera – Ile de Gomera* (1:35,000), published by Freytag & Berndt, also around €7. For simple tours around the island, *La Gomera* (1:50,000), by Distrimaps Telestar, costs about €3 and is easy to use. These maps are available in bookshops. The tourist office also gives out several decent, free maps of the island.

Newspapers

The local paper *El Correo de La Gomera* comes out once a week.

ACTIVITIES

La Gomera's varied landscape makes it an excellent destination for a walking or cycling holiday. Most people choose to spend just a day or two rambling through the green **Parque Nacional de Garajonay**, but there are enough trails across the island, both in and out of the central park, to make a week of hiking a viable option. Outfits such as **Timah** (☎ 922 80 70 37; www.timah.net) and **Tamaragua Tours** (☎ 900 70 52 22, 922 14 10 56; lagomera@tamaraguatours.com) organise guided hikes, while **Bike Center Gomera** (☎ 922 80 58 02; www.bikecenter-gomera.com) rents out bikes and leads cycling tours. For more information see p192.

There are a few pebbly beaches around, but La Gomera is not as focused on its coast as other Canary Islands are. Even so, you can take **boat cruises** starting from either Valle Gran Rey or Playa Santiago, and if you want to do some exploring in the water, contact the **diving school** at Hotel Jardín Tecina (p190).

ACCOMMODATION

With only a few dozen hotels and *pensiones* (guesthouses) across the island, most accommodation is in apartments and homes, the most tempting being the *casas rurales* (rural houses) scattered about. As on other islands, many of these charming country homes were abandoned by emigrants and have since been refurbished for tourists. For information, contact **Ecotural** (☎ 922 14 41 01; www.ecoturismocanarias.com/gomera).

If you arrive on the island without having booked accommodation, ask for the free *Guide to Holiday Service* from the tourist office, which has a fairly complete listing of lodging options.

Free camping is prohibited on the island. There's only one private camp site, **Camping La Vista** (☎ 922 88 09 49) near El Cedro (see p187).

GETTING THERE & AWAY
Air
The new **airport** (☎ 922 87 30 00) is just 3km outside the centre of Playa Santiago. Eight flights come through daily, all either arriving from or heading to Tenerife or Gran Canaria.

Boat
The port at San Sebastián is a busy place, with more than a dozen ferries coming in and out daily. Most people arrive on the quick jetfoils that hop over from Los Cristianos on Tenerife. **Fred Olsen** (☎ 922 62 82 00; www.fredolsen.es) makes the trip four times each way between 7.15am and 8pm (one way €16.90, 45 minutes).

The smaller company **Garajonay Exprés** (☎ 902 34 34 02; www.garajonayexpres.com in Spanish) links Los Cristianos with San Sebastián (€14.42) and Playa Santiago (€16.87) three times a day.

Trasmediterránea (☎ 902 45 46 45; www.trasmediterranea.es) makes the trip to and from San Sebastián to Los Cristianos at least twice daily, though it's a more leisurely ride (one way €15.19, 1½ hours).

Trasmediterránea also has a daily ferry to El Hierro, though some days the trip is via Los Cristianos.

GETTING AROUND
To/From the Airport
You can rent a car at one of several agencies at the airport or, if money is no object, take a taxi.

There is a bus stop at the airport, but buses are few and far between. From Monday to Saturday, bus No 5, heading towards San Sebastián, leaves at 8am and 5pm, while bus No 6, going to the Valle Gran Rey, leaves at 7am and 1pm.

Boat
Garajonay Exprés (see above) also runs ferries between San Sebastián, Playa Santiago and Valle Gran Rey.

Bus
The seven bus lines of **Servicio Regular Gomera** (☎ 922 14 11 01) do a good job of covering the main destinations, though getting around the island this way will require time and patience. The aqua-coloured buses set out from the ferry terminal at San Sebastián and stop by the bus station in town before heading around the island. Get a complete bus schedule from the tourist office or the San Sebastián bus station.

Car
There's several car-rental agencies around, and any will have a car waiting for you at the port or airport when you arrive if you book ahead. These include:
Cicar (☎ 922 14 11 46)
Rent-a-Car La Rueda (☎ 922 87 30 38)
Rent-a-Car Piñero (☎ 922 14 10 48)

Taxi
This is an expensive way to get around the island. The ride from San Sebastián to the airport costs €30, and from San Sebastián to Valle Gran Rey €40.

SAN SEBASTIÁN DE LA GOMERA

pop 4860
The capital and main entry point of La Gomera, San Sebastián is a friendly town that is known for its connections with Christopher Columbus. You will learn more about the famed explorer here than you ever did at school, as his every footstep (real or imagined) in the city has been well documented for visitors. Aside from Columbus relics, there are few interesting attractions here. However, the two shady squares in the town centre, Plaza Américas and Plaza Constitución, are congenial places to while away the day. The long Playa de San Sebastián caters to sun-worshippers, and the lush Parque Nacional de Garajonay, replete with excellent hiking trails, is a short drive away.

HISTORY
On 6 September 1492, after loading up with supplies from the island, Christopher Columbus led his three small caravels out of the bay and set sail westwards beyond the

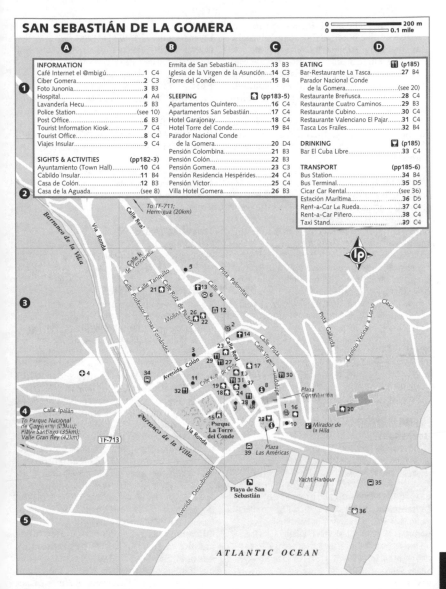

SAN SEBASTIÁN DE LA GOMERA

0 ━━━━━ 200 m
0 ━━━━━ 0.1 mile

INFORMATION
Café Internet el @mbigú...................1 C4
Ciber Gomera....................................2 C3
Foto Junonia.....................................3 B3
Hospital...4 A4
Lavandería Hecu...............................5 B3
Police Station..............................(see 10)
Post Office...6 B3
Tourist Information Kiosk.................7 C4
Tourist Office....................................8 C4
Viajes Insular....................................9 C4

SIGHTS & ACTIVITIES (pp182-3)
Ayuntamiento (Town Hall)..............10 C4
Cabildo Insular...............................11 B4
Casa de Colón.................................12 B3
Casa de la Aguada.....................(see 8)

Ermita de San Sebastián................13 B3
Iglesia de la Virgen de la Asunción....14 C3
Torre del Conde..............................15 B4

SLEEPING (pp183-5)
Apartamentos Quintero...................16 C4
Apartamentos San Sebastián..........17 C4
Hotel Garajonay.............................18 C4
Hotel Torre del Conde....................19 B4
Parador Nacional Conde
   de la Gomera...............................20 D4
Pensión Colombina.........................21 B3
Pensión Colón.................................22 B3
Pensión Gomera.............................23 C3
Pensión Residencia Hespérides......24 C4
Pensión Victor................................25 C4
Villa Hotel Gomera........................26 B3

EATING (p185)
Bar-Restaurante La Tasca...............27 B4
Parador Nacional Conde
   de la Gomera..........................(see 20)
Restaurante Breñusca.....................28 C4
Restaurante Cuatro Caminos..........29 B3
Restaurante Cubino........................30 C4
Restaurante Valenciano El Pajar.....31 C4
Tasca Los Frailes.............................32 B4

DRINKING (p185)
Bar El Cuba Libre............................33 C4

TRANSPORT (pp185-6)
Bus Station.....................................34 B4
Bus Terminal...................................35 D5
Cicar Car Rental.........................(see 36)
Estación Marítima..........................36 D5
Rent-a-Car La Rueda......................37 C4
Rent-a-Car Piñero..........................38 C4
Taxi Stand......................................39 C4

limit of the known world. When Columbus was on the island, San Sebastián had barely been founded. Four years earlier, in 1488, there had been a terrible massacre in the wake of the failed uprising against Hernán Peraza, the island's governor (see the boxed text on p183). When it was all over, what had been the Villa de las Palmas, on a spot

known to the Guanches as Hipalán, was renamed San Sebastián.

The boom in transatlantic trade following Columbus' journeys helped boost the fortunes of the city, which sits on a sheltered harbour and was one of the Canaries' best ports. Nevertheless, its population passed the 1000 mark only at the beginning of the

LA GOMERA

19th century. The good times also brought dangers as, like other islands, San Sebastián was regularly subjected to pirate attack from the English, French and Portuguese. In 1739, the English fleet actually landed an invasion force but the assault was repulsed.

The fate of the town was linked intimately with that of the rest of the island. Its fortunes rose with the cochineal boom in the 19th century, then collapsed with that industry, which was unable to compete with synthetic dyes.

ORIENTATION

If you arrive at the port at the eastern end of town, it's an easy drive or walk to the central square, Plaza Américas, the heart of San Sebastián. From here you can catch the main thoroughfare, Calle Real, also referred to as Calle Medio, which runs northwest. Most sights and services are on Calle Real or the busy street running parallel, Calle Ruiz de Padrón. A sandy black beach stretches down the western end of town; and there are a couple of bars and an exposition centre down here, but little else.

Maps

The free map given out by the tourist office is more than sufficient for poking around town, and all the major attractions are indicated.

INFORMATION
Bookshops

Foto Junonia (☎ 922 87 06 24; Avenida Colón 24) Stocks books, maps and guidebooks in Spanish and other languages (mostly German).

Emergency & Medical Services

Police Station (☎ 922 87 00 62; Plaza Américas) On the 1st floor of the *ayuntamiento* (town hall).
Hospital (☎ 922 14 02 00; Calle El Calvario 4) On the western side of town, across the Barranco de la Villa. As with the rest of Spain, call ☎ 112 in case of emergency.

Internet Access

Café Internet el @mbigú (☎ 922 8716 68; Plaza Américas 8; per hr €5.10; ⏰ 8am-1pm) This café has a few computer terminals where you can check email, but it's relatively expensive. Tasty sandwiches and pastries are also available.
Ciber Gomera (☎ 922 87 17 31; Calle Panama 1; per hr €2.50; ⏰ 9am-1.30pm & 4-9.30pm) A cheaper but less atmospheric option than Café Internet el @mbigú.

Laundry

Lavandería Hecu (☎ 922 14 11 80; Calle Real 76) This tiny place will wash and dry a load of up to 4.5kg for €9; a wash only is half the price.

Post

Post Office (☎ 922 87 10 81; Calle Real 60)

Tourist Offices

Main Tourist Office (☎ 922 14 15 12; www.gomera -island.com; Calle Real 4; ⏰ 9am-1pm & 4-6pm Mon-Sat summer, 9am-1.30pm & 3.30-6pm Mon-Sat, 10am-1pm Sun winter) A friendly, helpful place in the Casa de la Aguada.
Information Kiosk (Plaza Américas) This small kiosk supplies maps but little else.

Travel Agencies

Viajes Insular (☎ 922 87 14 50; www.viajesinsular.es; Calle Ruiz de Padrón 9) This island-based agency can help you with all your travel needs.

SIGHTS & ACTIVITIES

To get a good overview of San Sebastián, head up the road to the Parador Nacional Conde de la Gomera hotel (see p185), where the **Mirador de la Hila** showcases the coast, the square houses of town, and the rough, dry mountains beyond.

Back in the town centre, most of the interesting sites are somehow related to Columbus (in either real or contrived ways), and they form a route you can follow around town. Beginning at **Plaza Américas**, where you can get a juice in one of the terrace bars, cross through **Plaza Constitución**, shaded by enormous Indian laurel trees.

Just off the plaza is **Casa de la Aguada** (☎ 922 14 15 12; www.gomera-island.com; Calle Real 4; ⏰ 9am-1pm & 4-6pm Mon-Sat summer, 9am-1.30pm & 3.30-6pm Mon-Sat, 10am-1pm Sun winter), also referred to as Casa de la Aduana or Casa Condal, since at different times it served as the customs house and the count's residence. The tourist office fills one side of this traditional Canary home, but the back of it is dedicated to the exhibit 'La Gomera & the Discovery of America', an interesting account (though all in Spanish) of Columbus' trip and Gomeran culture in those times. Tradition says that Columbus drew water from the well that sits in the central patio, and used it to 'baptise America'.

Head up Calle Real to **Iglesia de la Virgen de la Asunción** (⏰ usually 6-8pm), the site where Columbus and his men supposedly came to pray before setting off for the New World. The original chapel was begun in 1450 but was destroyed by a fire. The 18th-century church here today has three naves and mixes *mudéjar* (Islamic-style architecture), Gothic and Baroque architectural styles. The simpler **Ermita de San Sebastián** (Calle Real), built in 1540, is a few blocks further on.

Nearby is **Casa de Colón** (Calle Real 56; ☯ 10am-1pm & 4-6.30pm Mon-Fri, 10am-1pm Sat), a house built on the site where Columbus supposedly stayed while on the island. Inside there's a collection of pre-Columbian ceramics from Peru and other parts of South America.

Set in a park just off the coast, **Torre del Conde** (☯ 10am-1pm Mon-Fri) is considered the Canary Islands' most important example of military architecture (built in 1447). Here Beatriz de Bobadilla, wife of the cruel and ill-fated Hernán Peraza, had to barricade herself in 1488 until help arrived (see the boxed text below). The fort was the first building of any note to be erected on the island. It is about the only one to have been more or less preserved in its original state.

The sandy volcanic **beach** is a nice place to relax and have a swim. It's also the site of some of the town's liveliest festivals, such as El Día de San Juan (St John's day; see below), when the beach is lined with bonfires.

FESTIVALS & EVENTS

The **Fiesta de San Sebastián**, the festival in honour of the town's patron saint, is cele-brated on 20 January, and Columbus' first voyage is commemorated on 6 September, in the **Fiestas Columbinas**, a week full of street parties, music and cultural events. The summer solstice is celebrated on 23 June, the night of **El Día de San Juan** (St John's Day), with bonfires all over town.

Every five years on 5 October (the next time is in 2008), the city celebrates the **Bajada de la Virgen de Guadalupe** (Procession of the Virgin of Guadalupe), when a flotilla of fishing boats escorts the statue of the Virgin Mary from the chapel of Punta Llana southwards to the capital.

SLEEPING

Most people don't stay in the capital for long, electing instead to head down to one of the beach resorts or to a rural house in the interior. With the exception of the lovely Parador Nacional hotel, accommodation options in San Sebastián lack the charm of hotels and rural housing elsewhere, though you won't be at a loss for options should you choose to stay a few nights.

Budget

Pensión Victor (☎ 607 51 75 65; fax 922 87 13 35; Calle Real 23; s/d €18/24) Here you'll find comfortable but old-fashioned rooms, some with their own bathroom. The house retains bits of its original charm in wooden floors and ceilings, though overall it seems a bit decayed. The owner is a friendly man who knows everyone in town – he's a great source of information.

WHAT A TANGLED WEB WE WEAVE...

Governor Hernán Peraza the younger had long been hated for his cruel treatment of the islanders. When in 1488 he broke a pact of friendship with one of the Gomero tribes and, openly cheating on his wife, began cavorting with Yballa, a local beauty and fiancée of one of the island's most powerful men, the natives rebelled. They surprised Peraza during one of his clandestine meetings with Yballa and killed him with a dart, communicating the news via Silbo (whistle) all over the island. They proceeded to attack the Spaniards in Villa de las Palmas, the precursor to modern San Sebastián, and locked up Peraza's deceived wife (the famed beauty Beatriz de Bobadilla) in the Torre del Conde, where she waited until help arrived.

Unfortunately, the story doesn't end there. 'Help' showed up in the form of Pedro de Vera, governor of Gran Canaria and one of the cruellest figures in Canary history. His ruthlessness was bloodcurdling. According to one account, de Vera ordered the execution of all Gomeran males above the age of 15 – in an orgy of wanton violence, islanders were hanged, impaled, decapitated or drowned. Some had their hands and feet lopped off beforehand, just for good measure. The women were parcelled out to the militiamen, and many of the children were sold as slaves. To complete the job, de Vera also ordered the execution of about 300 Gomeros living on Gran Canaria.

Pensión Gomera (☎ 922 87 02 35; Calle Real 59; d €25) Simple double rooms sharing a communal bathroom are spread around an interior patio overgrown with lush, green plants. A few blocks back from the busy centre, this *pensión* is quieter than most.

Pensión-Residencia Hespérides (☎ 922 87 13 05; Calle Ruiz de Padrón 25; s/d without bathroom €14/24, d with bathroom €27) This two-star *pensión* offers individual rooms with balconies, though some of the doubles look into a breezeless interior patio.

Also recommended are the convenient but no-frills **Pensión Colón** (☎ 922 87 02 35; Calle Real 59; s/d €20/25), and **Pensión Colombina** (☎ 922 87 12 57; Calle Ruiz de Padrón 83; s/d €20/32), with private bathrooms and a few rooms with balconies.

Mid-Range
HOTELS
Villa Hotel Gomera (☎ 922 87 00 20; fax 922 87 02 35; Calle Ruiz de Padrón 68; d/apt incl breakfast €50-60) This two-star hotel offers 16 simple but spacious rooms with street views and a nice

tiled bathroom. Apartments, for the same price, have a tiny kitchenette but ample living space.

Hotel Torre del Conde (☎ 922 87 00 00; fax 922 87 13 14; Calle Ruiz de Padrón 19; s €36-48, d €52-64) The rooms are clean and well cared for, but the best this three-star hotel has are the views of the Torre del Conde (see p183) and the pretty gardens that surround it; be sure to ask for a room with a view.

Hotel Garajonay (☎ 922 87 05 50; fax 922 87 05 54; Calle Ruiz de Padrón 17; s/d €38/44) Right next door to Hotel Torre del Conde, some of the small, bright rooms of the two-star Garajonay also have views of the tower, while others look onto the street. All are clean, with tiled floors, TV, and a clean, private bathroom.

APARTMENTS
Look out for signs around town that advertise apartment rental.

Apartamentos Quintero (☎ 922 14 17 44; Plaza Américas; 2-/3-/4-person apt €47/50/53) The one-bedroom apartments have sofa beds, so are roomy enough for two people, and a bit of

---

THE ISLE WHERE COLUMBUS DALLIED

A Genoese sailor of modest means, Cristoforo Colombo (as he is known in his native Italy – Christopher Columbus to the rest of us) was born in 1451. He went to sea early and was something of a dreamer. Fascinated by Marco Polo's travels in the Orient, he decided early on that it must be possible to reach the east by heading west into the sunset. After years of doors being slammed in his face, the Catholic monarchs of Spain, Fernando and Isabel, finally gave him their patronage in 1492.

On 3 August, at the head of three small caravels – the *Santa María*, the *Pinta* and the *Niña* – Columbus weighed anchor in Palos de la Frontera, Andalucia, on the Spanish mainland. But before heading across the ocean blue, he stopped off at La Gomera for last-minute provisions, unwittingly giving the island its biggest claim to fame and many future tourist attractions. One of the things he picked up for the journey was goats' cheese, one of La Gomera's star products to this day.

Columbus set sail on 6 September, a day now celebrated in San Sebastián with the Fiestas Columbinas (see p183). His ships didn't see land until 12 October, just as the ships' provisions and the sailors' patience were nearing their ends. The expedition 'discovered' several Caribbean islands on this trip and returned to Spain in March of the following year.

Columbus made three later voyages but died alone and bitter in Valladolid, Spain, in 1504, still convinced he'd found a new route to the Orient.

The Smitten Sailor...

Columbus had a single-minded focus on his explorations, but that didn't stop him from getting distracted by the beautiful widowed governess of La Gomera, Beatriz de Bobadilla (see p183). Legend has it that the two shared an intimate relationship, the cause of the one-month delay between Columbus' landing on the island and his final departure. On his two following expeditions, Columbus also passed through San Sebastián, though once he discovered that Beatriz had remarried, he never set foot on the island again.

Sunbathing on the black sand of Puerto Naos, La Palma (p212)

Cacti, La Palma

Balconies with Atlantic views in the old town of Santa Cruz de la Palma (p203)

Lagarto del Salmor (Lizard of Salmor), El Hierro (p221)

INGRID RODDIS

INGRID ROD

A typical farmer's house and garden, one of the Casas de Guinea at the Ecomuseo de Guinea, El Hierro (p230)

Hiking through the protected El Pinar pine forest, en route to Los Letreros, El Hierro (p228)

INGRID ROD

a squeeze for bigger groups. They also have a kitchen, balcony and, in some cases, an ocean view.

Apartamentos San Sebastián (☎ 922 87 10 90; Calle Real 20; 2-person apt €60) One of the nicer options in the town centre, this is a complex of fully furnished apartments ideal for self-caterers.

Top End
Parador Nacional Conde de la Gomera (☎ 922 87 11 00; gomera@parador.es; Calle Lomo de la Horca; s/d €98/122) Built to look like an old Canary mansion, the Parador is arguably the island's top hotel. The rooms are simply but elegantly furnished, with four-poster beds, rich wooden floors and marbled bathrooms. Most rooms look out onto the gardens, which have many examples of Canary plants and a small pool area overlooking the ocean. The hotel is on a hill above the port; follow signs from central San Sebastián to get here by car.

EATING
Budget
Restaurante Cubino (☎ 922 87 03 83; Calle Virgen Guadalupe 2; mains around €5) You'll find tasty grilled meat and fish at this friendly place. The dining room is intimate and informal, with wooden tables and the constant comings and goings that signify small-town success. A map of Cuba hangs on the wall.

Mid-Range
Bar-Restaurante La Tasca (☎ 922 14 15 98; Calle Ruiz de Padrón 57; mains €5-9.50, pizza €4-6) At this tavern, peninsular Spanish dishes such as gazpacho, omelettes and *calamares a la Romana* (fried squid) are served along with tasty pizzas.

Restaurante Breñusca (☎ 922 87 09 20; Calle Real 9; mains €5-9) Just across from the tourist office, Breñusca offers decent Canary-style dishes. Try the *potaje* (stew).

Restaurante Valenciano El Pajar (☎ 922 87 03 55; Calle Ruiz Padrón 26; mains €5-12) For the best paella in town, head to this tropical-feeling place with a fruit-bearing mango tree growing in the middle of it. It doesn't always look too clean, but locals come time and time again, so it must be OK.

Restaurante Cuatro Caminos (☎ 922 14 12 60; Calle Ruiz de Padrón 36; mains €8-9) Enjoy good international meat and seafood dishes in

a tiny patio dining room, where hanging plants drip from the ceiling.

Tasca Los Frailes (☎ 922 14 17 90; Calle Profesor Armas Fernández 1; mains €7-11) More upscale (in feel and price) than Cuatro Caminos, this quiet place has good gazpacho, several tapas-style starters, and a range of meat and fish dishes.

Top End
Parador Nacional Conde de la Gomera (☎ 922 87 11 00; Calle Lomo de la Horca; mains €14.50-17) The elegant restaurant of the Parador Nacional is without a doubt the most refined establishment in San Sebastián. Staff dress in local costume and the few but consistently good dishes are creative versions of traditional Canary favourites.

DRINKING
Bar El Cuba Libre (Plaza Americas 18) A juice bar in the heart of town, with great fresh fruit drinks and shakes. A glass of tropical juice costs €2.40.

GETTING THERE & AWAY
To/From the Airport
Two buses come and go from the airport on weekdays (see p180).

Boat
FERRY
A fun and fast alternative to tackling the hairpin curves of La Gomera's highways is the water taxi operated by **Garajonay Exprés** (☎ 902 34 34 50; www.garajonayexpres.com in Spanish; Muelle de Vueltas, Valle Gran Rey). Three daily ferries in each direction link San Sebastián with Playa Santiago (€2.45, 15 minutes) and Valle Gran Rey (€3.28, 35 minutes). The trip between San Sebastián and Playa Santiago takes 45 minutes by car, while the trip to Valle Gran Rey is one hour and 15 minutes, so water taxi is definitely the faster option.

GETTING AROUND
Bus
A few buses cross San Sebastián on their way to and from other places, but few dare to enter the narrow maze of streets in the town centre.

Travelling by bus within San Sebastián really isn't necessary anyway, as the town is easily walkable.

Car

Two rental agencies are set up in town – **Rent-a-Car Piñero** (☎ 922 14 10 48, 922 87 00 55; fax 922 14 13 90; Calle Real) and **Rent-a-Car La Rueda** (☎ 922 87 07 09, fax 922 87 01 42; Calle Real). Parking can be a pain in the town centre, but you'll need a car to get around the island easily.

Taxi

Ring for a taxi on ☎ 922 87 05 24. The taxi stand is on Avenida Descrubidores.

THE NORTH

Coming up from the parched lands around San Sebastián, you'll cross through a series of mountain tunnels on the highway, coming as if by magic into the greener, damper terrain of the north, where a permanent mist hangs in the air. It's thanks to that humidity that the valleys here are filled with banana plantations and the slopes lined with vines.

HERMIGUA

pop 475

The sleepy town of Hermigua, 16km outside San Sebastián, is strung out along the bottom of a ravine, its houses like beads on a chain running down the middle. The sign at the town entrance proudly proclaims 'we have the best climate in the world'. However, the truth is that it's often cloudy, which is partly why the valley is filled with palm trees and banana plants that threaten to take over the town with their big, lush leaves.

At the heart of the original village, to the right as you enter from San Sebastián, are the 16th-century **church** and **convent of Santo Domingo**, with an intricately carved *mudéjar* ceiling. Further down the ravine you'll find the modern town, centred around the **Iglesia de la Encarnación**. This church was begun in the 17th century and not completed until the 20th, partly due to the fact that the original construction crumbled in the early 18th century.

Hermigua winds down to the coast, where there's a rocky beach largely unsuitable for swimming and a **saltwater public pool** as the only option if you want to get wet. A better beach, **Playa de la Caleta**, is some 3km beyond; follow the signs from

the waterfront down a track that was being paved when we last stopped by. It's one of the prettier black-sand and pebble beaches in the north of the island.

Sleeping

There are several mid-range and top-end options in this pretty valley, making Hermigua a good base for those who want a taste of rural life with the comfort of a town's basic services.

Apartamentos Los Telares (☎ 922 88 07 81; apt €40-60) This reception office at the southern end of town, just off the highway, organises accommodation for apartments that are scattered all over town. The apartments vary widely in style, but all are clean and nicely decorated, and most have privileged views of the mountains or valley. Across the street from the reception is an artisan shop under the same ownership, where you can buy local crafts and visit a small loom museum.

Hotel Rural Villa de Hermigua (☎ 922 88 02 46; www.gomeraturismo.com; Carretera General 117; s/d incl breakfast €45/60) A lovely stone house with tasteful rooms. The wrought-iron bedposts and all-white linens give this small hotel rustic elegance. The common areas, including a kitchen and a rooftop terrace, are enchanting.

Ibo Alfaro (☎ 922 88 01 68; www.ecoturismocanarias.com/iboalfaro/ibo2uk.asp; s/d incl breakfast €55/67) Even better than Villa de Hermigua, the 17 romantic rooms here have gorgeous mountain views and an aroma of wood polish coming from the floors, ceilings and elegant furniture. The friendly German owner also runs the hotel restaurant. To get here, follow the signs up the unnamed rural road from beside Hermigua Rent-a-Car.

Apartamentos Playa (☎ 922 88 07 58, 922 14 40 64; 2-person apt €25) If you want to stay down by the coast, this is the place to come. The charming little apartments here each have an ocean view, terrace, kitchen and TV, and comfortable, if simple, décor.

Ecotural Gomera (☎ 922 14 41 01; Callejón Ordáiz 161) At the lower end of town, this organisation rents out rural houses and provides information on rural tourism.

Eating

El Silbo (☎ 922 88 03 04; Carretera General 102; mains €6-8) The best restaurant in town. Canary dishes such as *potajes* and local fish dominate the menu. A covered terrace with bright tablecloths and an abundance of hanging plants makes for a pleasant, if slightly jungle-like, dining experience.

Las Chácaras (☎ 922 88 10 39; 2nd fl, Lomo San Pedro 5; mains €5.50-9.50) At the other end of town from El Silbo, this place is known for its Gomeran specialities, especially local meats such as goat and rabbit. The dining room is dim and unremarkable, but the service is very friendly.

La Casa Creativa (☎ 922 88 10 23; Carretera General 54; mains €10-15) Located in the town centre, this is the place to head for a coffee or a drink. Tables are set up on a pretty outdoor terrace.

Downstairs, the fully fledged restaurant serves decent but slightly overpriced meals of international or local fare. The talking parrot adds a shrill spark of life.

AROUND HERMIGUA
El Cedro
Southwest of Hermigua, and on the national park border, El Cedro is a rural hamlet set amid farmed terraces and laurel thickets. The ravine and waterfall known as **Boca del Chorro** are beautiful, and the simple chapel, **Ermita de Nuestra Señora de Lourdes**, is a 1km wander out from the hamlet.

In El Cedro itself are four cottages for rent. Here too is **Camping La Vista** (☎ 922 88 09 49; camp sites per person €2), the island's only camp site. A friendly place open year-round, it has a bar and restaurant. The owners also run a nearby **refugio** (mountain hut; beds €12), which is complete with washing machine and TV.

To get to El Cedro from Hermigua, ask in town for the way to the *sendero* (trail) to El Cedro and be prepared for a two- to three-hour hike.

For bus information, see p190.

AGULO & LEPE
Five kilometres north of Hermigua, the village of Agulo was founded early in the 17th century. Along with the picturesque town of Lepe, it squats on a low platform beneath the steep, rugged hinterland that stretches back towards the Garajonay park.

The elegant **Iglesia de San Marcos** dominates the centre of Agulo. Built in 1912, it's a simple temple with a high ceiling and a few interesting pieces of art.

LAS ROSAS
Continuing past Agulo, on the main highway, next you'll come to Las Rosas, which sits at the foot of the national park. Just before the town centre is the turn-off for the park's **Juego de Bolas Visitors Centre** (see p189).

For a special treat, head high above Las Rosas to **Restaurante Roque Blanco** (☎ 922 80 04 83; Cruz de Tierno; mains €5-9; ☒ closed Mon), a casual, family restaurant perched above a gorgeous green valley. Enjoy the view, and the grilled meats paired with local wines. Easier to get to is the **Restaurante Las Rosas** (☎ 922 80 09 16; Carretera General; menú del día €10.80) on the main highway, where local specialities are served and you can hear an authentic demonstration of the Silbo Gomero whistle (see the boxed text on p179). The restaurant is run by Fred Olsen, a Norwegian company that owns some of the island's most important tourist infrastructures. It's popular and is often packed with day-trippers who arrive on tour buses.

VALLEHERMOSO
pop 1540
This truly is a 'beautiful valley', as its name translates. Small mountain peaks rise on either side of the deep gorge that runs through town, and the green, terraced hillsides dotted with palm trees complete the picture. The look is lovely, but the well-manicured terraces represent back-breaking work by the local farmers, since the steepness of the slopes means most work here has to be done without machines.

Like Hermigua, this makes a good home base for exploring the island on foot. The heart of town is **Plaza Constitución**; bars, services and much of the budget accommodation is around here. Take time to search out the stone **Iglesia de San Juan Bautista** behind the town centre.

Sleeping & Eating
Bar-Restaurante Amaya (☎ 922 80 00 73; Plaza Constitución 2; s/d without bathroom €11/20, with bathroom €18/30) Located on the plaza, this place has clean and simple rooms. The more expensive rooms (with private bathrooms) have TVs and views of the town. The bustling bar downstairs is a congenial place.

Tamahuche (☎ 922 80 01 76; www.ecoturismo canarias.com/hoteltamahuche; Calle Hoya 20; s/d incl breakfast €47/66) Just outside town, Tamahuche has the same owners as the Casa Bernardo (below). Rooms there are simple but elegant, with wooden floors and ceilings and lovely balconies.

Casa Bernardo (☎ 922 80 08 49; Calle Triana) The owner has houses and apartments scattered all over town, ranging in price and style but all well kept. Casa Bernardo serves as the reception for all the other places.

Agana (☎ 922 80 08 43; Avenida Guillermo Ascanio 5; mains €5.50-9) Head to this tavern for tasty Canarian dishes, including specialities such as *potaje de berros* (local stews) and *guisados* (boiled fish), served to you at small wooden tables.

AROUND VALLEHERMOSO

Just outside Vallehermoso towers the volcanic monolith of **Roque Cano**, whose rock walls rise up 650m. Head past the *roque* down to the coast, which is nice to look at but poor for swimming. There's a simple saltwater pool beside the ocean, however. Nearby is **Castillo del Mar** (☎ 922 80 56 54, 922 80 54 77; www.castillo-del-mar.com; ☽ 11am-sunset, closed Mon), an old banana-packaging factory that's been converted into a new cultural centre hosting concerts and exhibits.

Los Órganos

To contemplate this extraordinary cliffscape (something like a great sculpted church organ in basalt rising abruptly from the ocean depths), 4km north of Vallehermoso, you'll need to head out to sea. Boats making the trip actually set out from Valle Gran Rey (see p194) and Playa Santiago (see p190) in the southwest of the island. The columned cliff face has been battered into its present shape by the ocean.

Alojera

The main highway south of Vallehermoso snakes its way along the valley through farming villages (some abandoned) and up into the western extremity of the Parque Nacional de Garajonay. Shortly before the highway enters the park proper, a side road winds out, initially east then curling west, to Alojera. This sleepy settlement is sprawled out above the black-pebble Playa de Alojera. Tracks from here lead north to Tazo (about 5km) and Arguamul (8km). The best part of coming here is the spectacular drive down from the highway.

Tazo & Arguamul

In and around Tazo are some fine old farmhouses. The surrounding area also has the island's most extensive palm grove. The sap is used to make palm honey, a local speciality – the sap is boiled into a kind of thick, dark syrup.

Arguamul, 3km beyond, is another tiny hamlet. Walking trails lead on a kilometre to Playa del Remo, and you can also walk southeast up to the ridge dominated by the Teselinde peak (876m) and then follow the Barranco de la Era Nueva down into Vallehermoso.

In dry weather you can get a car down this road; in wet weather it is often impassable.

THE CENTRE

PARQUE NACIONAL DE GARAJONAY

La Gomera's star natural attraction is the ancient **laurisilva** (laurel forest) at the heart of the island's national park. Covering 10% of the island's surface, the 4000-hectare park forms a knot in its centre and is a haven for some of the planet's most ancient forest land. Although called *laurisilva*, there is much more to it than the several types of laurel that abound; as many as 400 species of flora, including Canary willows and Canary holly, flourish.

Up here on the roof of the island, cool Atlantic trade winds clash with warmer breezes, creating a constant ebb and flow of mist through the dense forest, something called 'horizontal rain'. The best place to see this in action is at the peak of the park, the **Alto de Garajonay** (1487m), where a single pine tree planted by the park rangers serves as an example of how the forest works. The dripping tree, which sits in a puddle of water that it has collected, acts like a sponge, trapping moisture in its green boughs. The pines' role in feeding the island's springs is one of the reasons why conservation here is so important.

Relatively little light penetrates the canopy, allowing moss and lichen to spread over everything. Among the trees you may happen to spot rare laurel trees and long-toed pigeons. Insect-lovers will have a field day here; there are nearly 1000 species of invertebrates in the park, and of these 150 are endemic.

The frosty fingers of the last Ice Age didn't make it as far as the Canaries, so what you see here was common across much of the Mediterranean millions of years ago. Humans have done more damage on the islands than has ice, but in this case, at least, we've acted to protect a good chunk of unique land before it was too late – Garajonay was declared a national park in 1981 and a Unesco World Heritage site in 1986.

Information

The **Juego de Bolas Visitors Centre** (☎ 922 80 09 93; La Palmita-Agulo Hwy; ☼ 9.30am-4.30pm) is actually located well outside the park and is hard to get to unless you arrive from the north. Nevertheless, it's worth the journey, as there are piles of information on the park and the island in general, including a very informative guidebook to the park (€8) and a 20-minute video. In the centre's gardens and interior patio flourish a microcosm of La Gomera's floral riches, and a small museum shows off island handicrafts and explains the park's geology and climate. The centre offers guided tours on Saturday; call ahead to reserve a spot.

Lighting fires in the park is forbidden, except in a few designated areas. Free camping is also prohibited. It can get cold here, and the damp goes right through to your bones, even when it is not raining. Bring walking boots, warm garments and a rainproof jacket (see p41).

Walking

Most trails running through the park were those historically used by the Gomeros. Though there are a few strenuous hikes, the majority are relatively light, and it's possible to get a solid view of the landscape without venturing too far.

Many independent visitors make for **Alto de Garajonay** (1487m), the island's tallest peak. From here, clouds permitting, you can see the islands of Tenerife, La Palma, El Hierro and sometimes even Gran Canaria. Another favourite stop is **La Laguna Grande**, just off the highway and ideal for picnics. The 'laguna' refers to a barren circle of land – now used as a recreational area – that has always held an air of mystery. Islanders say it's a mystical place and that witches once practised here. If you don't have much time to explore, you can take the short (20-

minute) circular route that begins here and serves as a decent, if too brief, introduction to the park. This route is a good place to spot the park's famous laurel trees.

For a more complete view, try the trail circuit leading to Alto de Garajonay via the path to El Cercado. Starting from behind the restaurant at La Laguna Grande, head first towards El Cercado, then bear left towards Los Llanos de Crispín. You'll walk among native vegetation and will head northwest, bearing right at the fork to reach the Alto de Garajonay. Return to the fork and follow the signs to get back to La Laguna Grande.

Several other popular walks will also get you up to Alto de Garajonay. Take bus No 1 from San Sebastián and get off at the Pajarito stop (where the bus turns south). From here it is about an hour's walk (signposted) to the peak. If you have your own transport or get a taxi, a much shorter trail (1.6km) leads up to the peak from El Contadero.

From El Contadero, another track, signposted Caserío de El Cedro, leads north. This is mostly descent and takes about 2½ hours to get down, and another three to return, leading you through the heart of the park and by some of its most emblematic flora.

If you haven't had enough of walking, there's a dirt track and walking trail of about 3.5km climbing from El Cercado to La Laguna Grande in the national park. You'll get to El Cercado on bus No 1. The route taken by the bus, which is the detour along the south of the park (most of it out of the park's border), is also full of interest. **Chipude**, with its 16th-century Iglesia de la Virgen de la

---

BY LEAPS & BOUNDS

So, hikers think they're pretty cool when they use a fancy walking stick. Bet they've never tried the *astia*, an ingenious invention of Gomeran shepherds that allowed them to quickly descend even the steepest slopes. A 2m-long pole made with sturdy holly or beech wood that ends in a sharp metal point, the *astia* is a difficult tool to use. The shepherds thrust the point into the slope below them, then slid down the slope. These days, few people know the art of the *astia*, and you will rarely see it being used on the island.

LA GOMERA

Candelaria, and **El Cercado**, known for its pottery production, are interesting stops. Both villages lie amid rows of intensively farmed terraces.

Getting There & Away

Unlike some other protected parks, Garajonay is extremely accessible. In fact, you won't be able to avoid it if you move much about the island, as the park exists at the island's major crossroads.

The TF-713 highway cuts east-west right through the park until it meets the TF-711 at the park's western extremity. Though wheeling through in your own car is certainly the quickest and most comfortable way to move about the park, there are four almost-daily buses between the capital and Valle Gran Rey that make a detour south along a secondary road, branching off shortly before Alto de Garajonay and continuing westwards along a decidedly tortuous route. They stop in such places as Igualero, Chipude and El Cercado before branching north again to rejoin the main road at Las Hayas.

Several secondary roads, mostly gravel tracks that will give your backside a ride it won't soon forget, meander through the park, sneaking in at points such as Cruce del Rejo in the northeast and Las Hayas in the west. Exploring this way can be an alternative to walking, though certainly it doesn't give you as much freedom.

A minor paved road connects the national park visitors centre in the north of the island to La Laguna Grande, about midway along the TF-713 between the park's eastern and western boundaries.

THE SOUTH

The sunburnt south is a land of dry hills, harsh rock cliffs and palm-filled ravines leading down to one of the island's most popular coastal resorts.

PLAYA SANTIAGO

pop 560

Though one of the island's most important tourist centres, Playa Santiago is a tiny place, really just a handful of shops and services huddled around a quiet, rocky beach. Until the 1960s this area was the busiest centre on the island, with factories, a shipyard and a port for exporting local bananas and tomatoes. But the farming crisis hit hard, and by the 1970s the town had all but shut down, its inhabitants having fled to Tenerife or South America.

Now tourism is coming to the rescue. A huge luxury hotel complex owned by Fred Olsen is doing more than its fair share to bring visitors this way, and the few pebbly beaches around also help. Things are looking up for Playa Santiago, but even with the arrival of tourism, agriculture and fishing are still important for the local economy.

Information

The **tourist office** (☎ 922 89 56 50; www.gomera -island.com; Edificio Las Vistas, Avenida Marítima; ☯ 9am-2pm Mon-Sat summer, 9am-1pm & 4-6pm Mon-Fri, 9am-1pm Sat winter) is on your right as you enter the town centre.

Your can connect to the Internet next door at the phone shop **Telefónica-Movistar** (☎ 922 89 51 56; Avenida Marítima; per hr €2).

All the town's services, including the post office, petrol station, laundrette, pharmacy, police station and medical centre, are clustered around Plaza Playa Santiago in the heart of town.

Activities

Excursion companies and travel agencies abound, so there's no shortage of hikes, boat rides and tours for which to sign up. Both **Timah** (☎ 922 80 70 37; www.timah.net) and **Tamaragua Tours** (☎ 900 70 52 22, 922 14 10 56; lagomera@tamaraguatours.com) charge between €20 and €30 to pick you up at your hotel and take you on one of several guided hikes around the island. Two large motorboats, **Tina** (☎ 922 80 58 85) and **Siron** (☎ 922 80 54 80), set out from the harbour daily on a coastal cruise to Los Órganos (p188). For details about the excursions, see p194.

There's a small **diving school** (☎ 922 89 59 02; www.gomera-dive-resort.com) set up in the Hotel Jardín Tecina (see p191). You can also buy tickets for various other excursions here.

If the rocky beach in town doesn't satisfy, you can head east, past Hotel Jardín Tecina, to three smaller beaches, Playas de Tapahuga, del Medio and de Chinguarime, which have some sand mixed in with the rocks. The three lie at the end of a bumpy gravel track and are known as hippy hang-outs.

Sleeping

Hotel Jardín Tecina (☎ 922 14 58 50; www.jardin -tecina.com; Playa Santiago; s/d incl breakfast €102/155; Ⓟ Ⓧ 🖳 🕾) This magnificent hotel dominates the lodging scene in a big way. Sprawled along a cliff above town (a lift goes down to the beach), the bungalow-like rooms are scattered throughout a green, well-kept landscape. All have balconies and most have ocean views. The hotel's restaurants – three of them – are noteworthy too (see below).

For those on a tighter budget, there are several options in the town centre.

Pensión La Gaviota (☎ 922 89 51 35; Avenida Marítima 33; d €24) This highly recommended place has cheerful rooms that are clean and well decorated. Some rooms have a balcony with an ocean view for the same price, so ask when booking. Obtain keys and information at the Bodegón del Mar next door.

Casanova (☎ 922 89 50 02; Avenida Marítima 6; apt €42) Not far from La Gaviota, Casanova rents out a few simple apartments with kitchenettes and views of the ocean.

Apartamentos Tapahuga (☎ 922 89 51 59; www.tapahuga.com; Avenida Marítima; apt €40-50; 🕾) At the far end of the Avenida, these spacious apartments boast beautiful wooden balconies and marble floors, well-equipped kitchens and a rooftop pool. Make sure you get an exterior apartment, as a few apartments open onto a cheerless and dark interior patio.

Eating

La Cuevita (☎ 922 89 55 68; Avenida Marítima; mains €8-10) This little restaurant has to be the most atmospheric place in town. Tucked into a natural cave beside the port, it somehow manages to be a cheery and cosy place; it's not the least bit dank or damp. House specials include fish (straight from the port) and local goat or rabbit meat.

Hotel Jardín Tecina (☎ 922 14 58 50; www.jardin -tecina.com; Playa Santiago; menú del día around €18) The three restaurants of this hotel (see above) are warmly recommended. Though each has its own style – grill, traditional or international – all serve tasty, creative dishes in beautiful open-air settings.

Casanova (☎ 922 89 50 02; Avenida Marítima 6; mains €5-7) According to the owner, the informal Casanova serves 'a little bit of everything', ranging from soups to local fish to saucy meats.

Avenida (☎ 922 89 54 98; Avenida Marítima; mains €5-9) The day's fresh fish is put on display at the door, and the small dining room looks out onto the ocean.

Self-caterers can head to Supermercado El Paso II (found off the main plaza) for groceries.

Getting There & Away

Bus No 2 heads to and from San Sebastián, and No 1 links Playa Santiago with Valle Gran Rey. The water taxis of **Garajonay Exprés** (☎ 902 34 34 50; www.garajonayexpres.com) will take you to San Sebastián (one way €2.45, 15 minutes) and Valle Gran Rey (one way €2.45, 20 minutes) more quickly.

ALAJERÓ

pop 325

The only sizable village outside Playa Santiago in the southeast of the island, Alajeró is a pretty, palm-tree-studded oasis on the road from the misty uplands down to the beach. The modest 16th-century **Iglesia del Salvador** is worth a quick look.

To visit the island's only surviving *drago* (dragon tree; see p37) if you're driving, take an unsigned left turn 1.25km north of Alajeró as far as an old farmhouse, from where a trail drops steeply. If you're on the bus, get off at the Imada stop and turn left down a cobbled track to join this side road. Either way, allow a good 45 minutes for the round trip.

Bus No 2 passes by Alajeró (the bus stop is on the main highway) four times daily.

Festivals & Events

In September Gomeros from far and wide converge on Alajeró to celebrate the **Fiesta del Paso**, a chirpy procession that dances its way down from the mountains.

BENCHIJIGUA

One of the prettiest and most tranquil areas of inland southern Gomera is the wide terraced bowl of the upper reaches of the Barranco de Santiago. Along its northern reaches is Benchijigua, a smattering of half-abandoned hamlets.

A cluster of **casas rurales** (☎ 922 62 83 84; www .fredolsen.es; 2-/3-/4-person houses €63/82/91) makes an excellent away-from-it-all base for a few days' walking. These renovated cottages are yet another initiative of Fred Olsen, and it's essential to reserve in advance. From Las Toscas on the San Sebastián–Playa Santiago highway (bus No 2 runs past), take a dirt road northwards for 4km.

From Benchijigua, a couple of trails lead north into the park and several others trace paths southwards along the ravines to the coast.

VALLE GRAN REY

pop 3440

Bet you can't make it all the way down to the shore without stopping at least once to sigh at the natural beauty of the 'Valley of the Great King'. You'll be hard-pressed to stop yourself snapping a picture of the green terraces that ascend like a staircase out of the valley floor.

The towns that form the island's major tourist centre run along the bottom of a deep gorge carved out of ancient inland rock. Bananas, tomatoes and, of course, tourists have made this area one of the island's most prosperous. If you speak German you'll be all the more comfortable, as most services here are geared towards the many German tourists in search of sunshine and nature.

As you descend into the valley, you could stop at the **Mirador César Manrique** near Arure, a lookout point affording incredible views of the gorge and the mountains that loom around it. The restaurant here is quite good. Also in Arure is the **Bodega Vino Tinto**, a good place to buy local wines, cheeses and *mojos* (sauces). Three kilometres further on is **Ermita de San Antonio**, a pretty white chapel whose best feature is the views from the plaza outside.

Orientation

Valle Gran Rey is really a collection of little hamlets with a grand name. The high part is known as La Calera. From here the road forks to descend to La Playa (right) and Vueltas (left). Both have small beaches and plenty of accommodation, and Vueltas also serves as the area's harbour.

Information

INTERNET ACCESS

Bar Internet (☎ 922 80 51 22; Edificio Normara 15, La Playa; per hr €3.50)

Ciberm@tika (☎ 922 80 59 99; Calle Vueltas, Vueltas; per hr €3.50)

POST

Post Office (☎ 922 80 57 30; Calle Vueltas)

TOURIST OFFICES

Tourist Office (☎ 922 80 54 58; www.gomera -island.com; Calle Lepanto, La Playa; ☉ 9am-1.30pm & 4-6.30pm Mon-Sat Oct-Jun, 9am-2pm Mon-Sat Jul-Sep) Pick up a map and local information here.

Servicios Integrados (☎ 922 80 58 66; www.gomera -service.com; Edificio El Contero, La Calera; ☉ 10am-1pm & 6-8pm Mon-Fri, 10am-1pm Sat) This useful agency can arrange everything from accommodation and car hire to hikes and donkey treks. The office is tucked behind the town hall, which you pass as you enter town.

La Paloma (☎ 922 80 60 43; www.gomera.de) Helpful, though aimed at German travellers, this agency offers assistance with air fares, ferry tickets and other travel needs.

Activities

Though the lush valley itself is perhaps the best the Valle Gran Rey has to offer, most people head straight to the shore. The beaches here are among La Gomera's prettiest, with real sand and lapping waves. The beach at La Playa is a long, sandy thing, with bars and a waterside boardwalk nearby. Heading towards Vueltas, the Charco del Conde is a quieter place to splash and swim. The Playa de las Vueltas, beside the port, is the least agreeable of the bunch.

To get off the sand and into the island, the well-established excursion outfit **Timah** (☎ 922 80 70 37; www.timah.net; La Puntilla; hikes €25-30; ☉ 11am-1pm & 6-9pm) organises small group hikes all over the island. Most hikes are in German, though the guides will translate into English or Spanish. Offering a similar service is **Tamaragua Tours** (☎ 900 70 52 22, 922 14 10 56; lagomera@tamaraguatours.com; hikes €21), though beware that if the hiking group isn't large enough Tamaragua will cancel the trip. Timah rarely cancels. **ÖkoTours** (☎ 636 23 18 17; www.oekotours.com in German; hikes €25-33) also leads hikes. Tamaragua and ÖkoTours don't have offices, but meet up at various hotels and apartments.

If trudging up a mountain seems too strenuous, you might like the all-downhill cycling tours. A van carries you and your bike up the mountain, and you enjoy the scenery as you wind down. The two arms of the same bike rental company – **Bike Centre Gomera** and **Alofi Rentals** (☎ 922 80 53 53, 922 80 58 02; www.bikecenter-gomera.com) – rent out bikes and also organise cycling tours at all levels.

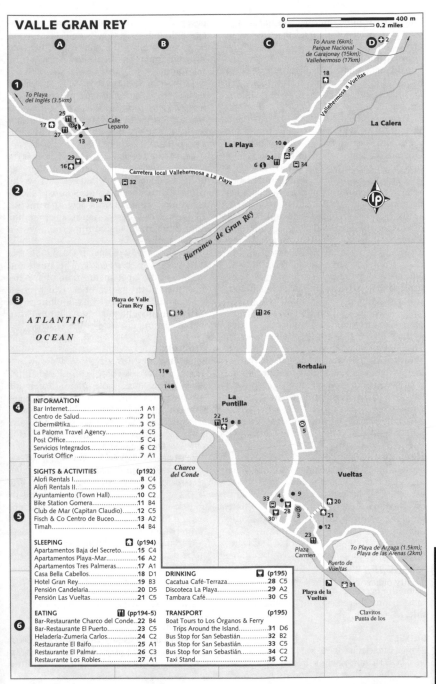

VALLE GRAN REY

0 — 400 m
0 — 0.2 miles

INFORMATION

Bar Internet.................................**1**	A1
Centro de Salud............................**2**	D1
Ciberm@tika.................................**3**	C5
La Paloma Travel Agency................**4**	C5
Post Office...................................**5**	C4
Servicios Integrados......................**6**	C2
Tourist Office **7**	A1

SIGHTS & ACTIVITIES (p192)

Alofi Rentals I...............................**8**	C4
Alofi Rentals II..............................**9**	C5
Ayuntamiento (Town Hall)............**10**	C2
Bike Station Gomera.....................**11**	B4
Club de Mar (Capitan Claudio).......**12**	C5
Fisch & Co Centro de Buceo..........**13**	A2
Timah..**14**	B4

SLEEPING (p194)

Apartamentos Baja del Secreto....**15**	C4
Apartamentos Playa-Mar.............**16**	A2
Apartamentos Tres Palmeras........**17**	A1
Casa Bella Cabellos....................**18**	D1
Hotel Gran Rey...........................**19**	B3
Pensión Candelaria.....................**20**	D5
Pensión Las Vueltas....................**21**	C5

EATING (pp194-5)

Bar-Restaurante Charco del Conde..**22**	B4
Bar-Restaurante El Puerto............**23**	C5
Heladería-Zumería Carlos.............**24**	C2
Restaurante El Baifo...................**25**	A1
Restaurante El Palmar.................**26**	C3
Restaurante Los Robles...............**27**	A1

DRINKING (p195)

Cacatua Café-Terraza..................**28**	C5
Discoteca La Playa......................**29**	A2
Tambara Café.............................**30**	C5

TRANSPORT (p195)

Boat Tours to Los Órganos & Ferry	
Trips Around the Island..............**31**	D6
Bus Stop for San Sebastián.........**32**	B2
Bus Stop for San Sebastián.........**33**	C5
Bus Stop for San Sebastián.........**34**	C2
Taxi Stand.................................**35**	C2

To Playa del Inglés (3.5km)

To Arure (6km);
Parque Nacional
de Garajonay (15km);
Vallehermoso (17km)

Calle Lepanto

La Calera

La Playa

Vallehermosa a Vueltas

Carretera local Vallehermosa a La Playa

La Playa

Barranco de Gran Rey

ATLANTIC OCEAN

Playa de Valle Gran Rey

Borbalán

La Puntilla

Charco del Conde

Vueltas

Plaza Carmen

Puerto de Vueltas

Playa de la Vueltas

To Playa de Argaga (1.5km);
Playa de las Arenas (2km)

Clavitos
Punta de los

LA GOMERA

One office is in La Puntilla, another is near the Charco del Conde, and the third is in central Vueltas.

There are also watery activities available. For diving, contact **Fisch & Co Centro de Buceo** (☎ 922 80 56 88; Calle Lepanto, La Playa; per dive €35; ☯ 5-7pm Sat-Thu), which offers dives throughout the day.

Two motorboats, **Tina** (☎ 922 80 58 85) and **Siron** (☎ 922 80 54 80), cruise daily around the south and west of the island, towards Los Órganos, a weird rock formation visible only from the water (see p188). The day-long trip could include some spontaneous whale or dolphin watching, as well as a little tuna fishing. A surprisingly good meal, partly prepared on board, is included in the price, and the boat will drop anchor in a scenic spot so that those aboard can have a swim. The trips themselves are fun, but apart from Los Órganos, there is little to see on La Gomera's cliff-strewn coast. The trips, which last upwards of seven hours, cost about €25.

To learn more about whales and dolphins, contact Capitan Claudio at the **Club de Mar** (☎ 922 80 57 59; Vueltas; boat cruises from €27). The *capitan* takes several short daily trips, always with a marine biologist on board, so that you can see and learn more about local marine life. You can also sign up for a day-long yacht cruise or an evening sunset cruise.

All the cruises set sail from the Vueltas port, a small and rather squalid place.

Sleeping

Most of the island's accommodation is here in Valle Gran Rey, and it's not hard to see why. Besides having the best beaches and breathtaking scenery, it makes a good base for those wanting to walk or cycle in the interior.

Accommodation, while simple and leaning towards the budget end, is abundant, so finding a room is usually no problem. Even if all the official lodgings were taken (something rather unlikely), it seems that most people here rent out rooms on the side, so ask around.

BUDGET
Pensión Candelaria (☎ 922 80 54 20; Puerto de Vueltas; s/d €20/30) A sprawling house with flowers on the front terrace, rooms here offer clean, tiled bathrooms and small kitchenettes, though they vary widely – some are large and sunny with a balcony, others are smaller. Try to see the room before getting settled.

Pensión Las Vueltas (☎ 922 80 52 16; Puerto de Vueltas; s €15, d €20-25) This charming house offers no-frills rooms, some with a kitchenette and all with private bathrooms and terraces. The décor is uninspired but clean and modern.

Casa Bellos Cabellos (☎ 922 80 51 82; La Calera; d €20-25, apt €30-40) Lush plants smother the pretty wooden balcony that runs across the front of this charming guesthouse. Pleasant double rooms and a few apartments, all with views of the landscape, are for rent. You'll pay €5 extra for a room with a private bathroom.

Apartamentos Playa-Mar (☎ 650 94 20 53/14; La Playa; studio/1-bedroom apt €25/40) The small and simple studio apartments don't have the amenities of the larger ones, which boast a large kitchen, a balcony looking onto the ocean and a big bedroom. But both are within spitting distance of the beach.

MID-RANGE
Hotel Gran Rey (☎ 922 80 58 59; www.hotel-granrey.com; La Puntilla; s €40-63.50, d €56.50-83; ℗ ⊠ ⊠) The area's only major hotel, it's just across from the beach. Rooms here are smallish but comfortable, with tiled floors, nice linens, a marbled bathroom and gorgeous views of either the mountains or (for a little extra) the ocean.

Apartamentos Baja del Secreto (☎ 922 80 57 09; bajadelsecreto@navegalia.com; Avenida Marítima, Charco del Conde; 2-/3-/4-/5-/6-person apt €46/52/58/64/76; ⊠) A charming, fortress-like building in traditional Canary style, apartments here include fully equipped kitchen, phone, TV and terrace with a view.

Apartamentos Tres Palmeras (☎ 922 80 57 93; www.trespalmeras.com; La Playa; apt €48-54; ℗ ⊠) A modern-looking hotel complex with a salt-water pool, apartments here have balconies (most with ocean views) and are spacious and well equipped.

Eating
Heladería-Zumería Carlos (☎ 922 80 50 52; La Calera; juice €2) For a glass of fresh juice or a cheap sandwich, nothing beats this sunny little café.

DETOUR

Some of La Gomera's prettiest scenery is in the southern interior of the island. From Playa Santiago, head north on the highway that leads towards San Sebastián via Las Toscas. This road is impressive in itself: hairpin curves sit atop deep ravines, and rock cliffs rise just beside the highway. In Las Toscas, take the small dirt road that leads to Benchijigua (p191), 4km on. This tranquil, green valley is one of the prettiest spots on the island, and from here several trails branch out, many heading north into the national park.

Next, get back to the main highway and continue north until you reach the TF-713 highway. Head west through the national park, stopping at the nearly half-dozen *miradores* (lookout points) that line the road.

When you reach the first major intersection, head south (left) towards Alajeró. The road winds sharply around the few houses dotting the dry countryside, and the ocean is often visible in the distance. Just over a kilometre before you reach Alajeró, take an unmarked road to the right to see the island's only ancient *drago* tree (p37). A steep trail to the tree itself begins at an old farmhouse, and the short hike will lead towards this large, weird tree whose blood-red sap reputedly has healing powers.

Back on the main highway, it's a quick trip back down to Playa Santiago.

Restaurante El Palmar (☎ 922 80 53 32; Borbalán; mains €6-12) Hidden among banana trees, a stone's throw from the main highway. It would easy to drive right by the Palmar, so keep an eye out for the road sign. Both the food and the atmosphere are comfy and welcoming. Try the *cazuela* (thick fish stew) and be sure to have a chat with the friendly owner.

Restaurante El Baifo (☎ 922 80 57 75; La Playa; menú del día €14) For something different, come to this Malaysian-French restaurant, where odd international mixes are served in a dining room with touches of Asian décor. Vegetarians will find lots of options, which is something rare around here.

Restaurante los Robles (☎ 922 80 61 61; Carretera Playa del Inglés; menú del día €6-9) An Argentinian restaurant featuring grilled meats, this place offers great value in a relaxed setting. The cheerful dining room has blue-tiled tables, and there's a small terrace.

Bar-Restaurante El Puerto (☎ 922 80 52 24; Puerta de Vueltas; mains €5.70-12) Specialising in – what else? – fresh fish, this pleasant place by the port offers local delicacies such as tuna in *mojo* (sauce), and grilled *peto* and *medregal* (local fish).

Bar-Restaurante Charco del Conde (☎ 922 80 54 03; Avenida Marítima; mains €6-10; ☯ closed Sun) There's an indoor-outdoor feel to this casual dining room, where you can order big portions of generic meat and fish dishes.

Drinking & Entertainment

Discoteca La Playa (La Playa) Beside the Apartamentos Playa-Mar (see p194), this place keeps the partying crowd going until late on summer nights. In winter it's open weekends only but is still a fun place to dance and to check out the crowd.

Tambara Café (Las Vueltas; ☯ 5pm-1am, closed Wed) A good place for a casual drink, this has a tiny terrace close enough to the beach to hear the waves breaking against the shore.

Cacatua Café-Terraza (Las Vueltas; ☯ 10am-11pm) Open all day, this relaxing place serves drinks, salads and sandwiches to a mixed crowd. There's a small bar area indoors, and outside is a large, shady patio with a few scattered tables.

Getting There & Away

Bus No 1 connects with San Sebastián (one hour and 45 minutes) several times a day and leaves from the various bus stops indicated on the map. Hop on the water taxi operated by **Garajonay Exprés** (☎ 902 34 34 50) to get to Playa Santiago (€2.45, 20 minutes, three times daily) or San Sebastián (€3.28, 35 minutes, three times daily) more quickly. The ferries leave from the port.

Getting Around

If your own two feet can't do the job, Alofi Rentals and Bike Station Gomera (see p192) rent out bikes, scooters and motorcycles.

LA GOMERA

La Palma

CONTENTS

With steep volcanic slopes, lush vegetation and some of the most beautiful coastline in the western Canaries, it's easy to see why La Palma has been dubbed La Isla Bonita (the Pretty Island). Rainfall and spring water are more plentiful here than on any other island, making the 708 sq km of San Miguel de la Palma (the island's full name) the greenest of the archipelago. Orchards, vineyards and forests flourish, and their soft beauty contrasts sharply with the harsh crags and peaks of the volcanic heights that run down the island's centre.

From the air, La Palma looks something like an arrowhead or an upside-down triangle. The north is tree-filled and scored with deep gorges, while the south is rockier and drier, proof of the still-breathing volcanoes at work on the land. The enormous depression Caldera de Taburiente dominates the centre of the island and is surrounded by a horseshoe-shaped rock wall. It was here that the native Benahoares had their last stand before the Spaniards took over the island.

The inhabitants of La Palma live fairly well off agriculture, fishing and the slowly growing tourist industry. But that hasn't always been the case, and until recently many Palmeros were forced to emigrate to South America or to other islands to make a living.

HIGHLIGHTS

- **Gazing**

  La Palma is one of the world's best spots for stargazing. When night falls, it's a feast for the eyes (p198)

- **Driving**

  The gorges that fall away beneath the LP-111 highway in the north are breathtaking (p216)

- **Sunbathing**

  Puerto Naos is the best beach on the island, where you can lounge beneath the swaying palms (p212)

- **Smelling Fresh**

  The talcum-powder festival in Santa Cruz de la Palma may be many things, but unhygienic it's not (p205)

- **Cratering**

  Walking the wall of the majestic Caldera de Taburiente is a must (p213)

| ▪ TELEPHONE CODE: 922 | ▪ POPULATION: 85,500 | ▪ AREA: 708 SQ KM |

HISTORY

La Palma was not incorporated into the Crown of Castilla until 1493, the year after Alonso Fernández de Lugo had finished off the island's native opposition. This he had achieved only after a stroke of trickery. He invited the leader of the Benahoares (the Guanche tribe on La Palma), Mencey Tanausú, to abandon his impregnable stronghold in the Caldera de Taburiente for talks, only to ambush him and his men at the spot now known as El Riachuelo. Tanausú was shipped to Spain as a slave, but went on a hunger strike on board the boat and never saw the Spanish mainland.

By the following century, the few Benahoares who had not been enslaved or wiped out had been joined by a motley assortment of Spanish, Portuguese, Italian and Flemish migrants. The main exports became sugar, *malvasía* (Malmsey wine) and honey. In the meantime, the abundant Canary pine provided timber for burgeoning shipyards. By the late 16th century, as transatlantic trade flourished, Santa Cruz de la Palma was considered the third most important port of the Spanish empire after Seville and Antwerp (in modern Belgium).

The fortunes of La Palma largely followed those of the other Canary islands, as one cash crop succeeded another. Today the banana remains a mainstay of the island's economy, although a wide range of crops is grown for local consumption. The cigars (half the menfolk seem to have one lodged permanently in a corner of the mouth) are of particular note and, according to locals, are nearly as good as their counterparts in Havana.

INFORMATION
Books & Maps

If you want to see every tiny gravel road and hiking path on the island, there's no substitute for the 1:50,000 map published by Ediciones David and created by Palmero Juan José Santos. The map costs around €5 and includes helpful text in several

---

THE WORLD'S LARGEST TELESCOPE

No, those round space-age-looking things squatting on the peak of Roque de los Muchachos aren't something from a theme park, and no, they're not alien spaceships come to explore earth. They are the telescopes of the island's astronomical observatory, which happens to be one of the world's best places to study the night sky. Tossed out in the Atlantic far from urban centres and city lights, La Palma is an ideal place to stargaze. Its high peaks allow cloud-free viewing, and even the wind here, which blows in straight layers and doesn't interfere much with images, gives the island an advantage. More than 75% of the nights here on El Roque are clear, a statistic that's hard to beat.

The Roque de los Muchachos Observatory is already home to Europe's largest telescope, the William Herschel, and will soon boast the world's largest, the mammoth Grantecan (Gran Telescopio Canario), a telescope with a diameter of 10m. For now, only observatories in Chile and Hawaii compete with La Palma, but when the new telescope is completed in 2005, 'the pretty island' will have the best astronomical technology on the planet. Studies here have been instrumental in discovering new planets, finding out how galaxies are formed, and learning how comets break up. Scientists working here also contributed to the ground-breaking theory that the universe will expand infinitely.

La Palma's observatory is linked with the Teide Astronomical Observatory in Tenerife (see p162), and together they form the Instituto de Astrofísica de Canarias (IAC), which is coordinated by the University of La Laguna. Scientists from all over the world come to La Palma to study, and the telescopes scattered about are owned by several different countries.

The people of La Palma support the astronomical studies as much as the scientific community does. The island has agreed to follow the 'law of the skies', which requires that all public lighting be yellow-tinted to allow for better night-time observation, and prohibits large factories above 1000m.

The observatory is normally closed to the public, but until 9pm you're free to drive around the complex and have a look at the looming telescopes on the hill. See p214 for information on how to get to the observatory.

ALMA

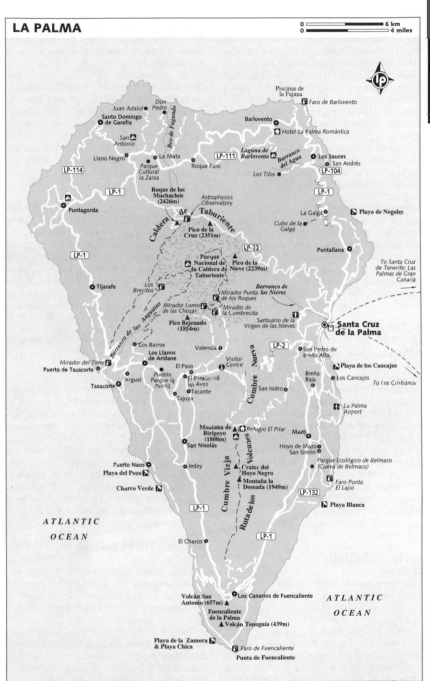

LA PALMA

0 — 6 km
0 — 4 miles

Piscinas de la Fajana
Faro de Barlovento
Juan Adalid • Don Pedro •
Santo Domingo de Garafía •
San Antonio
Barlovento
Hotel La Palma Romántica
Llano Negro •
La Mata •
LP-111
Laguna de Barlovento
Barranco del Agua
Los Sauces •
San Andrés
LP-114
Parque Cultural la Zarza
Roque Faro •
Los Tilos •
LP-104
Roque de los Muchachos (2426m)
Astrophysics Observatory
LP-1
LP-1
Caldera de Taburiente
La Galga •
Playa de Nogales
Puntagorda •
Pico de la Cruz (2351m)
Cubo de la Galga •
LP-1
LP-22
Parque Nacional de la Caldera de Taburiente
Pico de la Nieve (2239m)
Puntallana •
To Santa Cruz de Tenerife; Las Palmas de Gran Canaria
Tijarafe •
Los Brecitos
Mirador Punta las Nieves de los Roques
Barranco de las Nieves
Mirador Lomo de las Chozas
Mirador de la Cumbrecita
Santuario de la Virgen de las Nieves
Barranco de las Angustias
Pico Bejenado (1854m)
Santa Cruz de la Palma
Los Barros •
Valencia •
LP-2
San Pedro de Breña Alta •
Los Llanos de Aridane •
Mirador del Time
Visitor Centre
Playa de los Cancajos
Puerto de Tazacorte •
El Paso •
Cumbre Nueva
Breña Baja •
Los Cancajos •
Argual •
Pueblo Parque la Palma
El Paraíso de las Aves
San Isidro •
To Los Cristianos
Tazacorte •
Tacante •
La Palma Airport
Tajuya •
Montaña de Birigoyo (1808m)
Refugio El Pilar
Mazo •
San Nicolás •
Hoyo de Mazo •
San Simón •
Puerto Naos •
Jedey •
Cumbre Vieja
Cráter del Hoyo Negro
Parque Ecológico de Belmaco (Cueva de Belmaco)
Playa del Pozo
Ruta de los Volcanes
Montaña la Deseada (1949m)
Faro Punta El Lajio
Charco Verde
LP-132
Playa Blanca
LP-1
El Charco •
LP-1
ATLANTIC OCEAN

Volcán San Antonio (657m)
Los Canarios de Fuencaliente
ATLANTIC OCEAN
Fuencaliente de la Palma
Volcán Teneguía (439m)
Playa de la Zamora & Playa Chica
Faro de Fuencaliente
Punta de Fuencaliente

languages. A bit more manageable on the highway is the 1:100,000 *La Palma* map by Editorial Everest (€2.50), which also includes detailed maps of Santa Cruz and other major towns. The three hiking maps covering southern, central and northern La Palma given out for free at the tourist office give a good overview, but if you're a serious walker you should buy a hiking guide, such as *Landscapes of La Palma and El Hierro*, published by Sunflower Books, or one of the Discovery Walking Guides. *The Hiking Guide* (in English and Spanish), published by the tourist board, is helpful too.

Newspapers

Get the local news in *La Voz de la Palma*, which hits the shelves every two weeks. You can also pick up a copy of the free *Infomagazin*, which appears every three months in Spanish, English and German. Its website (www.lapalma-magazin.info) has loads of information about island culture and things to do.

ACTIVITIES

La Palma is a quiet sort of place, and the main activity is **walking** amid its solitude. The Parque Nacional de la Caldera de Taburiente has several trails that are well worth the effort it entails to hike among the rocks and inclines; the journey around the rim of the massive depression of the Caldera de Taburiente is an absolute must-do (see p214). Go with a guide (see p213) or take off on your own with one of the maps we recommend (see p198) or the map from the visitors centre.

To get off your feet, you can head to one of the **diving** outfits (see p207) or try **mountain biking** (p211 or p212), though the mountainous terrain makes for a strenuous excursion.

ACCOMMODATION
Camping

Free camping is prohibited on the island. There are a few basic camp sites, but to use them you need to apply in advance by phone.

For information on staying at the camp site inside the Parque Nacional de la Caldera de Taburiente, see p214. There are five camp sites outside the park. Phone the **Consejería de Política Territorial y Medio Ambi-**

ente (Department of the Environment; ☎ 922 41 15 83; fax 922 42 01 87) in Santa Cruz for those in Los Canarios de Fuencaliente in the south of the island, by the Refugio El Pilar in the north of the Cumbre Vieja, and at San Antonio, southeast of Santo Domingo de Garafía, in the northwest of the island. You need to apply at least a week in advance and collect your permit in person at least two days before you intend to camp.

The other two camp sites are outside Puntagorda (see p217) and beside the Laguna de Barlovento (see p216).

Casas Rurales

Although not for budget travellers, *casas rurales* (rural houses) are the best way to live like a local in La Palma, and in the rest of the Canaries, for that matter. Many of these homes were abandoned when their owners emigrated to South America. Now they have been refurbished and have gardens and a charm that is unmatched by any hotel. For more information contact the **Asociación de Turismo Rural** (☎ 922 43 06 25; www.islabonita.com; Casa Luján, Calle El Pósito 3, Puntallana), which has around 75 such places scattered across the island.

Hotels & Apartments

Thankfully, La Palma has not yet experienced the tourist boom of islands such as Tenerife and Gran Canaria. That means that it's calmer here but accommodation is a bit harder to find. Los Cancajos resort, outside Santa Cruz, and Puerto Naos, on the western coast, are the two tourist centres, though only a handful of large hotels are responsible for giving them the title. Elsewhere, *pensiones* (guesthouses), *casas rurales* and apartments make up the bulk of the lodging options.

GETTING THERE & AWAY
Air

Flying is an easy and a relatively inexpensive way to get to La Palma, although if you take into account the ridiculously short distances between islands, the €50-plus air fare doesn't seem so economical.

Binter (☎ 902 39 13 92; www.bintercanarias.es) connects **La Palma airport** (☎ 922 41 15 40) with the following destinations:
Tenerife Norte Average two flights daily; 30 minutes.
Gran Canaria Average five flights daily; 50 minutes.

El Hierro Two flights selected days only; 25 minutes.
Lanzarote One flight selected days only; 50 minutes.

Otherwise, traffic consists of one Iberia flight daily to Madrid, and direct chartered flights, mostly from Germany, Holland and the UK.

The airport, 7km south of Santa Cruz, has several car-rental agents, a currency exchange bureau and a small tourist office. Bus No 8 shuttles every 30 minutes between Santa Cruz and the airport from 8.15am to 5.45pm, and once an hour from 5.45pm to 9.15pm.

Boat

The ferry ride from Los Cristianos to Santa Cruz de la Palma takes about two hours with **Fred Olsen** (☎ 922 62 82 00; www.fredolsen.es). The daily trip leaves at 7.30pm and arrives at 9.30pm (one way €31 to €34). The trip back to Los Cristianos leaves at the unmerciful hour of 6.30am, arriving at 8.30am.

Trasmediterránea (☎ 902 45 46 45; www.trasme diterranea.es) makes a weekly run from Santa Cruz de Tenerife, leaving at 11.59pm on Thursday night and arriving at 8am on Friday morning (€28.10, eight hours). You can pay triple the price if you want a bed. In reverse, the boat leaves La Palma on Friday at 5pm and arrives at Tenerife at 11.15pm.

GETTING AROUND
To/From the Airport
For details of getting to/from Santa Cruz de Palma, see p206.

Bus
La Palma has a fairly good bus system (with 16 bus lines) that you can use to hop between the island's main towns. For complete route information, stop by a bus station or contact **Transportes Insular La Palma** (☎ 922 41 19 24; www.transporteslapalma.com). If you plan to use the bus often, you're better off buying a Bonobus card. Cards start at €12 and represent a discount of about 20% off normal individual fares. They are on sale at bus stations, newsstands and tobacco shops.

Car
In addition to the major chains (see p252), there are local car-rental agencies that often offer better prices. In Santa Cruz, try **Isla**

Bonita (☎ 922 41 57 53; Álvarez Abreu 62) or **La Palma** (☎ 922 41 24 49; Avenida Marítima 69).

Taxi
With taxis charging €0.70 per kilometre, they're an easy but awfully pricey way to get around. A one-way trip to Puerto Naos from Santa Cruz will burn a hole €35 wide in your pocket, more than a day's car rental!

SANTA CRUZ DE LA PALMA

pop 18,705

The island's capital and only major town, Santa Cruz de la Palma is full of historic Canary-style buildings and is one of the most pleasant places on the archipelago for a city stroll. Though it seems to have turned its back on the sea – the waterfront is dedicated to a huge car park and the commercial port – the interior is a maze of cobblestoned streets and small shops. From behind the city centre mountains grow majestically, and the white-walled villages that climb up them make for one of the island's most picturesque views.

HISTORY
In the 16th century, the dockyards of Santa Cruz earned a reputation as the best in all the Canary Islands. The town became so important that King Felipe II had the first Juzgado de Indias (Court of the Indias) installed here in 1558, and every single vessel trading with the Americas from mainland Spain was obliged to register.

The boom brought economic security, but it lead to problems as well. Santa Cruz was frequently besieged and occasionally sacked by a succession of pirates, including those under the command of Sir Francis Drake.

The worst attack came in 1553, when Francois le Clerc (aka Jambe de Bois, or Pegleg) unleashed a merciless assault on the town.

ORIENTATION
The historical centre of Santa Cruz runs parallel to the waterfront, which is like a wide smile curving into the town. Santa Cruz is easily walkable, although as you

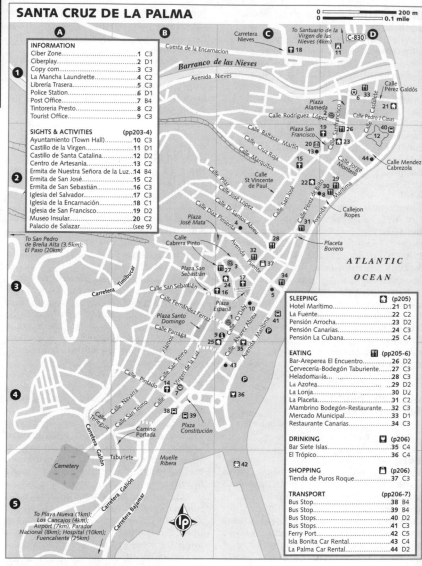

SANTA CRUZ DE LA PALMA

0 ____ 200 m
0 ____ 0.1 mile

INFORMATION
Ciber Zone..1 C3
Ciberplay...2 D1
Copy com...3 C3
La Mancha Laundrette......................4 C2
Librería Trasera.................................5 C3
Police Station....................................6 D1
Post Office...7 B4
Tintorería Presto...............................8 C2
Tourist Office....................................9 C3

SIGHTS & ACTIVITIES   (pp203-4)
Ayuntamiento (Town Hall)..............10 C3
Castillo de la Virgen........................11 D1
Castillo de Santa Catalina................12 D2
Centro de Artesanía.........................13 C2
Ermita de Nuestra Señora de la Luz..14 B4
Ermita de San José...........................15 C2
Ermita de San Sebastián..................16 C3
Iglesia del Salvador..........................17 C3
Iglesia de la Encarnación.................18 C1
Iglesia de San Francisco...................19 D2
Museo Insular...................................20 C2
Palacio de Salazar.........................(see 9)

To San Pedro
de Breña Alta (3.5km);
El Paso (20km)

SLEEPING   (p205)
Hotel Marítimo.................................21 D1
La Fuente..22 C2
Pensión Arrocha...............................23 C3
Pensión Canarias..............................24 C3
Pensión La Cubana...........................25 C4

EATING   (pp205-6)
Bar-Areperea El Encuentro...............26 D2
Cervecería-Bodegón Taburiente.......27 C3
Heladomanía...................................28 D2
La Azotea...29 D2
La Lonja...30 D2
La Placeta..31 C2
Mambrino Bodegón-Restaurante....32 C3
Mercado Municipal...........................33 D1
Restaurante Canarias.......................34 C3

DRINKING   (p206)
Bar Siete Islas..................................35 C4
El Trópico...36 C4

SHOPPING   (p206)
Tienda de Puros Roque.....................37 C3

TRANSPORT   (pp206-7)
Bus Stop...38 B4
Bus Stop...39 B4
Bus Stop...40 D2
Bus Stops...41 C3
Ferry Port...42 C5
Isla Bonita Car Rental......................43 C4
La Palma Car Rental.........................44 D2

ATLANTIC
OCEAN

To Playa Nueva (1km);
Los Cancajos (4km);
Airport (7km); Parador
Nacional (8km); Hospital (10km);
Fuencaliente (25km)

head further from the coast the hills get steeper. The heart of activity here is Calle O'Daly, aka Calle Real, a long pedestrian boulevard lined with shops and colonial-era houses.

Most interesting sites, restaurants and shops are around O'Daly on the grid of pedestrian streets that fill the centre.

Maps

The tourist office gives out a free map of Santa Cruz, but it's not that easy to follow. Your best bet is to either use the map in this guidebook or purchase the Editorial Everest 1:100,000 map of La Palma, which contains a detailed (1:5000) map of Santa Cruz.

INFORMATION

Bookshops

Librería Trasera (☎ 922 41 18 15; Calle Álvarez Abreu 27) This great, little, intimate bookshop stocks good literature and lots of titles on La Palma. However, most are in Spanish.

Internet Access

Ciber Zone (☎ 650 82 65 98; Calle Apurón 8; per 30 min €1.20; ⊙ closed Aug)
Copy.com (☎ 922 41 32 36; Calle A Cabrera Pinto 15) This place has just four computers, but you can also send and receive faxes and make photocopies.
Ciberplay (☎ 922 41 15 10; Calle San Francisco 1; per hr €2.70) Just off Plaza Alameda.

Laundry

La Mancha (☎ 922 41 21 98; Calle Díaz Pimienta 10)
Tintoreria Presto (☎ 922 41 80 69; Calle Pérez de Brito 44) A wash, dry and fold costs €10.

Medical Services

Hospital (Hospital General de las Nieves; ☎ 922 18 50 00) The new hospital is an easy 10km drive or bus ride from town. Bus No 9 makes the trip once per hour.

Post

Post Office (☎ 922 41 17 02; Plaza Constitución; ⊙ 8.30am-8.30pm Mon-Fri, 9.30am-1pm Sat) Located by the big roundabout. It seems like an awfully big building for the postal needs of such a tiny island!

Tourist Offices

Tourist Office (☎ 922 41 21 06; www.lapalmaturismo .com; Calle O'Daly 22; ⊙ 9am-7.30pm Mon-Fri, 9am-3pm Sat, 9am-2pm Sun) Stocks lots of information about the town and the island, whether you're interested in hiking, festivals, history or gastronomy. The building itself, the Palacio de Salazar (below), is worth a look too.

SIGHTS & ACTIVITIES

Old Town

Calle O'Daly runs parallel to the coast and is the main artery of Santa Cruz. Named for an Irish trader who made La Palma his home, the street is full of shops, bars and some of the town's most impressive architecture. Late-Renaissance **Palacio de Salazar** (17th century) is on your left soon after you enter the street from Plaza Constitución. The palace now houses the tourist office.

Wander north along Calle O'Daly and you'll come to the **Plaza España**, considered the most important example of Renaissance architecture in the Canary Islands. To one side sits the imposing **ayuntamiento** (town hall), built in 1559 after the original was des- troyed by French pirates. Across the plaza is the ornate **Iglesia del Salvador**, closed for restoration at the time of publication. Though the church's exterior seems more fortress than house of worship, the interior boasts numerous neoclassical altars, an intricate *mudéjar* (Islamic-style architecture) ceiling and several fine sculptures, among them the 16th-century Flemish carving of the crucifixion, *Cristo de los Mulatos*, in the Capilla de Ánimas side chapel. The square itself is flanked by grand mansions. You'll see more such noble houses, most of them adorned with balconies in a variety of styles, as you head north along Calle Pérez de Brito.

Balcony-lovers should head to the waterfront, just north of Avenida Puente, to see a series of wonderful, gaily painted **old houses**. Some date back to the 16th century and all sport balconies in a variety of styles. This penchant for balconies came with Andalucian migrants and was modified by Portuguese influences. The style was also exported, and similar balconies can be seen on houses in Venezuela, Cuba and Peru, where they came to be part of the so-called 'colonial style'.

It's lucky that the balconies are still there at all; King Felipe II of Spain apparently disapproved of balconies and sent orders to the islands that they be torn down. But the ship carrying the royal command never made it to La Palma, so the good citizens of Santa Cruz maintained their prized balconies, safe in their ignorance.

From the rise behind Plaza Constitución (trudge up the steps about 100m south of the post office), the modest chapel **Ermita de Nuestra Señora de la Luz** stands watch over the harbour – appropriately so since the chapel is also dedicated to San Telmo, patron saint of sailors and fishermen, whose guild paid for its construction in 1680. Inside is a rich Baroque altarpiece, illuminated and visible through a window in the eastern door, even when the chapel is closed.

The *ermita* is one of several small 16th- and 17th-century chapels, most of them originally attached to monasteries, that the Dominicans and Franciscans established in the popular quarters of Santa Cruz, beyond the choicer noble and bourgeois quarter nearer the coast. Another chapel, the **Ermita de San Sebastián** (Calle San Sebastián), is behind the Iglesia de San Salvador. Yet another is **Ermita de San José** (Calle San Jose), which has given its name to the street on which it stands.

Around Barranco de las Nieves

The **Iglesia de San Francisco** (Plaza San Francisco), another Renaissance church, is equally rich in works of art, the majority unmistakably Baroque. The plaque on the floor just inside the eastern portal commemorates Baltasar Martín, who was killed while defending the church against assault by Pegleg and his French pirates in 1553.

The restored convent next door is architecturally interesting and worth a visit for its own sake. The small band of Franciscan monks who arrived with the conquering Spanish force began the convent's construction in 1508, after having lived in straw huts for 15 years. Nowadays it houses the **Museo Insular** (☎ 922 42 05 58; admission €1.80; ⏰ 9am-2pm & 4-6pm Mon-Fri Oct-Jun, 9am-2pm Mon-Fri Jul-Sep), the island's museum. Here you'll find everything from Guanche skulls to cupboards of sad stuffed birds, pickled reptiles and a great portrait of Franco with a feathery hat. Also on the square is **Centro de Artesania** (☎ 922 41 21 29; ⏰ 8am-3pm Mon-Fri Oct-Jun, 8am-2pm Jul-Sep), which has a small exhibition of handicrafts for sale.

Gaze north across leafy Plaza Alameda (a good place to sip a *café cortado* – an espresso with a splash of milk) and you'll think Christopher Columbus' ship, the *Santa María*, became stranded here. But no, it's actually a rather weird idea for the town's **Museo Naval**, known as 'El Barco de la Virgen' ('the Virgin's Boat') to the locals. It was closed at the time of publication, but until it reopens it makes for a great photo opportunity.

On the seafront, the **Castillo de Santa Catalina** was one of several built in the 17th century to fend off pirate raids. Across the ravine and higher is a smaller one, the **Castillo de la Virgen**. Tucked away on the same hill is the 16th-century **Iglesia de la Encarnación**, the first church to be built in Santa Cruz after the Spanish conquest.

Santuario de la Virgen de las Nieves

A 2km hike or 4km drive north of town leads to La Palma's main object of pilgrimage, the 17th-century **Santuario de la Virgen de las Nieves**

(☎ 922 41 63 67, 922 41 50 14; ⏰ 8.30am-8pm). To walk from Plaza Alameda, follow the road, which becomes a dirt track, westwards up the gorge of the Barranco de las Nieves. It will take nearly 45 minutes to walk up, but coming back is faster. By car, follow signs from the Avenida Marítima where it crosses the barranco (ravine).

The church sits in a peaceful spot surrounded by trees, green slopes and a handful of pilgrim hostels, all in typical Canarian colonial style. The church is simple outside, but the interior is truly ornate, with a beautiful *mudéjar* ceiling and an organ. The Virgin Mary herself, surrounded by a glittering altar, is a 14th-century sculpture, the oldest religious statue in the Canary Islands. It was probably brought by merchants before the arrival of the Spaniards. Every five years the Virgin is brought down to Santa Cruz in a grand procession (below).

You'll also find a bar-restaurant in the church's grounds. Bus No 10 (€0.92) comes up hourly from the town centre.

Playa Nueva

Just 1km south of town, past the port and the shipyards, is the new beach, aptly named Playa Nueva (New Beach). It's a wide, sandy beach with volleyball nets and football goals, and it's an easy walk or drive from the centre. Park along the highway.

FESTIVALS & EVENTS

During the **Fiesta de Nuestra Señora de las Nieves** (Feast Day of Our Lady of the Snows), celebrated on 5 August, Santa Cruz puts on its party clothes for the celebration of the island's patron saint. It's the island's principal fiesta – finding a place to stay at this time without having booked in advance is just about impossible.

Don't miss the parade of giants and 'fat heads' (fanciful, rather squatty characters with exceptionally large heads), though the high point is the dance of the dwarves, which has been performed here since the early 19th century.

Every five years (next time in 2005), the **Bajada de la Virgen de las Nieves** (Descent of the Virgin of the Snows) is celebrated. It's a religious procession where the islanders take the Virgin around the island throughout July and August, celebrating her arrival in each important town with a big party.

ALMA

THE SWEETEST-SMELLING BATTLE

Tenerife and Gran Canaria are known for their, ahem, lively celebrations of Carnaval (see p138 & p69), but unassuming Santa Cruz de la Palma also has a wild side. There's music, dancing, drinking and, of course, talcum powder. On Carnaval Monday, the good citizens of La Palma bring buckets of white, fragrant powder down to the centre of Santa Cruz and prepare to do battle with their neighbours. After loosening up with a few drinks and a little music, the snowy spectacle begins. Anyone is a target in this all-out war, and the town ends the night coughing and blinking furiously, covered head to toe with talcum powder. The tradition began to mock the *los indios*, Canary emigrants who became wealthy in the Americas and returned to the island decked in white suits and Panama hats. Now it's just another excuse for a fiesta.

The processions for **Easter Week**, when members of lay brotherhoods parade in their blood-red robes and tall, pointy hoods, march down Calle O'Daly. This street again becomes party central during **Carnaval**, which takes place in early to mid-February. If you're around during this pre-Lent celebration, don't forget your bottle of talcum powder (see the boxed text above).

SLEEPING

There aren't many lodging options in Santa Cruz itself, but most of what's available is low-priced. Though you might get lucky, it's always a good idea to reserve ahead of time, especially if you're arriving on the late ferry from Tenerife or plan to arrive outside of regular business hours.

Budget

Pensión Canarias (☎ 922 41 31 82; Calle Cabrera Pinto 27; s/d €20/28) Clean, modern rooms are cheap and come with their own bathrooms and TV sets at this two-starred *pensión*. Its location on a quiet side street just out of the town centre is a big plus.

Pensión La Cubana (☎ 922 41 13 54; Calle O'Daly 24; s/d €20/26) This 200-year-old house has beautiful wooden floors and pretty windows

with latticework. The seven rooms with shared bathroom are rustic and give off a summer-camp air.

Pensión Arrocha (☎ 922 41 11 17; Calle Pérez de Brito 77; s/d €15/22) The cheapest rooms in town are set around a typical Canary patio. Touches such as floral bedspreads and posters on the walls lend a cheery touch to the otherwise stale rooms. The communal bathroom looks rather worn but, comfortingly, smells of bleach.

La Fuente (☎ 922 41 56 36; Calle Pérez de Brito 49; 1-2-/3-person apt €37/45) The 11 apartments are all different, but each is decorated in a casual, beachy style with modern bathroom. There is no elevator but those willing to climb to the 4th floor are rewarded with amazing sea and town views.

Mid-Range & Top End

Hotel Marítimo (☎ 922 42 02 22; www.hotelmari timo.com; Avenida Marítima 75; s/d €53/90) Right on the waterfront, the look is standard hotel, with sea-green carpets, comfy beds and a small bathroom. Rooms have a sitting area with two hard-backed chairs and views of the avenida (so yes, there is traffic noise).

Parador Nacional (☎ 922 43 58 28; lapalma@ parador.es; Carretera de Zumacal, Breña Baja; s/d €75.50/94; P ⓧ ⓡ) About 8km south of town, this elegant hotel looks like a huge Canary farmhouse overlooking the ocean. There is a pretty pool surrounded by grass, and rooms are spacious and sun-filled, with a sitting area and lovely views.

EATING

Budget

Mercado Municipal (Avenida Nieves 3-4) If you're self-catering or just want to prepare a picnic, there is no place like the local market, where fresh veggies, fish, meat and cheese await every morning until 2pm.

Bar-Arepera El Encuentro (☎ 922 41 10 44; Calle Perez de Brito; arepas €1.50) For a taste of the popular Venezuelan *arepas* (hot pockets made of corn or flour and filled with meat or cheese), come to this atmospheric little bar just off Plaza Alameda. Iron tables are set up on the shady plaza.

Heladomanía (☎ 922 42 07 64; Calle Vandale 8; per ice-cream scoop €1) For some of the smoothest kilojoule-rich ice cream you've had in a while, pop into Heladomanía, where the artisanal ice cream is made on the spot.

Mid-Range

Mambrino Bodegón-Restaurante (☎ 922 41 18 73; Avenida Puente 19; mains €5-9, menú del día €7.80) This simple tavern makes a real effort to serve mainly island goods, with a great selection of local cheeses, cured meats and wines.

Cervecería-Bodegón Taburiente (☎ 922 41 64 42; Calle Pedro Poggio 7; mains €9) The menu here changes according to the season and the available ingredients. The bar, open all day, is the main focus of the restaurant's interior, which has just a few tables scattered about.

Restaurante Canarias (☎ 922 41 10 00; Avenida Marítima 28; mains €5.50-10) Seafood and fish in various sauces dominate the menu. The ambience is nothing special – cafeteria-esque, with linoleum floors and square tables – but the food is good and the prices fair. There's also a children's menu.

Top End

Parador Nacional (☎ 922 43 58 28; Carretera de Zumacal, Breña Baja; mains €14-18) Serving local specialties and island wines, the *parador's* elegant restaurant is a great place for a special dinner. Sitting on a hill overlooking the ocean, the setting is unbeatable.

La Placeta (☎ 922 41 52 73; Calle Borrero 1; mains €6.80-12; ☒ closed Sun) A charming little bistro on a tiny square, La Placeta has a small menu but quality options, including lots of vegetarian dishes.

La Lonja (☎ 922 41 52 66; Avenida Marítima 55; mains €10-13) Set in an old Canary house, La Lonja is a bit more upscale. Enjoy dishes such as cod, and beef fillets in sauce, around the central interior patio. The salads here – very fresh and generous – offer cheaper eating at €3.60 to €6.

La Azotea (☎ 922 41 20 33; Avenida Marítima 55; mains €8-12) Next door to La Lonja, and sharing its street number, La Azotea is a refined restaurant where you can sit on a pretty rooftop terrace or in the elegant, wood-beamed main dining room. Seafood is the speciality here.

DRINKING & ENTERTAINMENT

Santa Cruz can't exactly be called a night-life hot spot. After dark, most people find a quiet terrace bar where they can nurse a drink or two, or they join the younger crowd at the local football or basketball game. You'll find a bit more life along Avenida Marítima, which is lined with cafés,

zumerías (juice bars) and a few night-time bars. In town, **Bar Siete Islas** (☎ 922 41 76 35; Calle Álvarez Abreu 65) is a hamburger joint that looks like a cave and has music until late on weekends. **El Trópico** (Avenida Marítima 4) pulls in weekend revellers but isn't usually open during the week. Both places are active from July to mid-October but this can't be guaranteed for the rest of the year.

SHOPPING

Cigars are one of the island's most famed products. They may not be Cuban but they are made with fine ingredients and rolled using traditional methods. Even the most rabid antismoker might enjoy poking their nose into **Tienda de Puros Roque** (Calle Péres Volcán 10), a small temple to nicotine in its finest form, and sniffing its rich aromas. The shop's founder, Señor Roque, as the photos in his workshop attest, provided *puros* (cigars), the finest and the fattest, to Sir Winston Churchill, among other luminaries.

Otherwise, stroll along Calle O'Daly, which has a number of interesting shops.

GETTING THERE & AWAY
To/From the Airport

Bus No 8 leaves every 30 minutes (hourly on weekends) on the quarter hour to/from the airport and takes about 20 minutes, stopping at Los Cancajos. The fare is €0.95.

A taxi to the airport costs about €15.

Bus

Transportes Insular La Palma buses keep Santa Cruz well connected with the rest of the island. The bus stops are near Plaza Constitución and along the Avenida Marítima. Destinations include Los Llanos de Aridane (No 3, one way €5.50) and Puntallana (No 11, one way €1.30).

Car

There are plenty of car-hire places in town, particularly along Avenida Marítima. See p201 for details.

GETTING AROUND

The best way to get around Santa Cruz is by foot. If you come in by car, try to find a parking spot in the large lot by the waterfront, as the narrow streets of town are much better enjoyed while walking. If you're in a hurry you can catch one of the buses that run up and down the Avenida Marítima (fare around €1) or hop in a taxi. Since Santa Cruz is not big, you'd have to try very hard to run up a big taxi fare here.

THE SOUTH

Heading down the coast from Santa Cruz, the LP-1 highway makes for some of the smoothest and straightest driving in all the island, although that's not saying much. The landscape in the south is largely dry, due to the numerous volcanoes spread throughout the south, though banana plantations along the coast add shots of green.

LOS CANCAJOS

A small volcanic beach on a windy cove is the *raison d'être* for this growing coastal resort, 4km south of Santa Cruz. The town itself is mostly comprised of apartment buildings, with a handful of restaurants and bars, but the rugged waterfront is beautiful. There's a short maritime promenade and a hiking trail that runs along the coast.

Activities
Several activity outfits are set up in town. Dive with **Buceo Sub** (☎ 922 18 11 13; www.buceos -sub.com; dives incl equipment €29; ✆ 9am-5pm), based beside the H10 Costa Salinas apart-hotel (a hotel with apartment-like rooms), or **La Palma Diving Center** (☎ 922 18 13 93; www.la -palma-tauchen.de; dives €29; ✆ 10am-7pm Mon-Sat), in the cave-like Centro Cancajos shopping centre (on your left as you enter town from Santa Cruz).

You can rent bikes from **Damian** (☎ 922 43 46 88; Centro Cancajos, local 211; ✆ 9am-1pm & 5-7pm Mon-Fri, 9-11.30am Sat) or sign up for a hike with **Natour Trekking/Senderos Canarios** (☎ 922 43 30 01; www.natour-trekking.com; Apartamentos Valentina 4; ✆ 9am-1pm & 5-7pm).

Plenty of tour operators are also set up here. **Tours Viva** (☎ 922 43 53 00; Urbanización San Antonio del Mar; ✆ 9am-7pm Mon-Fri, 10am-1pm Sat) organises bus and hiking trips.

Sleeping & Eating
Most accommodation options here are apartments, except for H10 Taburiente Playa.

H10 Taburiente Playa (☎ 922 18 12 77; www .h10.es; Playa de los Cancajos; s/d €120.20/174.30; P ⊠

⊠ ⛄ ⛱) A comfortable beachside hotel popular with package tourists. The prices quoted here are enormously inflated compared with what most people pay through tour operators.

H10 Costa Salinas (☎ 922 43 43 48; www.h10.es; 1-bedroom apt €50/105, 2-bedroom apt €63-118.50; P ⛄ ⛱) Owned by the same hotel chain as H10 Taburiente Playa, the apartments at this apart-hotel are well equipped and have water views and a large pool complex.

Lago Azul (☎ 922 43 43 05; lagoazul-recepcion@telef onica.net; 2–3-person apt €42-54; P ⛱) You'll find simple apartments here.

Meson Canarias (☎ 922 43 43 52; Centro Cancajos, local 314; mains €6-12) Head here for quality Canarian dishes – it's low on atmosphere, but dependable.

La Marina (☎ 922 43 43 04; Urbanización Lago Azul; mains €8-11) At the far southern end of town, beside the Lago Azul apartments, La Marina specialises in crepes. Eat in a little courtyard or inside the elegant dining room.

Cafetería Agua Viva (☎ 922 43 43 04; Urbanización Lago Azul; mains €4-9) Upstairs from La Marina, and under the same ownership, this is an informal place with pretty ocean views and an international menu with the likes of pizza, chicken and pasta among other familiar foods.

The area around Centro Cancajos has several casual restaurants and bars, many with terraces.

Drinking & Entertainment
At night, head to **Trébol** (Urbanización Lago Azul), a disco that pulls in the young crowd from Santa Cruz. Other options include **Pepé's** (Centro Cancajos) and **Pub Guantanamera** (Centro Cancajos), where there is often live music on weekends.

Getting There & Away
Bus No 8 passes through every 30 minutes on its way from Santa Cruz to the airport; a second No 8 bus does the route in reverse. The main bus stop is at the Centro Cancajos shopping centre. The airport fare is €0.95.

MAZO
pop 5000
A peaceful village 13km south of Santa Cruz, Mazo is surrounded by green, dormant volcanoes. The town is known for the cigars and handicrafts made here.

As soon as you enter town, make a left to head down to **Museo Casa Roja** (☎ 922 42 85 87; Calle Maximiliano Pérez Díaz; adult/child €2/0.75; ☽ 10am-2pm & 3-6pm Mon-Fri, 11am-6pm Sat, 10am-2pm Sun), a lovely pinkish-red mansion (built in 1911) with exhibits on embroidery and Corpus Cristi – a festival the town celebrates with particular gusto (below). The house itself has an impressive imperial staircase and ornate tiled floors.

Beyond the museum is **Escuela Insular de Artesanía** (☎ 922 42 84 55; ☽ 8am-3pm Mon-Fri Oct-Jun, 8am-2pm Mon-Fri Jul-Sep), the island handicrafts school that runs a shop where you can buy tobacco, embroidery, ceramics, baskets and other goods. To get to the shop, head into the school's main patio and up the stairs on your right. In the afternoons, you can peek in on the students at work.

Down the hill from the school is the **Templo de San Blas**, Mazo's 16th-century church, which sits on a small plaza overlooking the ocean. Inside, the church boasts a Baroque altarpiece and several interesting pieces of Baroque art.

Get a bite to eat in **San Blas** (☎ 922 42 83 60; Calle Maria del Carmen Martínez Jerez 4; mains €5.50-10), where local dishes such as goat with *papas* (potatoes) are served on an outdoor terrace.

Festivals & Events
Mazo's celebration of **Corpus Cristi** in June is a fragrant, flowery affair. Islanders from surrounding towns descend on Mazo just before Corpus and decorate the streets with elegant 'carpets' made of flower petals, seeds and soil. The designs are intricate and require an artistic eye and a lot of work. Just as labour-intensive are the beautiful banners, also made of flowers and seeds, that the people carry in religious processions. It seems almost a crime that these creations are trampled and destroyed at the end of the day.

Getting There & Away
Mazo is on the LP-1 highway. Get here by bus No 3, which links Los Llanos, Fuencaliente and Santa Cruz (€1.35 to €1.60, depending on origin).

PARQUE ECOLÓGICO DE BELMACO
Ecological Park is a rather misleading name for this centre, dedicated to a small but archaeologically important cave once

inhabited by Benahoare tribespeople who left behind petroglyphs (patterns of whorls and squiggles etched in the cave walls). The **Cueva de Belmaco** (☎ 922 44 00 90; adult/child €2/0.75; ☽ 10am-6pm Mon-Fri winter, 10am-8pm Mon-Fri summer, 10am-3pm Sun year-round) was the first such site to be discovered and recorded on the island, back in 1752. There are four sets of engravings, and experts remain perplexed about their meaning.

The place is badly signposted from the LP-1 highway. Heading south from Santa Cruz, your best bet is to take the first left after the Mazo exit and then turn right (south) onto the LP-132. It's about 1km beyond San Simón. A few buses from Santa Cruz head down this way via Hoyo de Mazo. The nearest bus stop is about 400m south of the cave.

PLAYA BLANCA
Just 1.3 kilometres north up the LP-132 highway from the Cueva de Belmaco is the unmarked dirt road that leads down to **Playa Blanca** (White Beach, though it's not that white and there's not much beach). A perfect picnic spot, here you'll find a tiny hamlet with a few summer homes, a tranquil beach and calm waters in which to swim (though the rocks can be uncomfortable to walk on). Permanent umbrellas made with wood dot the beach, and you can see La Gomera and Tenerife from the shore.

LOS CANARIOS DE FUENCALIENTE
pop 1728
If you keep heading south from Parque Ecológico de Belmaco, the LP-132 highway joins with the larger LP-1 and leads to Fuencaliente. The area gets its name from hot springs that were long ago buried by fiery volcanoes. Don't think that the volcanoes have calmed down; the last eruption was in 1971, when Volcán Teneguía's lava flow added a few hectares to the island's size.

Sights & Activities
The volcanoes are the major draw here, and you shouldn't miss the short but breathtaking walk along the rim of **Volcán San Antonio** (☎ 922 44 46 16; adult/child under 13 €3/free; ☽ 9am-8pm Jun-Sep, 9am-6pm Oct-May). It takes just 20 minutes to walk the gravel path halfway around the yawning chasm of this great black cone, which last blew in 1949 and is now being

repopulated by hardy Canary pines. Afterwards, take a look at the small visitors centre, where a machine that constantly measures volcanic movement in the area shows a boring but comforting straight line.

From the visitors centre, a signposted trail leads you to **Volcán Teneguía**, whose 1971 eruption was the archipelago's most recent. The easy walk there and back takes about two hours.

The town's other claim to fame is its wine. Across the highway from Volcán San Antonio you can visit **Vinos Carballo** (☎ 922 44 41 40; Carretera de Las Indias 44; ⊗ 11am-7pm Mon-Sat), a small winery known for its *malvasía* (see the boxed text). In town is the larger winery **Bodegas Teneguía** (☎ 922 44 40 78; www.vinosteneguia.com; Los Canarios s/n; ⊗ 8am-2pm Mon-Fri), whose white, red and sweet wines are sold all over the island and beyond. There's also a good restaurant in the winery (below).

Sleeping & Eating

Apartamentos & Pensión Los Volcanes (☎ 922 44 41 64; Carretera General 84; s/apt €20/24) A nice surprise, with newish, tasteful décor, private bathrooms and some rooms with a small balcony. Apartments are studio style, with a kitchenette, sitting area and bed all in the same room.

Pensión Central (☎ 922 44 40 18; Calle Yaiza 4; s/d €17/21, apt €25-35) This place has basic but comfy rooms (tiled floors, wooden bedposts, private bathroom). To get information and/or keys, you have to stop by the owner's house, under the sign for the now-defunct Imperial Pensión on Calle San Antonio 1.

The best eats in town are at **El Patio del Vino** (☎ 922 44 46 23; Los Canarios s/n; mains €7-9), behind the Bodegas Teneguía. House soups and local game dishes are served in a tranquil and spacious dining room.

Tasca La Era (☎ 922 44 44 75; Carretera Antonio Paz y Paz 6; mains €7-9) is not as refined, but the setting – in a red farmhouse – is a plus, and the menu is varied, with an emphasis on grilled meats.

Getting There & Away

Every two hours (less often on Sunday and school holidays), Bus No 3 stops here on its way from Los Llanos to Santa Cruz (€2.95). The Santa Cruz to Los Llanos route has roughly the same schedule, though between 12pm and 2pm there's a bus every hour.

NECTAR OF THE GODS

Since the early 16th century, when Spanish conquerors planted the first vines on the island, La Palma has been known for its sweet *malvasía* (Malmsey wine), which pairs superbly with desserts. Thanks to the merchants and colonists that came in and out of La Palma's ports, the wine acquired fame throughout Europe, and some referred to the tasty stuff as 'the nectar of the gods'. Even Shakespeare wrote about sweet Canary wine, making it Falstaff's favourite in *Henry IV* and calling it a 'marvellous searching wine' that 'perfumes the blood'.

These days, producers also make a dry *malvasía*, and the volcanic soil also gives birth to a variety of reds, whites and rosé wines, especially in the areas of Fuencaliente and Hoyo de Mazo. For more information visit www.malvasiadelapalma .com.

PLAYA DE LA ZAMORA & PLAYA CHICA

The coast around Fuencaliente is largely inaccessible, with banana plantations, rocky outcrops and steep cliffs lining much of it. There are a few beaches around, though, mostly small rocky affairs at the ends of gravel roads. Two pleasant exceptions are **Playa de la Zamora** and **Playa Chica**, black beaches tucked in coves side by side. They're no secret but are rarely crowded. To get here, take the Carretera de Las Indias past the San Antonio volcano until the road stops. Turn right (there's a signpost for the *playas*) onto a rural road and make another left at the sign for Kiosk Zamora, the small snack shop that's down by the beaches.

FUENCALIENTE TO PUERTO NAOS: THE SOUTHWESTERN COAST

The road up the west coast from the bottom tip of the island is full of open curves that swoop past green hills dotted with cacti and low shrubs. The highway runs along a ridge, leaving the glittering ocean a blue haze to the left. Other than the view, there's not much here, unless you count the **mirador** (lookout), which has a small bar. Find it 6km out of Fuencaliente in the tiny town of El Charco.

Keep heading north and you'll zip through a series of tiny, almost uninhabited villages. Stop in **San Nicolás** (1km past the village of Jedey) to eat at **Bodegon Tamanca** (☎ 922 49 41 55; Carretera General; mains €5-11; ☻ closed Mon), a fun restaurant located in a spacious, natural cave. This is a meat-lover's kind of place, whether you like it grilled, cured or stewed.

THE CENTRE

The well-kept LP-2 highway links Santa Cruz and the east coast with Los Llanos and the west. The highway skirts the southern rim of the Parque Nacional Caldera de Taburiente, and from the road you can sometimes see the characteristic cloud blanket that fills the interior of the caldera and spills over its sides like an overboiling pot. When you reach the west coast, banana plantations fill the valleys. The peaks of the Taburiente are ever present, covered in a green blanket of pines and scored with deep ravines. With so many ruts on the exterior, the mountains look like colossal ant hills.

BREÑA ALTA

A sprawling valley with no real town centre, this is a tranquil area known for its artisan cigars and natural beauty. To see some of that beauty contained in a great little zoo, visit **Maroparque** (☎ 922 41 77 82; www.maroparque.com; Calle Cuesta 28; adult/child €9.70/4.90; ☻ 10am-6pm), where 300 species of animals and lots of local vegetation make for a pleasant afternoon.

Better yet, head to the **El Pilar recreational area** (☎ 922 41 15 83), a park with a camp site. From here begins the **Ruta de Los Volcanos**, a hiking trail that leads south along the mountain ridge, through the heart of volcanic territory and towards Fuencaliente, where you can get a bus back to Santa Cruz. Allot six to seven hours for the trek – it's demanding and should be undertaken only in good weather. It's worth the effort, though; the trail meanders through ever-changing volcanic scenery and gives privileged views of both coasts.

EL PASO

pop 7192

You hear a lot about El Paso because the national park's visitors centre is nearby,

but there's really not much to this town. You could visit the **silk workshop** (☎ 922 48 56 31; Calle Manuel Taño 6; ☻ 10am-1pm Mon-Fri, 5-7pm Tue & Thu), where silk is made according to traditions that have barely changed since the silk industry arrived on the island in the 16th century.

The restored 18th-century **Ermita de la Virgen de la Concepción de la Bonanza** ('La Bonanza') is a curiously painted little chapel whose renovations mercifully left intact the splendid *mudéjar* ceiling above the altar.

On the highway heading towards Los Llanos you'll see a sign leading off to **El Paraíso de las Aves** (☎ 922 48 57 01; adult/child €6/3; ☻ 10am-5pm Mon-Sat), a park dedicated to endangered birds and island flora.

Just 1km out of town towards Los Llanos (before you reach the bird park) is **La Cascada** (☎ 922 48 57 27; Carretera Cumbre; mains €6-10; ☻ closed Thu), a hearty restaurant popular with local workmen (always a sign of fair prices and filling food). From the highway you can smell meat sizzling on the grill.

LOS LLANOS DE ARIDANE

pop 20,238

La Palma's second-largest town isn't as charming as the capital or some of the waterfront resorts, but chances are you'll pass through more than once, if only to access the Caldera de Taburiente or to cross from the east coast to the west. One of the island's few centres of commerce, it's set in a fertile valley and its economy depends largely on local banana and avocado plantations, though as tourism strengthens that is slowly changing.

Information
MEDICAL SERVICES
Centro de Salud (Calle Princesa Dacil)

POST
Post Office (Avenida Tanausú)

TOURIST OFFICES
Tourist Office (☎ 922 40 18 99; Avenida Dr Fleming; ☻ 8am-3pm Mon-Fri, 8am-2pm in summer)

Sights & Activities
At the heart of Los Llanos is the charming little haven of Plaza España. Shaded by mature laurel trees, its main feature is the gleaming white **Iglesia de Nuestra Señora de**

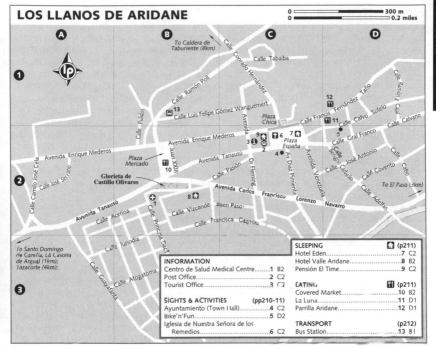

LOS LLANOS DE ARIDANE

INFORMATION	
Centro de Salud Medical Centre........1 B2	
Post Office.................................2 C2	
Tourist Office.............................3 C2	

SIGHTS & ACTIVITIES	(pp210-11)
Ayuntamiento (Town Hall)..............4 C2	
Bike'n'Fun................................5 D2	
Iglesia de Nuestra Señora de los	
Remedios...............................6 C2	

SLEEPING	(p211)
Hotel Eden...............................7 C2	
Hotel Valle Aridane.....................8 B2	
Pensión El Time.........................9 C2	

EATING	(p211)
Covered Market.........................10 B2	
La Luna..................................11 D1	
Parrilla Aridane........................12 D1	

TRANSPORT	(p212)
Bus Station.............................13 B1	

los Remedios, built in the Canarian colonial style. The surrounding streets, particularly Calle Francis Fernández Taño, still preserve much of their traditional character.

Cyclists should check out **Bike'n'Fun** (☎ 922 40 19 27; Calle Calvo Sotelo; ⏰ 10am-1pm & 6-8pm Mon-Fri, 6-8pm Sat). It rents out mountain bikes starting at €12 per day, and organises day rides around the island from €40 (including transport to the start of the route, and bike and equipment hire).

Sleeping

Pensión El Time (☎ 922 46 09 07; Plaza España; s/d €19/32) This no-frills *pensión* has the look of a 1950s hospital ward, but rooms are attractively laid out around a central patio, and there is an impressive winding stone staircase leading to the 2nd floor.

Hotel Eden (☎ 922 46 01 04; www.hoteledenlapalma .com; Plaza España; s/d €20/35) At the eastern end of the square, this is a better bet than Pensión El Time if it's comfort rather than aesthetics you're after. The single rooms share the hall bathroom, but the larger doubles get a private one, and some also have balconies.

Hotel Valle Aridane (☎ 922 46 26 00; www.hotel vallearidane.com; Glorieta Castillo Olivares 5; s/d €31/38). Popular with walkers, this place has three stars, which is surprising. Rooms are worn and not terribly attractive, but they're clean.

Eating

Parrilla Aridane (☎ 922 46 43 14; Calle Francis Fernández Taño 29; mains €7-10; ⏰ closed Mon) Head here for a filling meal with grilled meat specialities, and a nice patio to boot.

La Casona de Argual (☎ 922 40 18 16; Plaza Soto Mayor 6; mains €12-16; ⏰ closed Thu) Just opposite the Casa Massieu van Dalle in Argual, 1km west of town, this restaurant is in a beautiful early-18th-century house. Dishes focus on local ingredients and Palmero specialities.

Covered market (Plaza Mercado; ⏰ 8am-2pm Mon-Sat) If you're catering for yourself, a browse around this small covered market can be rewarding.

La Luna (☎ 922 40 19 13; Calle Francis Fernández Taño) Head here at night for creative cuisine and, later, drinks. On Thursday at 9.30pm there's live music.

Getting There & Away

The bus station is on Calle Luis Felipe Gómez Wanguemert. Bus No 4 runs to Puerto Naos (€1.15) and bus Nos 1 and 3 go to Santa Cruz, between the two of them running about every half-hour. No 3 (€5.50) makes more stops than No 1 (€3.90). Buses also run frequently to Tazacorte.

PUERTO DE TAZACORTE

This small, planned community looks like a little toy village, with Canary-style houses painted in bright colours and a perfect grid of narrow streets. Most people come for the long, sandy beach and the calm waters of the town's shorefront.

Get out on the water with the motorboats **Fancy II** (☎ 609 53 13 91; www.lp-b.com/fancy in Spanish; adult €22-46, child €12-30; ☟ 9am-8pm) or **Agamenon** (☎ 699 66 20 84; adult/child €19.50/9.75; ☟ 10am-3.30pm). Both make several excursions daily to see whales, to explore coastal caverns or to deep-sea fish.

In town, you have the choice of several basic apartments by the beach. Try **Apartamentos Luz y Mar** (☎ 922 40 81 63, 922 42 85 02; apt €44; ☒), where apartments have kitchens, balconies and ocean views, or **Apartamentos Miramar** (☎ 922 46 34 39; apt €30), where apartments also have balconies and kitchens. Both are a short walk from the ocean.

There are several restaurants along the waterfront. **Taberna del Puerto** (☎ 922 40 61 18; Plaza Castilla 1; mains €7-11) has an attractive, rustic feel and an enviable ocean view.

PUERTO NAOS

A sandy black beach dotted with palm trees, a glittering ocean, gentle waves...this is as close to coastal paradise as La Palma gets. Puerto Naos is a small but growing tourist centre huddled around a rounded bay and protected on either side by tall rock cliffs. Calm and quiet but with plenty of services for travellers, the town makes a good base for sun-lovers who want easy access to the north and interior.

Activities

With all the activities going on here, there's no excuse not to stay busy. **Wanderzentrale** (☎ 922 40 81 29; wandern@teleline.es; Calle Jose Guzman Pérez y Pérez; guided hike €33; ☟ 10am-1pm & 4-6pm Mon-Fri, 10am-1pm Sat) offers walking routes all over the island.

For the daring, paragliding is available through **Kiosko Playa Morena** (☎ 610 69 57 50; paragliding €70-120; ☟ noon-7pm Thu-Tue), set up on the boardwalk behind the beach. **Bike Station** (☎ 922 40 83 55; Avenida Cruz Roja, local 3; ☟ 9am-1pm & 6-8pm Mon-Sat) rents out mountain bikes starting at €13 per day. It also offers a range of challenging guided mountain-bike rides for between €34 and €42, including bike and equipment hire and transport.

Take a trip with **Yellow Fin Sport Fishing** (☎ 686 92 06 24) to search out marlin, tuna and sharks deep in the ocean.

Viajes Yadir (☎ 922 40 81 06; Avenida Marítima) offers a bit of everything, from car hire to bus trips.

Sleeping & Eating

The town centre is full of apartment blocks, most of them family-run affairs advertising vacancies with a small sign on the door. You are best off contacting **Tamanca** (☎ 922 40 81 47; www.tamanca.com; Calle Mauricio Duque Camacho 46a), an agency that rents out properties in and around Puerto Naos. If you don't want to self-cater, try **Sol La Palma** (☎ 922 40 80 00; www.solmelia.com; Punta del Pozo s/n; Playa de Puerto Naos; s €43-73, d €86-146, apt €71-116; P ☒ ☒ ☒).

For Canarian fare, the local favourite is **Orinoco** (www.islalapalma.com/orinoco; Calle Manuel Rodriguez Quintero 1; mains €3-5; ☟ 11am-10pm, closed Wed), just off Avenida Marítima. Simple but homey, its house speciality is fresh fish, though save room for the traditional Palmero desserts. For both Canarian and peninsular dishes try **Mesón Don Quijote** (☎ 922 40 80 45; Edificio La Palma; mains €8-12), one block up from the beach.

Getting There & Away

Bus No 4 comes and goes regularly from Los Llanos (€1.15).

PARQUE NACIONAL DE LA CALDERA DE TABURIENTE

Scan the enormous stone walls of this natural fortress from the south and you can appreciate how the terrain challenged the invading Spaniards back in the late 15th century. Here the last of the Benahoares, under Mencey Tanausú, took refuge, and there was precious little Alonso Fernández de Lugo could do to dislodge them. Luckily for the Spaniards, the chief had faith in the honour of his opponents and was tricked into abandoning his stronghold for 'talks' that proved to be nothing less than an old-fashioned ambush.

The **Caldera de Taburiente** itself is a mammoth circular pit surrounded by sheer rock walls that soar up to 2000m and are topped by shafts of rock called *roques*. Its massive, broken wall of volcanic rock is about 8km in diameter and the only real opening, the aptly named Barranco de las Angustias (Gorge of Fear), lies to the southwest. The park, cloaked at its lower levels in dense thickets of Canary pine, covers 4690 hectares and was created in 1954.

All may seem impressively stoic and still, but the forces of erosion are hard at work. Landslides and collapsing *roques* are frequent, and some geologists believe it will finally disappear in just 5000 years. An excellent place to see this fast erosion is near the **Mirador de la Cumbrecita** (see p214), where a group of pines stands atop a web of exposed roots, clinging miraculously to the hilltop. These trees were once planted firmly in the ground, but more than 2m of soil already has been lost during their lifetime.

In 1825 the German geologist Leopold von Buch applied the Spanish term *caldera* (cauldron) to what he assumed to be a massive volcanic crater, the Caldera de Taburiente. The word 'caldera' stuck, and was to be used as a standard term for all such volcanic craters the world over. However, this caldera, although largely made up of volcanic rock, was not in fact the result of a massive eruption, but has rather been slowly excavated by erosion over the millennia.

Water flows mainly along underground channels but occasionally crashes headlong in waterfalls down the caldera's many steep ravines. It flows to the southwest coast along the Barranco de las Angustias and is siphoned off to irrigate the lowlands beyond the park.

Information

The helpful **visitors centre** (☎ 922 49 72 77; Carretera General de Padrón; ⏰ 9am-2pm & 4-6.30pm) is 5km outside El Paso on the LP-2 highway. The centre's 20-minute film on the park is worth seeing; you can mill around the small museum here until they play the English version on the half-hour. A government-published guidebook (in English) is on sale for €8 and contains a wealth of information

about the park and hiking around it. Helpful, though less detailed, maps and information are available for free.

Just across from the visitors centre is the **Pensión Nambroque** (☎ 922 48 52 79), closed at the time of publication but due to reopen someday (when is anyone's guess). Bus No 1 linking Santa Cruz and Los Llanos stops here hourly, though within the park you need your own transportation (or own two feet) to get around.

Walking

The free map and brochure *La Caldera de Taburiente*, given out at the visitors centre, gives a helpful overview of the park and should be fine if you're attempting short, straightforward hikes. The guidebook (see Information, previous, for details) provides more complete details on altitude, possible dangers, flora, fauna etc. The trails are generally in very good shape, though signposts can be a little confusing. You should be OK with a map or guidebook, but before starting out, see the boxed text on p41.

In summer, park rangers offer free **guided walks**, leaving from the camp site at 10am.

THE SOUTHERN END

From the Mirador de la Cumbrecita (see earlier) there's a short (45 minutes) and easy (part is accessible to wheelchairs and strollers) hike to the **Mirador Lomo de las Chozas**, which gives you a peek further into the park. It's not as spectacular as the trails in the interior but is a good, quick introduction. You can also head down the considerably steeper trail to the **Mirador Punta de los Roques** and back (allow 1¼ hours for the circuit), or combine both walks (about two hours).

A more challenging hike begins just before the Mirador Punta de los Roques and heads north-northwest to El Escuchadero, up inside the eastern wall of the caldera. Reckon on it taking a good two hours each way.

A popular way to hike to the camp site and back is to leave your car at the car park in the Barranco de las Angustias and take a **taxi** (per person €10; ⏰ 9am-12pm) to Los Brecitos. That lets you make the two-hour hike to the camp site and the four-hour trek down the gorge without having to backtrack.

If you'd rather stay at the camp site and explore the park further, there are several trails that branch off from here and head north into the park.

From the visitors centre another possibility is to follow the fork in the road to Valencia. Once you reach a flat section of the road, a walking trail heads to the **Pico Bejendado** (1854m). Plan on it taking 2½ hours there and back – you'll enjoy the reward of taking in one of the least visited yet most inspiring views over the caldera.

THE NORTHERN END

You can hike along the tops of the rock walls that form the caldera. To reach one of the most spectacular sections, take the LP-1032 from just north of Santa Cruz and leave your car at the turn-off for Pico de la Nieve.

After 20 minutes' walking towards the Pico de la Nieve summit, you can strike out along a narrow path in one of two directions: southeast to the Ermita de la Virgen del Pino and on to the visitors centre beside the LP-2 highway (six to seven hours) or, for something even more spectacular, northwest up to the **Roque de los Muchachos** (four to five hours), where you'll need to organise a car to collect you. Less strenuously, press on to the summit of **Pico de la Nieve** (2239m), where, unless cloud obscures the valley, you'll have a panorama as splendid as any in the park. Then return to your vehicle – the round-trip hike takes under two hours.

After the shorter walk you could continue driving west, where there are several opportunities to stop at lookouts and lean out over one of nature's most remarkable balconies before pushing on to the distinctive rock figures of the 'lads' (*muchachos*) that constitute the Roque de los Muchachos.

Sleeping & Eating

If you want to stay in the park itself, the only available option is the camp site, which offers basic services for 100 people and incredible views of the caldera's interior. To stay here, contact the visitors centre 15 days in advance to request a permit. The maximum stay is three days and you'll need to show your passport to pick up the permit. You'll need to bring, and take away, your own food (see the boxed text on p42 for responsible walking tips).

Getting There & Away

No roads run through the park, and there are only three ways to access it. The easiest and most popular is via the visitors centre off the LP-2 highway. Beside the visitors centre is the turn-off for Mirador de la Cumbrecita. The 7km drive passes turn-offs for the Pista de Valencia and the Ermita del Pino, leading you through a peaceful pine forest to the *mirador* that has sweeping views of the pine-filled valley.

Another option is to head up the steep dirt trail from Los Llanos to Los Brecitos. Follow the signs first to Los Barros and then on to Los Brecitos. Be warned – this is a rough and winding dirt track, recommended only for cars (and drivers) equipped for off-road driving. That said, plenty of tiny Fiat Puntos and the like have made it to the end, but we wouldn't try it. From Los Brecitos, it's a 6km hike to the camp site (above).

Option three is to head into the park from the north. The LP-1032 branches off the LP-1 highway 3km north of Santa Cruz and snakes its way across the island, skirting the rim of the park and its northern peaks. Several hikes (some very demanding) begin on this side. For those who just want to get a sense of the park, the Roque de los Muchachos lookout (follow the signs to the observatory – see p000) offers a fabulous view – when the caldera isn't full of cloud soup, that is. At 2426m it's the highest point on the island. You'll have to drive up here, as no buses make the trek.

THE END OF THE WORLD AS WE KNOW IT?

According to scientists, the volcanic activity on La Palma could bring an end to the world as we know it. A fatalistic prediction, to be sure. But experts say that if there's another big eruption on the island, it could cause erosion-weakened mountains to simply break away and slide into the sea. The effect of a massive piece of volcano hitting the ocean would cause a tidal wave so enormous that it could destroy parts of the United States and South America. According to some estimations, the wave could be as tall as 650m and would travel at 720km/h towards Florida. Fortunately, there's no sign of this happening any time soon.

THE NORTH

La Palma's north is the kind of island paradise you think exists only on the covers of glossy travel magazines. Rocky cliffs plunge into sapphire waters, deserted black beaches are surrounded by palms trees, and tiny towns have cobblestoned streets and whitewashed walls. The drive north along the LP-1 highway is a curvy but lovely one, with the glistening ocean always at your side and the landscape alternating between pastoral green hills and fresh pine forests. There are plenty of lookout points to stop and soak in the view.

PUNTALLANA

pop 2308

One of the first things you'll see as you head into this friendly little town is the **Iglesia de San Juan Bautista**, with its stone bell tower and cheery yellow exterior. Just before the church, turn right down a steep road to find the **Casa Lujan**, a traditional Canary house that's now home to the rural tourism office and a small ethological **museum**. The museum was closed at the time of publication, but the town hall says it will reopen soon.

There's not much else in Puntallana, but nearby **Playa de Nogales** is worth a detour. From town, follow the signs to Bajamar, then take the turn-off to the Playa. Head down the steep, windy road and you'll arrive at a car park on a cliff where a trail leads down to the beach, a sandy black strip backing up to a rock cliff.

SAN ANDRÉS & LOS SAUCES

pop 5226

Technically, San Andrés and Los Sauces are united under the same town hall, but the two villages could not be more different.

San Andrés, 3km off the main LP-1 highway, is like something from a storybook, with hilly, cobblestoned streets that lead past low, whitewashed houses. The **Iglesia de San Andrés** has its origins in 1515 and is one of the first churches the Spanish conquerors built on the island, though most of what you see today was built in the 17th century. Inside, take a look at the lavish Baroque altarpieces and the coffered ceiling.

If you feel like staying a spell, ring the **Pensión Martín** (☎ 922 45 05 39; Carretera General;

s/d/apt €15/21/30), where the simple rooms have views of the owners' garden and the mountains behind. The three rooms share a bathroom, and the place is clean and friendly. A few steps down the highway that runs through town, **Pensión Las Lonjas** (☎ 922 45 07 36; d €24) is a charming, Canary-style house. Rooms are modern, though, and while comfortable, their ground-level doors open directly onto the highway. That wouldn't be so bad if those doors weren't also the rooms' only ventilation.

From the church plaza there is a pretty ocean view, bordered by valley palm trees. On the plaza itself are two cosy little restaurants, **San Andrés** (☎ 922 45 17 25; mains €6-9; closed Wed), serving up tasty tenderloin steaks and fresh fish outside by the plaza fountain, and **El Montadito** (☎ 630 60 56 53; menú del día €11.50), which specialises in tapas-style *montaditos* (bread topped with everything from cheese to anchovies). You can eat outside or on the picnic tables in the dining room.

Los Sauces is a modern town with two pretty central squares (or one big one bisected by the highway, depending on how you look at it). The grand church **Nuestra Señora de Montserrat** is on the square and has some valuable Flemish artwork inside. Named for the patron of Catalunya, this church is evidence of the many Catalans who participated in the island's conquest.

More important (and more interesting) than anything in Los Sauces itself is the Los Tilos biosphere reserve just out of town (see p216).

Bus No 11 comes by once an hour on its way between Santa Cruz and Santo Domingo. Bus No 12 travels from Los Sauces, stopping in San Andres (€0.95). It runs at irregular intervals six times a day on weekdays and four times a day on weekends.

CHARCO AZUL

Beyond San Andrés on the LP-104 highway is a sign pointing the way to Charco Azul, a beautiful swimming hole 3km further on. A bit of tastefully applied concrete has been added to the volcanic rocks along the shore, to make a series of natural-looking saltwater pools with sunbathing platforms between them.

Past Charco Azul, construction work is underway on the **Puerto Espindola**. When it's finished (and no-one's making guesses on when that will be) it will have a nice beach, a garden and a small recreational port.

LOS TILOS

One of the prettiest spots on the island is the Unesco-protected **biosphere** at Los Tilos, a cool, damp forest. Declared a biosphere reserve in 1983, the nearly 14,000 hectares here are home to an impressive range of ecosystems and the largest *laurisilva* (laurel) forest on the island (see p36 for more information about *laurisilva*).

At the **visitors centre** (☎ 922 45 12 46; www.lapal mabiosfera.com; ☼ 8.30am-2pm & 2.30-5pm Nov-Jun, 8.30am-2pm & 2.30-6.30pm Jul-Oct) there's a video about the biosphere and a small museum. A bar and restaurant are nearby.

Several hiking trails run through the area. To the left behind the visitors centre begins a one-hour (1.5km) round-trip trail involving some 800 steps up. It will take you to the **Mirador Topo de las Barandas**, where there is a spectacular view of the gorge. For those prepared for walking steep hills, a tougher hike (3½ to four hours, or 11km, one way) leads southwest to the Corderos spring.

Getting There & Away

Coming from Santa Cruz, turn off 1km before Los Sauces, and head 3km up the Barranco del Agua, a lush gorge. No buses venture up here, so you'll need either your own wheels or strong legs to arrive.

BARLOVENTO

pop 2685

As a local farming centre, most things of interest lie outside the town itself.

About 5km east of Barlovento, on the LP-1 highway, take the turn-off for **Piscinas de la Fajana**, natural saltwater pools set among volcanic rocks. The coast is starkly beautiful, with reddish-tinged rocks and a savage ocean. Bring snorkelling gear to appreciate the underwater scenery. Dine on fresh local fish at **La Gaviota** (☎ 922 18 60 99; mains €4.50-5.50), a restaurant set inside a cave above the beach. If you want to linger longer, you can stay at **Apartamentos La Fajana** (☎ 922 18 61 62; 2-/4-person apt €36/45), with cosy, whitewashed apartments with balconies and one of the best ocean views on the island.

On the south side of Barlovento, there are signs to the **Laguna de Barlovento** (☎ 922

69 60 23; ☼ 9am-8pm), a camp site and recreational area set beside an ugly agricultural holding tank (that is, the *laguna*) built inside the crater of an extinct volcano. You can't swim here, but you can stop by the *laguna*'s **restaurant** and **artisan centre**, where local crafts are for sale. To camp here you should call ahead to request permission.

For more creature comforts and the only three-star hotel this side of Santa Cruz, head to **Hotel La Palma Romántica** (☎ 922 18 62 21; www.hotellapalmaromantica.com; Las Llanadas s/n, Barlovento; s/d €78/108; ℗ ◙), a rural hotel with an elegant restaurant and sweeping views of the valley. The 44 rooms are spacious, with high ceilings, terraces and lounge chairs, and a sitting area. They could have used some of that space for the bathrooms, though – they're tiny.

LP-111 RURAL HIGHWAY

If you like driving, keep going straight (past the *laguna*) along the LP-111 highway, which runs parallel to the larger LP-1. Both are spectacular and pass countless deep ravines, but the LP-111 is something special. The road skims the base of a rock cliff and gives heart-fluttering views of tree-filled gorges, which spread out like skirts below you. There are a few (though not enough!) lookout points where you can stop and marvel at the glory of nature. Several hiking trails also cut across this highway. It takes more than an hour to drive from the *laguna* to the end of the LP-111, where it meets up with the main highway.

PARQUE CULTURAL LA ZARZA

Two Benahoare petroglyphs (rock carvings) are the reason for **Parque Cultural La Zarza** (☎ 922 69 50 05; adult/child €1.80/0.90; ☼ 11am-7pm summer, 11am-5pm winter). Heading west out along the LP-1 towards La Mata, the park is 1km past the turn-off for La Mata (it's on a curve and easy to miss – keep an eye out for the signpost). To actually see the geometric-shaped etchings, take the 1.5km circuit into the park itself. Back at the visitors centre, you can watch an informative 20-minute video about the life of the aborigines and take a tour around the interactive museum.

A few kilometres past the park on the main road is **Restaurante La Mata** (☎ 922 40 00 74; Carretera General; mains €5.50-12; ☼ closed Wed), a humble little place that doesn't call much attention to itself but offers some of the best eating around, all based on freshly grilled meats.

THE NORTHWEST

There isn't much to see or do on the journey from La Mata to Puerto de Tazacorte (on the central coast). The northwest coast is a solitary, tranquil place that was largely isolated from the rest of the island until recent times. You'll see deep ravines, lots of Canary pines and, closer to the coast, banana plantations. Historically, this corner of the island was the wealthiest, producing wine, fruit and timber, but with economic problems of the mid-20th century, many farmers here were forced to emigrate.

If you get hungry and have time for a not-so-scenic detour, head to **Santo Domingo de Garafía**, a rural town that sits at the end of a winding road 7km from Llano Negro. **Restaurante Berengal** (☎ 922 40 04 80; Calle Díaz y Suárez 5; mains €5-9; ☾ lunch only) is great value, with sumptuous fresh fish, grilled meat and

the house speciality, fish pâté. Try the local wine – *vino de tea*. The wine is fermented in *tea* (heart of pine) wood and has a taste of resin. While you're in town, take a stroll around the 16th-century **Iglesia de la Virgen de la Luz**.

The small towns of **Puntagorda** and **Tijarafe** are worth a brief stop, if only to wander the streets of their historic centres. There is a **camp site** (☎ 922 49 33 06; www.airelibrelapalma .org; camping per person €5, tent rental per day €3) at Puntagorda, which is also a centre dedicated to ecology and nature preservation. You can join guided hikes or sign up for one of the ecology workshops. Tijarafe is home to a small **museum** (☎ 922 49 00 72; Casa del Maestro; ☾ 8am-2pm & 3-9pm Mon-Fri) dedicated to traditional culture. To get to the museum, follow the signs to the Casa del Maestro from the main highway.

Several lookout points offer privileged vantage points of the northwest coast's inspiring scenery. Just south of Tijarafe is **Mirador de Garome**, overlooking a majestic gorge. Further south, **Mirador del Time** looks out over Puerto de Tazacorte.

El Hierro

EL HIERRO

The westernmost point of Europe and the smallest island in the Canary archipelago, El Hierro was the end of the known world until 1492. Although it's now connected to the rest of the planet via air, boat and TV, this tiny boomerang-shaped island will always feel remote. In fact, that's its major drawcard. Covered with broad plains of volcanic badlands (*malpaís*; deeply eroded barren areas), rocky coasts where waves roar, and vegetation twisted and tortured by the wind, the island's unique landscape – so unique that it was declared a Unesco biosphere reserve – is as tough as its people, and neither take kindly to tourists who look to be entertained with nonstop activity.

Those who come to El Hierro want to escape crowds (the biggest town has a whopping 1630 residents), get away from traffic (there's not a single traffic light on the island) and rest in the silence of El Hierro's natural spaces.

EL HIERRO

HIGHLIGHTS

- **Splashing**

  Tamaduste's natural cove is perfect for swimming (p226)

- **Cruising**

  A peaceful, winding road travels through the protected pine forest of El Pinar (p228)

- **Dining**

  The Mirador de la Peña offers views of El Golfo, courtesy of Cesar Manrique's designs, as well as creative local dishes (p227)

- **Hiking**

  The magnificent trail down from the Mirador de Jinama to La Frontera is an old donkey track (p227)

- **Lounging**

  The red-sand beach of Playa del Verodal lies below the volcanic badlands of La Dehesa (p232)

Tamaduste ★
★ Mirador de la Peña
★ Mirador de Jinama
★ Playa del Verodal
El Pinar ★

- TELEPHONE CODE: 922
- POPULATION: 10,002
- AREA: 269 SQ KM

HISTORY

El Hierro hasn't always been the tiny tot of the Canaries. About 50,000 years ago the area was hit by an earthquake so massive that a third of the island was ripped off the northern side – it slipped away beneath the waves, creating the crescent-shaped coast of El Golfo. It must have been a very dramatic event – the ensuing tidal wave may have been more than 100m high and probably crashed as far off as the American coast.

The last eruption was 200 years ago, but the island is still littered with about 500 volcanic cones (and 300 more were covered up by lava flows).

How the island got its name is anyone's guess; there isn't a speck of iron *(hierro)* ore

on the island. Perhaps the original inhabitants, the Bimbaches, called it *hero*, meaning 'milk'. Ptolemy identified the western edge of the island as the end of the known world in the 2nd century AD and it remained the Meridíano Cero (Meridian Zone) until replaced by the Greenwich version in 1884.

After the Spanish conquest in the 15th century, a form of feudalism was introduced and Spanish farmers gradually assimilated with those locals who had not been sold into slavery or died of disease. In the subsequent quest for farmland, much of El Hierro's forests were destroyed.

Today, the island's economy is based on cheese, fishing, fruit-growing, livestock and tourism.

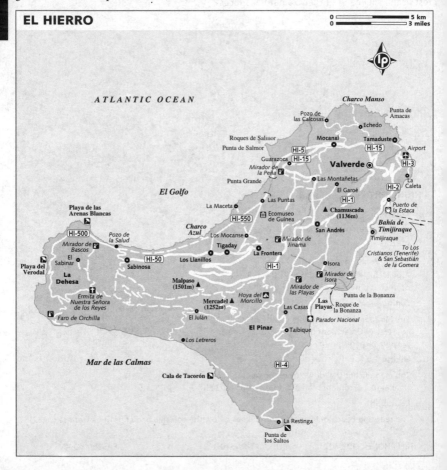

THE GIANT LIZARD

Imagine the Spaniards' surprise when they began to explore El Hierro and, among the native birds, juniper trees and unusual volcanic rock, they discovered enormous lizards as large as cats. Greyish-brown and growing up to 45cm long, the lizards aren't poisonous or harmful, though according to one early chronicler they're 'disgusting and repugnant to behold'.

By the 1940s, these giant lizards were almost extinct, their species all but snuffed out by human encroachment on their habitat, the introduction of non-native predators (such as cats) and climatological factors. A few survived on the Roques de Salmor rock outcropping off the Gulf coast (giving the species its name, 'Lizard of Salmor'), but before long, those too had disappeared. Though it's doubtful that the island farmers mourned their passing, scientists believed that they'd lost a species forever.

Then, in the 1970s, herdsmen began reporting sightings of large, unidentified animal droppings and carcasses of extra-long lizards that had been killed by dogs. To the delight of conservationists, a small colony of the giant lizards had survived on a practically inaccessible mountain crag, the Fuga de Gorreta. One herdsmen was able to capture a pair of the reptiles, beginning the species' journey back to life.

In 1985, the Giant Lizard of El Hierro Recovery Plan was put into place. These days you can see it in action at the Lagartario (p230), where the lizards are bred in captivity and released into a supervised wild area. There are now about 1500 lizards living near the Lagartario, in a protected nature reserve, though experts insist that the species is not out of danger yet.

At the Lagartario, you can spy on a few specimens in their glassed-in cages as they soak up the sun or snack on vegetation. A guide explains the recovery efforts and the history of the giant lizard.

INFORMATION

Maps

In late 2003, a brand-new highway tunnel connecting Valverde with La Frontera was built, and the island changed the names of all its major highways. At the time of publication, none of those changes appeared on maps. Nevertheless, the following maps are usable, if you take into account the existence of the tunnel and the fact that some highway names will have changed. The Michelin map to the western Islas Canarias (at 1:125,000 and 1:50,000 for Tenerife) is OK for highways, but for more detail use the *Tourist Map El Hierro* (1:50,000) by Turquesa, with text in English, German and Spanish. If you're tempted to strike out on random dirt paths, take along the extra-detailed *El Hierro* (1:30,000) published by Freytag & Berndt. The maps given out free by the tourist office are more than sufficient for making simple tours around the island.

Newspapers

Most Herreños read papers from Tenerife, such as the *Diario de Avisos* and *El Día*. On the island, a few monthly and bi-monthly newsletters keep the locals informed of town happenings and island politics. You can find them in bookstores or by asking around.

ACTIVITIES

Activities here include splashing around in the natural volcanic-rock pools, fishing off the shore, hiking, and...hiking.

ACCOMMODATION

With fewer than 1000 beds available across the island, you may want to book in advance, especially at Christmas, around Easter, and in August. Aside from the lovely Parador Nacional hotel (see p226), most of what's on offer is simple and rustic. Privately owned apartments are far more numerous than the *pensiones* (guesthouses) and rural hotels that are scattered through the larger towns.

The most appealing lodging option is the *casas rurales*, restored farm homes that are especially suited for groups of four or more. Contact **Meridiano Cero** (☎ 922 55 18 24; www .ecoturismocanarias.com; Calle Barlovento 89, Valverde) for reservations.

There is only one legal campsite – at Hoya del Morcillo (p228). Elsewhere, camping is prohibited.

GETTING THERE & AWAY
Air
The island's small **airport** (☎ 922 55 37 00) is 12km outside Valverde. Up to four daily flights connect the island with Tenerife, and on a more sporadic basis there are flights to Gran Canaria and La Palma as well.

At the airport you'll find car rental offices, a bar, and a shop selling maps and local products.

Boat
Fred Olsen (☎ 922 62 82 00; www.fredolsen.es) runs a daily ferry to Los Cristianos in Tenerife (one way €28.70, four hours). It leaves El Hierro at 3.30pm.

Trasmediterránea (☎ 902 45 46 45; www.trasmed iterranea.es) also runs a ferry to Tenerife (one way €21.75, eight hours). It leaves at one minute to midnight Sunday through Friday and arrives in Los Cristianos at 8am the next morning. In the other direction, the ferry leaves Los Cristianos at 7pm and takes between four and five hours depending on the day. From Los Cristianos, it is a quick hop by ferry to La Gomera. In the other direction, the trip from La Gomera to El Hierro sometimes, but not always, has a stop in Los Cristianos. El Hierro's Puerto de la Estaca was under construction at the time of publication (see p226).

GETTING AROUND
To/From the Airport
The easiest way to get to and from the airport is your own four wheels; car rental agencies are happy to have a car waiting for you at the airport if you call ahead (see under Car later). Taxis are a simple but pricey way to move about. Though getting to nearby Valverde should cost less than €10, the price of a taxi from the airport to La Restinga, for example, will cost more than one day's car rental. Getting to the airport by bus is cheap (€1.20) but complicated, as the routes there are extremely limited. The one almost-daily bus (there is no Sunday or holiday service) leaves Valverde at 8.15am and returns from the airport at 8.55am. That said, the schedule is liable to change without notice.

Bus
The island's buses are run by the **Servicio Insular de Guagua** (☎ 922 55 07 29; fax 922 55 14 96), whose small fleet runs on a very limited schedule around the island's main towns Monday through Saturday.

Ask at the tourist office for a complete bus schedule. Bus rides cost between €1.20 and €3.16 on a very limited schedule Monday through Saturday. For example, just one 12pm bus connects Valverde and La Frontera and you will have to wait a day to return: the first and only bus out of La Frontera leaves at 6.45am. The routes among other island towns are similarly limited, and all are liable to change without notice.

Car
There are many car rental firms in Valverde, and if you reserve ahead they'll have a car waiting for you at the airport or port when you arrive. In addition to the large chains renting throughout the Canaries (see p252), El Hierro has a few local companies that usually work out to be cheaper (around €20 per day), though their cars are older.

Autos Bamir (☎ 922 55 01 83)

Autos Cooperativa (☎ 922 55 07 29; fax 922 55 11 75) Has the cheapest cars (and those most likely to break down).

Autos Rosamar (☎ 922 55 04 22; www.rosamar-sl.com in Spanish)

Cruz Alta Rent-A-Car (☎ 922 55 03 49, 922 55 00 04)

Be sure to fill up the petrol tank before leaving Valverde, as there are only three petrol stations on the island! One is in the capital, a second in La Frontera and a third on the highway towards La Restinga.

PRESERVING EL HIERRO

Dry and rocky, El Hierro might not strike you as the most beautiful of the Canary Islands, but it is home to some of the most unusual plant and animal life, a distinction that has earned the entire island the label of Unesco biosphere reserve. Environmentalists' attention is mainly focused on protecting the marine reserve in the Mar de las Calmas (p229), the unique juniper trees in El Sabinar (p233) and the quiet El Pinar pine forest (p228), but the whole island benefits, as Unesco funds go to helping the island use its unique natural resources in a sustainable way.

Taxi

Taxis are part of the Autos Cooperativa, the same company that has cheap car rental (see earlier). They are an expensive way to get around the island; a ride from Valverde to La Restinga will cost around €30.

VALVERDE

pop 1630

From the valley below, Santa María de Valverde, the only landlocked Canary capital, looks like a white strip painted across the mountain. Its low white houses, situated on two main streets that run across a mountain ridge, aren't as scenic as those historic, balconied mansions of the other capitals, but when clouds don't interfere the town offers some pretty valley views, and on rare clear days you can see Tenerife's El Teide and La Gomera perfectly from the centre. Nevertheless, most of the time the fog and wind make Valverde a rather depressing place. It's not worth strolling for its aesthetic value, but you'll doubtlessly have to come through, as it's the island's centre of commerce and services.

HISTORY

Though Jean de Béthencourt conquered the island in 1405, Valverde only really came into being following a devastating hurricane in 1610. Many of the islanders fled to this small inland hamlet seeking shelter, beginning a relative boom that would eventually see the town be made the seat of a *municipio* (town council) that covered the whole island. In 1926 the island's first *cabildo insular* (local government) was established here.

ORIENTATION

At the time of publication, Valverde was immersed in major construction work, with cranes in the streets and noise all around, making it a little harder to find your way. But normally getting around this small capital is uncomplicated.

In town there are only two important streets, both with one-way traffic, one going south, and the other heading north. Coming in from the airport or port, you'll follow one long street with several different names (Calles Valverde, Constitución,

Doctor Quintero, Licenciado Bueno and San Francisco) past the town centre and most of the important services, including the tourist office. When the road ends, you can either head south to San Andrés and La Restinga, or you can curl back right and head back through town on the northbound Calle Dacio Darias.

INFORMATION
Emergency
Police Station (☎ 922 55 00 25; ⏱ 8.30am-2pm & 3.30-9.30pm, Closed in the afternoon on weekends in summer) Situated inside the *ayuntamiento* (town hall).

Internet Access
Ciscom (☎ 922 55 19 08; Calle Doctor Quintero 6; per hr €2)
Urban Ciber Net (☎ 922 55 15 49; Calle San Francisco 4; per hr €1.60) Here you're charged by the minute.

Medical Services
Hospital (☎ 922 59 29 90; Calle Santiago) The area's brand-new hospital is just outside the town centre.

Post
Post Office (☎ 922 55 02 91; Calle Correos 3)

Tourist Offices
Local Tourist Office (☎ 922 55 03 02; www.el hierro.org; Calle Doctor Quintero 11, ⏱ 8.30am-2.30pm Mon-Fri, 9am-1pm Sat in winter, 8.30am-2pm Mon-Fri, 9am-1pm Sat in summer) Not overly helpful, but you can get maps and information about a few island attractions.

Travel Agents
Viajes Ecotours (☎ 922 55 14 59; fax 922 55 15 50; Calle Pérez Galdós 2)
Viajes Insular (☎ 922 55 00 38; fax 922 55 12 61; Calle San Juan 1) Flights, ferries, car rentals, excursions...it is all covered. There are offices all over the islands, including one in La Frontera.

DANGERS & ANNOYANCES

The only real annoyance to speak of is the windy weather: it's constantly blowing and makes for a chilly day even when the sun is out.

SIGHTS

The prettiest part of Valverde is behind Calle Doctor Quintero, where the sprawling **Plaza Quintero Nuñez** (known locally as the Plaza Cabildo) is sandwiched between the **ayuntamiento** (town hall) and the church

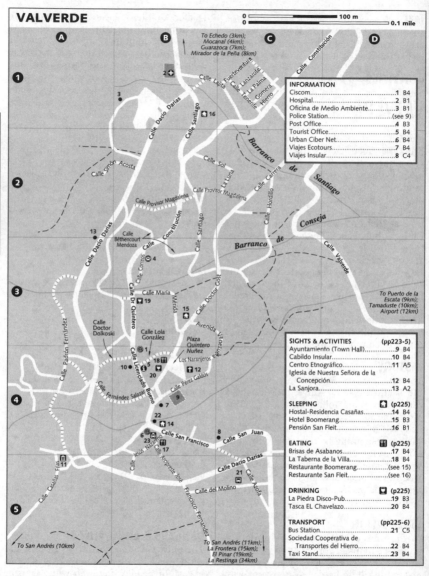

VALVERDE

0 — 100 m
0 — 0.1 mile

To Echedo (3km);
Mocanal (4km);
Guarazoca (7km);
Mirador de la Peña (8km)

Calle Lajita Fuerteventura
Calle Lanzarote Calle La Palma
Calle Tenerife Gomera Hierro
Calle Constitución

Calle Dacio Darias
Calle Santiago
Calle Simón Acosta
Calle Sol
Calle Luna
Calle Provisor Magdalena
Calle Provisor Magdalena
Calle Carrera
Calle Hordilla
Barranco de Santiago
Calle Béthencourt Mendoza
Calle Constitución
Calle Correos
Calle Santiago
Barranco de Conseja
Calle Valverde
Calle Dr Quintero
Calle Maria
Mérida
Calle Doctor Gost
Calle Doctor Dolkoski
Calle Lola González
Avenida Venezuela
Plaza Quintero Nuñez
Los Naranjeros
Calle Padrón Fernández
Calle Licenciado Bueno
Calle Fernández Salazar
Calle Pérez Galdós
Calle Jesús Nazareno
Calle San Francisco
Calle San Juan
Calle Dacio Darias
Calle Arcipreste José
Calle Azofa
Calle Casalás-Frías
Calle del Molino
Francisco Fernández

To Puerto de la
Estaca (9km);
Tamaduste (10km);
Airport (12km)

To San Andrés (10km)

To San Andrés (11km);
La Frontera (15km);
El Pinar (19km);
La Restinga (34km)

INFORMATION
Ciscom	1 B4
Hospital	2 B1
Oficina de Medio Ambiente	3 B1
Police Station	(see 9)
Post Office	4 B3
Tourist Office	5 B4
Urban Ciber Net	6 B4
Viajes Ecotours	7 B4
Viajes Insular	8 C4

SIGHTS & ACTIVITIES (pp223-5)
Ayuntamiento (Town Hall)	9 B4
Cabildo Insular	10 B4
Centro Etnográfico	11 A5
Iglesia de Nuestra Señora de la Concepción	12 B4
La Sanjora	13 A2

SLEEPING (p225)
Hostal-Residencia Casañas	14 B4
Hotel Boomerang	15 B3
Pensión San Fleit	16 B1

EATING (p225)
Brisas de Asabanos	17 B4
La Taberna de la Villa	18 B4
Restaurante Boomerang	(see 15)
Restaurante San Fleit	(see 16)

DRINKING (p225)
La Piedra Disco-Pub	19 B3
Tasca EL Chavelazo	20 B4

TRANSPORT (pp225-6)
Bus Station	21 C5
Sociedad Cooperativa de Transportes del Hierro	22 B4
Taxi Stand	23 B4

EL HIERRO

Nuestra Señora de la Concepción. When the clouds aren't too thick, there are peaceful views of the rounded, bald mountains and the valley that spreads out below town. The church itself is a simple three-knave structure built in 1767 and crowned by a bell tower whose railed-off upper level serves as a lookout. Inside, the polychrome *Purísima Concepción* is the town's most prized piece of artwork.

Beside the church is the construction site of a planned *museo insular* (island museum), but construction was stalled when we last visited, and there's no completion date in sight. For now the town's only museum is the **Centro Etnográfico** (☎ 922 55

20 26; Calle Armas Martel; admission €3; ☺ 9am-2pm Mon-Fri, 10.30am-1.30pm & 4.30-6.30pm Sat), where exhibits about local history and culture are displayed in a small stone house.

ACTIVITIES

To arrange day hikes, rock climbing, canyoning, biking or paraskiing, contact **La Sanjora** (☎ 922 55 18 40; www.islaelhierro.com; Calle Dacio Darias 65).

FESTIVALS & EVENTS

If you're around for the 15 May, **Fiesta de San Isidro** (Saint Isidro's Feast Day), be sure to get a look at the *lucha canaria* (Canarian wrestling; see p27) showcase in the afternoon. Another festival worth being here for is the **Fiesta de la Virgen de la Concepción** (Virgin of the Conception's feast day), celebrated on 8 December in the capital. The night before is marked with fireworks and a lively town party, while the day itself is devoted to religious celebrations, concerts and various cultural acts.

SLEEPING

As in the rest of El Hierro, accommodation in Valverde is largely limited to simple, budget *pensiones* and hotels.

Pensión San Fleit (☎ 922 55 08 57; Calle Santiago 18; s/d €21.50/27.50) Here you'll find cosy, well-kept rooms with their own baths. The *pensión* is on the edge of town, with a small diner of the same name next door (see Eating following).

Hostal-Residencia Casañas (☎ 922 55 02 54; Calle San Francisco 9; s/d €25.20/31.50) A two-star *pensión* with exceptionally clean rooms. Everything looks new and each room has its own bathroom and TV. A few rooms have a balcony for the same price.

Hotel Boomerang (☎ 922 55 02 00; fax 922 55 02 53; Calle Doctor Gost 1; s/d €37/49.50) Rooms are small and the décor old-fashioned, but the place is clean and comfortable, and the staff is friendly. A plus is the restaurant next door (see Eating following), but a minus is the fact that it's inconveniently located at the bottom of a steep hill. This is also the place to get information about Apartamentos Boomerang in Tamaduste (see p226).

EATING

Valverde doesn't stand out for its fine cuisine, but there are a few agreeable places.

Here we've listed our favourites, though any bar will do for a quick drink and a *bocadillo* (bread roll with filling).

La Taberna de la Villa (☎ 922 55 19 07; Calle General Rodriguez y Sánchez Espinoza 10; tapas €4-9, mains €4.50-12) The most popular spot in town for the young crowd, this is a tavern-like place that serves pizzas, pastas and tapas until midnight. Out of all the restaurants in Valverde, this is the only one that has taken care with the ambience, and the result is a laid-back atmosphere perfect for groups. It turns into a pub from 12am until 2am at weekends.

Restaurante Boomerang (☎ 922 55 02 00; Calle Doctor Gost; mains €7-10) Located beside the hotel of the same name, Boomerang offers classic Canarian specialities plus something a bit different – homemade Indian dishes made by the owner's Hindu wife. Call ahead if you want to try them.

Brisas de Asabanos (☎ 922 55 12 50; Calle Jesús Nazareno 1; mains €7-10; ☺ closed Mon) Generally considered the nicest restaurant in town (and a great date place), it's set above a pharmacy, with picture windows looking down onto the main street. Specialities include pork fillet with Herreño cheese and a fillet of the local *pez gallo* (literally, 'rooster fish') in burgundy sauce.

Restaurante San Fleit (☎ 922 55 08 57; Calle Santiago 18; mains €7.50-10) You can get tasty sandwiches and fresh fish from this casual little diner on the edge of town. The long bar is a hangout for locals who come to shoot the breeze over a drink.

DRINKING & ENTERTAINMENT

It doesn't get much more humdrum than Valverde, and during the week you'll likely find the places listed below closed pretty early. But the locals follow a routine route Friday and Saturday nights, heading first to **Tasca El Chavelazo** (☎ 607 57 29 96; Calle General Rodriguez y Sánchez Espinoza 8) for an after-dinner drink, and then continuing on to **La Piedra** (Calle Doctor Quintero 2) disco and pub for more drinking and dancing.

GETTING THERE & AWAY

The bus station is at the southern end of town on Calle Molino. See p222 for route information and for details about taxis and car rental as well as for getting to/from the airport.

Getting Around

You'll find a taxi stand on the Calle San Francisco, just in front of the island transportation co-op (Sociedad Cooperativa de Transportes del Hierro). Taxi fares start at €2.21 and climb slowly up from there. If you're in a hurry to get across town, a taxi is a relatively inexpensive way to do it.

You can hire bikes from La Sanjora (for details, see p225).

AROUND THE ISLAND

Covering an area of just 269 sq km, El Hierro is an easy place to explore, and in theory you could tour the entire island in a day, though curves and poor pavement would take their toll. A much better idea is to rent a car for at least three days, which lets you leisurely explore the island and, if you like, take time out for hiking or diving.

THE EAST COAST
Echedo

Only 3km from Valverde, Echedo is at the heart of the wine-growing region. Its vineyards are planted behind quaint volcanic rock walls which help to block the wind that often swirls through. Continue past the town to the **Charco Manso**, natural saltwater pools that lie at the end of a curvy, lonely stretch of bitumen that winds down among shrubs and volcanic rock. When the tide is out, the exposed rocks make it hard to swim, but otherwise the waters are calm. There's a small picnic area with barbecues too.

Tamaduste & La Caleta

The resort of choice for people with means from Valverde (10km to the west), **Tamaduste** is little more than a cluster of houses around a pretty natural cove made of volcanic rock.

There is absolutely nothing interesting about the town itself, but the rock pools in the cove are perfect for swimming, fishing, crabbing and in general escaping from the outside world. At high tide the cove fills with water and kids dive head-first into the waves. At low tide, the rough waves dry up, leaving nothing more than still pools. This is the perfect time to collect crabs and ocean snails.

A kilometre or so further on is **La Caleta**, another tiny town centred around a cove. The calm waters here are especially good for kids, and there are natural saltwater pools formed by the volcanic rock (and a bit of cement too). You can follow the steps beyond the pool to a basalt rock face bearing much-weathered Bimbache rock carvings (see p228 for more Bimbache rock carvings).

If you want to stay, the best option in town is **Apartamentos Boomerang** (☎ 922 55 02 00; Calle El Cantil; 1-/2-bedroom apt €54/60), which is right on the ocean and has balconies to let in the breeze.

Puerto de la Estaca & Las Playas

The island's most important port (in fact, its only port), **Puerto de la Estaca** (☎ 922 55 09 03) is a sleepy, rather sad little place that only wakes up twice a day to greet the ferries coming in from Tenerife. At the time of publication, major construction work was under way, giving hope for a better port in the future but making the present one all the more dreary. When construction work is finished, El Hierro will have a spacious recreational port, facilities for cruise ships and a few new beaches.

The drive out to Las Playas (10km past the port) is through a no-man's land of rocky shores and rockier hillsides. You'll pass the little town of **Timijiraque**, where there is a small beach (watch the undertow here) and two informal restaurants. **Bahía** (☎ 922 55 00 20; Carretera General 4; mains €6-9) is known for its grilled *chocos* (cuttlefish) and **Casa Guayana** (☎ 922 55 04 17; Carretera General; menú del día €9) offers a variety of tasty fresh fish. The latter also rents out a few no-frills **rooms** (s/d €15/30) that each have their own toilet but a shared shower.

Most of those who make the trek out here end up at the **Parador Nacional** (☎ 922 55 80 36; hierro@parador.es; Las Playas; s/d €89/110; P X X X) which sits on the edge of a rocky beach. This is the island's top hotel, and rooms are lovely, with hardwood floors, cool blue décor and balconies (ask for one with an ocean view), though the best they offer is the lullaby of the waves crashing.

The *parador*'s **restaurant** (mains €14-16) is elegant as well, with big picture windows looking onto the ocean and creative takes on traditional Canarian dishes.

THE NORTH
Mocanal to Mirador de la Peña

The near-permanent blanket of mist and fog that smothers northern El Hierro makes this quiet, rural area seem almost spooky in its solitude. That may be good for ambience, but it makes for difficult driving, so keep your eyes on the road and off the landscape of low hills and occasional pine forests. Though not a lush area, the soil here is rich and farmers cultivate almonds, figs and fruit, cereals, cabbages and other crops.

Take the HI-5 5km out of Valverde towards **Mocanal**, one of several farming villages that line the highway. Just before the town itself, a well-marked turn leads right down to the **Pozo de las Calcosas**, a coastal hamlet whose claim to fame is an oceanside rock pool that sits at the end of a steep path. There's also a **mirador** (lookout), a tiny **stone chapel** and a few restaurants. **Mesón La Barca** (☎ 922 55 08 82; mains about €15) is a cheerful place, painted yellow and with a few rustic dining rooms. Fresh fish is the speciality of the house. Beside it is **Casa Carlos** (☎ 922 55 11 53; mains €4.50-6.50), which serves a similar fresh-fish menu but on plastic tablecloths.

Back on the main highway, continue a few kilometres more and turn left onto the HI-15. Just past **Guarazoca**, another agricultural hamlet, you can hear the whinnies of the 'happy donkeys' at **Los Burros Felices** (☎ 922 55 11 11; ⏱ 11am-4pm Wed, Fri & Sun), a haven for aging or abandoned asses. The slogan – 'our happy donkeys are looking forward to seeing you' – says it all.

One of El Hierro's top sites – the **Mirador de la Peña** – is just 500m further on. The *mirador*'s vantage points provide great views (mist permitting!) of the Gulf coast and the valley. Wander around short paths connecting the lookouts and then dine at the elegant **restaurant** (☎ 922 55 03 00; mains €9-11), which was designed by Lanzarote-born César Manrique (see p117 for more on this famed designer). The dining room is dominated by a huge window that looks out over the Gulf. The menu is focused on creative ways to use local ingredients, with results like Herreño pineapple stuffed with shellfish.

From the *mirador*, a steep walking trail leads down to Las Puntas (see p230). Allow a good 2¼ hours. Another track trails off northwards towards **Punta de Salmor** and, offshore, **Los Roques de Salmor** (see p230).

Las Montañetas to Mirador de Isora

The largely abandoned houses of **Las Montañetas**, one of the island's oldest villages, are scattered around a bend in the road as you head toward San Andrés. Although a few farmers continue to work the land, the thin soil and harsh, damp climate has pushed most of them away.

As the road enters a pine forest, take a signed left turn toward **El Garoé** (⏱ 10.30am-2.30pm & 5-7pm Tue-Sat, 11am-2pm Sun), the ancient holy tree of the Bimbaches. According to legend the tree, which sits at the end of 2.5km of rough dirt track, miraculously spouted water, providing for the islanders and their animals. Today we know that it's really no miracle – mist in the air condenses on the tree's leaves and gives fresh water. The tree itself is rather unremarkable, especially taking into account that the original, a variety of laurel, was felled by a hurricane in 1610; the one here today was planted in 1949. There's a small visitors centre near the tree.

After so many highway signs, one would expect more from **San Andrés**, the next dot on the map. To get here, make a left just after the Garoé turn-off. The town is made up of a few buildings scattered on either side of the highway; one of them is **Casa Goyo** (☎ 922 55 12 63; mains €6-8.50), a homey restaurant serving up filling local fare to locals and hungry passers-by.

In June, the **Fiesta de la Apañada** (Festival of the Clever!) takes place here, where farmers gather for a livestock sale and the smartest extract the best prices.

A couple of kilometres southwest of San Andrés, stop at the **Mirador de Jinama** for magnificent views over the fertile plains of El Golfo (or over a big pot of cloud soup, depending on the day). From here, you can take a glorious 3.5km walk down an old donkey track to La Frontera. Wear walking shoes (it's a little rough in places) and allow around 1½ hours.

Another walking trail meanders its way south from San Andrés towards the cheese-producing village of **Isora**. If you're driving, take the secondary road that branches off the HI-1 highway (also known as the TF-912), just northeast of San Andrés. Beyond

EL HIERRO

Isora, perched high on El Risco de los Herreños ridge, is the **Mirador de Isora** with its awesome panorama of Las Playas and the ocean. A steep track allows hikers to descend to the coast (reckon on at least an hour to get down). Otherwise, you can follow another road southwest back to the highway and turn left (south) to follow signs for La Restinga. If you do the latter, you'll soon pass the **Mirador de las Playas**, with an equally spectacular view of the coast.

EL PINAR & THE SOUTHEAST

A peaceful, paved road winds through El Pinar, the protected pine forest that cuts through the centre of the island in a wide east–west strip. It's possible to drive from the eastern rim of El Pinar through to the Ermita de Nuestra Señora de los Reyes (see p232) on the western side of the island.

Hoya del Morcillo & Around

A shady recreational area with a football field, a playground and a picnic area, **Hoya del Morcillo** (☼ 9am-9pm) is the perfect spot to rest among the pines. Don't miss the large-scale map of El Hierro, made with logs. It's a great way for kids (and directionally challenged adults) to get their bearings on the island.

Nearby is the island's only **campsite** (per person per day €4.50). It has space for 300 and is well equipped, but you must request permission at the Hoya del Morcillo information booth, at the tourist office (p223), or at the Oficina de Medio Ambiente (Environment Office; ☎ 922 55 00 17; fax 922 55 02 71; Calle Trinista 1), both in Valverde. If you send in your request ahead of time, the Environment Office will fax you a permit before you even leave home.

Continuing into the El Pinar forest, you come across **El Julán**. If you're up to it, this is the place to begin the trail to **Los Letreros**, a scattering of petroglyphs (*petroglifos*; rock carvings) scratched into a lava flow by the Bimbaches. Like the rest of the Bimbache carvings, this one is still puzzling the experts about its meaning and why it was made here. The hike is a long one that leaves behind the pine forest and heads into dry, volcanic territory. At the end (or sometimes along the trail) a guide will ask you to show your passport. Ask the guide to point out the carvings; if you don't know

where to look you may pass right by the faded etchings and not know it.

If you head west past El Julán, after about 6km you'll come to a dirt road on your right that will eventually lead you up to the foot of **Malpaso** (1501m), the island's highest peak. The 9km of rough dirt track make for slow going, but the ride is all an adventure. The track is suitable for almost any vehicle (carry a spare tyre just in case).

Las Casas & Taibique

The small towns **Las Casas** and **Taibique** form a small county that, like the nearby pine forest of Hoya del Morcillo (see earlier), is known as El Pinar. The two towns run into each other and seem to be sliding precariously downhill.

On the main highway in Taibique you'll find the two-star **Hotel Pinar** (☎ 922 55 80 08; fax 922 55 80 90; s/d €35/42), where appealing rooms with private bathrooms, TV and phone are excellent value. Some rooms have balconies for the same price.

Just below the hotel, **Restaurante Luis El Taperio** (mains €7-10) is a friendly bar and restaurant with cheap lunches and tapas in addition to the hearty entrées of fish and grilled meats.

Cala de Tacorón

Halfway between El Pinar and La Restinga, you'll pass the turn-off to **Cala de Tacorón**. The road winds through a harsh volcanic landscape to reach a rocky coast with lake-like calm waters. This is a great area for diving (many of La Restinga–based companies come here; see Activities later) and is popular with kayakers too.

The **Cala de Tacorón** is a cove that is perfect for swimming; bring lunch to eat at the rustic covered picnic area, made with logs and branches, à la Swiss Family Robinson. There is a small bar down here too, serving snacks and drinks from 1pm to 8pm, except Thursday.

La Restinga

The road down to La Restinga rambles through volcanic badlands. Take time to look at the funny lava shapes, ranging from *pahoehoe* or *lajial*, smooth rock that looks like twisted taffy, to badlands of hard, crumbling rock that looks like wet oatmeal. The gleaming sea lays out before you as you descend into the town, and you can clearly make out the line between the glassy Mar de las Calmas (Sea of Calm) and the windblown open ocean to the west, which is rough and choppy. Part of the sea is a marine reserve, and both fishing and diving are restricted in an effort to provide fish with a safe place to breed.

The town itself is a hodge-podge of dull, modern constructions, many still unfinished. The best the area has to offer is scuba diving, and you can't go a block without finding an outfitter trying to lure you into a wetsuit. The island's only fishing port is here and, though it's made La Restinga into the island's boating and fishing capital, it's also blocked the ocean view with an ugly concrete wall. Oh well, that's the price of progress.

Two volcanic beaches sit right on the port. The water is calm but not always clean, though that doesn't seem to bother the bathing crowd.

ACTIVITIES

There's no shortage of diving companies offering their services to divers and to diver hopefuls, and everyone is offering pretty much the same thing – a €25 dive around the Mar de las Calmas. The opening hours change daily, according to the weather and the number of dives planned. Companies include:

Arrecifal (☎ 922 55 71 71; arrecifal@arrakis.es; Calle La Orcilla 30)

Buceo La Restinga (☎ 922 55 71 67; Calle Juan Gutierrez Monteverde 21)

Centro de Buceo El Hierro (☎ 922 26 18 38; www.centrodebuceoelhierro.com in Spanish; Avenida Marítima)

Centro de Buceo Meridiano 0 (☎ 922 55 70 76; fax 922 55 71 59; Avenida Marítima)

El Hierro Taxi Diver (☎ 922 55 71 42; www.elhierrotaxidiver.com; Avenida Marítima)

El Submarino (☎ 922 55 75 75; Avenida Marítima)

So fins aren't your thing? Head to **@ctivos** (☎ 922 55 71 17; activos@ya.com; Calle Las Calmas), a centre for adventure sports. Located three blocks up from the waterfront, the young Austrian owner organises bike excursions, guided hikes, kayak trips and car tours. Prices vary, but bike rental starts at €18 per day, while a two-hour kayak trip is €20 per person.

FESTIVALS & EVENTS

La Restinga's two most important (and most fun) fiestas are the **Fiesta de San Juan**, on 24 June, a celebration of the longest night of summer, and the **Fiesta de la Virgen del Carmen**, on 16 July, honouring the town's patroness saint. To celebrate San Juan the islanders congregate here and build huge bonfires where they eat and party until late into the night. The Fiesta de la Virgen del Carmen is celebrated on the weekend closest to 16 July, the actual feast day. On Saturday night a town dance and often a dinner kick off the party, while Sunday is a more serious affair, with a religious procession that takes the Virgin out onto the water in a small boat.

SLEEPING

The accommodation options in town are nearly all apartments, and unless you have an extremely tight budget, they are the better choice.

Casa Kai (☎ 922 55 70 34; Calle Varadero 6; s/d €22/23) An exception to the predominant apartments is this old white house on the beach that offers minuscule rooms with their own bathrooms (if you can call a toilet in one closet and a stall shower in another a real bathroom). Miraculously, the place has two stars, but it's none too clean and scores low on the charm scale.

La Marina (☎ 922 55 90 16; Avenida Marítima; 2-bedroom apt €42-45) On the waterfront, this newish building has three apartments for rent. All have big balconies, TV and a small kitchenette.

Apartamentos Rocamar (☎ 922 55 70 83; Avenida Marítima 20; 1-bedroom apt €33) Also on the waterfront, this has been around for a while, but the apartments are clean and well equipped.

Rocamar II (☎ 650 193 397; Calle Juan Gutierrez Monteverde; 1-/2-bedroom apt €33/45) Situated in town, this is under the same ownership as Apartamentos Rocamar. Though not on the water, the construction is new and very attractive.

EATING

Hope you like fish, as it's the main food on offer.

Casa Juan (☎ 922 55 71 02; Calle Juan Gutierrez Monteverde 23; mains €5-9) A simple restaurant with a large variety of local fish, all quite good and fairly priced. A friendly place popular with locals, it's one of the most warmly recommended in all the island.

El Refugio (☎ 922 55 70 29; Calle La Lapa 1; mains €6-9) Serving fresh fish and seafood (the restaurant has its own fishing boat), this is one block up from the waterfront.

EL GOLFO

From La Restinga, you could head north back to the HI-1, which follows the ridge along the volcanic wall that overlooks El Golfo then zigzags down to the plain. The route is scenic, but tortuously curved. A much simpler option is to head back to Valverde and take the HI-5, which connects to El Golfo via a new tunnel cut into the mountain. The tunnel puts La Frontera just 15km away from the capital. Coming through the tunnel, you're faced with the gulf spread out before you and the taller, greener and more rugged mountains that are particular to this side of the island.

Las Puntas

The first town you come across is Las Puntas; take the HI-55 turn-off to head down to this coastal town. Surprisingly, the town has no real access to the coast. Beautiful rugged rock cliffs, the soothing sound of crashing waves and good fishing possibilities are about all that's on offer, though construction is underway on a new aquatic park that should open by the time you read this.

Meanwhile, the closest place for a swim is **La Maceta**. To reach here you have to get back on the main highway (HI-5) and take the next turn right onto the HI-550. From the road, signposts lead you to La Maceta, a series of natural saltwater pools built along the coast. At high tide, the ocean swallows the pools, making swimming dangerous.

For such a small place there is an abundance of lodging options in Las Puntas, the most famous being a four-room hotel that once held the Guinness world record of being the smallest hotel in the world: **Hotel Puntagrande** (☎ 922 55 90 81; s/d €47/57), an old stone port building perched on a rock outcropping. From here there is a clear view of **Los Roques de Salmor**, an important nesting spot for various bird species and the last stand of the primeval Lagarto del Salmor (Lizard of Salmor), which now only survives in captivity (see Ecomuseo de Guinea, following, and the boxed text on p221).

You could also stay in the charming **Bungalows Los Roques de Salmor** (☎ 922 55 90 16; up to 4 people €54), a series of white-walled small bungalows on your left as you enter town. New and well kept, they have tile roofs, stone detailing and tasteful décor.

Apartamentos & Pensión Caribe (☎ 922 55 92 21; d/apt €24/36) offers small apartments, and rooms so cramped you will have trouble squeezing past the bed into the bathroom. The décor hasn't been updated for a few decades, but the place is clean enough and has a nice rooftop terrace.

Get a bite to eat at **El Tejerde** (☎ 696 38 24 58; Calle Cascadas de Mar 3; mains €10-11), a cheery place with green checked tablecloths and daily specials (fish, mostly) scrawled on a chalk board. You can hear fish sizzling on frying pans as you walk in.

FESTIVALS & EVENTS

The **Fiesta de San Juan**, a celebration of the longest night of the year, is celebrated here and in other towns on 24 June throughout the islands (for example, La Restinga, p229).

Ecomuseo de Guinea

Off to your left past La Maceta is this **museum** (☎ 922 55 50 56; one centre €4.50, both centres €7.50), which is really two centres in one. The **Casas de Guinea** (☯ 10am-2pm & 4-6pm Tue-Sat, 11am-2pm Sun, 10.30am-2.30pm & 5-7pm Tue-Sat, 11am-2pm Sun in summer), which encompasses 20 houses (four of which are visitable), represents lifestyles of the islanders through the centuries. The **Lagartario** (☯ 10am-2pm & 4-6pm Tue & Thu, 11am-2pm Sun, 10.30am-2.30pm & 5-7pm Tue-Thu, 11am-2pm Sun in summer) is a recuperation centre for the giant lizard of El Hierro (see the boxed text on p221). You can only visit the Lagartario with a guide, so arrive at least an hour before closing time to make sure there's time for a visit. Don't miss the gift shop selling lizard-themed jewellery, ash trays and art.

Tigaday & La Frontera

Like most people, you may get confused when you hear everything on the gulf coast referred to as 'La Frontera'. That's because although on the map La Frontera is just a dot indicating a single town, it's also the name of the municipality that covers this side of the island.

About 5km southwest of the Ecomuseo de Guinea is **Tigaday**, the nerve centre of the La Frontera municipality. It's a pleasant place, with trees lining the highway that leads into town and a sunnier climate than Valverde and the north. El Hierro's second town, Tigaday is the only place on the island with shops and services to rival the capital. It even has one of the island's three petrol stations! Most shops and bars are along Avenida Ignacio Padrón. Here you'll find **Beep** (☎ 922 55 94 00; per min €0.05), where you can check your email. A pharmacy, supermarket and travel agency are all on this street too.

In town, the **Pensión Guanche** (☎ 922 55 90 65; Calle Cruz Alta 1; s/d €15/21) is a one-star *pensión* that has unremarkable rooms with private bathroom. Some rooms have a balcony for the same price.

There are also some apartments around. The best seems to be **Apartamentos Frontera** (☎ 922 55 92 46; Carretera General 19; 2-/4-person apt €35/45, extra bed €6), which has roomy, modern places with kitchenettes and safes.

Up the hill behind Tigaday is **La Frontera**, though it's hard to tell where one town ends and the other begins. The most important thing here is the **Iglesia de Nuestra Señora de la Candelaria**, a 17th-century construction that was redone in 1929. Inside, the three-nave church has two rows of pretty stone columns and an ornate golden altar. It sits on the **Plaza de la Candelaria**, a charming square with benches and a fountain. Behind the church, you can walk to the empty **stone chapel** perched on the hill. It's a short but steep climb, and from the top the gulf valley spreads out before you like a patchwork quilt of fields and banana plantations.

Just in front of the church, **Joapira** (☎ 922 55 98 03; Plaza de la Candelaria; mains about €7) is a bar with a covered terrace that also serves simple food, such as fried squid and grilled chicken. Across the street, the slightly more upscale **Bar-Restaurante Candelaria** (☎ 922 55 50 01; Calle de la Candelaria 1; mains €5-7.50), where the walls are covered with knick-knacks and local paintings and there are flowers on the pavement out front.

Stay at the **Hotelito Ida Inés** (☎ 922 55 94 45; www.hotelitoidaines.com; El Hoyo 2; s/d €63/76). There are just 12 rooms in this quaint hotel, all clean with floral bedspreads, TV, phone, coffee and tea facilities, nice bathrooms and balconies with splendid views.

FESTIVALS & EVENTS

Around 15 August La Frontera celebrates the **Fiesta de la Virgen de la Candelaria** (The Feast of the Virgin of Candelaria) with a religious procession and a showcase of *lucha canaria* (see p27). Afterwards there's a lively dance in the Plaza Tigaday.

Sabinosa & Around

After Tigaday, the HI-5 meets up with the HI-50 and heads toward Los Llanillos and Sabinosa. **Los Llanillos** won't detain you for long, but there is a good restaurant at the town's entrance. The **Asador Artero** (☎ 922 55 50 37; Calle Artero; mains €5-11) is a cosy yet busy place popular with locals and specialising in grilled meats and chicken, though there are a few more elaborate dishes too.

In town there's the turn-off for **Charco Azul**, a natural cove with calm pools for swimming.

Leaving Los Llanillos, get ready for a beautiful drive along a coastal mountain ridge. The hairpin curves can be challenging though, especially if you're tempted to admire the scenery of the ocean laid out at your feet and the surrounding rugged volcanic mountains.

Some 7km further on is **Sabinosa**. This remote little village feels as though it's at the end of the world, and in a way it is. The most western town in all Spain (all Europe, in fact), it is the last inhabited place before the great expanse of the Atlantic.

If you want to stay, your only option is the **Pensión Sabinosa** (☎ 922 55 93 55; Calle Valentina Hernández 7; s/d €15/22, d with private bathroom €24). It's at the bottom of a steep road that will challenge even the most experienced drivers. Rooms are simple, but the owners are especially friendly.

The **Pozo de la Salud** (Well of Health), and beside it the hotel-spa **Hotel-Balneario Pozo de la Salud** (☎ 922 55 95 61; fax 922 55 98 01; s €49-53, d €60-69), are 4km further down the winding highway. You can walk down to the small *pozo* (well), whose waters are said to cure a variety of ills, but it's all closed up and there's not much to see. If you like, you can do as the Herreños do and bring an empty jug to fill up for free in the hotel.

The hotel is a stately building that seems out of place in the rustic wilderness of western El Hierro. Rooms have views of either the ocean or the mountains and are simple but comfortable. There are 1st-floor rooms prepared for the elderly or disabled. The **spa** (◷ 9am-8pm; massage per hr €33) offers a variety of water-based treatments, as well as standards like massages and algae facials, and the prices are a lot better than what you'd find in mainland Europe. Anyone can get treatments here, but be sure to reserve a few days ahead, even earlier during busy times like summer and Christmas.

There are plans to pave a flat coastal road between Los Llanillos and the *pozo*, which will make the journey here quicker and safer, though it will also take away some of the lost-world quality that makes this place so alluring.

Just west of the hotel, down the HI-500, is **Playa de las Arenas Blancas** (White Sands Beach). Take a short road down to the coast where indeed there are a few whitish grains of sand. They quickly melt into volcanic rock at the water's edge though, and the beach is unremarkable although remote and often deserted. The rolling waves are generally safe to swim in, if you don't go out too far, but you may need to wear shoes to cross the rocks.

LA DEHESA

The road from Sabinosa arches all the way around the west coast to what is known as **La Dehesa** (The Pasture), cutting through volcanic badlands where only a few low shrubs dare to survive. The landscape here, which looks like a rock graveyard, is impressive for its lunar-like bareness.

Some 10km past the Pozo de la Salud is the **Playa del Verodal**, a curious red-sand beach that backs up to a majestic rock cliff. The beach itself is 1km off the main highway (follow the signs) and is often deserted, leaving you with your own private paradise. The winds here are a bit tamer than in other spots on the coast and the waves are calm

enough to swim in, though it's still a good idea to keep the kiddies in shallow waters.

Shortly after, you reach the turn-off for the most southwesterly point of all Spanish territory: the **Faro de Orchilla** (Lighthouse of Orchilla). Long ago robbed of its status as Meridíano Cero by Greenwich in the UK (a title the island still uses in its tourist promotion), the lighthouse is still the first or last contact with land for mariners navigating the rough Atlantic waters between Africa or Europe and the Americas. The 4.5km of dirt track down to the lighthouse make for a bumpy ride – you need to have a fervent love of lighthouses or a particular sense of place to bother.

Festivals & Events

On 25 April the locals honour the shepherds who bought the Virgin de los Reyes (Virgin of the Kings), the island's patroness saint, from European sailors in 1545. The **Fiesta de los Pastores** (The Shepherd's Feast) is celebrated with a religious procession that carries the Virgin out of her current home in the Ermita de los Reyes to the cave where she was first kept.

Ermita de Nuestra Señora de los Reyes

Back on the main highway, head inland a few kilometres to reach this pretty white **chapel** *(ermita)* made all the more interesting because of the history and tradition behind it.

The chapel contains the image of the island's patroness saint, named Nuestra Señora de los Reyes (Our Lady of the Kings) because local shepherds bought her from foreign sailors on Three Kings Day, 6 January (1545). The people attribute several miracles to the Virgin, including ending droughts and epidemics.

Every four years (2005, 2009 etc), the Virgin is taken out of the chapel in a lively

---

HERE COMES THE VIRGIN

The fiesta par excellence on El Hierro is the Bajada de la Virgen de los Reyes (Descent of the Virgin), held in early July every four years (2005, 2009 etc). Most of the island's population gathers to witness or join in a procession bearing a statue of the Virgin, seated in a sedan chair, from the Ermita de Nuestra Señora de los Reyes in the west of the island all the way across to Valverde. Her descent is accompanied by musicians and dancers dressed in traditional red and white tunics and gaudy caps, and celebrations continue for most of the month in villages and hamlets across the island.

procession around the island (see the boxed text p232).

El Sabinar & Beyond

From the *ermita*, follow the road, which soon becomes a firm dirt track, up this windswept height named after the *sabinas* (junipers) that grow up here in very weird ways. Along one part of the road, the way is lined with *sabinas* – though beautiful, these are not as spectacular as the wind-twisted trees further down the road at El Sabinar, which have become the island's symbol. You'll pass a turn-off to the left at a signpost indicating El Sabinar. Park here and wander among some of the most unusual trees you'll have ever seen. They have been sculpted by nature into wild shapes that look frozen in time.

Supposedly there is a path among these tortured figures, but it's impossible to follow. Wear long pants if you want to hack your way through the brush and get close to the trees, which are scattered on the hillside. These wonderfully weird *sabinas* are part of the reason that Unesco declared the entire island of El Hierro a biosphere reserve (see p222).

Once back at the fork, you could curl north for a further 2km to reach the **Mirador de Bascos**, a spectacular lookout that's unfortunately often cloaked in cloud. If it's a clear day, prepare for a breathtaking view. If not, don't bother.

EL HIERRO

Directory

CONTENTS

ACCOMMODATION

The short, sad advice to those who prefer to travel independently and keep their options open is that it's easier and a lot cheaper to buy a Canaries package, including flight and accommodation, before leaving home.

Unless it's the nightlife you're after, you might want to pick one of the smaller and quieter resorts. But don't think that, once you've arrived, you're trapped for the whole of your stay; on Tenerife and Gran Canaria, buses fan out all over the island and car hire, on whichever island you land at, is less expensive than in mainland Europe.

The accommodation listings within this guide are ordered as follows: budget (under €40 per double per night); mid-range (€40

PRACTICALITIES

- **Electricity** 220V, 50Hz – plugs have two round pins. Make sure you bring plug adapters for your appliances.

- **Newspapers & Magazines** Local *Diario de Avisos, La Gaceta de Canarias, Canarias 7* and *La Provincia*; English-language local *Island Connections*; Spanish *El País* and *El Mundo*; Foreign *International Herald Tribune, Hello!* and all the English and German tabloids.

- **Radio** Radio Nacional de España has four stations. Local FM stations abound on the islands and the BBC World Service can be found mainly on 6195kHz and 12095kHz.

- **TV** The Canaries receives the mainland's big channels (TVE1, La 2, Antena 3, Tele 5) and has a few local stations that are of very limited interest.

- **Weights & Measures** The metric system is used. Decimals are indicated with commas and thousands with points.

---

to €100 per double per night) and top end (over €100 per double per night). Generally speaking, budget facilities will comprise simple rooms sometimes with private bathroom. Most of the lodgings in the Canary Islands fall into the mid-range bracket and, while there are some variations between standards (even from island to island), you'll find most perfectly comfortable. Top end is just that – anything that appears under this category will have all the mod cons you need.

Some places have separate price structures for the *temporada alta* (high season), *temporada media* (midseason) or *temporada baja* (low season), all usually displayed on a notice in reception or nearby. Hoteliers are not actually bound by these displayed prices.

Any time is tourist time in the Canaries. But the high season here is in winter, when the Canaries can offer sunshine, warmth and an escape from the rigours of the northern European winter. Winter runs from about December to April (including the Carnaval period of February/March), and this is when you are likely to find accommodation at its most costly – and elusive. Semana Santa (Easter Week) is another peak time. Summer (July to September) can also be busy as mainland Spaniards turn up in full force. If you can visit during the rest of the year, you'll find less pressure on accommodation, with many of those same hotels and apartments offering reductions of about 25%.

Note that options in individual towns fill up quickly when a local fiesta is on, and those on the smaller islands can be fully taken during important celebrations. See p240 for details on festivals and events.

The overwhelming majority of visitors to the Canary Islands come with accommodation booked. This has certain advantages, especially in high season, when going it alone can be difficult. Advance booking for independent travellers really does pay off, even if it's no more than a phone call on the morning of the same day.

Virtually all accommodation prices are subject to IGIC, the Canary Islands' indirect tax, charged at a rate of 5%. This tax is often included in the quoted price at the cheaper places, but less often at the more expensive ones. In some cases you will only be charged the tax if you ask for a receipt.

Apartments

Apartments for rent are much more common than hotels. Quality can vary greatly, but they can be more comfortable than a simple *pensión* and more economical, especially if there are several of you and you plan to self-cater. The two principal categories are *estudios* (studios), with one bedroom or living room and bedroom in common, and the more frequent *apartamento*, where you get a double bedroom and separate lounge. Both have separate bathroom and a kitchenette.

The downside for the independent traveller is that, particularly in the main western-island resorts, many apartment complexes are completely in thrall to tour operators. Obeying the terms of their contract, they can't rent you a room, even if it's empty, since the tour company has snapped up every last one for the season. Even those apartment complexes that do rent to independent travellers may insist upon a minimum stay of three nights.

In many cases the owner doesn't live in the building so there's little point in just turning up – you generally need to call. This is particularly the case in the three western-most islands, La Gomera, El Hierro and La Palma, where small operators predominate. Contact phone numbers will usually be posted at the entrance.

Apartments are officially categorised as one to three keys. At the bottom of the scale they can cost as little as €40 for a double per night. At the top you're looking at anything up to €90. Look for signs like *apartamentos de alquiler* (apartments for rent).

You should get hold of each island's hotel/apartment guide from tourist offices as soon as you can after arrival, because of the peculiar difficulties sometimes associated with apartments, and the need in most cases for a phone number. These guides are often far from complete, the majority giving only contact details, but at least they give you some information to work with.

Camping

For a place with so much natural beauty, there are precious few places to camp in the Canary Islands. Most islands have just one token official campsite, and free camping is largely prohibited. In all cases, you'll have to request permission in advance to camp. Generally, the protocol is this: call or fax in a request ahead of time (best if it's before you even leave home) and your permit will either be faxed back or you will have to pick it up in person. Some of the smaller campgrounds are geared toward trekkers and only allow one-night stays.

Note that Camping Gaz is the only common brand of camping gas. Other kinds of canisters are nearly impossible to find.

Casa Rurales

Converted farmsteads or village houses sometimes form the only accommodation option in out-of-the-way places. They are often a highly agreeable option for those seeking to escape the bustle of the resorts, but it's essential to call ahead as they usually offer limited places and there may be no-one in attendance. Many *casas rurales* are distant from public transport so check

---

CANARY PACKAGES

The overwhelming majority of people who end up in apartments are package tourists who book their accommodation with flights from home. Make sure you scan the tour company's brochure carefully before committing yourself. What services does the apartment being offered have? Is there a pool? A bar? Children's facilities? Is the beach within walking distance if you've a couple of toddlers in tow?

---

whether a hired car is necessary or desirable. They usually represent excellent value for the charm of their setting and facilities. Each island has its own organisation or you can reserve centrally through **Acantur** (Asociación Canaria de Turismo Rural; ☎ 922 80 12 48; www.ecoturismocanarias.com). To get an idea of the kind of properties available, visit their website or check out www.canary-islands.com.

Hotels, Hostels & Pensiones

Officially, all these establishments are either *hoteles* (one to five stars), *hostales* (one to three stars) or *pensiones* (one- or two-star guesthouse).

Compared with mainland Spain, there are precious few of any of these around. Since the bulk of the islands' visitors arrive with accommodation booked in advance – usually in villas or self-catering apartments – the demand for more standard hotels is low.

The one-star *pensión* usually offers no discount for single occupancy. Two-star usually means there is at least a wash basin in the room. *Hostales* are often little different from *pensiones*.

Hoteles range from simple places to luxurious, five-star establishments. Even the cheapest ones may have a restaurant, and most rooms will have a bathroom attached.

Paradores

The *paradores*, a Spanish state-run chain of high-class hotels with six establishments in the Canary Islands, are in a special category. These can be wonderful places to luxuriate. They also offer a range of discounts for senior citizens, under-30s and those staying more than one night. The organisation has accommodation on Tenerife and the three easternmost islands. You can find current

offers at www.parador.es, or by contacting their central reservation service, the **Central de Reservas** (☎ 91 516 66 66; info@parador.es; Calle Requena 3, 28013 Madrid).

ACTIVITIES

The Canaries are a great destination for some 'fun in the sun' and there is a diverse range of activities offered for young and old. For more details, see the Outdoors chapter (p41).

BUSINESS HOURS

Generally, business hours are 9am to 2pm and 5pm to 8pm Monday to Friday. Having said that, a lot of government offices don't bother with afternoon opening.

Shops and travel agencies usually open these same hours Monday to Saturday, although some skip the afternoon session on Saturday.

Supermarkets often stay open from about 9am to 9pm Monday to Saturday.

Banks mostly open 8.30am to 2pm Monday to Friday, and 9am to 1pm Saturday. Some don't bother opening on Saturday.

Big-city post offices open 8.30am to 8.30pm Monday to Friday and 9.30am to 1pm on Saturday. Most others open from 8.30am to 2.30pm Monday to Friday and 9.30am to 1pm on Saturday.

Restaurants are open 1pm to 4pm and 9pm until late. Locals go to small bars for breakfast, which open from around 8am.

Many places give hours as summer/ winter, with summer as June through September and winter as the rest of the year. In the Canaries the winter is the high season, often with longer opening hours.

CHILDREN

Children are welcome at all kinds of accommodation and in virtually every café, bar and restaurant. Having children with you can often open doors to contact with local people who you otherwise may not have the opportunity to meet.

Many bars and cafés have outside tables, allowing drinking adults to indulge in their favourite tipples while their little ones run around and play. Local kids are quite used to staying up late and at fiestas it's commonplace to see even tiny ones toddling the streets at 2am or 3am.

Travelling with children usually implies taking a different approach to your holiday. Fortunately, the Canaries are, in this sense, an ideal location – only those determined to see all seven islands at lightning speed would be tempted to subject themselves, let alone their children, to day after day of tiring movement. Hanging around the one spot for a few days at a time, or choosing a permanent base from which to make excursions, creates a sense of familiarity.

Practicalities

Many of the islands' hotels will happily supply a cot for infants, although it's always a good idea to arrange this in advance. With advance warning, the well-known car-hire companies can provide safety seats for children, but you might find it difficult to arrange this with some of the smaller operators. High chairs and nappy-changing facilities are rare, but the laid-back, friendly attitude to children on the islands means that this needn't be a dilemma.

Larger hotels and tourist resorts will be able to arrange child minding, and will often have a specific 'kids club' to keep the littlies occupied during the day and early evening.

Infants generally travel free on ferries and other boats, and those aged two to 12 years go for half price. Similar reductions apply at most commercial attractions, museums and on public transport.

There are no particular health precautions you need to take with your children in the Canaries. That said, kids tend to be more affected than adults by unfamiliar heat, changes in diet and sleeping patterns.

Nappies (diapers), creams, lotions, baby foods and so on are all as easily available on the islands, as in any Western country, but if there's some particular brand you swear by, it's best to bring it with you. Breastfeeding in public is not frowned upon by locals.

Lonely Planet's *Travel with Children* has lots of practical advice on the subject and first-hand stories from many Lonely Planet authors and others who have done it.

Sights & Activities

Children will be cheered by the discovery that the Canaries are not overly laden with museums and other grown-up delights that so often engender desperate, yawn-inducing boredom for the young.

Instead, much of the stuff put on for tourists appeals to kids. Animal reserves (such as Tenerife's Loro Parque) and all the water and theme parks on the bigger islands provide fun for all the family.

Tenerife's southern stretches are especially popular family-friendly destinations, and recent efforts to get rid of drunken rowdiness have met with publicity and approval.

Plenty of seaside activities are suitable for the young too, with many companies welcoming children keen to learn how to surf, snorkel and the like.

CLIMATE CHARTS

Yes, it really is like a permanent spring in the Canary Islands, with a particularly benign climate putting a smile on your face as soon as you hit the tarmac. Mean temperatures

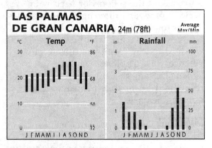

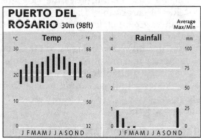

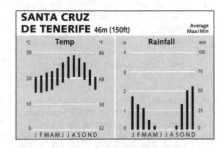

range from 18°C in the winter to about 24°C in summer. Daily highs can easily reach mid-30°C in summer. Even on a hot day at the beach, however, it can be pleasantly cool higher up, and the snow atop Teide is a clear enough reminder that, in winter at any rate, some warm clothing is essential.

COURSES

A Spanish class in the Canary Islands is a great way to learn something and meet people. With a little *castellano* under your belt, you'll be able to better appreciate the local culture.

Check the index for courses listed in this book. You can also check out the local yellow pages for Academias de Idiomas to find private language schools throughout the islands. If you're looking for a personal tutor, ask at the schools or keep your eyes peeled for adverts offering Spanish classes. Expect to pay around €15 per hour.

It's worth asking whether your course will lead to any formal certificate of competence. The Diploma de Español como Lengua Extranjera (DELE) is a qualification recognised by Spain's Ministry of Education and Science.

CUSTOMS

Although the Canary Islands is part of Spain, for customs purposes they are not considered part of the EU. For this reason, allowances are much less generous than for goods bought within EU countries.

You are allowed to bring in or take out, duty free, a maximum of 2L of still wine, 1L of spirits (or 2L of fortified wine), 60mL of perfume, 250mL of *eau de toilette*, 200 cigarettes and up to €175 worth of other goods and gifts.

DANGERS & ANNOYANCES

The vast majority of travellers to the islands risk little more than sunburn, hangovers and overspending. Petty theft can be a problem in Las Palmas de Gran Canaria and the big south-coast resorts of Tenerife and Gran Canaria, but with a few simple precautions you can minimise the danger.

Carry valuables under your clothes if possible – certainly not in a back pocket or in a day pack or anything that could be snatched away easily – and keep your eyes open for people who get unnecessarily close to you.

Never leave anything visible in cars. If possible, don't even leave anything valuable in the boot (trunk). Hire cars are targeted.

Take care with your belongings on the beach. Lone travellers should consider investing in a waterproof neck pouch so that they can keep lightweight valuables with them even while swimming.

Don't leave anything valuable lying around your room and use a safe if there is one available, even though you'll almost always have to pay for such a thing.

If anything valuable is stolen or lost, you must report it to the police and get a copy of the report if you want to make an insurance claim.

If your passport has gone, contact your embassy or consulate for help in issuing a replacement. Before you leave home, write your name, address and telephone number inside your luggage, and take photocopies of your important documents.

Travel insurance against theft and loss is another good idea; see Insurance (p241).

Party animals should be aware that some other party animals, when drunk enough, can become quite unpredictable. In most cases, we are talking loud and drunken louts ferried in on charter flights from northern Europe, some of whom can't resist a good fight.

Scams

You may well come across timeshare touts if you hang around the main resorts in the Canary Islands. If you like the islands enough, timeshare may be worth considering – but be careful about how and what you choose. You need to have all your rights and obligations in writing, especially where management companies promise to sell your timeshare for you if you decide to buy a new one. A number of 'free' sightseeing tours throughout the islands are little more than a quick trip to a theme park and then a solid round of the hard sell, as touts pressure you to buy time in a property. If you're not into this, say so up front and save yourself the hassle.

DISABLED TRAVELLERS

Sadly, the Canary Islands is not geared towards smooth travel for disabled people. Most restaurants, shops and tourist sights are not equipped to handle wheelchairs, although the more expensive accommodation options will have rooms with appropriate facilities. Transport is tricky, although you should be able to organise a specially modified hire car from one of the international hire companies (with advance warning). In fact, advance warning is always a good idea; start with your travel agent and see what they can offer in terms of information and assistance. In the archipelago's cities, such as Las Palmas and Santa Cruz, some buildings (eg museums or government offices) have Braille in the lifts, and some specially textured floors before stairs, but not much else. Few concessions are made in the public infrastructure for deaf people.

In the UK, **Holiday Care** (☎ 0845 124 99 71; www.holidaycare.org.uk) can send you a fact sheet on hotels and other accommodation in the Canary Islands that cater for the disabled, as well as travel agents who can help organise trips.

DISCOUNT CARDS

If you're a full-time student, a teacher or under 26 years old, you can get discounts on everything from airfare and car rental to public transportation and museum entry. The International Student Identity Card (ISIC) and International Youth Travel Card (IYTC) cost €6 each, and the International Teacher Identity Card (ITIC) costs €11. Get details about how to apply at www.isic.org. You can buy and use the cards almost anywhere in the world.

EMBASSIES & CONSULATES

It's important to realise what your own embassy – the embassy of the country of which you are a citizen – can and can't do to help you if you get into trouble. Generally speaking, it won't be much help in emergencies if the trouble you're in is remotely your own fault. Remember that you are bound by the laws of the country you are in. Your embassy will not be sympathetic if you end up in jail after committing a crime locally, even if such actions are legal in your own country.

In genuine emergencies you might get some assistance, but only if other channels have been exhausted. For example, if you need to get home urgently, a free ticket home is exceedingly unlikely – the embassy would expect you to have insurance. If you

have all your money and documents stolen, it might assist with getting a new passport, but a loan for onward travel is out of the question.

Some embassies used to keep letters for travellers or have a small reading room with home newspapers, but these days the mail-holding service is rarely offered, and even newspapers tend to be out of date.

Spanish Embassies

The following is a selection of Spanish embassies abroad:

Australia (☎ 02-6273 3555; www.embaspain.com; 15 Arkana St, Yarralumla, Canberra 2600, ACT)
Canada (☎ 613-747 2252; www.docuweb.ca; 74 Stanley Ave, Ottawa, Ontario K1M 1P4)
France (☎ 01 44 43 18 00; ambespfr@ mail.mae.es; 22 Avenue Marceau, 75008 Paris)
Germany (☎ 030-254 007 215; www.spanischebotschaft.de in German; Lichtensteinallee 1, 10787 Berlin)
Ireland (☎ 01-269 1640; www.mae.es/embajades /dublin/; 17A Merlyn Park, Balls Bridge, Dublin 4)
Netherlands (☎ 070-302 49 99; www.claboral.nl in Dutch; Lange Voorhout 50, 2514 EG, The Hague)
UK (☎ 020-7235 5555; embespuk@mail.mae.es; 39 Chesham Place, London SW1X 8SB)
USA (☎ 202-452 0100; www.spainemb.org; 2375 Pennsylvania Ave NW, Washington, DC 20037)

Embassies & Consulates in the Canary Islands

The following countries all have their main diplomatic representation in Madrid but also have consular representation in Las Palmas de Gran Canaria:

France (Map pp62-3; ☎ 928 29 23 71; Calle Néstor de la Torre 12)
Germany (Map pp62-3; ☎ 928 49 18 80; Calle José Franchy Roca 5)
Netherlands (Map pp62-3; ☎ 928 24 23 82; Calle León y Castillo 244)
UK (Map pp62-3; ☎ 928 26 25 08; Calle Luis Morote 6)
USA (Map pp62-3; ☎ 928 27 12 59; Calle Martínez de Escobar 3)

Countries with consular representation in Santa Cruz de Tenerife include:
France (Map pp140-1; ☎ 922 23 27 10; Calle José María 1)
Ireland (Map pp140-1; ☎ 922 24 56 71; Calle Castillo 8)
Netherlands (Map pp140-1; ☎ 922 24 35 75; Calle Marina 7)
UK (Map pp140-1; ☎ 922 28 66 53; Plaza General Weyler 8)

DIRECTORY

FESTIVALS & EVENTS

Like many of their mainland cousins, Canarios love to let it all hang out at the islands' numerous fiestas and *ferias* (fairs). Carnaval is the wildest time, but there are many others throughout the year – August alone has more than 50 celebrations across the islands.

The great majority of these fiestas have a religious background (nearly every town has a patron saint's day) but all are occasions for having fun. *Romerías* (pilgrimages) are particularly noteworthy. Processions head to/from a town's main church to a chapel or similar location dedicated to the local patron saint or the Virgin Mary.

Many local fiestas are noted in city and town sections of this book and tourist offices can supply more detailed information. A few of the most outstanding include:

FEBRUARY
Virgen de la Candelaria (Festival of the Patron of the Archipelago) This intense festival, celebrated in Candelaria (Tenerife) on 2 February, derives from the supposed apparition of the Virgin Mary before the Guanches (indigenous Canarios). This festival is also celebrated on 15 August.

FEBRUARY/MARCH
Carnaval Several weeks of fancy-dress parades and merry-making across the islands end on the Tuesday, 47 days before Easter Sunday. Carnaval is at its wildest and most extravagant in Santa Cruz de Tenerife.

JULY
Bajada de la Virgen de las Nieves (Descent of the Virgin of the Snows) This fiesta is held only once every five years in Santa Cruz de la Palma (La Palma) on 21–30 July. The processions, dances and merrymaking constitute the island's premier religious festival.

Bajada de la Virgen de los Reyes (Descent of the Virgin) Held in early July every four years (2005, 2009 etc) in El Hierro, most of the island's population gathers to witness or join in a procession bearing a statue of the Virgin.

Día de San Buenaventura (Saint Buenaventura's Day) Betancuria (Fuerteventura) celebrates the town's patron saint on 14 July.

Romería de San Benito Abad (Pilgrimage of San Benito Abad) This festival is held on the first Sunday of the month in La Laguna (Tenerife).

AUGUST
Día de San Ginés (Saint Ginés day) This is held 25 August in Arrecife (Lanzarote).

Fiesta de la Rama This fiesta is held in Agaete (Gran Canaria) on 4 August.

Fiesta de Nuestra Señora de las Nieves (Feast Day of Our Lady of the Snows) Celebrated on 5 August, this is La Palma's principle fiesta.

Romería de San Roque (Pilgrimage of Saint Roch; dates vary) This annual festival fills Garachio's streets (Tenerife) with pilgrims and partygoers.

SEPTEMBER
Fiesta de la Virgen del Pino (Feast day of the Virgin of the Pine) Held in Teror (Gran Canaria) in the first week of September, this is the island's most important religious celebration. Festivities begin two weeks before these final key days.

Fiesta del Santísimo Cristo (Feast of the Holy Christ) This fiesta is held 7–15 September in La Laguna (Tenerife).

OCTOBER
Romería de Nuestra Señora de la Luz (Pilgrimage of Our Lady of Light) Held in mid-October in Las Palmas de Gran Canaria, this festival is marked by a boat procession.

13 DECEMBER
Día de Santa Lucía (Saint Lucía's Day) Celebrations occur all over Gran Canaria.

Arts Festivals

As well as an abundance of local festivals, the islands also host several important arts festivals every year, including the following:

JANUARY/FEBRUARY
Festival de Música de Canarias (Canary Music Festival) Celebrated simultaneously throughout the islands, particularly on Gran Canaria and Tenerife.

FEBRUARY/MARCH
Festival de Ópera (Opera Festival) Gran Canaria.

MAY
Festival de Ballet y Danza (Ballet and Dance Festival) This festival is well worth seeing (Gran Canaria).

AUGUST
Festival Son Latino Held in August in Playa de las Américas (Tenerife), this arts festival draws pop musicians from throughout Latin America. The festival is wildly popular, but residents sick and tired of the hordes of drunk concert-goers are trying to put an end to it.

SEPTEMBER
Encuentro Teatral Tres Continentes (aka Festival Internacional de Teatro de los Tres Mundos; Three Continents Theatre Encounter) Attracts theatre companies from Europe, South America and Africa to Agüimes (Gran Canaria).

OCTOBER/NOVEMBER
Festival Internacional de Cine (International Film Festival) Gran Canaria.

FOOD

Our Eating reviews feature the price ranges for main courses as a guide. That is, if a restaurant's cheapest main course costs €6 and its most expensive costs €20, our practicalities listing will record the following: mains €6 to €20. Prices for *menús del día* (set menus) may be included instead and occasionally we'll list such specialities as tapas instead of main courses. Check out the Food & Drink chapter on p47 for details on Canarian culinary delights.

GAY & LESBIAN TRAVELLERS

Gay and lesbian sex are both legal in Spain and hence in the Canary Islands. The age of consent is 16, the same as for heterosexuals. The Playa del Inglés, on the southern end of Gran Canaria, is where the bulk of Europe's gay crowd heads when holidaying in the Canaries, and the nightlife here bumps and grinds year-round. By day, nudist beaches are popular spots to hang out.

Spanish people generally adopt a 'live and let live' attitude to sexuality, so you shouldn't have any hassles in the Canary Islands. That said, some small rural towns may not know quite how to deal with overt displays of affection between same-sex couples. Gay magazines in Spanish and on sale at some newsstands include the monthly *Mensual*, which includes listings for gay bars, clubs and the like in the Canary Islands. Visit *Mensual* on line at www.mensual.com (Spanish only). Another worthwhile website is www.guiagay.com (in Spanish).

For information about gay groups in the islands, you might like to write in advance to: Colectivo de Gays y Lesbianas de Las Palmas, Apartado de Correos 707, 35080 Las Palmas de Gran Canaria.

HOLIDAYS

There are at least 14 official holidays per year in the Canary Islands. When a holiday falls close to a weekend, locals like to make a *puente* (bridge) – meaning they take the intervening day off too. On occasion, when a couple of holidays fall close to the same weekend, the *puente* becomes an *acueducto* (aqueduct)!

The eight main national holidays, observed throughout the islands and the rest of Spain (though the authorities seem to change their minds about some of these from time to time), are:

1 January Año Nuevo (New Year's Day)
March/April Viernes Santo (Good Friday)
1 May Fiesta del Trabajo (Labour Day)
15 August La Asunción de la Virgen (Feast of the Assumption)
12 October Día de la Hispanidad (National Day)
1 November Todos los Santos (All Saints' Day) Gets particular attention on Tenerife.
8 December La Inmaculada Concepción (Feast of the Immaculate Conception)
25 December Navidad (Christmas)

In addition, the regional government sets a further five holidays, while local councils allocate another two. Common dates include:

6 January Epifanía (Epiphany) or Día de los Reyes Magos (Three Kings' Day) Children receive presents on this day.
February/March Martes de Carnaval (Carnival Tuesday)
19 March Día de San Juan (St John's Day)
March/April Jueves Santo (Maundy Thursday)
30 May Día de las Islas Canarias (Canary Islands Day)
June Corpus Cristi (the Thursday after the eighth Sunday after Easter Sunday) In Las Palmas de Gran Canaria, La Laguna and La Orotava (Tenerife), locals prepare elaborate floral carpets to celebrate this feast day; the celebration is also big in Mazo and El Paso (La Palma).
25 July Día de Santiago Apóstol (Feast of St James the Apostle, Spain's patron saint) In Santa Cruz de Tenerife the day also marks the commemoration of the defence of the city against Horatio Nelson.
8 September Día del Pino (Pine Tree Day) This is particularly important on Gran Canaria.
6 December Día de la Constitución (Constitution Day)

INSURANCE

A travel-insurance policy to cover theft, loss and medical problems is a good idea. Some policies offer lower and higher medical-expense options; the higher ones are chiefly for countries such as the USA, which have extremely high medical costs. There is a wide variety of policies available, so check the small print.

Some policies specifically exclude 'dangerous activities', which can include scuba diving, motorcycling, even trekking. A locally acquired motorcycle licence is not valid under some policies.

You may prefer a policy which pays doctors or hospitals directly rather than you having to pay on the spot and claim later. If you have to claim later make sure you keep all documentation. Some policies ask you to call back (reverse charges) to a centre in your home country where an immediate assessment of your problem is made.

Check that the policy covers ambulances or an emergency flight home. See the Insurance section of the Health chapter (p254) for further details.

INTERNET ACCESS

If you plan to carry your notebook or palm-top computer with you, remember that the power-supply voltage in the countries you visit may vary from that at home, risking damage to your equipment. The best investment is a universal AC adapter for your appliance, which will enable you to plug it in anywhere without frying the innards.

Phone jacks in the Canary Islands are the standard American style RJ-11, which should make modem connection easy. All you need to ensure is that your accommodation has a phone connection in your room.

Many of the Canary Islands' resorts have at least one place where you can log onto the Internet and access your emails. Don't assume that every town, or even every island capital, can provide this. You'll generally pay about €2 per hour to log on.

Another option for collecting mail is to open a free email account on line with ekno. You can then access your mail from anywhere in the world from any Internet-connected machine running a standard Web browser. For more information, visit the ekno website at www.ekit.com.

LEGAL MATTERS

Should you be arrested, you will be allotted the free services of a *abogado de oficio* (duty solicitor), who may speak only Spanish. You are also entitled to make a phone call. If you use this to contact your embassy or consulate, it will probably be able to do no more than refer you to a lawyer who speaks your language. If you end up in court, the authorities are obliged to provide a translator.

Spanish *policía* (police) are, on the whole, more of a help than a threat to a law-abiding traveller. Most are certainly friendly enough to be approached for directions on the street. Unpleasant events, such as random drug searches, do occur but not frequently. There are three main types of *policía* – the Policía Nacional, the Policía Local and the Guardia Civil.

Should you need to contact the police, don't agonise over which kind to approach; any of them will do, but you may find that the Policía Local is the most helpful. The Government of the Canary Islands provides a toll-free telephone number (☎ 112), which ensures that any emergency situation can be attended to by the nearest police action. You can also call ☎ 902 10 21 12, a multilingual assistance line.

MAPS

You'll find driving and walking maps in bookshops, newsstands and in tourist offices. In general, these basic maps will do

---

DRUGS

Cannabis is the only legal drug, and only in amounts for personal use – which means very little.

Public consumption of any drug is, in principle, illegal, yet there are some bars where people smoke joints openly. Other bars will ask you to step outside if you light up. The only sure moral of these stories is to be very discreet if you do use cannabis.

Although there's a reasonable degree of tolerance when it comes to people having a smoke in their own home, it would be unwise in hotel rooms or guesthouses and could be risky in even the coolest of public places. The Canary Islands' proximity to northern Africa means that customs officers and the police are vigilant about putting the brakes on the drug trade between the two areas – you'd be a fool to get caught up in this business.

Be aware that some so-called 'public relations officers' for nightclubs in southern Tenerife's Las Americas area are little more than drug dealers, and it's best to avoid buying drugs from them. Authorities in the island's south are starting to come down heavily on those who sully the 'family friendly' image they're trying to cultivate for the region.

just fine to guide you through the large towns and around the islands' highways, though if you want more there are plenty of options.

To see all the Canaries together, Firestone's *Islas Canarias* map (1:150,000) is a good one and costs upwards of €7. The map is fine for getting oriented but the waters of the Atlantic take up so much space that detail is limited. Michelin also does excellent multi-island maps for about the same price, each showing blowups of major tourist centres. Check out *Tenerife, El Hierro, La Gomera & La Palma, Lanzarote & Fuerteventura*, and *Gran Canaria* (scales vary).

For walking or doing a bit of off-highway exploring, the German company Freytag & Berndt does some excellent maps of the western islands. Another option for the western islands are the high-quality maps Canario Juan José Santos publishes in various scales through Ediciones David. If you plan to hike alone then a descriptive hiking guidebook is invaluable. The national parks publish in-depth descriptions of hikes within their borders, and for hiking outside the parks, Discovery Walking guides, which publish books covering all islands except Fuerteventura, and Sunflower guides are both reliable.

To buy maps before you leave home, check out travel bookshops or the Spanish Bookstore on line at www.teachertrading .co.uk.

MONEY

You can get by easily enough with a single credit or debit card that allows you to withdraw cash from ATMs, but you may also want to take some travellers cheques and a second card (if you have it). This combination gives you a fallback if you lose a card or it lets you down.

Spain's currency is the euro. Notes come in denominations of €500, €200, €100, €50, €20, €10 and €5. Coins are €0.50, €0.20, €0.10, €0.5, €0.2 and €0.1.

To check exchange rates between the euro and other currencies, visit the website www.oanda.com.

ATMs

Like any good tax haven, the Canary Islands has a surfeit of banks, pretty much every one with a multilingual *cajeros automáticos* (ATMs). Honestly, you'll be amazed at some of the backwaters where'll you find ATMs.

Cash

Even if you're using a credit card you'll make a lot of your purchases with cash, so you need to carry some all the time. Small restaurants and shops may not accept cards.

Credit Cards

All major *tarjetas de crédito* (credit cards) and debit cards are widely accepted. They can be used for many purchases (including at petrol stations and larger supermarkets, who sometimes ask to see some form of ID) and in hotels and restaurants (although smaller establishments tend to accept cash only).

Cards can also be used in ATMs displaying the appropriate sign or, if you have no personal identification number (PIN), to obtain cash advances over the counter in many banks. Visa and MasterCard are among the most widely recognised for such transactions.

Be sure that you report a lost or stolen card immediately:

American Express (☎ 902 37 35 37)
Diner Club (☎ 91 547 74 00 in Madrid)
MasterCard/Eurocard (☎ 900 97 12 31)
Visa (☎ 900 97 44 45)

Moneychangers

You'll find exchange facilities at most air and sea ports on the islands. In resorts and cities that attract swarms of foreigners you'll find them easily – they're usually indicated by the word *cambio* (exchange). Most of the time they offer longer opening hours and quicker service than banks, but worse exchange rates. Wherever you change money, ask from the outset about commission, the terms of which differ from place to place, and confirm that exchange rates are as posted. A typical commission is 3%. Places that advertise 'no commission' usually make up the difference by offering poorer exchange rates.

Travellers Cheques

These are safe and easily cashed at banks and exchange offices (take along your passport) throughout the Canary Islands. Always keep the bank receipt listing the cheque numbers separate from the cheques themselves and log those you have already cashed. This will ease things if they're lost or stolen.

If your travellers cheques are in euros, you should pay no exchange charge when cashing them.

POST

Stamps are sold at every post office (*oficina de correos* or *correos*), most *estancos* (tobacconist shops; look for the yellow-on-brown 'Tabacos' sign) and some newsagents.

A postcard or letter weighing up to 20g costs €0.25 to send within the islands and to mainland Spain, €0.50 to other European countries, €0.75 to North America, Australia or New Zealand.

Delivery times aren't great: mail to other EU countries takes about a week, and sometimes just as long to the Spanish mainland; 10 days to North America and; about two weeks to Australia or New Zealand.

Poste restante (general delivery) mail can be addressed to you at *lista de correos* anywhere in the Canary Islands that has a post office. In the few towns on the islands with more than one post office, it will arrive at the main one unless another is specified in the address.

Take your passport when you go to pick up mail. It helps if people writing to you capitalise or underline your surname, and include the postcode. A typical *lista de correos* address looks like this:

Jane SMITH,
Lista de Correos
35080 Las Palmas de Gran Canaria
Islas Canarias, Spain

SOLO TRAVELLERS

Travellers heading out alone should have no qualms about the Canary Islands, though neither should they forget common-sense safety (see p238). Cost-wise, you may end up paying a little more, since most package deals base per-person prices on shared double rooms. Nevertheless, most *pensiones* and hotels offer either single rooms or discounts for single occupancy of a double room.

Solo travellers have endless options for activities to keep busy. Though hiking alone is not a good idea, you can sign up

for a guided, group hike, which can also be a good way to get to know other travellers. Boat cruises, bike excursions, scuba diving trips (see p41) and Spanish classes (see p238) are other options.

TELEPHONE

Pay phones once stood at nearly every corner, but the popularity of mobile phones has reduced their number considerably. Still, you won't have trouble spotting the distinctive blue boxes in even the smallest towns. You can use coins with most pay phones, though some require you to use a *tarjeta telefónica* (phonecard), which you can buy at tobacco stands or newsstands. In large towns, an alternative option is a telephone centre, a shop with various phone booths offering special rates.

Using the phone in Spain has no hidden secrets. If you're calling within the country (including the Canaries), all numbers have a total of nine digits beginning with 9. In the Canary Islands, numbers beginning with ☎ 928 are for the province of Gran Canaria, while ☎ 922 numbers are for the Tenerife province (see Phone Codes, following). Signs and business cards will often print just the last six digits of a phone number, confident that locals know the islands' phone codes.

Even local calls can be expensive, especially if you're calling from a hotel, where random fees can be tacked on. In general, a three-minute local call from a pay phone will cost about €0.20.

Contact a domestic operator by dialling ☎ 1009. A reverse-charge (collect) call is called *una llamada por cobro reverso*. For directory inquiries dial ☎ 11818, which has a charge of €0.30, though the call is free from a phone box.

Mobile Phones

Mobile telephones are widely used in the Canary Islands, as in the rest of Spain. The Canary Islands use GSM 900/1800, which is compatible with the rest of Europe and Australia but not with the North American GSM 1900 or the totally different system in Japan (though some North Americans have GSM 1900/900 phones that do work here). If you have a GSM phone, check with your service provider about using it on the islands, and beware of calls being routed internationally (very expensive for a 'local' call).

Spaniards, Canarios included, use mobile phones constantly, though it's considered bad form to talk on your mobile phone in restaurants or in packed public spaces like buses.

Phone Codes

Numbers that begin with ☎ 900 and ☎ 902 are toll-free and those that begin with '6' are mobile numbers.

El Hierro ☎ 922
Fuerteventura ☎ 928
Gran Canaria ☎ 928
La Gomera ☎ 922
La Palma ☎ 922
Lanzarote ☎ 928
Tenerife ☎ 922

Phonecards

Lonely Planet's ekno global communication service provides low-cost international calls; for local calls, and calls to mainland Spain, you're usually better off with a local phonecard. Ekno also offers free messaging services, email, travel information and an on-line travel vault, where you can securely store all your important documents. You can join on line at www.ekno.lonelyplanet .com, where you will find the local-access numbers for the 24-hour customer service centre. Once you have joined, always check the ekno website for the latest access numbers for each country and updates on new features.

TIME

Like most of Europe, the Canaries operate on the 24-hour clock, which for those accustomed to 'am' and 'pm' can take some getting used to.

The Canary Islands are on Greenwich Mean Time (GMT/UTC), plus an hour in summer for daylight-saving time. The islands keep the same time as the UK, Ireland and Portugal, and are always an hour behind mainland Spain and most of Europe. Neighbouring Morocco is on GMT/UTC year-round – so in summer it is an hour behind the Canary Islands even though it's further east!

Daylight-saving (summer) time starts on the last Sunday in March, when clocks are put forward one hour. Clocks are put back an hour on the last Sunday in October. When telephoning home you might also need to make allowances for daylight-saving time in your own country.

When it's noon in the islands, it's 1pm in Madrid and Paris, 4am in San Francisco, 7am in New York and Toronto, 8pm in Perth, 10pm in Sydney, and midnight in Auckland. See also the World Time Zones map (p256).

TOILETS

Public toilets are not common and rarely inviting. The easiest option is to wander into a bar or café and use its facilities. The polite thing to do is to have a coffee or the like before or after, but you're unlikely to raise too many eyebrows if you don't. This said, some curmudgeonly places in popular tourist areas post notices saying that their toilets are for clients only.

The cautious carry some toilet paper with them when out and about as many toilets lack it. If there's a bin beside the loo, put paper and so on in it – it's probably there because the local sewage system has trouble coping.

TOURIST INFORMATION

All major towns have a tourist office, and while you may have to wait patiently and politely to be attended, you can eventually get very good maps and information about the area. Though the Canary Government offers some region-wide information on their excellent website (www.canarias.org), the tourist offices themselves are run by the *cabildos* (governments) of each island. Contact them at each islands' Patronatos de Turismo (Head Tourist Office):

El Hierro (☎ 922 55 00 78; www.el-hierro.org; Calle Doctor Quintero Magdaleno 11, Valverde)
Fuerteventura (☎ 928 53 08 44; Calle Constitución 5, Puerto del Rosario)
Gran Canaria (☎ 928 21 96 00; www.turismograncanaria.com; Calle Leon y Castillo 17, Las Palmas de Gran Canaria)
La Gomera (☎ 922 14 15 12; www.gomera-island.com; Calle Real 4, San Sebastián)
La Palma (☎ 922 42 33 40, 922 41 21 06; www .lapalmaturismo.com; Avenida Marítima 34, Santa Cruz de la Palma)
Lanzarote (☎ 928 80 24 75; www.turismo lanzarote.com in Spanish; Calle Blas Cabrera Felipe, Arrecife)
Tenerife (☎ 922 23 95 92; www.webtenerife.com; Plaza de España, Santa Cruz)

VISAS

The Canary Islands are part of Spain. Hence all rules (on passports, visas, residency etc) that are pertinent to Spain apply equally here too.

Spain is part of the Schengen Convention, an agreement whereby all EU member countries (except the UK and Ireland) plus Iceland and Norway have abolished checks at common borders for nationals of those countries included in the agreement. Legal residents of one Schengen country do not require a visa for another such country. In addition, nationals of a number of other states, including the UK, Canada, Ireland, Japan, New Zealand and Switzerland, do not require visas for tourist visits of up to 90 days to any Schengen country.

Various other nationals not covered by the Schengen exemption can also spend up to 90 days in Spain without a visa. These include citizens of Australia, Israel and the USA. If you are from a country not mentioned in this section, you should check with a Spanish consulate whether you need a visa.

The standard tourist visa issued by Spanish consulates is the Schengen visa, valid for up to 90 days. It's generally good for travel in all other Schengen countries. However, individual Schengen countries may impose additional restrictions on certain nationalities. It is therefore worth checking visa regulations with the consulate of each Schengen country you plan to visit.

You must apply for the visa in your country of residence. In principle, if you are going to visit more than one Schengen country, you are supposed to apply for the visa at a consulate of your main destination country, or else the first country you intend to visit. It's worth applying early, especially in the busy summer months.

Those needing a visa must apply *in person* at the consulate. Postal applications are not accepted. You can't apply for more than two visas in any 12-month period and you cannot renew them once inside Spain. Options include 30- and 90-day single-entry visas, 90-day multiple-entry visas and various transit visas. Schengen visas are free for spouses and children of EU nationals.

Since passports are often not stamped on entry (unless you arrive by air from outside the Schengen area), the 90-day rule can generally be quite flexible, because no one can prove how long you have been in the country.

WOMEN TRAVELLERS

Harassment is much less frequent than the stereotypes of Spain would have you believe, and the country has one of the developed world's lowest incidences of reported rape. Any unpleasantness you might encounter is more likely to come from drunken northern European yobs in the big resorts than from the locals.

In towns you may get the occasional unwelcome stare, catcall or unnecessary comment, to which the best (and most galling) response is indifference. Don't get paranoid about what's being called out; the *piropo* – a harmless, mildly flirty compliment – is deeply ingrained in Spanish society and, if well delivered, even considered gallant.

The advice is really just the commonsense stuff you need to keep in mind anywhere. Think twice about going alone to isolated stretches of beach, lonely country areas or dark city streets at night. Where there are crowds – as there often are very late into the night in towns and cities – you're usually safer. It's inadvisable for a woman to hitchhike alone and not a great idea even for two women together.

Topless bathing and skimpy clothes are generally OK at the coastal resorts, but otherwise a little more modesty is the norm. Quite a few local young women feel no compunction about dressing to kill, but equally feel absolutely no obligation to respond to any male interest this arouses.

Transport

CONTENTS

THINGS CHANGE...

The information in this chapter is particularly vulnerable to change. Check directly with the airline or a travel agent to make sure you understand how a fare (and ticket you may buy) works and be aware of the security requirements for international travel. Shop carefully. The details given in this chapter should be regarded as pointers and are not a substitute for your own careful, up-to-date research.

GETTING THERE & AWAY

ENTERING THE CANARY ISLANDS

Citizens of the European Union (EU) member states and Switzerland can travel to the Canary Islands with just their national identity card. Nationals of the UK have to carry a full passport (UK visitor passports are not acceptable). All other nationalities must have a full valid passport.

Check that your passport's expiry date is at least some months away, or you may not be granted a visa, should you need one.

By law you are supposed to have your identity card or passport with you at all times in the Canaries, in case the police ask to see it. In practice this is unlikely to cause trouble. You might want to carry a photo-copy of your documentation instead of the real thing. You often need to flash one of these documents for registration when you take a hotel room.

As unfortunate as it is, you'll encounter far less hassle at immigration as a white European than as a black European or African. In general though, you are likely to find the whole deal of flying into a Canary Islands airport remarkably lackadaisical.

AIR
Airports & Airlines

Dozens of airlines, many of which you'll never have heard of, fly into the Canary Islands. All seven islands have airports. Tenerife, Gran Canaria and Lanzarote absorb nearly all the direct international flights and those from mainland Spain, while the others are principally for interisland hops.

There are two main airports on Tenerife. Tenerife Norte (Los Rodeos) handles just about all interisland flights and most of those to the Spanish mainland. The remainder of the scheduled flights and virtually all charter flights to the island are channelled to the more modern Tenerife Sur (Reina Sofía). Gran Canaria's airport is 16km south of Las Palmas. Lanzarote's Guasimeta airport lies a convenient 6km southwest of the capital, Arrecife.

The bulk of international flights serving the islands directly are charters. Remember that for charter flights you are obliged to ring to confirm your flight within 72 hours of departure.

For more details on airline services to/from each island, see Getting There & Away in the separate island chapters.

Tickets

Full-time students and those aged under 26 (under 30 in some countries) have access to better deals than other travellers. You have to show a document proving your date of birth or a valid International Student Identity Card (ISIC) when buying your ticket and boarding the plane.

Generally, there is nothing to be gained by buying a ticket directly from the airline.

DEPARTURE TAX

Departure tax is factored into the cost of your ticket, so you won't need to worry about last-minute cash searches as you prepare to fly home.

Discounted tickets are released to selected travel agents and specialist discount agencies, and these are usually the cheapest deals going.

One exception to this rule is booking on the Internet. Many airlines offer some excellent fares to Web surfers.

Another exception is a 'no-frills' carrier, which normally only sells tickets directly to travellers (again, usually over the Internet). Unlike the full-service airlines, no-frills carriers often make one-way tickets available at around half the return fare, so it is easy to put together an open-jaw ticket.

The cheapest time to fly is midweek on a night flight. Always check the arrival and departure times on these flights, as inconvenience is usually part of the price you pay for a low fare. You should not be surprised, in peak times at any rate, to find your flight delayed. Remember too that, once booked, you cannot alter your charter flight details. If you miss a charter flight, you have lost your money.

From Africa

There are weekly flights from Morocco with **Royal Air Maroc** (www.royalairmaroc.com) and from Senegal with **Air Senegal International** (www.air-senegal-international.com).

From Australia & New Zealand

There are no direct flights from Australia to the Canaries, so you'll have to book connecting flights via Madrid, Barcelona or another European capital. High-season return fares to Madrid or Barcelona cost from around A$2500. You then have to tack on the cost of the return flights between Europe and the Canaries.

From New Zealand, flights to Europe are via the USA and Asia. You can also fly from Auckland to pick up a connecting flight in either Melbourne or Sydney. Expect to pay at least NZ$3000 for a return flight to Barcelona or Madrid during the high season.

From Canada

There are no direct flights from Canada to Spain, let alone to its offshore islands. To reach the Canaries, you'll need to travel via the USA or a European hub. The thing to do is work out the best possible route/fare combination; a direct flight to London combined with an onward charter or package can often work out to be the cheapest and simplest method of reaching the Canaries.

From Continental Europe

There are plenty of packages and flights available in Continental Europe for the Canary Islands. Munich is a haven for discount travel agents and more mainstream budget-travel outlets. Parisian travel agents should also be able to put you in touch with some good deals.

From Spain, Air Europa, Iberia and Spanair all fly to the Canary Islands. They connect the islands with international destinations, usually via Madrid or Barcelona:
Air Europa (☎ 902 40 15 01; www.aireuropa.com)
Iberia (☎ 902 40 05 00; www.iberia.com)
Spanair (☎ 902 13 14 15; wwwspanair.com)

Lufthansa's subsidiary airline, **Condor** (☎ 928 57 92 93; www.condor.de in German), has frequent flights from many towns in Germany to Tenerife Sur, Las Palmas de Gran Canaria, Santa Cruz de la Palma, Arrecife (Lanzarote) and Puerto del Rosario (Fuerteventura).

Other airlines with frequent direct flights between Germany and the Canary Islands include:
Aero Lloyd (www.aerolloyd.com in Spanish)
Air Berlin (www.airberlin.de)
Germania (www.europe.tiscasli.co.uk)
Hapag-Lloyd Flug (www.hlx.com)
LTU (www.ltu.com)

Amsterdam is another popular departure point. **Martinair** (www.martinair.com) and **Transavia Airlines** (www.transavia.com) have several direct flights between Amsterdam and Tenerife Sur each week.

From South America

There's only one scheduled direct flight per week between the Canaries and South America – Iberia's Monday run between Caracas (Venezuela) and Tenerife. You can pay as little as €459 for a discount return ticket or as much as €1310 unrestricted one way. For all other transatlantic destinations, you will need to go via Barcelona or Madrid.

From the UK & Ireland

Discount air travel is big business in London. Check the weekend broadsheet papers for specials deals. Iberia flights all go via Madrid, and the standard return fare from London to Gran Canaria is around UK£300. At the time of writing, high-season return fares with British Airways were £250 (low-season £200). The discount travel agents can get you across for much less, usually on charter flights.

Air Europa (☎ 0870 240 1501; www.air-europa.co.uk) has flights from London (Gatwick) to both Gran Canaria and Tenerife via Madrid. **Monarch** (☎ 0870 040 5040; www.monarch-airlines.com), principally a charter company, also offers scheduled flights to Tenerife.

In the low season, discount fares to the Canaries can fall as low as UK£99 return. If your quotes are still way above this, you might try calling the **Air Travel Advisory Bureau** (☎ 020-7636 5000). If you tell the bureau your destination, it provides a list of relevant discount travel agents that it has on its books.

You needn't necessarily fly from London; many good deals are just as easily available from other major centres in the UK.

If you're travelling from Ireland, several charter flights leave every weekend for the Canary Islands. Check them out, then perhaps compare what is available with prices from London – getting across to London first might save you a few quid.

From the USA

There are no direct scheduled flights from the USA to the Canary Islands. The options are to take a package trip with a charter airline or to fly to mainland Spain or another European destination and take a connecting flight to the islands. It is also worth considering getting a cheap flight to Europe and then finding a package deal or charter flight to the Canaries from there.

If your European trip is not going to be confined to the islands, consult your travel agent about how best to incorporate them into your vacation.

Iberia flies nonstop between Madrid and New York. One-way fares cost around US$2318. You may get a better deal with another airline if you are prepared to fly via other European cities, so shop around. Spain's **Air Europa** (☎ 902 40 15 01; www.air europa.com) occasionally has good deals between Madrid and New York.

The very cheapest way of getting from the USA to Europe is by stand-by or courier flights. Stand-by fares are often sold at 60% of the normal one-way price.

Courier flights are where you accompany a parcel to its destination. Courier prices can be 10% to 40% below scheduled fares and tend to drop if you are prepared to fly at short notice. You'd be very lucky to get anything directly to the islands, but a New York–Madrid or New York–London return on a courier run can cost under US$400 in the low season (more expensive from the west coast). Always check conditions and details with the company.

SEA

Just about everyone flies to the Canaries. The only other alternative (apart from a very long swim!) is to take the **Trasmediterránea** (☎ 902 45 46 45; www.trasmediterranea.com) ferry, which carries vital supplies and cars to the islands. It sets out from Cádiz, on Spain's Mediterranean coast, every Tuesday at 6pm. After a long and often bumpy voyage, it arrives at Las Palmas de Gran Canaria at 8.45am on Thursday. It then proceeds to Santa Cruz de Tenerife, arriving at 3pm and hanging around until about midnight before sailing on to Santa Cruz de La Palma, which it reaches around 8am on Friday.

The boat back to the Spanish mainland leaves Santa Cruz de La Palma on Friday at 5pm and arrives in Santa Cruz de Tenerife at about 11pm. It leaves there at 10am on Saturday and calls by Las Palmas de Gran Canaria (2.30pm Saturday) and Arrecife on Lanzarote (9.30pm Saturday), from where it sets sail at 10pm for the Spanish mainland, arriving back in Cádiz at 10.45am on Monday.

Unless you particularly like rough ocean voyages for their own sake, or have a car that you simply must get to the islands, you're much better off just hopping on a plane.

Ferry fares range from €208 to €444 per person depending on the type of cabin and – we should hope so at such prices – include all meals. A car up to 2m long costs €174 one way, a motorcycle costs €73 and bicycles are free. You generally need to book at least a month in advance if you want to get a car aboard.

GETTING AROUND

AIR

Flying isn't the cheapest way to get around but, for longer interisland trips, it can work out substantially quicker than taking a ferry. **Binter** (☎ 902 39 13 92; www.bintercanarias.es) connects all seven islands with regular flights.

Another airline that flits between the islands is the modest **Islas Airways** (☎ 902 47 74 78; www.islasairways.com in Spanish), which flies Gran Canaria–Fuerteventura, Tenerife–La Palma, Tenerife–Gran Canaria, Tenerife–Fuerteventura, and La Palma–Gran Canaria.

Two other airlines serving the Spanish mainland have a few flights connecting the bigger islands. They are Air Europa (which flies to Tenerife, Gran Canaria, Lanzarote) and Spanair (to Tenerife, Gran Canaria, Lanzarote and Fuerteventura).

BICYCLE

Biking around the island is an extremely pleasant way to see the sights, but don't nec-

essarily expect drivers to accommodate you (or have much grasp of what it's like to be a cyclist tackling a hairpin bend uphill). Sadly, bicycle lanes in the urban environment are nonexistent, although beachside boulevards will generally include space for bike riding.

If you plan to bring your own bike, check with the airline about any hidden costs and whether it will have to be disassembled and packed for the journey. Taking your bike on the ferries is pretty straightforward – it's either free or very cheap, say around €3.

Fill all your water bottles, and then add one more: it can be hot on the open road and, more often than not, you won't find any water between villages.

Hire

You can rent mountain bikes and city bikes in various resorts and in the more tourist-orientated areas of the islands. Expect to pay €8 per day for the simplest machine and about €12 to €15 for a mountain bike. A deposit of around €50 is standard. Rental rates will include a helmet and some basic equipment.

BOAT

The islands are connected by ferries, 'fast ferries', and jetfoils. There are three main

FERRY Route	Duration	One-way Fare
Las Palmas de Gran Canaria–Santa Cruz de Tenerife	3½hr	€22.40
Las Palmas de Gran Canaria–Puerto del Rosario (Fuerteventura)	8hr	€28
Las Palmas de Gran Canaria–Arrecife (Lanzarote)	10hr	€28
Las Palmas de Gran Canaria–Morro Jable (Fuerteventura)	3¾hr	€29.50
Las Palmas de Gran Canaria–Santa Cruz de la Palma	20hr	€37
Arrecife (Lanzarote)–Puerto del Rosario (Fuerteventura)	1½hr	€14
Playa Blanca (Lanzarote)–Corralejo (Fuerteventura)	¾hr	€14.20
Santa Cruz de Tenerife–Agaete/Puerto de las Nieves (Gran Canaria)	1½hr	€29.70
Santa Cruz de Tenerife–Santa Cruz de la Palma	8hr	€28.10
Los Cristianos (Tenerife)–Santa Cruz de la Palma	5hr	€35
Los Cristianos (Tenerife)–Puerto de la Estaca (El Hierro)	5½hr	€21.75
Los Cristianos (Tenerife)–San Sebastián de la Gomera	¾hr	€16.90
San Sebastián de la Gomera–Puerto de la Estaca (El Hierro)	3hr	€21.75
JETFOIL Route	Duration	One-way Fare
Las Palmas de Gran Canaria–Santa Cruz de Tenerife	1hr 20min	€49.35-62.65
Las Palmas de Gran Canaria–Morro Jable	1½hr	€49.35-62.65

companies: **Naviera Armas** (☎ 902 45 65 00; www.navieraarmas.com), **Fred Olsen** (☎ 901 10 01 07; www.fredolsen.es) and **Trasmediterránea** (☎ 902 45 46 45; www.trasmediterranea.com). See the inter-island ferry and jetfoil tables on p250 for more information.

Do bear in mind that times, prices – even routes – can and do change. This isn't so important on major routes where there's plenty of choice, but it can mean a big delay if you're planning to travel a route which has only a couple of boats per day, or even week. See the colour map at the front of the book for interisland ferry routes.

BUS
A bus in the Canary Islands is called a *guagua*, pronounced 'wa-wa'. If you've bounced around Latin America, you'll be familiar with the term. Still, if you ask about *autobuses*, you'll be understood.

Every island has its own interurban service. One way or another they can get you to most of the main locations, but in many cases there are few runs each day. This is especially so on the smaller islands where the population is low and most people are obliged to have their own wheels.

The bigger islands of Tenerife and Gran Canaria each have an impressive public transport system that covers the whole island. Frequency, however, varies enormously: from a regular service between major towns to a couple of runs per day for transporting workers and school kids to/from the capital.

Check the timetable carefully before you travel at the weekend. Even on the bigger islands' major runs, a frequent weekday service can trickle off to just a few departures on Saturday and one, or none, on Sunday.

In the larger towns and cities, buses leave from an *estación de guaguas* (bus station). In villages and small towns, they usually terminate on a particular street or plaza. You buy your ticket on the bus. Bus companies include:

Arrecife Bus (☎ 928 81 15 22) Good service for Lanzarote's tourist areas, but minimal elsewhere.
Global (☎ 902 38 11 10; www.globalsu.net in Spanish) Excellent service all over Gran Canaria.
Servicio Insular de Guagua (☎ 922 55 07 29; fax 922 55 14 96) El Hierro's modest bus service.
Servicio Regular Gomera (☎ 922 14 11 01; www.servicioregulargomera.com) La Gomera's service.

Tiadhe (☎ 928 85 21 66) Limited service, with 13 lines operating on Fuerteventura.
TITSA (☎ 922 53 13 00; www.titsa.com) Excellent, comprehensive service on Tenerife.
Transportes Insular La Palma (☎ 922 41 19 24; www.transporteslapalma.com) La Palma's service.

Bus Passes
On some of the islands you can buy a Bonobus card (called a Tarjeta Insular on Gran Canaria), which usually costs €12. They're sold at bus stations and shops such as newsagents. Insert the card into the machine on the bus, tell the drivers where you are going and they will deduct the fare from the card. You get about 30% off standard fares with one, so they are a good investment if you intend to use the buses a lot.

Costs
Fares, especially if you invest in a Bonobus card, are reasonable. Destinations within each island are calculated pro rata according to distance.

CAR & MOTORCYCLE
Bringing Your Own Vehicle
Unless you're intending to settle on the islands, there's no advantage whatsoever in bringing your own vehicle. Transport costs on the ferry from Cádiz in mainland Spain are savage and car hire rates on the islands are significantly cheaper than in most EU countries. If you're one of the very rare visitors to bring their own vehicle, you will need registration papers and an International Insurance Certificate (or a Green Card). Your insurance company will issue this.

Driving Licence
Be sure to pack your driving licence if you intend to hire a car in the Canary Islands. EU licences are recognised here, as throughout Spain. Other foreign licences should be accompanied by an International Driving Permit (in practice, your own driving licence will more often than not suffice), which are available from automobile clubs in your country and valid for 12 months.

Fuel
Gasolina is much cheaper in the Canary Islands than elsewhere on Spanish territory because it's free from normal consumer taxes.

You will not find leaded petrol anywhere nowadays, but *sin plomo* (lead-free) petrol is available pretty much everywhere. Prices vary slightly between service stations and fluctuate according to oil tariffs, OPEC (Organisation of the Petroleum Exporting Countries) arm twisting and tax policy. The following prices can serve only as a guide: lead free (95 octane) costs €0.60 and 98 octane super (sometimes known as Súper Star) costs around €0.65. You can pay with major credit cards at most service stations.

Hire

If you're contemplating this, remember to pack your driving licence, which is required for any vehicle over 50cc. You need to be at least 21 years old and have held a driver's licence for a minimum of two years. It's easier, and with some companies obligatory, to pay with a credit card – although they do then have a hold over you if something goes wrong. Out on the road, always drive with your licence, passport and rental agreement on board.

All the big international car-rental companies are represented in the Canary Islands and there are plenty of local operators too. If you intend to stay on one island for any length of time, it might be worth booking a car in advance, for example in a fly/drive deal.

No matter what you rent, make sure you understand what is included in the price (unlimited kilometres, tax, insurance, collision damage waiver and so on) and what your liabilities are, and that you examine the rental agreement carefully – difficult if it is in Spanish only!

Multinational companies such as **Hertz** (☎ 901 10 07 77; www.hertz.es), **Avis** (☎ 902 18 08 54; www.avis.com), **Europcar/BC Betacar** (☎ 922 37 28 56; www.europcar.is) operate on all or most of the islands. Local operators worth trying include **Cicar** (☎ 928 82 29 00; www.cicar.com).

It's well worth shopping around and picking up a few brochures. In the big resorts some operators quote rates that are seductively and misleadingly low. That's because insurance, which can more than double the cost, isn't included. There are other incidentals (some optional) such as collision damage waiver, extra passenger cover and 5% IGIC (General Indirect Tax to the Canary Islands) to look out for.

Generally, you can't take a hire car from one island to another without the company's explicit permission. An exception for most companies is the Fuerteventura–Lanzarote sea crossing – most have no problem with you taking your car from one to the other, and in some cases you can hire on one island and drop the car off on the other.

Check before you set out that the phone number of the rental company features on the copy of the rental agreement that you should be given (you're required by law to carry this with you). Some agents also offer a 24-hour mobile phone contact.

Insurance

For a small extra fee you can usually boost the travel insurance coverage on your vehicle – and it's a good idea to do so. The number of dinged-up hire cars certainly makes you wonder if anyone's getting a nasty shock when the credit card bills come in. All the car hire companies have insurance, and you will have to pay for it in one way or another. Driving on a dirt road will generally render your policy null and void, so take this into account.

Purchase

Only residents of Spain can buy a car in the Canaries, and only those who can prove residence in the Canary Islands may avail themselves of the local tax breaks to buy a car cheaply.

Road Conditions

Road conditions are generally excellent, with plenty of roadworks keeping up the high standards. Driving, even in the biggest cities of Las Palmas de Gran Canaria and Santa Cruz de Tenerife, doesn't present particular difficulties, although the traffic can be a little intense. Parking, however, can be more problematic. Most city centres and several smaller towns operate restricted meter parking. Otherwise, there are several paying carparks in the two capitals.

Road Rules

The minimum age for driving cars is 18. If fitted, rear seatbelts must be worn – there are fines for failure to comply with this. Driving takes place on the right-hand side of the road.

Motorcyclists should use headlights at all times, though few locals do. Crash helmets are obligatory when riding any motorised bikes. The minimum age for riding bikes and scooters up to 50cc is 16 (no licence required). For anything more powerful, you'll need to produce your driving licence.

In built-up areas the speed limit is generally 40km/h, rising to a maximum of 100km/h on major roads and 120km/h on *autovías* (motorways).

The blood-alcohol limit is 0.08% and random breath-testing is carried out.

TAXI

You could tour around an island by taxi but it's a very expensive way to go. A (very) few taxi drivers operating between towns are sharkish and reluctant to set the meter. It's wise to confirm the fare (in most cases there are set tariffs) before taking (or being taken for) a ride.

TRANSPORT

Health

CONTENTS

BEFORE YOU GO

Prevention is the key to staying healthy while abroad. Some predeparture planning will save trouble later. See your dentist before a long trip, carry a spare pair of contact lenses and glasses, and take your optical prescription with you. Bring medications in their original, clearly labelled, containers. A signed and dated letter from your physician describing your medical conditions and medications, including generic names, is also a good idea. If carrying syringes or needles, be sure to have a physician's letter documenting their medical necessity.

INSURANCE

For EU citizens, an E111 form, available from health centres (and UK post offices), covers most medical care. It doesn't cover nonemergencies or emergency repatriation home. You'll still have to pay for medicine bought from pharmacies, even if prescribed, and perhaps for a few tests and procedures. An E111 is no good for private medical consultations and treatment in the Canaries; this includes most dentists and some of the better clinics and surgeries.

Citizens from other countries should find out if there's a reciprocal arrangement for free medical care between their country and the Canaries. If you need health insurance, strongly consider a policy that covers for the worst possible scenario, such as an accident requiring an emergency flight home.

Find out in advance if your insurance plan will make direct payments to providers or reimburse you later for overseas health expenditures. The former option is usually preferable, since it doesn't require you to pay out of pocket in a foreign country.

RECOMMENDED VACCINATIONS

No jabs are required to travel to Spain. The World Health Organisation (WHO), however, recommends that all travellers should be covered for diphtheria, tetanus, measles, mumps, rubella and polio, regardless of their destination. Since most vaccines don't produce immunity until at least two weeks after they're given, visit a physician at least six weeks before departure.

ONLINE RESOURCES

The WHO's publication *International Travel and Health* is revised annually and is available online at www.who.int/ith/. Other useful websites include www.mdtravel health.com (travel-health recommendations for every country; updated daily), www.fitfor travel.scot.nhs.uk (general travel advice for the layperson), www.ageconcern.org.uk (advice on travel for elderly people) and www.mariestopes.org.uk (information on women's health and contraception).

IN TRANSIT

DEEP VEIN THROMBOSIS

Blood clots may form in the legs during plane flights, chiefly because of prolonged immobility. The longer the flight, the greater the risk. The chief symptom of deep vein thrombosis (DVT) is swelling or pain in the foot, ankle or calf, usually, but not always, just on one side. When a blood clot travels to the lungs, it may cause chest pain and breathing difficulties. Travellers with any of these symptoms should immediately seek medical attention.

To prevent the development of DVT on long flights, you should walk about the cabin, contract the leg muscles while sitting, drink plenty of fluids and avoid alcohol and tobacco.

JET LAG
To avoid jet lag (common when crossing more than five time zones), drink plenty of nonalchoholic fluids and eat light meals. Upon arrival, seek exposure to natural sunlight and readjust your schedule (for meals, sleep and so on) as soon as possible.

IN THE CANARY ISLANDS
AVAILABILITY OF HEALTH CARE
If you need an ambulance call ☎ 112 (the pan-European emergency telephone number, which can be called for urgent medical assistance). An alternative emergency number is ☎ 061 for Urgencias Salud (Medical Emergencies). For emergency treatment go straight to the *urgencias* (casualty) section of the nearest hospital.

Good health care is readily available. For minor, self-limiting illnesses, pharmacists can give valuable advice and sell over-the-counter medication. They can also advise when more specialised help is required and point you in the right direction.

The standard of dental care is usually good; however, it is sensible to have a dental checkup before a long trip.

TRAVELLER'S DIARRHOEA
If you develop diarrhoea, be sure to drink plenty of fluids, preferably an oral rehydration solution such as Dioralyte. If diarrhoea is bloody, persists for more than 72 hours or is accompanied by fever, shaking, chills or severe abdominal pain, you should seek medical attention.

ENVIRONMENTAL HAZARDS
Heat Exhaustion
Heat exhaustion occurs following excessive fluid loss with inadequate replacement of fluids and salt. Symptoms include headache, dizziness and tiredness. Dehydration is already happening by the time you feel thirsty – aim to drink sufficient water to produce pale, diluted urine. To treat heat exhaustion, replace fluids through water and/or fruit juice, and cool the body with cold water and fans.

Insect Bites & Stings
Mosquitoes are found in most parts of Europe. They may not carry malaria, but they can cause irritation and infected bites. Use a DEET-based insect repellent.

Bees and wasps cause real problems only to those with a severe allergy (anaphylaxis). If you have a severe allergy to bee or wasp stings, carry an 'epipen' or similar adrenaline injection.

Scorpions are mercifully rarer on the Canary Islands than in mainland Spain. Their sting can be distressingly painful but isn't fatal.

In forested areas watch out for the hairy reddish-brown caterpillars of the pine processionary moth. They live in silvery nests in the pine trees and, in spring, leave the nest to march in long lines (hence the name). Touching the caterpillars' hairs sets off a severely irritating allergic skin reaction.

Check for ticks if you have been walking where sheep and goats graze: they can cause skin infections and other more serious diseases.

TRAVELLING WITH CHILDREN
Make sure children are up to date with routine vaccinations. Discuss possible travel vaccines well before departure, as some are not suitable for children under a year old. Lonely Planet's *Travel with Children* includes travel-health advice for younger children.

WOMEN'S HEALTH
Travelling during pregnancy is usually possible but there are important things to consider. Always seek a medical checkup before planning your trip. The most risky times for travel are during the first 12 weeks of pregnancy and after 30 weeks.

SEXUAL HEALTH
Condoms are readily available but emergency contraception may not be, so take the necessary precautions. When buying condoms, look for a European CE mark, which means they have been rigorously tested, and then keep them in a cool, dry place or they may crack and perish.

HEALTH

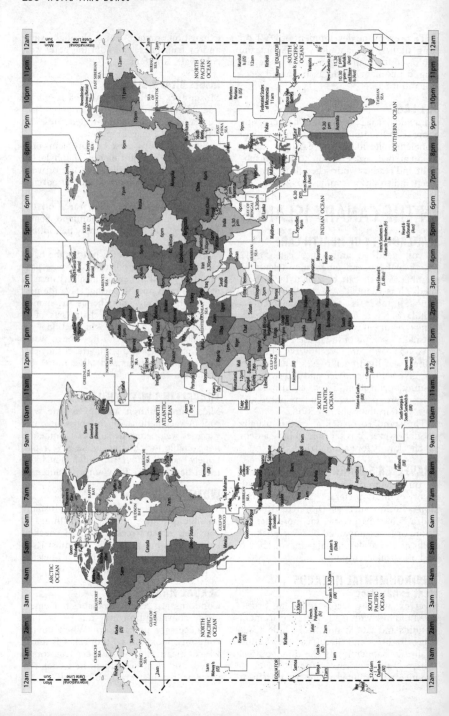

Language

CONTENTS

The language of the Canary Islands is Spanish *(español)*, which many Spanish people refer to as *castellano* (Castilian) to distinguish it from other mainland tongues such as Basque and Catalan. Spanish is the most widely spoken of the Romance languages – the group of languages derived from Latin, which includes French, Italian, Portuguese and Romanian.

See the Food & Drink chapter (pp47–55) for information on food and useful words and phrases for use when ordering at a restaurant (Eat Your Words, p52). For a more comprehensive guide to the language than we're able to offer here, pick up a copy of Lonely Planet's *Spanish phrasebook*.

If you'd like to learn the language in greater depth, courses are available in Las Palmas de Gran Canaria (see p68) and La Laguna (p148). See p238 for more information on language courses.

PRONUNCIATION

Spanish spelling is phonetically consistent, meaning that there's a clear and consistent relationship between what you see in writing and how it's pronounced. In addition, most Spanish sounds have English equivalents, so English speakers shouldn't have much trouble being understood.

Those steeped in the *castellano* of the central and northern mainland will be surprised by the Latin American lilt of the Canaries accent. It also bears a closer to the resemblance to what you hear in Andalucía than to mainland Spanish.

The lisp (like 'th' in 'thin') you'd normally expect with **z** and **c** before vowels is pronounced more as a sibilant 's', and **s** itself is hardly pronounced at all – it's more like an aspirated 'h' – for example, Las Palmas sounds more like Lah Palmah! The swallowing of consonants like this is a marked feature of Canaries Spanish, and even solid speakers of the language may find themselves wondering just how much they really understood on hearing a lively *charla* (chat) among Canarios.

Vowels

a	as in 'father'
e	as in 'met'
i	as in 'marine'
o	as in 'or' (without the 'r' sound)
u	as in 'rule'; the 'u' is not pronounced after **q** and in the letter combinations **gue** and **gui**, unless it's marked with a diaeresis (eg *argüir*), in which case it's pronounced as English 'w'
y	at the end of a word or when it stands alone, it's pronounced as the Spanish **i** (eg *ley*); between vowels within a word it's as the 'y' in 'yonder'

Consonants

As a rule, Spanish consonants resemble their English counterparts, with the exceptions listed below.

While the consonants **ch**, **ll** and **ñ** are generally considered distinct letters, **ch** and **ll** are now often listed alphabetically under **c** and **l** respectively. The letter **ñ** is still treated as a separate letter and comes after **n** in dictionaries.

b	similar to English 'b', but softer; **b** is referred to as 'b larga'
c	as in 'celery' before **e** and **i**; otherwise as English 'k'
ch	as in 'choose', although in the Spanish of the Canaries it can sound more like a 'y'. For example, Guanche is often pronounced 'Guanye'

d as in 'dog' when initial or preceded by **l** or **n**; elsewhere as the 'th' in 'then'. Often not pronounced at all when at the end of a word.

g as the 'ch' in the Scottish *loch* before **e** and **i** ('kh' in our guides to pronunciation); elsewhere, as in 'go'

h always silent

j as the 'ch' in the Scottish *loch* (written as 'kh' in our guides to pronunciation)

ll as the 'y' in 'yellow'

ñ as the 'ni' in 'onion'

r a rolled 'r'; longer and stronger when initial or doubled

rr very strongly rolled

v similar to English 'b', but softer; **v** is referred to as 'b corta'

x as the 'x' in 'taxi' when between two vowels; as the 's' in 'say' when preceding a consonant

z as the 's' in 'sun' (not as the 'th' in 'thin' as in most of mainland Spain)

Word Stress

Stress is indicated by italics in the pronunciation guides included with all the words and phrases in this language guide. In general, words ending in vowels or the letters **n** or **s** have stress on the next-to-last syllable, while those with other endings have stress on the last syllable. Thus *vaca* (cow) and *caballos* (horses) both carry stress on the next-to-last syllable, while *ciudad* (city) and *infeliz* (unhappy) are both stressed on the last syllable.

Written accents indicate a stressed syllable, and will almost always appear in words that don't follow the rules above, eg *sótano* (basement), *porción* (portion).

GENDER & PLURALS

In Spanish, nouns are either masculine or feminine, and there are rules to help determine gender (there are of course some exceptions). Feminine nouns generally end with **-a** or with the groups **-ción**, **-sión** or **-dad**. Other endings typically signify a masculine noun. Endings for adjectives also change to agree with the gender of the noun they modify (masculine/feminine **-o/-a**). Where both masculine and feminine forms are included in this language guide, they are separated by a slash, with the masculine form first, eg *perdido/a*.

If a noun or adjective ends in a vowel, the plural is formed by adding **s** to the end. If it ends in a consonant, the plural is formed by adding **es** to the end.

ACCOMMODATION

I'm looking for ...	Estoy buscando ...	e·stoy boos·kan·do ...
Where is ...?	¿Dónde hay ...?	don·de ai ...
a hotel	un hotel	oon o·tel
a boarding house	una pensión/ residencial/ un hospedaje	oo·na pen·syon/ re·see·den·syal/ oon os·pe·da·khe
a youth hostel	un albergue juvenil	oon al·ber·ge khoo·ve·neel
I'd like a room.	Quisiera una habitación ...	kee·sye·ra oo·na a·bee·ta·syon ...
double	doble	do·ble
single	individual	een·dee·vee·dwal
twin	con dos camas	kon dos ka·mas
How much is it per ...?	¿Cuánto cuesta por ...?	kwan·to kwes·ta por ...
night	noche	no·che
person	persona	per·so·na
week	semana	se·ma·na

Does it include breakfast?
¿Incluye el desayuno? een·kloo·ye el de·sa·yoo·no
May I see the room?
¿Puedo ver la habitación? pwe·do ver la a·bee·ta·syon

MAKING A RESERVATION
(for phone or written requests)

To ...	A ...
From ...	De ...
Date	Fecha
I'd like to book ...	Quisiera reservar ... (see the list under 'Accommodation' for bed and room options)
in the name of ...	en nombre de ...
for the nights of ...	para las noches del ...
credit card ...	tarjeta de crédito ...
number	número
expiry date	fecha de vencimiento
Please confirm ...	Puede confirmar ...
availability	la disponibilidad
price	el precio

I don't like it.
No me gusta.   no me *goos*·ta
It's fine. I'll take it.
OK. La alquilo.   o·*kay* la al·*kee*·lo
I'm leaving now.
Me voy ahora.   me *voy* a·*o*·ra

full board	pensión	pen·*syon*
	completa	kom·*ple*·ta
private/shared	baño privado/	*ba*·nyo pree·*va*·do/
bathroom	compartido	kom·par·*tee*·do
too expensive	demasiado caro	de·ma·*sya*·do *ka*·ro
cheaper	más económico	mas e·ko·*no*·mee·ko
discount	descuento	des·*kwen*·to

CONVERSATION & ESSENTIALS

When talking to people familiar to you or younger than you, it's usual to use the informal form of 'you', *tú*, rather than the polite form *Usted*. The polite form is used in all cases in this guide; where options are given, the form is indicated by the abbreviations 'pol' and 'inf'.

In Canaries Spanish the standard second person plural pronoun of mainland Spain, *vosotros* (you), is rarely heard. Instead, the more formal *Ustedes* is used.

Hello.	Hola.	o·la
Good morning.	Buenos días.	*bwe*·nos *dee*·as
Good afternoon.	Buenas tardes.	*bwe*·nas *tar*·des
Good evening/	Buenas noches.	*bwe*·nas *no*·ches
night.		
Goodbye.	Adiós.	a·*dyos*
Bye/See you soon.	Hasta luego.	*as*·ta *lwe*·go
Yes.	Sí.	see
No.	No.	no
Please.	Por favor.	por fa·*vor*
Thank you.	Gracias.	*gra*·syas
Many thanks.	Muchas gracias.	*moo*·chas *gra*·syas
You're welcome.	De nada.	de *na*·da
Pardon me.	Perdón/	per·*don*
	Discúlpeme.	dees·*kool*·pe·me

(before requesting information, for example)

Sorry. Lo siento.   lo see·*en*·to
(when apologizing)
Excuse me. Permiso.   per·*mee*·so
(when asking permission to pass, for example)

How are things?
¿Qué tal?   ke tal
What's your name?
¿Cómo se llama Usted?   *ko*·mo se *ya*·ma *oo*·ste (pol)
¿Cómo te llamas?   *ko*·mo te *ya*·mas (inf)

My name is ...
Me llamo ...   me *ya*·mo ...
It's a pleasure to meet you.
Mucho gusto.   *moo*·cho *goos*·to
Where are you from?
¿De dónde es/eres?   de *don*·de es/e·res (pol/inf)
I'm from ...
Soy de ...   soy de ...
Where are you staying?
¿Dónde está alojado?   *don*·de es·*ta* a·lo·*kha*·do (pol)
¿Dónde estás alojado?   *don*·de es·*tas* a·lo·*kha*·do (inf)
May I take a photo?
¿Puedo hacer una foto?   *pwe*·do a·*sair* *oo*·na *fo*·to

DIRECTIONS

How do I get to ...?
¿Cómo puedo llegar a ...?   *ko*·mo *pwe*·do lye·*gar* a
Is it far?
¿Está lejos?   es·*ta* *le*·khos
Go straight ahead.
Siga/Vaya derecho.   *see*·ga/*va*·ya de·*re*·cho
Turn left.
Doble a la izquierda.   *do*·ble a la ees·*kyer*·da
Turn right.
Doble a la derecha.   *do*·ble a la de·*re*·cha
I'm lost.
Estoy perdido/a.   es·*toy* per·*dee*·do/a
Can you show me (on the map)?
¿Me lo podría indicar   me lo po·*dree*·a een·dee·*kar*
(en el mapa)?   (en el *ma*·pa)

here	aquí	a·*kee*
there	allí	a·*yee*
avenue	avenida	a·ve·*nee*·da
street	calle/paseo	*ka*·lye/pa·*se*·o
traffic lights	semáforos	se·*ma*·fo·ros
north	norte	*nor*·te
south	sur	soor
east	este	*es*·te
west	oeste	o·*es*·te

SIGNS	
Entrada	Entrance
Salida	Exit
Abierto	Open
Cerrado	Closed
Información	Information
Prohibido	Prohibited
Prohibido Fumar	No Smoking
Comisaría	Police Station
Servicios/Aseos	Toilets
Hombres	Men
Mujeres	Women

LANGUAGE

EMERGENCIES

Help!	¡Socorro!	so·ko·ro
Fire!	¡Incendio!	een·sen·dyo
Go away!	¡Vete!/¡Fuera!	ve·te/fwe·ra

Call ...!	¡Llame a ...!	ya·me a
the police	la policía	la po·lee·see·a
a doctor	un médico	oon me·dee·ko
an ambulance	una ambulancia	oo·na am·boo·lan·sya

It's an emergency.
Es una emergencia.   es oo·na e·mer·khen·sya
Could you help me, please?
¿Me puede ayudar,   me pwe·de a·yoo·dar
por favor?   por fa·vor
I'm lost.
Estoy perdido/a.   es·toy per·dee·do/a
Where are the toilets?
¿Dónde están los baños? don·de es·tan los ba·nyos

HEALTH

I'm sick.
Estoy enfermo/a.   es·toy en·fer·mo/a
I need a doctor.
Necesito un médico   ne·se·see·to oon me·dee·ko
(que habla inglés).   (ke a·bla een·gles)
Where's the hospital?
¿Dónde está el hospital? don·de es·ta el os·pee·tal
I'm pregnant.
Estoy embarazada.   es·toy em·ba·ra·sa·da
I've been vaccinated.
Estoy vacunado/a.   es·toy va·koo·na·do/a

I'm allergic to ...	Soy alérgico/a a ...	soy a·ler·khee·ko/a a ...
antibiotics	los antibióticos	los an·tee·byo·tee·kos
penicillin	la penicilina	la pe·nee·see·lee·na
nuts	las fruta secas	las froo·tas se·kas
peanuts	los cacahuetes	los ka·ka·we·tes

I'm ...	Soy ...	soy ...
asthmatic	asmático/a	as·ma·tee·ko/a
diabetic	diabético/a	dya·be·tee·ko/a
epileptic	epiléptico/a	e·pee·lep·tee·ko/a

I have ...	Tengo ...	ten·go ...
a cough	tos	tos
diarrhea	diarrea	dya·re·a
a headache	un dolor de cabeza	oon do·lor de ka·be·sa
nausea	náusea	now·se·a

LANGUAGE DIFFICULTIES

Do you speak (English)?
¿Habla/Hablas (inglés)? a·bla/a·blas (een·gles) (pol/inf)
Does anyone here speak English?
¿Hay alguien que   ai al·gyen ke
hable inglés?   a·ble een·gles
I (don't) understand.
Yo (no) entiendo.   yo (no) en·tyen·do
How do you say ...?
¿Cómo se dice ...?   ko·mo se dee·se ...
What does ...mean?
¿Qué quiere decir ...? ke kye·re de·seer ...

Could you please ...?	¿Puede ..., por favor?	pwe·de ... por fa·vor
repeat that	repetirlo	re·pe·teer·lo
speak more slowly	hablar más despacio	a·blar mas des·pa·syo
write it down	escribirlo	es·kree·beer·lo

NUMBERS

1	uno	oo·no
2	dos	dos
3	tres	tres
4	cuatro	kwa·tro
5	cinco	seen·ko
6	seis	says
7	siete	sye·te
8	ocho	o·cho
9	nueve	nwe·ve
10	diez	dyes
11	once	on·se
12	doce	do·se
13	trece	tre·se
14	catorce	ka·tor·se
15	quince	keen·se
16	dieciséis	dye·see·says
17	diecisiete	dye·see·sye·te
18	dieciocho	dye·see·o·cho
19	diecinueve	dye·see·nwe·ve
20	veinte	vayn·te
21	veintiuno	vayn·tee·oo·no
30	treinta	trayn·ta
31	treinta y uno	trayn·ta ee oo·no
40	cuarenta	kwa·ren·ta
50	cincuenta	seen·kwen·ta
60	sesenta	se·sen·ta
70	setenta	se·ten·ta
80	ochenta	o·chen·ta
90	noventa	no·ven·ta
100	cien	syen
101	ciento uno	syen·to oo·no
200	doscientos	do·syen·tos
1000	mil	meel
5000	cinco mil	seen·ko meel

SHOPPING & SERVICES

I'd like to buy ...
Quisiera comprar ... kee-*sye*-ra kom-*prar* ...
I'm just looking.
Sólo estoy mirando. so-lo es-*toy* mee-*ran*-do
May I look at it?
¿Puedo mirar(lo/la)? pwe-do mee-*rar*-(lo/la)
How much is it?
¿Cuánto cuesta? kwan-to kwes-ta
That's too expensive for me.
Es demasiado caro es de-ma-*sya*-do *ka*-ro
para mí. pa-ra mee
Could you lower the price?
¿Podría bajar un poco po-*dree*-a ba-*khar* oon po-ko
el precio? el pre-syo
I don't like it.
No me gusta. no me *goos*-ta
I'll take it.
Lo llevo. lo ye-vo

Do you accept ...?	*¿Aceptan ...?*	a-sep-*tan* ...
credit cards	*tarjetas de crédito*	tar-*khe*-tas de kre-dee-to
travellers cheques	*cheques de viajero*	che-kes de vya-*khe*-ro

less	*menos*	me-nos
more	*más*	mas
large	*grande*	gran-de
small	*pequeño/a*	pe-*ke*-nyo/a

I'm looking for the ...	*Estoy buscando ...*	es-*toy* boos-*kan*-do
ATM	*el cajero automático*	el ka-*khe*-ro ow-to-*ma*-tee-ko
bank	*el banco*	el ban-ko
bookstore	*la librería*	la lee-bre-*ree*-a
embassy	*la embajada*	la em-ba-*kha*-da
laundry	*la lavandería*	la la-van-de-*ree*-a
market	*el mercado*	el mer-*ka*-do
pharmacy/ chemist	*la farmacia/ la botica*	la far-*ma*-sya/ la bo-*tee*-ka
post office	*correos*	ko-*re*-os
supermarket	*el supermercado*	el soo-per-mer-*ka*-do
tourist office	*la oficina de turismo*	la o-fee-*see*-na de too-*rees*-mo

What time does it open/close?
¿A qué hora abre/cierra? a ke o-ra a-bre/sye-ra
I want to change some money/travellers cheques.
Quiero cambiar dinero/ kye-ro kam-*byar* dee-*ne*-ro/
cheques de viajero. che-kes de vya-*khe*-ro

What is the exchange rate?
¿Cuál es el tipo de kwal es el *tee*-po de
cambio? kam-byo
I want to call ...
Quiero llamar a ... kye-ro lya-*mar* a ...

airmail	*correo aéreo*	ko-*re*-o a-e-re-o
letter	*carta*	*kar*-ta
registered mail	*correo certificado*	ko-*re*-o ser-tee-fee-*ka*-do
stamps	*sellos*	se-los

TIME & DATES

What time is it?	*¿Qué hora es?*	ke o-ra es
It's one o'clock.	*Es la una.*	es la *oo*-na
It's seven o'clock.	*Son las siete.*	son las sye-te
midnight	*medianoche*	me-dya-*no*-che
noon	*mediodía*	me-dyo-*dee*-a
half past two	*dos y media*	dos ee me-dya

now	*ahora*	a-o-ra
today	*hoy*	oy
tonight	*esta noche*	es-ta *no*-che
tomorrow	*mañana*	ma-*nya*-na
yesterday	*ayer*	a-yer

Monday	*lunes*	*loo*-nes
Tuesday	*martes*	mar-tes
Wednesday	*miércoles*	*myer*-ko-les
Thursday	*jueves*	khwe-ves
Friday	*viernes*	*vyer*-nes
Saturday	*sábado*	sa-ba-do
Sunday	*domingo*	do-*meen*-go

January	*enero*	e-*ne*-ro
February	*febrero*	fe-*bre*-ro
March	*marzo*	mar-so
April	*abril*	a-*breel*
May	*mayo*	ma-yo
June	*junio*	khoo-nyo
July	*julio*	khoo-lyo
August	*agosto*	a-*gos*-to
September	*septiembre*	sep-*tyem*-bre
October	*octubre*	ok-*too*-bre
November	*noviembre*	no-*vyem*-bre
December	*diciembre*	dee-*syem*-bre

TRANSPORT
Public Transport

What time does ... leave/arrive?	*¿A qué hora sale/llega ...?*	a ke o-ra sa-le/ye-ga ...?
the bus	*el autobus*	el ow-to-*boos*
the plane	*el avión*	el a-*vyon*
the ship	*el barco*	el *bar*-ko
the train	*el tren*	el tren

airport	el aeropuerto	el a·e·ro·pwer·to
train station	la estación de tren	la es·ta·syon de tren
bus station	la estación de autobuses	la es·ta·syon de ow·to·boo·ses
bus stop	la parada de autobuses	la pa·ra·da de ow·to·boo·ses
luggage check room	guardería/ equipaje	gwar·de·ree·a/ e·kee·pa·khe
taxi	taxi	de tak·see
ticket office	la taquilla	la ta·kee·lya

The ... is delayed.
El ... está retrasado.   el ... es·ta re·tra·sa·do
I'd like a ticket to ...
Quiero un billete a ...   kye·ro oon bee·lye·te a ...
Is this taxi free?
¿Está libre este taxi?   e·sta·lee·bre es·te tak·see
What's the fare to ...?
¿Cuánto cuesta hasta ...? kwan·to kwes·ta a·sta ...
Please put the meter on.
Por favor, pong el taxímetro.   por fa·vor pon·ga el tak·see·me·tro

a ... ticket	un billete de ...	oon bee·lye·te de ...
one-way	ida	ee·da
return	ida y vuelta	ee·da ee vwel·ta
1st class	primera clase	pree·me·ra kla·se
2nd class	segunda clase	se·goon da kla·se
student	estudiante	es·too·dyan·te

Private Transport

I'd like to hire a/an ...	Quisiera alquilar ...	kee·sye·ra al·kee·lar ...
4WD	un todoterreno	oon to·do·te·re·no
car	un coche	oon un ko·che
motorbike	una moto	oo·na mo·to
bicycle	una bicicleta	oo·na bee·see·kle·ta

Is this the road to (...)?
¿Se va a ... por esta carretera?   se va a ... por es·ta ka·re·te·ra
Where's a petrol station?
¿Dónde hay una gasolinera?   don·de ai oo·na ga·so·lee·ne·ra
Please fill it up.
Lleno, por favor.   ye·no por fa·vor
I'd like (20) liters.
Quiero (veinte) litros.   kye·ro (vayn·te) lee·tros

diesel	diesel	dee·sel
leaded (regular)	gasolina normal	ga·so·lee·nor·mal
petrol	gasolina	ga·so·lee·na
unleaded	gasolina sin plomo	ga·so·lee·na seen plo·mo

ROAD SIGNS	
Acceso	Entrance
Aparcamiento	Parking
Ceda el Paso	Give way
Despacio	Slow
Desvío	Detour
Dirección Única	One-way
Frene	Slow Down
No Adelantar	No Overtaking
Peaje	Toll
Peligro	Danger
Prohibido Aparcar/ No Estacionar	No Parking
Prohibido el Paso	No Entry
Vía de Accesso	Exit Freeway

(How long) Can I park here?
¿(Por cuánto tiempo) Puedo aparcar aquí?   (por kwan·to tyem·po) pwe·do a·par·kar a·kee
Where do I pay?
¿Dónde se paga?   don·de se pa·ga
I need a mechanic.
Necesito un mecánico.   ne·se·see·to oon me·ka·nee·ko
The car has broken down (in ...).
El coche se ha averiado (en ...).   el ko·che se a a·ve·rya·do (en ...)
The motorbike won't start.
No arranca la moto.   no a·ran·ka la mo·to
I have a flat tyre.
Tengo un pinchazo.   ten·go oon peen·cha·so
I've run out of petrol.
Me he quedado sin gasolina.   me e ke·da·do seen ga·so·lee·na
I've had an accident.
He tenido un accidente.   e te·nee·do oon ak·see·den·te

TRAVEL WITH CHILDREN

I need ...	Necesito ...	ne·se·see·to ...
Do you have ...?	¿Hay ...?	ai ...
a car baby seat	un asiento de seguridad para bebés	oon a·syen·to de se·goo·ree·da pa·ra be·bes
a child-minding service	un servicio de cuidado de niños	oon ser·vee·syo de kwee·da·do de nee·nyos
a children's menu	un menú infantil	oon me·noo een·fan·teel
a creche	una guardería	oo·na gwar·de·ree·a
(disposable) diapers/nappies	pañales (de usar y tirar)	pa·nya·les de oo·sar ee tee·rar

an (English-speaking) babysitter	*un canguro (de habla inglesa)*	oon kan·*goo*·ro (de *a*·bla een·*gle*·sa)
formula (milk)	*leche en polvo*	*le*·che en *pol*·vo
a highchair	*una trona*	*oo*·na *tro*·na
a potty	*un orinal de niños*	oon o·*ree*·nal de *nee*·nyos
a stroller	*un cochecito*	oon ko·che·*see*·to

Do you mind if I breast-feed here?

¿Le molesta que dé de pecho aquí?	le mo·*les*·ta ke de de *pe*·cho a·*kee*

Are children allowed?

¿Se admiten niños?	se ad·*mee*·ten *nee*·nyos

Also available from Lonely Planet:
Spanish phrasebook

Glossary

A
abierto – open
aficionado – enthusiast
apartado de correos – post office box
artesonado – coffered ceiling
autovía – motorway
ayuntamiento – town hall

B
barranco – ravine or gorge. Most of the islands are rippled by ravines that cut paths from the mountainous centres to the coast.
barrio – district, quarter (of a town or city)
Bimbaches – indigenous Herreños
bocadillo – bread roll with filling
bodega – traditional wine bar
bote – local variety of shuttle boat developed to service offshore vessels
buceo – scuba diving
butaca – armchair seating on ferries

C
cabildo – government
cabildo insular – island government
cabra – goat
cabrito – kid
cajero automático – ATM
caldera – cauldron
calle – street
cambio – exchange
cañades – flatlands
Canariones – people from Gran Canaria
Carnaval – festival celebrating the beginning of Lent, 40 days before Easter
casa rural – a village or country house or farmstead with rooms to let
caserío – traditional farmhouse or hamlet
catedral – cathedral
cena – dinner
centro comercial – shopping centre, usually with restaurants, bars and other facilities for tourists
chiringuito – kiosk
churros – doughnuts
comedor – dining room
comida – lunch
Conejeros – people from Lanzarote
Corpus Christi – festival in honour of the Eucharist, held eight weeks after Easter
correos – post office

cruz – cross
Cruz Roja – Red Cross
cueva – cave

D
denominación de origen – appellation certifying a high standard and regional origin of wines and certain foods
desayuno – breakfast
drago – dragon tree

E
ermita – chapel
estación – terminal, station
estación de guaguas – bus terminal/station
estación marítima – ferry terminal
estancos – tobacconist shops
este – east

F
faro – lighthouse
feria – fair
fiesta – festival, public holiday or party
finca – farm

G
godo – goth, the name Canario name for Spaniards
gofio – ground, roasted grain used in place of bread in Canarian cuisine
Gomeros – people from La Gomera
goth – see godo
gran – great
guagua – bus
guanarteme – island chief
Guanches – indigenous Canarians

H
Herreños – people from El Hierro
horario – timetable
hostal – pl *hostales*; commercial establishment providing accommodation in the one-to-three star range; not to be confused with youth hostels (of which there is only one throughout the islands)
hoteles – one-to-five star hotel

I
IGIC – Impuesto General Indirecto Canario (local version of value added tax)
iglesia – church

J
jamón – cured ham
juego del palo – stick game

L
lagarto – lizard
laurisilva – laurel
lavandería – laundry
librería – bookshop
lista de correos – poste restante
lucha canaria – Canarian wrestling

M
Majoreros – people from Fuerteventura
malpaís – volcanic badlands
malvasía – Malmsey wine
marcha – action, nightlife, 'the scene'
menú del día – set menu
mercado – market
meseta – plateau
mirador – pl *miradores*; lookout point
mojo – spicy salsa sauce made from red chilli peppers
montaña – mountain
mudéjar – Islamic-style architecture
muelle – wharf or pier
municipio – town council
museo – museum, gallery

N
norte – north

O
oeste – west
oficina de turismo – tourist office

P
Paginas Amarillas – Yellow Pages
Palmeros – people from La Palma
papas arugadas – wrinkly potatoes
parador – pl *paradores*; chain of state-owned upmarket hotels
parque nacional – national park
paseo marítimo – seaside promenade
pensión – pl *pensiones*; guesthouse (one/two star)
piscina – swimming pool
plateresque – silversmith-like
playa – beach

pozo – well
presa canario – Canary dog; see also *verdino*
pueblo – village
puenta – bridge
puerta – door
puerto – port

R
ración – large tapas
rastro – flea market
retablo – altarpiece
romería – festive pilgrimage or procession

S
sabina – juniper
Semana Santa – Holy Week, the week leading up to Easter
señorío – island government deputising for the Spanish crown
s/n – sin numero (without number); sometimes seen in street addresses
sur – south

T
taberna – tavern
tapas – bar snacks traditionally served on saucer or lid *(tapa)*
taquilla – box office
tarjeta de crédito – credit card
tarjeta telefónica – phonecard
tasca – pub, bar
terraza – terrace; outdoor cafe tables
thalassotherapy – warm sea-water treatment designed to remove stress and physical aches
timple – type of ukulele and the musical symbol of the Canary Islands
Tinerfeños – people from Tenerife

V
valle – valley
vega – plain, flatlands
verdino – Canary dog (from a slightly greenish tint in its colouring); see also *presa canario*
volcán – volcano

Z
zumería – juice bar

Behind the Scenes

THIS BOOK

The first edition of *Canary Islands* was written by Damien Simonis and the second edition was revised and updated by Miles Roddis. This third edition was written by Sally O'Brien and Sarah Andrews. The Health chapter was written by Dr Caroline Evans.

THANKS from the Authors

Sally O'Brien Thanks to Sarah Andrews for her wonderful work and email camaraderie over the months that this book took to shape. Canarians who deserve a round of applause include Juan and Pedro and various staff at tourist offices, bars, restaurants, shops and hotels who gave information, tips and gossip. Thanks to everyone at Lonely Planet who helped with this book (especially Fionnuala Twomey, Katrina Webb, Simon Williamson, Heather Dickson and Kusnander) and to Gerard Walker for companionship on the road (and reassurance during those first few days of driving around Gran Canaria!). Finally, thanks to Miles Roddis for the previous edition, his tips and the long-overdue beer in Sydney.

Sarah Andrews A million thanks to Sally O'Brien for being such an easy-going, patient and all-round wonderful coauthor. You made my first Lonely Planet book much less stressful than I feared it would be! Another pile of thanks go to Heather Dickson and the rest of the office crew, for many of the same reasons. You kept everything on track. Both during my trip preparations and on the road, the Spanish and Canary tourist offices were supportive and helpful at every step. I appreciate all of their efforts and believe the book is better for them. Special thanks to Ana Castañera in La Palma and Pilar Vico at Tourspain. Last but certainly not least, *un beso* for my husband Miquel, who acted alternately as navigator, chauffer, encourager and co-*mojo* taster – *gracias.*

CREDITS

Canary Islands 3 was commissioned and developed in Lonely Planet's London office by Heather Dickson. It was coordinated by Fionnuala Twomey and Katrina Webb (editorial), Kusnandar (cartography) and Pablo Gastar (colour and layout). Overseeing production were Ray Thomson and Andrew Weatherill (project managers), Bruce Evans and Martin Heng (managing editors), Mark Griffiths and Corinne Waddell (managing cartographers), and Adriana Mammarella (layout manager). Quentin Frayne compiled the Language chapter. Editorial assistance was provided by Melanie Dankel, Nancy Ianni, Brooke Lyons, Joanne Newell, Stephanie Pearson and Simon Williamson. Yvonne Bischofberger and Tamsin Wilson assisted with layout, and Kate McDonald assisted with layout checks. The cover was designed by Simon Bracken and the artwork was produced by James Hardy.

Series Publishing Manager Susan Rimerman oversaw the redevelopment of the regional guide series with help from Virginia Maxwell and Maria Donohoe. Regional Publishing Manager Katrina Browning steered the development of this title. The series was

---

THE LONELY PLANET STORY

The story begins with a classic travel adventure: Tony and Maureen Wheeler's 1972 journey across Europe and Asia to Australia. There was no useful information about the overland trail then, so Tony and Maureen published the first Lonely Planet guidebook to meet a growing need.

From a kitchen table, Lonely Planet has grown to become the largest independent travel publisher in the world, with offices in Melbourne (Australia), Oakland (USA), London (UK) and Paris (France).

Today Lonely Planet guidebooks cover the globe. There is an ever-growing list of books and information in a variety of media. Some things haven't changed. The main aim is still to make it possible for adventurous travellers to get out there – to explore and better understand the world.

At Lonely Planet we believe travellers can make a positive contribution to the countries they visit – if they respect their host communities and spend their money wisely.

SEND US YOUR FEEDBACK

We love to hear from travellers – your comments keep us on our toes and help make our books better. Our well-travelled team reads every word on what you loved or loathed about this book. Although we cannot reply individually to postal submissions, we always guarantee that your feedback goes straight to the appropriate authors, in time for the next edition. Each person who sends us information is thanked in the next edition – and the most useful submissions are rewarded with a free book.

To send us your updates – and find out about LP events, newsletters and travel news – visit our award-winning website: **www.lonelyplanet.com**.

Note: We may edit, reproduce and incorporate your comments in Lonely Planet products such as guidebooks, websites and digital products, so let us know if you don't want your comments reproduced or your name acknowledged. For a copy of our privacy policy visit www.lonelyplanet.com /privacy.

designed by James Hardy, with mapping development by Paul Piaia. The series development team included Shahara Ahmed, Jenny Blake, Anna Bolger, Erin Corrigan, Nadine Fogale, Dave McClymont, Leonie Mugavin, Rachel Peart, Lynne Preston, Howard Ralley, Valerie Sinzdak and Bart Wright.

THANKS from Lonely Planet

Many thanks to the travellers who used the last edition and wrote to us with helpful hints, useful advice and interesting anecdotes:

B Rob Bakker, Julie Barrie, N Bell, F Benkina, Almer Bolman, John Bowman, Irène Buonocore **C** Margaret Cabrera, Joe Cawley, Ian Clifford, Phil Coates, Ben Coleman, Mark Corbluth **D** Josephine Daly, Olaf Draper, GCM Dunbar **E** Pieter van Es **F** Julia Fiehn, Caroline Forder **G** Bastiaensen Gilbert, Gylaine Gilmore, Mark Gilmore, Eirik Gjonnes, Hennie Goddard, Maria Gonzalez Alvarez **H** Jackie Homer, Julian Hopkins, Bela Horvath **J** Dominic Jacobs **K** Johan Kaberg, Peter Keller, Roy Kellett, Roger Kember, Cathelijne van Kemenade, Edwin Koopmanschap, Pam Krist **L** Aoife Lawler, Martin Lawson, Frank Learner, Manual Oscar Lopez-Figueora **M** Silvie Marinovova, Ash Mather, Alex Matshevich, Karen McAuliffe, Fernando Mennella, Gustavo F Migoya, BA Mills, Caterina Moschieri, Tony Murphy **N** Anja Nerrings, Liz Northcott, Ray Northcott **P** Andrea N Patriquin, Nancy Pease, Simon Pecovnik **R** Glenn Read, David Redding, Volker Renz, JT Rigsbee, Malcolm Robinson, Hendrik Roesel **S** Jeff Sale, Gail Scott Spicer, Timur Shtatland, Bernice Siager, Benkina Siebe, K Siebe, Mark Spurlock, S Stenger, Dr Peter G Stone, George Swan **T** Terence Tam, Andrea Terbijhe, Rick Toth, Jo Thomas Treaua, Heini Tiinonen, Cecile Troth **V** Joost van Bellen, Ewald van der Hoop, Luk Van Sand, JDR Vernon **W** Richard Wadsworth, Roy Ward, Judith Winter, Thomas Winter **Y** Helen Yates

Index

000 Map pages
000 Location of colour photographs

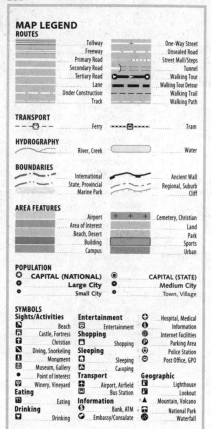

MAP LEGEND
ROUTES

Tollway	One-Way Street
Freeway	Unsealed Road
Primary Road	Street Mall/Steps
Secondary Road	Tunnel
Tertiary Road	Walking Tour
Lane	Walking Tour Detour
Under Construction	Walking Trail
Track	Walking Path

TRANSPORT

Ferry	Tram

HYDROGRAPHY

River, Creek	Water

BOUNDARIES

International	Ancient Wall
State, Provincial	Regional, Suburb
Marine Park	Cliff

AREA FEATURES

Airport	Cemetery, Christian
Area of Interest	Land
Beach, Desert	Park
Building	Sports
Campus	Urban

POPULATION

◉ CAPITAL (NATIONAL)	◎ CAPITAL (STATE)
● Large City	● Medium City
● Small City	○ Town, Village

SYMBOLS

Sights/Activities	Entertainment		Hospital, Medical
Beach	Entertainment		Information
Castle, Fortress	Shopping		Internet Facilities
Christian	Shopping		Parking Area
Diving, Snorkeling	Sleeping		Police Station
Monument	Sleeping		Post Office, GPO
Museum, Gallery	Camping		
Point of Interest	Transport	Geographic	
Winery, Vineyard	Airport, Airfield		Lighthouse
Eating	Bus Station		Lookout
Eating	Information		Mountain, Volcano
Drinking	Bank, ATM		National Park
Drinking	Embassy/Consulate		Waterfall

LONELY PLANET OFFICES

Australia
Head Office
Locked Bag 1, Footscray, Victoria 3011
☎ 03 8379 8000, fax 03 8379 8111
talk2us@lonelyplanet.com.au

USA
150 Linden St, Oakland, CA 94607
☎ 510 893 8555, toll free 800 275 8555
fax 510 893 8572, info@lonelyplanet.com

UK
72–82 Rosebery Ave,
Clerkenwell, London EC1R 4RW
☎ 020 7841 9000, fax 020 7841 9001
go@lonelyplanet.co.uk

France
1 rue du Dahomey, 75011 Paris
☎ 01 55 25 33 00, fax 01 55 25 33 01
bip@lonelyplanet.fr, www.lonelyplanet.fr

Published by Lonely Planet Publications Pty Ltd
ABN 36 005 607 983